READING AND THE ELEMENTARY SCHOOL CHILD

Selected Readings on Programs and Practices

VIRGIL M. HOWES

HELEN FISHER DARROW

Research and Development Division
Institute for Development of Educational Activities, Inc.
Los Angeles

THE MACMILLAN COMPANY, NEW YORK
COLLIER-MACMILLAN LIMITED, LONDON

Second Printing, 1970

Library of Congress catalog card number: 68–16764

THE MACMILLAN COMPANY
866 THIRD AVENUE, NEW YORK, NEW YORK 10022
COLLIER-MACMILLAN CANADA, LTD., TORONTO, CANADA

Printed in the United States of America

PREFACE

The field of reading in the elementary school is one of the most prolific in the production and use of new teaching approaches, materials, programs, techniques, and organizational procedures. These developments present tantalizing alternatives for reading instruction in the elementary school classroom. Some of the developments suggest fundamental changes, others appear as refinements to existing practices, some function merely as safe notebook ideas, and others arouse much controversy and conflict.

Just as no method can be understood apart from the values and objectives that the method makes operational, so no proposal for the teaching of reading can be understood apart from the purposes and values not only of reading in particular but of childhood education in general. If beginning students as well as experienced teachers are to avoid being buffeted from one alternative to another without perspective or direction, they need to understand the various developments in terms of such underlying values and objectives. The task is threefold: (1) to become aware of emerging developments, (2) to clarify the implications of each in terms of operational values and objectives, and (3) to compare the operational values and objectives with societal and personal values and goals for childhood education.

The task is not easy. It includes a thorough examination of the current literature, which is not only extensive but scattered in innumerable sources. Journal reports, curriculum guides, pamphlets, research reports, conference reports, and workshop proceedings are not easily accessible to classroom teachers. Overburdened library facilities or limited library resources confront students in many institutions. Even where ample materials are available for teachers and

students, much time and energy is consumed in locating and review-
ing references for relevance and significance.

The present volume was planned to help in this task. As a result
of intensive search and review of hundreds of articles and papers
published within the past decade, the editors have brought together
in book form some of the especially significant materials. The selections chosen present timely, insightful, and relevant points of view,
and give as broad a picture as possible of the many alternatives.

The volume should contribute to a clear understanding of reading
as an integral part of elementary education. Preceding each chapter,
an introductory statement includes questions and issues that point up
basic values and goals, and provide background information for the
reader's own critical examination of the selections that follow.
Throughout the book, the content focuses on the child as a person
who grows in reading power throughout his elementary school life
and beyond. The child's success as a confident reader has been emphasized. Every attempt has been made to build an understanding of
methodology as a flexible means to achievement of goals, rather than
as an end.

The authors are indebted to many authorities and their publishers
whose material appears in this book. School districts were most cooperative in providing material. Special thanks go to Mrs. Sheila
Candioty for her invaluable assistance in retrieval of material, correspondence, typing, and preparing the manuscript for production.

V. M. H.
H. F. D.

READING AND THE ELEMENTARY SCHOOL CHILD

Selected Readings on
Programs and Practices

CONTENTS

vii

READING AND THE ELEMENTARY SCHOOL CHILD

Selected Readings on Programs and Practices

Chapter 1

READING IN THE CHILD'S WORLD

Reading can be one of man's deepest pleasures. It can carry him to distant lands and acquaint him with people he would otherwise not know. It extends his experiences, giving him a glimpse of the world's excitement, pleasure, and wisdom.

Through reading, man can ponder the mysteries of the world, explore accumulated knowledge, and contemplate the unknown. From this search, he begins to uncover some answers to questions; he is stimulated to raise more questions and to continue his pursuit for deeper understanding.

Through reading, man can move backward and forward through time and space. Reading can take him into the lives of people who lived a thousand years ago or project him into times yet to emerge. Through reading, man can learn to understand himself as he learns of others.

Reading does different things for different people, bringing different kinds of results. It can bring new skills and increase knowledge. Interests and appreciation can be expanded and deepened, powers of problem-solving and critical thinking can be improved and developed. Reading can have an impact on one's life by helping him to become a self-fulfilling person, to gain new social and personal insights, and to understand and strengthen his values. Reading is one of man's ingredients for blending his inner psychological world with the outer social world, and emerging into a new world of thought, imagination, and reality. It becomes an avenue for growth to the degree to which it stimulates both intellectual and emotional aspects of personal and group living.

Then what is reading to be for the child? Doesn't what the child reads become as important to his development as how he reads; doesn't why he reads become as significant to his growth as when he reads? Is reading to be separated from life? Can it be separated from the entire matrix of communication? These are only some of the questions to be examined by the teacher. How they are examined depends, perhaps, upon whether the teacher chooses to look upon the child as a growing reader who responds to his environment or upon reading as a subject to be taught.

READING AS CONTACT *

Dorris May Lee

THE TEACHING of reading in our schools today is lost in a jungle of detail and outdated beliefs and procedures. There is a tremendous need to climb to a point where the essence of what we now know about children and how they learn and our contemporary understandings of what reading really is, and its true goals can put the acquisition of the art of reading into more accurate perspective. From such a vantage point we can set our course to reach our goals as directly and effectively as possible.

In all our normal, natural, self-directed aspects of living, we determine our objective and move toward it as directly as possible, detouring around roadblocks as necessary. Only in our highly contrived cloverleaf highway construction do we turn east to go west. Here we must give up dependence on our own knowledge and expertise and give ourselves over to the direction of others—the signs. Too many of our procedures in reading start children out, like the cloverleaf, in opposite or unuseful directions unrelated to real goals, which, unlike the cloverleaf, may hinder or prevent expeditious arrival at the destination.

Our goal in reading, as virtually all will agree—even though we may not express it in these terms—is to achieve maximum communication with such pleasure and satisfaction that individuals choose it with regularity and for a wide variety of purposes from a range of readily available alternatives.

COMMUNICATION

The key in reading is "communication," communication of ideas, feelings, understandings and information. We now realize that effective communication takes place through either oral or written media to the extent that the individual can bring personal meaning to *these* ideas in *this* context. Personal meaning is developed through contact. This experience must be direct and personal until such time as enough background has been accumulated in each type of situation that it may be synthesized by the individual. Only then can it provide a basis for bringing personal meaning to the reading vicariously. Individuals may be able to attach similar verbalizations to various situations but this may only reflect others' statements and carry virtually no real meaning.

This does not happen automatically, even with experienced adults. One

* REPRINTED with permission of the Association for Supervision and Curriculum Development and Dorris May Lee from *Educational Leadership*, Vol. 24, February, 1967, pp. 413–17. Copyright © 1967 by the Association for Supervision and Curriculum Development.

must first be able to abstract or generalize meaning from the experience, for only generalizations transfer. Next, one must see the relationship between the experiences. Both of these abilities require considerable maturity and familiarity with the situations. Many times adults fail to be able to use transferred meanings as vicarious experience to bring meaning to new situations. Expecting children to make abstractions in the first place and transfer them to a new situation they do not understand very well is highly questionable.

PLEASURE AND SATISFACTION

Referring to our previously stated goal, the next important concept is "pleasure and satisfaction." A common rather cynical interpretation of what brings pleasure and satisfaction to children has developed too much out of experience with them when confined to the quite indefensible situations existing in far too many of our classrooms. Here the *teacher* determines goals and purposes, the materials and activities which *he* decides the children are to use to reach them, and *his* evaluation of how well each had learned what *he* wanted them to learn. This results in children's finding pleasure and satisfaction in something non-school. "What do you like best about school?" "Recess."

However, children must have a significant part in planning and deciding on the activities which will result in their needed learnings. As they feel some measure of success in their own accomplishment, they gain great satisfaction and pleasure, since these activities hold personal meaning for the child. In these situations we more often hear, "Can I stay in at recess to finish my project?"

Today we know that children can successfully become increasingly self-directing, self-evaluating and that their greatest drive is toward a feeling of adequacy. This knowledge must be put to use in all learning situations.

Back to our goal for teaching reading, we find next the real basis for evaluation of success—"that individuals choose it with regularity for a wide variety of purposes from a range of readily available alternatives." The one who *can* read but *does not* may well be worse off than the one who cannot but wants to. The former first must overcome his feelings of discomfort, disinterest or inadequacy which have become associated with his experience with reading. He has found it too hard, or too easy, or meaningless, because of its inanity, or his lack of contact with the ideas or situations involved, or because reading was always a threatening situation since he never felt he could do as well as the teacher expected.

On the other hand, any child who has learned to talk *can* learn to read for it is a far less difficult process. That is, he can if he has normal use of his eyes, if it can be as meaningful an experience for him and if the school situation does not set up too many activities which are confusing and meaningless to him or demand responses beyond what he feels he can perform.

We have looked at goals for the teaching of reading and explored a little each part of the statement. Now let us see what some of the implications may be for setting our course to reach these goals.

Since our first concern is communication, each child must be able to bring personal meaning to what is to be read. He must have had personal contact with a reasonable proportion of the concepts and situations involved. One criterion is that *no one can read what he cannot talk about in some meaningful way.* The more immature the reader, the more this is true.

Personal Meaning

There are several implications if schools are going to insure that each child can bring personal meaning to his reading:

1. More of the school time needs to be devoted to real experiences not already a part of those particular children's lives, to which each can bring meaning, thereby enriching each child's personal contacts with his world.

2. The school should help children explore and clarify their contacts with their physical and social world by providing opportunities to express them freely, both orally and in writing. (This may first be by pictures and dictation until the physical writing skills come more easily.)

3. Since each child is the only one who really knows what is meaningful to him, he must have free choice of what he is to read and write. This is just as important in the content areas of the curriculum as in "reading class." One cannot read "reading." What is read is *about* something whether fictional or informational. The child should be aware of the purpose *he* has for reading though it may only be a sincere, "I want to"; not "I'm supposed to." As various experiences and real life situations are discussed, some aspects seem more important to some children than to others. For some reason, often hard to identify, certain aspects of a problem have more personal meaning. Material a child finds related to these concerns will be read with far more learning, of both process and content, than material which has been assigned.

As he feels free to express himself, every person, child or adult, is eager to talk about that with which he is involved. As he has opportunity to write about it in a non-threatening way (he is helped but not criticized—does not have errors pointed out), he seeks the help *he* feels he needs. He also eagerly looks for and reads related materials and seeks help as he needs it for better understanding. This describes the child every teacher hopes to have: self-directing, self-evaluating and taking the responsibility and initiative for his own learning.

An Approach to Reading

If this is natural behavior for children, and we believe it is, then why does it not happen more often? What are some logical natural ways we might explore to secure such behavior?

1. Provide a variety of activities or opportunities for experience from which each child may choose, or accept his own chosen activities which may be different from any provided.

2. Help children plan together how they can live and work together, using any problem situations as bases for their rethinking or extended thinking on the matter.

3. Help children recognize their goals and purposes and plan with them ways of implementing these. Such planning can enable children much more effectively to structure their own time to meet their own real needs. It can also free much teacher time for helping individuals or small groups who have a particular need at a particular time.

4. Help children learn more effectively to evaluate their learning and to identify their own needs. If we are to be able to do this usefully, teachers will need to look at *all* a child's performance as evidence of his present learning—real learning which results in significant changes in what he does and how he feels. When evaluation is viewed in this way then mistakes become cues for learning not yet achieved, not behavior to be punished.

Children see much sincere teacher correction as punishment; words corrected in oral reading, red marks on papers, being sent out of the room for reading help, having to "read" twice a day when most only read once, having to have a different book from what everyone else has. Instead, all children need opportunity to participate in choosing their own materials, encouragement in helping one another, and in asking the teacher's help, not to get his answer but to explore what it is he needs to know and through what experiences he can best learn it. As the teacher and child agree on what needed learning he has not yet achieved, the teacher can effectively teach—arrange needed contact—so that the child can effectively learn.

Children, before their entrance to school and each day afterward, have learned so much just from living in this world, that it is highly presumptuous for anyone to say in advance that all children in a class need the same experiences. Such teaching results inevitably in a tremendous amount of wasted time. What is worse, children who already have passed the need for such teaching, those for whom it has no personal meaning, and those who have solved the problem by a different route are confused or may reject it and are thus not only wasting time but are also thereby less able to learn.

As teachers provide opportunities for individuals and small groups to meet pinpointed needs, while others work ahead on their own identified concerns, the effectiveness of learning increases tremendously. We can think of this as personal contact at point of need.

There is another way that involvement, eagerness and enthusiasm, resulting from meaningful experiences in a rich school environment, increase reading effectiveness. As children become more interested in more things they search for more and more related reading materials, to find out more or just for the pleasure of contact with this area of involvement. As they search they learn to make increasingly better choices, choosing what is meaningful to them, what they feel communicates best, what most effectively provides them with what they need. And having contacted such material they have a better basis for choice.

Since we know that no one can make anyone really learn anything, why do we not stop requiring? Why not, instead, provide inviting situations in which children can be psychologically comfortable, widely increase their personal contact with many aspects of their world, and follow their natural desires to extend their personal meaning and therefore the learning that it brings?

READING AND THE SELF-CONCEPT *

Alma Cross Homze

Reading is the school subject most discussed by educators and laymen today. It is written about in journals and books, spoken about on radio and television, and heard about in conferences and meetings. Yet reading is usually attacked from one vantage point, "How is it done?" An overabundance of new formulae for teaching reading continually appear. They are, in turn, advertised as panaceas for the problems involved in making our nation literate.

While we abound in these "How to Do It" books, we are oblivious of the paucity of thoughtful information emphasizing such basic questions as, "What are the effects of reading?" We develop different methodologies for different reading levels, while we often fail to consider the relationship between the child's development and his reading.

One aspect of child development, the self-concept, is being explored in terms of motivation and learning but not specifically in terms of reading. It is my purpose to describe briefly the research in the general effects of reading and the development of the self-concept, and then draw a hypothetical relationship between the two.

---

* REPRINTED with the permission of the National Council of Teachers of English and Alma Cross Homze from *Elementary English*, Vol. 39, March, 1962, pp. 210–15.

I. THE EFFECTS OF READING

In spite of the necessity of including "effects" in a consideration of reading, that aspect of interpretation of the printed page is grossly neglected. In Betts' bibliography of 8278 articles and studies, there was only a limited reference to research studies on the effects of reading.[1] The studies which did relate to the effects of reading stressed mass media. They included investigations of newspaper and magazine reading, and effects of TV on reading rather than emphasizing the direct effects of reading on the child.[2] Russell clarifies the point further:

Studies in the effects of reading are the present no man's land of this large domain in the language arts area. Since at least the 1880's starting with Janal and Cattell, the psychology of the reading act has been charted with considerable care. Beginning a little later, the problems of reading behavior and instruction have been explored and analyzed by Buswell, Dearborn, Gates, Gray, McKee, Thorndike, and by their students and other workers. It is in the third large area, the investigation of the effects of reading that large unknown regions and unmapped territories exist today.[3]

There are, of course, valid reasons for the neglect of research in the effect of reading on the individual. The teacher places greater emphasis in her reading program on the "process" or "methodology" of reading rather than the "product" of reading. The large classes prevent her from following through the complete reading cycle so that she can observe the effects of reading on the child. The second reason for the neglect of this area is inherent in the problem: the task is a complex one. Many factors are related to changes in reading and "it is rarely possible to discover one immediate effect linked to a single cause."[4] The research that has been done concerns the effects of reading on personality, attitudes and groups of people.

In *What Reading Does to People*, Douglas Waples reports the results of his studies of the effects of reading on groups of people. He has identified five general areas:

a. The instrumental effect: the results of reading for knowledge, information
b. The prestige effect: the results of reading for self-approval
c. The aesthetic effect: the results of reading for the beauty of expression
d. The respite effect: the results of reading that relieves tension
e. The reinforcement effect: the results of reading that inforces our attitudes [5]

[1] Emmett Albert Betts, E. W. Dolch, Arthur Gates, and David H. Russell, "Unsolved Problems in Reading: A Symposium I," *Elementary English*, Vol. 31 (October, 1954), p. 335.
[2] *Ibid.*, p. 336.
[3] *Ibid.*, p. 335.
[4] *Ibid.*
[5] Douglas Waples, Bernard Berelson, and Franklin R. Bradshaw, *What Reading Does to People* (Chicago, Ill.: University of Chicago Press, 1940), p. 114.

Although Waples' work chiefly concerns groups, his five effects should be kept in mind as we develop a relationship between reading and the self-concept.

It has been believed for many years that reading would develop "a desirable" personality. The Colonial days fostered the reading of *The Bible* for this reason. While recent studies have given impetus to this theory, Louise Rosenblatt stresses the "value of books in terms of their effects upon the pupils' personal life and adjustment" in *Literature as Exploration*.[6]

In the book *The Reader's Guide to Prose Fiction*, Elbert Lenrow presents a comprehensive compilation of "lists of books designed to aid pupils in understanding themselves and their personal environment, in comprehending social problems and issues, and in finding 'escape' or entertainment." [7] Evalene Jackson tried to determine the effects of reading on race prejudices. She measured racial attitudes, advised the group to read a particular book which dealt with the problem, readministered the racial attitude questionnaire and compared the "pre" and "post" measures. She found a small but significant shift from a less, to a more favorable attitude towards Negroes.[8] However, the effect was not a lasting one which may indicate that in order to change attitudes more than one book during one time period is necessary.

I have considered only the "book" partner of the "man-book" team necessary for reading. Perhaps the effects of books depend more on the receptivity of the individual rather than the content of the book, or perhaps the process is more one of total interaction. Certainly the predisposition of the readers must be considered. Waples lists the following factors as determinants of the response to, and the effects of literature.

a. The age of the person: We go through reading stages at particular ages. Children's interests are generally uniform because of the similarity of their experiences.
b. The sex of the person: There are differences in selections of reading material between men and women. See Douglas Waples' book, *What People Like to Read*.
c. The education of the person: The educational background determines the types of study and reading habits and the levels of vocabulary one has.
d. The occupation of the person: Various occupations encourage us to read certain types of literature.
e. The income level of the person: The income may limit the number and type of material available. (The rise of paperback books may alter this factor.)
f. The group membership of the person: The people one contacts through family, school friends, vocational associates, church, club and sport groups may all help explain interests in types of reading material.[9]

[6] Paul Witty, "Relationship of Reading to Personality Development," *Supplementary Educational Monograph*, 72 (October, 1950), 173.
[7] *Ibid.*
[8] Evalene P. Jackson, "Effects of Reading Upon Attitudes Toward the Negro Race," *Library Quarterly*, 14 (January, 1944), 53.
[9] Waples, *op. cit.*, p. 89.

The group membership factor may be, for a child, the most important of the six personal factors. His group determines, to a large extent, many of the actions and opinions that later become part of his self-concept. His group also determines to some extent, according to Waples, his reading choices. This too becomes part of his self-concept. How then does reading relate more specifically to the child's self-concept?

II. The Child's Self-Concept

The self-concept is defined as the "person as known to himself, particularly stable, important and typical aspects of himself as he perceives them." [10] The social forces which act on children and help them form their self-concepts are widely varied. At first, the child's contact with the world is through empathy. This is the child's form of communication, and a rather nebulous one.

When language develops, the child has a more precise form with which to contact people. It is in this early language growth that the child is beginning to recognize himself. At first, his needs are all directed towards himself; they are "mine" and "me." The child is establishing his identity through bodily possessions, material possessions, and abstract possessions. First, he identifies his nose; next he can identify his shoes; finally he identifies his responsibility. All three are parts of the child's self-concept.

The child continues through the "mine-me" stage until he begins to recognize and accept others around him.[11] He no longer can rely on "mine-me"; he begins to recognize the power of "his-hers" and his position with other people becomes clearer. His self-concept has evolved from the time when he was alone most of the time, to the period when he was identifying himself as a person, to his beginning socialization. This probably takes place when he reaches school age and is placed in a situation with a great number of children his own age. The development of his self-concept is now as dependent on his social contacts as on his language development.

The roles of his peers determine much of what behavior the child will assume. The roles of his peers become his life-models. He is about the same stage of development as his playmates so he can more easily identify with his young companion than he can with an older neighbor.

This ability to *identify* with others is perhaps the most important factor in the development of his self-concept. The child selects those parts of others which he desires for himself and adapts them to himself. As the child selects actions which he wants to use as part of his self-concept he also recognizes certain patterns of action, or roles, which he may assume so that he can be effective with different people. We are all familiar with the child who has a role at

[10] Ira J. Gordon and Arthur W. Combs, "The Learner: Self and Perception," *Review of Educational Research*, 28 (December, 1958), 433.

[11] M. Sherif and H. Cantril, *The Psychology of Ego-Involvements* (New York: John Wiley and Sons, Inc., 1947), p. 179.

home with his parents and assumes a different role when he comes to school. Different approaches are more successful with different people, and the child recognizes it.

The actions he assumes which are satisfying and socially rewarding are adopted by the child as part of his self, and as each is chosen to be part of the self, so the next choice is influenced. The process is an overlapping and a continuous one. As he grows, the more successfully the child can relate the actions of others to himself and understand how they concur with or alter his own actions, the more successful he will be in understanding his self-concept.

Although this article is primarily concerned with the relationship between reading and the self-concept, the implications of the self-concept for all of education are pointed out in the doctoral dissertation of Hugh V. Perkins.

Specifically the self-concept can be used in education: a) as a psychological construct which enables teachers, counselors, parents, and others to achieve with training deeper understandings and insights into the behavior and development of children, and b) as a vital and important aspect of learning and development which the school through its educational processes seeks to promote and foster in every child.[12]

III. The Hypothetical Relationship

How are reading and the self-concept related? How does reading ability affect the self-concept? How does the self-concept affect reading performance?

Reading has various effects on the reader. Waples has described these effects and the personal factors of the reader which permit or prevent these effects from taking place. If we accept that some of these effects do take place to varying degrees depending on the reader, then it may be the individual's ability to *identify* that produces the greatest effects. It is that ability to identify that transmits the effects of reading to the self-concept.

Before he reads, the child identifies most readily with people. He uses people as models for his behavior or thinking. He adapts and adopts portions of their behavior for his own. He uses them to define and develop his self-concept. The child acts as a mirror to a wide variety of actions from a wide variety of people. From this image-making the child is formulating what he is as a person, and this becomes his self-concept.

As the child learns to read, he selects some of his models from the books he reads.[13] He identifies with a central character, a family, a problem, or a desire he shares with characters in the books.

A child may read of a character who ran away from home and ask himself, "Why did he do it?" "How did he feel?" "How would I feel?" or "What

[12] Hugh V. Perkins, "Teachers and Peers Conceptions of Children's Self-Concepts," *Child Development*, 29 (June, 1958), 204.

[13] Ethel J. Alpenfels, "All Children Need to Identify," *Childhood Education*, 25 (May, 1949), 394.

would I do?" He is internalizing the motives of the book character, searching his own thinking, and arriving at a better understanding of why some children do run away from home. If the child can ask himself, "Would I do that?" and arrive at an answer, then he is using reading to examine himself. He can, in this way, begin to recognize and to build on his self-concept. The child may not be aware that this is taking place, but the next time he encounters either a real or a fictitious character who ran away from home, or if he ever feels the urge himself, he will be better prepared to understand the situation. He becomes able to give a meaning to things that will happen to him and things that have happened to him.[14] He begins to build and clarify his self-concept through reading.

In the article, "The Personal and Social Values of Reading," Nila Smith presents the results of a study of children in grades 4 through 8. She asked the children if they "remembered any book, story, or poem which had changed their thinking or attitudes in any way." Of 502 responses, 60 per cent indicated that they had experienced changes in their attitudes as a result of reading. An additional 10 per cent said that they had also felt changes in their behavior.[15] It is possible that such changes indicate changes in the basic way the children perceive themselves—in their self-concept.

However, two factors must be present for such changes, a child's receptivity to the change and the stimulus for the change. Beyond that, we really cannot be sure what character or plot will encite a change in a child's attitude or behavior. No book would produce the same effects on any two children: good! A great part of reading is exploring; let the children ramble through many different kinds of books until each child finds the models that give him satisfaction.

In addition to considering what a child reads, we must also consider how well he reads, for this too influences his self-concept. If the child is highly proficient in extracting ideas from the printed page and he recognizes this, he will have a positive approach to reading. He is able to read, therefore his concept of himself is as a "reader." He is more apt to read widely; he will attempt more difficult material; he will have great pleasure in reading. Since his self-concept is that of a reader he reads more widely, and he does become more of a reader; the cycle is complete.

However, if the child has great reading problems, and he experiences little success in reading, his concept of himself will be that of a "non-reader." He has difficulty with word recognition; he struggles to glean ideas from groups of words; he may not like reading at all; a vicious cycle develops. The child experiences little success in reading and his self-concept becomes such that he feels he is not a reader. Since the conception he has of himself in reading is a

[14] Arthur T. Jersild, *In Search of Self* (New York: Teachers College, Columbia University, 1952), p. 17.
[15] Nila Banton Smith, "The Personal and Social Values of Reading," *Elementary English*, 25 (December, 1948), 490.

negative one, he fails to make the progress necessary for him to experience success and improvement.

It is readily understandable that the remedial work we give such children sometimes has little or no effect. A child with reading difficulties once said to me, "I can't read because I don't have a reading head." Previous attempts at remedial reading with this child had proven unsuccessful. It was not until the child was helped to succeed in simple reading experiences that she began to see herself as a reader. Consequently, succeeding attempts in building skills also included strong encouragement to help the child see herself as a reader. In this way, the child's reading skills improved as did her attitude towards herself as a reader. The gradual and slight change in the child's self-concept helped her improve the necessary reading skills; the relationship is, again, interdependent.

Implications For Education

The interdependence of reading and the self-concept has important implications for education. Educators must become more aware of the kinds of books children need. Then they must provide a wide variety of materials for all children of all ages. The children must have many different types of characters from which to select models. They must have a wide variety of story situations in which they can place themselves. Most of all, they must have freedom to select the book that best fills their immediate appetite. Then, books will help children in understanding themselves.

Educators must add a second dimension to all remedial reading programs. This would stress developing the child's attitude towards himself as a reader as well as developing reading skills. Such a program would include many successful reading experiences to help build the child's confidence. It would include discussions which would help the child relate the reading to his personal life. Only then will the "reluctant reader" find that reading is a part of himself, and only then will he improve because he does see himself as a reader.

Educators must provide *time* for every child to read. That is not the "six pages of the second story beginning on page 31" type of reading time. There must be a time in every day when a child can pull himself up in his own place and say, "Now, book, you belong to me, and I belong to you!" Let the child meet someone in that book. Let him go somewhere in that book. Let him see something in that book. He will enjoy reading just for that chance.

The pleasure will not be the same for every child: "Undoubtedly, individual children vary greatly in the amount and type of their identification . . . but the possibilities exist even in later childhood. Juvenile literature must be considered as one of the more important avenues for identification from early childhood. . . ." [16] The problems involved in examining this facet of reading

[16] David H. Russell, "Identification Through Literature," *Childhood Education*, 25 (May, 1949), 397.

are fascinating ones. They are open for exploration. Well then, what does reading do to you?

SELECTED BIBLIOGRAPHY

1. Alpenfels, Ethel J., "All Children Need to Identify," *Childhood Education*, 25 (May, 1949), pp. 394–396.
2. Betts, Emmett Albert, E. W. Dolch, Arthur Gates and David H. Russell, "Unsolved Problems in Reading: A Symposium I," *Elementary English*, 31 (October, 1954), pp. 325–337.
3. Gordon, Ira J., and Arthur W. Combs, "The Learner: Self and Perception," *Review of Educational Research*, 28 (December, 1958), pp. 433–440.
4. Jackson, Evalene P., "Effects of Reading Upon Attitudes Toward the Negro Race," *Library Quarterly*, 14 (January, 1944), pp. 47–54.
5. Jersild, Arthur T., *In Search of Self*, New York: Teachers College, Columbia University, 1952.
6. Perkins, Hugh V., "Teachers and Peers Conceptions of Children's Self-Concepts," *Child Development*, 29 (June, 1958), pp. 203–220.
7. Russell, David H., "Identification Through Literature," *Childhood Education*, 25 (May, 1949), pp. 397–401.
8. Sherif, M. and H. Cantril, *The Psychology of Ego-Involvements*, New York: John Wiley and Sons, Inc., 1947.
9. Smith, Nila Banton, "The Personal and Social Values of Reading," *Elementary English*, 25 (December, 1948), p. 490.
10. Waples, Douglas, Bernard Berelson and Franklin Bradshaw, *What Reading Does to People*, Chicago, Ill.: University of Chicago Press, 1940
11. Witty, Paul, "Relationship of Reading to Personality Development," *Supplementary Educational Monograph*, 72 (October, 1950), pp. 172–177.

READING INSTRUCTION:
A RECONCEPTUALIZATION *

John R. Kinzer

Reading can no longer be considered merely as a "school subject" which some people might be privileged to learn and wear as an adornment. Speaking, for example, is not a school subject; it has for many millenia been too pervasive. Speaking is something one learns because everyone is doing it, and

* REPRINTED by permission of the publisher from the *Peabody Journal of Education*, Vol. 39, July, 1961, pp. 20–23.

speaking is a skill absolutely necessary to human survival. I know of no non-talking human groups. This symbolic behavior is the primary difference between man and the other animals. Man can carry the most important parts of his world with him, both in time and in place. Today reading has joined speaking as a completely necessary skill, and it is linked with speaking as an integral part of child development in almost all societies.

Reading and talking, and their complementary aspects, writing and listening, are all parts of a complete inter-communication skill matrix. These various skills can hardly be broken down or abstracted even for purposes of instruction. Hence, our emphasis in recent years upon "the language arts." I will try to deal with the combination of speaking and reading because many of the difficulties presently encountered in learning to read English can be lessened by considering the intimate connection between a child's speech and beginning reading.

The present controversy about reading instruction could not occur except for the fact that speaking and reading are separated for instructional purposes. It is time that we not only consider them together but know why they must be considered together. In order to do this I must present some history. The controversy in the field of reading instruction came about because of two facts. The parties to the controversy singled out a single fact as fundamental and devised instructional procedures on the assumption that the one fact chosen could be used with little regard for the other. This is a prime example of over-simplifying something that is not simple. These two facts do not stand as separate entities.

The first fact is that English is a language with an alphabet. True, but English is not like Spanish or Italian, it is more like French in that the letters and combinations do not stand for unique sounds. There is no definite sound-to-letter relationship in English. However, it was assumed since English is an alphabetic language that it should be possible to construct the written language out of these alphabetic elements. This can be done if proper regard is given to the multitude of exceptions and complexities occasioned by English being a hybrid language. It would be much better to consider the alphabet and word analysis as an abstract process which could ultimately be helpful in learning to write and spell, but not much help in the beginning in relating written symbols to spoken symbols, as indeed it isn't. The connecting of oral symbols with objects, followed by connecting written symbols with objects is the temporal order in which language is learned. English, it turns out, is only partially phonetic, and therein lies the difficulty in using an alphabetic or phonetic analysis as the basis for beginning reading instruction.

The second fact, and the notion upon which most present reading instruction in America is based, is the discovery that printed words have characteristic shapes and are recognizable as unitary wholes. This is true, but it is *not a sufficient basis* for the development of a self-contained instructional method for teaching beginning reading. I am referring to the discovery by James McKeen

Cattell in 1883 in Leipzig while he was a graduate student of psychology in the laboratory of Wilhelm Wundt, namely that it takes almost twice as long to read both words and letters which have no connections than those which are embedded in a meaningful context. This means that one can identify a whole word just as easily and as quickly as any single letter comprising it.[1]

By the 1920's this important discovery had influenced some American educators to the point where they were willing to junk the old phonetic system of teaching reading and to emphasize a "look and say" approach to beginning reading. It works. But in junking the phonetic approach a difficulty was introduced which had not been a problem under the old method. The old method had its own problems. The "look and say" method is just fine for the very beginners, but one cannot possibly live long enough to develop much of a vocabulary, and one does not learn how to analyze and discover new words. This latter feature was the greatest value of the older approach. This is where phonetic analysis must come back into the picture. The problem is to get these two aspects into the proper developmental sequence. These two facts must be brought into relationship with the process of learning within a given individual.

Reading can be learned only as an aspect of total language development along the dimension of time. Speech comes first. Oral language is learned by infants in contact with their parents and their siblings. Speech sounds become symbols for objects and associations are established quite naturally. Children are able to respond to many thousand orally presented symbols by the age they enter upon formal schooling. The ubiquitarian printed words are also symbols for objects.

Another fact now enters the picture. Children are curious, unless that curiosity has been prematurely removed by conventional schooling and other forms of acculturation. The child will want to know what those little black marks are. Here is the transition point.

The members of the child's family must teach the child that these printed marks also represent objects. An object not only has a noise associated with it, but a little black mark can also be associated with an object. (Do not fear anthropomorphising at this point.) It is perfectly proper to refer to the little black mark as "saying" something just as a sound says something. Now the child has two associations for the same object. Words can be either spoken or written, as we well know. Help the child to associate both the sounds and the little black marks with objects. This is the place to emphasize the shape of the little black marks that are the whole word. This is not the place to talk about ABC's or engage in phonetic analysis. The child will single those parts out as soon as he is aware of them and not before.

Here you can see that my emphasis is upon the learner and not upon the teacher or the teaching process. Reading can be understood only as a learning

[1] Cattell, James McKeen. "Ueber die Zeit der Erkennung and Benennung von Schriftzeichen, Bildern und Farben." *Philosophische Studien*, 1885, 2, 635–650.

situation for an individual. The important elements are thrown entirely out of perspective by an emphasis upon teaching and teaching methods. The parents and teachers are facilitators of learning and development; to assure any other role can be disastrous to the learner. Many teachers, many parents, and most critics of school practices do not understand that language development in a child is behavioral and that the study of language in children is primarily psychological in nature and not mechanical. Development cannot be forced, but it can be nurtured by those who understand the learning process in children.

Hence, we must attend to the temporal sequence in language learning. First, and always, there are experiences. Second, these experiences must become associated with oral speech. Third, written symbols are also experiences and must be shown to be connected with experiences as oral words are. The important generalization here is the temporal sequence.

The parents and teachers must know that children are developing a world of language and that education is the formal means whereby that world is constructed.

A quotation from Roger Brown indicates the problem: [2]

> A symbol cannot represent its meaning to
> someone who has no experience with the thing
> signified. The writer and his reader must
> see the same world in the same way.

Teachers must understand the rationale of this proces as well as they know the techniques of teaching. Teachers know about experience charts and other paraphernalia, but they must understand the rationale of their methods. Education is world-building.[3] Language makes it possible for us to have a much more complex world, but it is a world of one's own making and all of us should understand that fact.

[2] Brown, Roger. *Words and Things:* An Introduction to Language. 1958, Glencoe, Illinois, The Free Press, p. 59.

[3] Davidson, Thomas. *Education as World-Building.* 1925, Cambridge, Massachusetts, The Harvard University Press.

RESEARCH ON THE PROCESSES
OF THINKING WITH SOME
APPLICATIONS TO READING *

David H. Russell

Research on the so-called "higher mental processes" has been a dubious, even precarious enterprise in this country for much of this century. Scholars in most disciplines, and even psychologists themselves, have had doubts about attempts to study cognitive functioning. In the *Scientific American*, Barron (4) reports sending letters to writers asking them to contribute to studies of creative thinking. He comments as follows on the replies:

In trenchant and not particularly orderly prose, about a fifth of those who responded to our original letter pointed out the intrinsically evil character of psychological research. The objections to such research are mainly on these counts: it is vivisection; it is an expression of the effort of organized society to encroach upon the individual and rob him of his freedom; it is presumptuous because it seeks to describe and to understand what is intrinsically a mystery.

The suspicion of studies of thinking has extended beyond artists, writers, college professors, and atomic scientists to psychologists themselves. Despite the brilliant exceptions of James, Thorndike, and the transplanted Lewin, American psychologists in general have been wary of studies of mental life. We have careful laboratory investigations of conditioning eye-blink and elegant procedures for recording the maze-running ability of rats, but we have often shied away from the study of the complex intellectual life of children and adults. This has probably not been true of European psychology to nearly the same degree. The Gestaltists, and Burt, Bartlett, and Piaget have been concerned with cognitive processes. Here in America, as Edna Heidbreder put it, we have not always been asking the important questions about human behavior—or at least not until quite recent times. Within the last ten years, however, there has been a discernible shift of emphasis in psychological research toward some of the many phases of intellectual functioning.

It is now about ten years since I attempted to put together, in some sort of organized fashion, the scattered work of the last sixty years on higher mental processes. In the book *Children's Thinking* (45) I agreed with Johnson (30) that, in surveying research on children's thinking, it is possible to distinguish

---

* REPRINTED with the permission of the National Council of Teachers of English from *Elementary English*, Vol. 42, April, 1965, pp. 370–78+.

between the materials of thinking, which are multitudinous, and the processes of thinking, which are very few. I suggested that it is feasible to describe, and to some extent to discover, unique characteristics of each of six types of thinking. These categories I am using in this article because I believe they all can be applied directly to the learning of language abilities and especially to learning to read, the area from which my examples will be drawn. Here then is the hypothesis—that most thinking behavior can be categorized into one or more of the six categories: perceptual thinking, associative thinking, concept formation, problem solving, critical thinking, and creative thinking. It is not the purpose of this article to be taxonomic—to define and distinguish these types—although this can be done. Instead, I should like to indicate a few outstanding researches or research results in the various categories, with an occasional hint of how these may be applied to the process of reading. There are, of course, many other labels that could be used—thinking has been described as relational, fluent, logical, structural, scientific, evaluative, inferential, deductive, and artistic. Spearman (51) wrote of education of relations and correlates. Guilford (22) uses terms like convergent and divergent thinking. Bruner (7) distinguishes between intuitive and analytic thinking. The possibilities are many but this paper uses six labels which are particularly relevant to the work of the teacher.

1. *Perceptual Thinking.* Perceptual thinking is learned; it goes beyond relatively unlearned sensation to an awareness of objects and events which are interpreted. It may be relatively simple as in pitch discrimination or complex as in a recognition of emotional meanings. It may be objective as in naming a primary color or subjective as in interpreting pictures or in the "Johnson image" during an election. Perceptual research flourished early in this century, moving from introspection to nicely controlled laboratory responses. Applications to letter, word, and phrase recognition are obviously related to reading and therefore researches and theories of perception probably need more attention in educational psychology.

Some of the theories of perception are physiologically based as in Hebb's (24) cell-assembly theory and some are functionally based as in Helson's (26) adaptation level or Brunswik's (10) perceptual constancy. The last ten years has seen emphasis on the influence of set, attitude, and other personality factors in perception as in the work of Ames (2), Bruner and Postman (9), and Blake and Ramsey (5). The well-known Ames' studies illustrated the influence of habit in visual perception of space relationships. The Bruner-Postman three-step cycle of expectancy, input of information, and checking of hypothesis would seem to offer many leads to reading research. For example, they say the stronger the set or hypothesis, or category, the less information needed to confirm it, the more needed to change it. The Blake and Ramsey book explores some of the relationships between perception and personality.

More recent summaries of research on perception are represented by Wohlwill's (60) review of the development of perception abilities in childhood and by the Gibson and Olum (18) chapter on experimental methods of studying perception in children. They find that the research on the question of part *versus* whole discrimination is inconclusive with results depending upon the materials used in the experiments. Langman (33) listed sixteen visual perception skills and five auditory· perception skills needed in reading and added seventeen generalizations used in letter-sound analysis. Gibson (19) studied the role of grapheme-phoneme correspondences in perception of words and concluded that pseudo-words constructed according to rules of invariant spelling-to-sound correlation are perceived more accurately in tachistoscopic presentation than their matched words with variable spelling-sound prediction. Gibson also reports several other studies in the volume by Levin *et al* (34), which contains accounts of twenty-two separate studies, most of them dealing with some form of perception. In the collection Levin has two other studies of variable grapheme-phoneme correspondences and, in addition to the study mentioned, Gibson deals with the perception of letters.

The analysis of some of the more complex perceptions of children as they read paragraphs or stories is currently not an active area. Earlier studies by McKillop (39), Groff (21), and others illustrated that perception of the meaning of paragraphs may be affected by attitudes toward the subject matter read. Reed (44) has traced some of the relationships between personality scores and reading choices in the sixth grade. Studies are needed, for example, of children's perceptions of different types of fictional characters or of different kinds of poems.

2. *Associative Thinking.* Associative thinking is a broad term which includes such theories or constructs as conditioning, S-R bonds, primacy, and reinforcement. With the exception of the study of reinforcement, research on this topic has declined from the interest of the 1920's but there seems little doubt that the label describes much thinking of a rather routine sort in which simple relationships are established. It may be the most accurate description of children's learning names of letters or a sight vocabulary.

Both McCreary (38) and Otto (43) have studied associative learning in relation to reading ability. A number of other studies within this framework have been reported in the new publication *The Journal of Verbal Learning and Verbal Behavior*.

In his book, *Learning Theory and Personality Dynamics*, Mowrer (41) extended the concept of association in a two-factor exposition to include both contiguity theory and drive-reduction theory. Current interest in the area is also evident in Skinner's reinforcement theory and its application to teaching machines. In the Soviet Union, Luria (36) is continuing the Pavlov tradition with studies of children's thinking based on theories of conditioning and association.

3. *Concept Formation.* Research in this area goes back at least to the 1890's and G. Stanley Hall. It has always been pursued with some diligence and has recently flourished with even more prominence as certain scientists, mathema-

ticians, and scholars in structural linguistics have become interested in the concepts children can learn. One problem nagging today's primary teacher is whether young children understand more than they did a generation ago as a result of television, travel, and other phases of modern life. Another problem in curriculum planning is that of selection of the most important concepts in a discipline. A third one concerns the current tendency to introduce concepts earlier; children can learn them sooner than we once thought but is the earlier gain worth the extra effort?

Research on concept formation has been summarized in general articles by Russell (46) and by Carroll (12) and in specific subject-matter fields by research workers with interests in particular areas. The research on concepts can be divided into three categories: 1) concept discovery, 2) gradual concept attainment and enrichment, and 3) children's knowledge of concepts at various age levels. Carroll believes the first phenomenon is the result of inductive thinking, the second of deductive thinking. The first is usually used in laboratory experiments; the second and third are closely related to the usual teaching and learning procedures in school.

The laboratory studies of concept discovery began with the work of Hull (27) in 1920 on learning nonsense names for pseudo-Chinese characters. This type of study was continued in the 1940's by Heidbreder (25) and expanded in the book, A *Study of Thinking* by Bruner, Goodnow, and Austin (8). Bruner hypothesizes that the subjects use different "selection strategies" and "reception strategies" in sorting out a sequence of events or group of examples so they can categorize them. He uses such terms as simultaneous-scanning, conservative-focusing, and focus-gambling to describe ways the category may be established. In many of his more recent books Piaget has been concerned with concept discovery in simple science experiments. Although the relationship between concept discovery and the reading process is not clear, Kress (32) has shown that there are differences between good and poor readers, who have been matched on general intelligence, in the ability to discover concepts in some of the well-known, clinical type non-verbal sorting tests. The retarded readers preferred concrete to functional or abstract methods and scored lower on versatility and flexibility in concept formation.

The second main area of concept acquisition seems to have much significance for reading instruction. Undoubtedly many children beyond the ages of seven or eight learn many concepts, at least partially, by reading about them. The series of studies by Welch and Long (58) suggest that children can use a two-step hierarchy between two and four years and that most kindergartners can grasp a three-step hierarchy (people-man-soldier). In the spiral curriculum or through reading, children may add "layers of meaning" to their concepts. The most important work in the area of concept learning is that of Piaget who is also concerned with the third division of concepts typically known at various developmental levels. His numerous experiments have been summarized and evaluated in part by Flavell (16) and by Hunt (28).

There are scores, perhaps hundreds, of respectable investigations of concepts known, or not known, at various stages. For example, Russell (48) has summarized some doctoral studies at the University of California on the development of social concepts, conservation concepts, the self concept, the concepts of liberty and justice (as contained in the Pledge of Allegiance), concepts of God, and concepts understood by middle class and culturally deprived children. Among other things, in *The Measurement of Meaning*, Osgood (42) suggests the importance of connotative meanings and personality factors in any analysis of a store of concepts.

Such investigations raise theoretical questions of interest. For example, if certain concepts, as in mathematics or science, are not typically grasped at some age level, should the teacher, forsaking all others, make strenuous efforts to have the children understand these concepts if they have been labelled important by the mathematicians or scientists? Since some concepts seem to be harder than others, but also more fundamental than others, in what sequence should concepts be studied? A third question is whether children, adolescents, and adults think alike or differently in concept formation. There is considerable agreement in the literature that thinking is similar at all levels. In *The Process of Education*, for example, Bruner (7) writes of a central conviction "that intellectual activity anywhere is the same whether at the frontier of knowledge or in a third-grade classroom" (p. 14). On the other hand, Piaget believes that the preschool child relies on what he calls "intuitive thought" based largely on perceptual experience, that the child of elementary school ages shifts into a stage of "concrete operations" or ways of getting information which begin with the objective world but are internalized and symbolized. It is not until eleven or twelve years, Piaget believes, that the child becomes capable of "formal operations," of understanding "reversibility," or grasping possibility as effectively as reality. It is therefore not until this stage, Piaget believes, that the child can fully grasp the abstractions of mathematics or physics or other disciplines. These problems are examples of some of the questions about concept formation which must be studied in relation to the whole curriculum, including reading.

4. *Problem Solving.* The psychological view of problem solving is one of a complex operation involving several specific types of thinking. Problems may exist in any field, including those on the printed page, where there may be a question for the child of deciphering strange words, of grasping an author's argument, or of judging a fictional character. Modern psychology still accepts Dewey's (13) classic five steps in problem solving but regards them as a general, somewhat idealized picture rather than an exact description of some of the frustrations and circumlocutions of the individual who cannot find an immediate solution. For example, today we use many labels to describe the solver's behavior. These include 1) relational thinking (Maier's combining the essentials of two isolated experiences), 2) logical reasoning (Guilford tests for this factor), 3) rigidity (Werner and Kaplan and Bloom and Broder find this a

useful concept, but some research indicates it is a specific rather than a general trait), and 4) anxiety (Fattu reports a negative relationship between anxiety and number of problems solved). A number of studies such as that of McNemar (40) have found that good problem solvers excel poor problem solvers in ability to overcome an induced set and to do deductive thinking. Harootunian (23) found that reading ability, intelligence, judgment, and problem recognition were important predictors of problem solving ability; closure, word fluency, and ideational fluency made little independent contribution to variance in problem solving ability.

As indicated elsewhere, the research suggests that problem solving behavior varies with 1) the nature of the problem, 2) the methods of attack used, 3) the characteristics of the solver, and 4) the group or social factors in the situation. Problem solving has been studied most thoroughly in science situations (14, 29) and with mathematical materials (Wertheimer, 59), but each of these four areas may apply in the reading situation. For example, the first (the nature of the problem), might include the numbers of unknown words in the selection, the second (methods of teaching), the pupil's ability to outline, the third, the attitudes of the reader to the content, and the fourth (influence of the group), may be of interest in terms of current views about individualized and group reading. What we know about the dynamics of groups (6, 31) has not been tested in groups organized for reading instruction. But a number of writers including Stauffer (52) have shown that problem solving in the areas of word recognition and simple comprehension may be encouraged as early as the first grade.

5. *Critical Thinking.* From the psychological point of view, critical thinking is the most dubious of the six labels by which I am attempting to summarize research in thinking. Usually it is part of some other process, as in evaluating the kinds of evidence collected in problem solving or judging the original result in creative thinking. The nearest the psychologist comes to allowing the term is in his use of the word *judgment.* Educational writings, on the other hand, are full of the two words, and the term "critical thinking" is especially the darling of the social studies people. One trouble in educational writing has been that critical thinking has had so many meanings. It has been made synonymous with the ability to abstract and organize information, to draw inferences, to search for relevant materials, to evaluate data, to compare sources, to employ a from-Missouri attitude, to distinguish fact from opinion, to detect propaganda, and to apply the rules of logical reasoning (49). Perhaps the time has arrived when we should be critical of our use of the phrase "critical thinking."

As a research area, the field of critical thinking accordingly suffers from this lack of precision. The exploratory study of Glaser (20) is still about the best at the high school level. A number of studies of propaganda analysis are closely related to reading. The bulletin published by the National Conference on Research in English and entitled *Critical Reading* (50) is correctly sub-titled as an introduction. Some of the confusion in terms is shown in the book from England by Abercrombie (1) entitled *The Anatomy of Judgment* and subtitled "An Investigation into the Processes of Perception and Reasoning." This may be one more bit of evidence that psychologists confuse terms, or the whole picture may be interpreted to mean that critical thinking is not a separate process so much as part of other cognitive functioning. Like some psychologists in this country, Abercrombie reasons that in receiving information from a given stimulus pattern we select from the total amount of information available and from our own store of information. Thus the perceptual process involves selection and judgment with the subject sometimes deliberate, sometimes unaware of what he is doing. Abercrombie used a tape recorded, group discussion method with university students and found that some of the factors influencing judgment became apparent and the judgments improved. The group discussion method may be one way of getting at assumptions or preconceptions and thus of improving critical thinking.

Recent attempts to clarify the concept of critical thinking have been made by Ennis (15) who divides the activity into some twelve overlapping categories along logical, critical, and pragmatic dimensions, and by Saadeh (49) who related his analysis to some of the rules of logic. Saadeh taught critical skills to sixth graders with considerable success as did Lundsteen (35) in another investigation of the possibility of teaching critical listening abilities.

6. *Creative Thinking.* In these days of emphasis upon intellectual attainment, curricular rigor and the "pursuit of excellence," creative thinking, and creativity are fashionable topics. In addition to individual researches, well-supported team studies are being made in a half-dozen centers throughout the country. Guilford includes creativity in his studies using factor-analysis at the University of Southern California. At Chicago, Getzels and Jackson (17) have differentiated between adolescents scoring high on intelligence tests and adolescents rated as creative, but have not studied cases where the two groups overlap. In Berkeley, MacKinnon and his associates (37) have a series of studies of personality factors related to creativity in various professions, and in Minnesota, Torrance (56, 57) is heading work on a group of studies more closely related than most to creative behavior in classroom settings. Such studies assume that creative thinking is not the province of a gifted few but exists on some sort of continuum for much of the population. In addition to certain skills, production of originality in some of these studies seems to involve three general factors which may be labelled perceptual, integrative, and emotional. MacKinnon finds different amounts of these in artistic creativity, scientific creativity, and what he terms "overlapping" creativity. Artistic creativity involves externalization of an internal state; emotion and personality may be heavily involved. In scientific creativity the scientist functions as a mediator between an external problem and its solution and is, presumably, less involved

emotionally. Creativity in the "overlapping" category includes performers, interpreters, and high-grade individuals in such pursuits as architecture and engineering.

In some of their research memoranda, Torrance and his students report trouble in establishing the reliability of his tests of creativity in elementary school children but have certain findings about the personalities of children rated as creative. As some of us might suspect, the so-called creative child is not well accepted by his peers or his teachers in the first four grades; he is often rated as limelighty and bossy. By the sixth grade a better status has usually been achieved.

On the positive side, the upsurge of interest in creativity may be documented by the publication, within five years, of at least six substantial volumes collected by various editors and reporting research in various aspects of creativity. Alphabetically by editor or author, these include Anderson's *Creativity and Its Cultivation* (3), MacKinnon's *The Creative Person* (37), Stein and Heinze's *Creativity and the Individual* (53), Taylor's *Creativity: Progress and Potential* (54), Taylor and Barron's *Scientific Creativity: Its Recognition and Development* (55), and Torrance's *Creativity: Second Conference on Gifted Children* (56). Combined with scores of research articles, the books represent increasing interest in, instead of final conclusions from the empirical study of creativity.

In the above research, two important problems are unsolved: the unique characteristics of creativity in childhood and youth, and some valid and reliable measures of creativity itself. As one reviewer put it, "creativity is a construct in search of a generally acceptable objective referent." Most of the tests of creativity have been developed by Guilford and his associates or adapted from his work. These lend themselves to factor analysis, which may be regarded as one step on the way to complete understanding, but some of them do not seem to correlate highly either with retest scores, with teachers' or supervisors' judgments of creativity, or with rating of students' creative products by independent judges.

The books and articles are samples of work in progress which suggest four domains of research in creativity: 1) the nature of the creative process, 2) the characteristics of the creative person, 3) the qualities of creative products, and 4) the social-cultural milieu, including classrooms, which block or foster creative responses. The whole area of creative thinking thus bristles with problems. Is there such a thing as teaching creativeness? Does creativity in play, rhythms, and language occur before creative thinking about social or scientific problems and are they different things? What can teachers do to achieve some sort of balance between conformity and spontaneity in the classroom? How can we get more "discovery" into a reading lesson? What are the places of production *versus* appreciation in reading and in other curricular areas?

The act of reading has usually been regarded as a receptive process rather than a creative one. There seems to be some justification, however, for the use of the term "creative reading" to signify behavior which goes beyond word identification or understanding of literal meaning to the reader's interpretation of the printed materials (47). Such reading may be productive of new ideas, critical of old ones, or appreciative of the art of literature. Research studies suggest that certain mechanics of reading must be well in hand before the child or adolescent achieves these higher levels of reading and that they, like the skills, can be developed by the right kinds of instruction.

CONCLUSION

The above examples suggest that language abilities should be defined not merely as perceptual skills nor as the ability to grasp a communication, nor as competence in solving verbal problems. Probably all types of thinking are involved in the learning and use of language and these I have subsumed under six labels. Other general descriptive terms could be used and more precise designations of specific verbal behavior are undoubtedly needed. Furthermore, this account neglects such topics as emotional factors in thinking, the role of memory, and attempts to derive a comprehensive theory or model of thinking as in the work of Burt (11) or Guilford (22). It is probably not too important in the study of the reading process, from which the examples are drawn, to distinguish between the types of thinking, here called perceptualizing and conceptualizing. Behavior which involves the apprehension of events or objects such as printed symbols may be profitably conceived as a categorizing, whether perceptual or conceptual. As Bruner has put it, "There are examples in which it is almost impossible to differentiate perceptual and conceptual categorizing, notably in language learning" (8). In addition to its use in the discovery of concepts, reading seems to be one of the best ways we have of deepening and enriching concepts.

Similarly, there is overlap of critical thinking with the processes of problem solving and creative thinking. A child or a scientist must be critical of his proposed solutions to a problem. An adolescent or an adult must sometimes be critical about his creative production, whether an original story or an interpretation of A. E. Housman. Despite this blending of critical thinking into problem solving and creative thinking, it is my bias that some aspects of critical thinking can be taught directly as such. Similarly, I believe the other five types of thinking can, to some extent, be isolated and taught in relation to the school curriculum, including reading.

In reading instruction of the past, most of a reading teacher's time and energy have gone into perceptual aspects of word identification and conceptual responses to literal meaning. These are necessary bases for more sophisticated approaches to reading, but perhaps the time has come when we can use our psychological knowledge of the processes of problem solving and critical and creative thinking to help teachers develop a more demanding set of goals for reading instruction.

SELECTED BIBLIOGRAPHY

1. Abercrombie, M. L. Johnson, *The Anatomy of Judgment*. London, England: Hutchinson, 1960.
2. Ames, Adelbert, "Visual Perception and the Rotating Trapezoidal Window," *Psychological Monographs* 65: No. 324, 1951.
3. Anderson, Harold H., (ed.), *Creativity and Its Cultivation*. New York: Harper, 1959.
4. Barron, Frank, "The Psychology of Imagination," *Scientific American* 199: 151–166, September, 1958.
5. Blake, Robert R. and G. V. Ramsey, (eds.), *Perception: An Approach to Personality*. New York: Ronald, 1951.
6. Blake, Roy, "Small Group Research and Cooperative Teaching Problems," *National Elementary Principal* 43:31–36, February, 1964.
7. Bruner, Jerome S., and Leo Postman, "Symbolic Value as an Organizing Factor in Perception," *Journal of Social Psychology* 27:203–208, May, 1948.
8. ——, Jacqueline Goodnow, and G. A. Austin, *A Study of Thinking*. New York: Wiley, 1956.
9. ——, *The Process of Education*. Cambridge: Harvard University Press, 1960.
10. Brunswik, Egon, *Perception and the Representative Design of Psychological Experiments*. Berkeley: University of California Press, 1956.
11. Burt, Cyril, "The Differentiation of Intellectual Ability," *British Journal of Educational Psychology*, 24:76–90, June, 1954.
12. Carroll, John B., "Words, Meanings and Concepts," *Harvard Educational Review*, 34:178–202, Spring, 1964.
13. Dewey, John, *How We Think*. Boston: Heath, 1910.
14. Duncker, Karl, "On Problem Solving," trans. by Lynne S. Leer, *Psychological Monographs*, 58, No. 27, 1945.
15. Ennis, Robert H., "A Concept of Critical Thinking," *Harvard Educational Review*, 32:81–111, Winter, 1962.
16. Flavell, John H., *The Developmental Psychology of Jean Piaget*. Princeton, N.J.: Van Nostrand, 1963.
17. Getzels, Jacob W., and Philip W. Jackson, *Creativity and Intelligence*. New York: Wiley, 1962.
18. Gibson, Eleanor N. and V. Olum, "Experimental Methods of Study in Perception in Children," P. H. Mussen (ed.), *Handbook of Research Methods in Child Psychology*. New York: Wiley, 1960.
19. Gibson, Eleanor, *et al.*, "The Role of Grapheme-Phoneme Correspondences in the Perception of Words," *American Journal of Psychology*, 75:554–570, December, 1962.
20. Glaser, Edward M., *An Experiment in the Development of Critical Thinking*. Contributions to Education No. 843. New York: Teachers College, Columbia University, 1941.
21. Groff, Patrick J., *Children's Attitudes Toward Reading and Their Critical Reading Abilities in Four Content-Type Materials*, doctoral dissertation, University of California, Berkeley, 1955.

22. Guilford, Joy P., "Three Faces of Intellect," *American Psychologist* 14:469–479, August, 1959.
23. Harootunian, B., and M. B. Tate, "The Relationship of Certain Selected Variables to Problem Solving Ability," *Journal of Educational Psychology*, 51:326–33, December, 1960.
24. Hebb, Donald O., *The Organization of Behavior: A Neuropsychological Theory*. New York: Wiley, 1949.
25. Heidbreder, Edna, "The Attainment of Concepts: IV, The Process," *Journal of Psychology*, 24:93–138, July, 1947.
26. Helson, Harry (ed.) and others, *Theoretical Foundations of Psychology*. New York: Van Nostrand, 1951.
27. Hull, Clark A., "Quantitative Aspects of the Evolution of Concepts," *Psychological Monographs*, 28, No. 123, 1–86, 1920.
28. Hunt, Joseph McV., *Intelligence and Experience*, New York: Ronald, 1961.
29. Inhelder, Barbel and Jean Piaget, *The Growth of Logical Thinking from Childhood to Adolescence*. New York: Basic Books, 1958.
30. Johnson, Donald M., "A Modern Account of Problem Solving," *Psychological Bulletin*, 41: 201–229, April, 1944.
31. Kelley, H. H. and J. W. Thebaut, "Experimental Studies of Group Problem Solving and Process," *Handbook of Social Psychology*, Vol. II (Gardner Lindzey, ed.). Cambridge, Mass.: Addison-Wesley, 1954.
32. Kress, Roy, "An Investigation of the Relationship Between Concept Formation and Achievement in Reading." Abstract of Dissertation; private communciation from author, 1960.
33. Langman, Muriel P., "The Reading Process: A Descriptive, Interdisciplinary Approach," *Genetic Psychology Monographs*, 62:3–40, August, 1960.
34. Levin, Harry, Eleanor Gibson, and others, *A Basic Research Program in Reading*. Cooperative Research Project No. 639. Ithaca, New York: Cornell University, 1963. (Mimeo.)
35. Lundsteen, Sara W., *Teaching Abilities in Critical Listening in the Fifth and Sixth Grades*, doctoral dissertation, University of California, Berkeley, 1963.
36. Luria, Aleksandr R., *Speech and the Development of Mental Processes in the Child*. London, England: Staples Press, 1950.
37. MacKinnon, Donald W. (ed.), *The Creative Person*. Proceedings of Conference of IPAR and University Extension. Berkeley: University of California Extension Division, 1961.
38. McCreary, Anne P., "A Study of Association, Reinforcement and Transfer in Beginning Reading," *Journal of Experimental Education*, 31:285–290, Spring, 1963.
39. McKillop, Ann S., *The Relationship Between the Reader's Attitude and Certain Types of Reading Responses*. New York: Bureau of Publications, Teachers College, Columbia University, 1952.
40. McNemar, Olga W., "An Attempt to Differentiate Between Individuals with High and Low Reasoning Ability," *American Journal of Psychology*: 68:20–36, March, 1955.
41. Mowrer, O. Hobart, *Learning Theory and Personality Dynamics*. New York: Ronald, 1950.

42. Osgood, Charles E., G. J. Suci, and P. H. Tannenbaum, *The Measurement of Meaning*. Urbana: University of Illinois Press, 1958.
43. Otto, Wayne, "The Acquisition and Retention of Paired Associates of Good, Average and Poor Readers," *Journal of Educational Psychology*, 52:241–248, October, 1961.
44. Reed, Charles H., *Relationships of Personality and Reading Choices of Sixth-Grade Children*, doctoral dissertation, University of California, Berkeley, 1962.
45. Russell, David H., *Children's Thinking*. Boston: Ginn, 1956.
46. ———, "Concepts," *Encyclopedia of Educational Research*, 3rd edition, (C. W. Harris, ed.). New York: Macmillan, 1960.
47. ———, *Children Learn to Read* (2nd ed.). Boston: Ginn, 1961.
48. ———, "Six Studies of Children's Understanding of Concepts," *Elementary School Journal*, 63:255–260, February, 1963.
49. Saadeh, Ibrahim Q., *An Evaluation of the Effectiveness of Teaching for Critical Thinking in the Sixth Grade*, doctoral dissertation, University of California, Berkeley, 1962.
50. Sochor, E. Elona (ed.), *Critical Thinking: An Introduction*. Bulletin of the National Conference on Research in English, Champaign, Illinois: National Council of Teachers of English, 1959.
51. Spearman, Charles E., *The Abilities of Man*. New York: Macmillan, 1927.
52. Stauffer, Russell G., "Children Can Read and Think Critically," *Education* 80:522–525, May, 1960.
53. Stein, M. I., and S. J. Reinze, (eds.), *Creativity and the Individual*. Glencoe, Ill.: The Free Press, 1960.
54. Taylor, Calvin W., *Creativity: Progress and Potential*. New York: McGraw-Hill, 1964.
55. ———, and Frank Barron. (eds.). *Scientific Creativity: Its Recognition and Development*. New York: Wiley, 1963.
56. Torrance, E. Paul, (ed.), *Creativity: Proceedings of the Second Minnesota Conference on Gifted Children*. Minneapolis: University of Minnesota Extension Division, 1959.
57. ———, (ed.), *Talent and Education: Present Status and Future Directions*. Minneapolis: University of Minnesota Press, 1960.
58. Welch, Livingston, and L. Long, "The Higher Structural Phases of Concept Formation in Children," *Journal of Psychology*, 9:59–95, January, 1940.
59. Wertheimer, Max, *Productive Thinking*. New York: Harper, 1945.
60. Wohlwill, Joachim, "Developmental Studies of Perception," *Psychological Bulletin*, 57:249–288, July, 1960.

THE NATURE OF THE READING
PROCESS AND BUILDING BALANCED
READING PROGRAMS *

By way of introduction I should like to review briefly a few points of the history of this conference. During the summer of 1932 the conference began as a feeble infant. Its first expression was, however, a cry of protest against the traditional restrictive practices then operative with concern for reading.

Like another babe in history, it was left floating among the academic bull-rushes in the hope that some understanding and sympathetic soul might find it and nurture it to maturity. Within a brief time a group of modern Pharaoh's daughters, viz.; Alpha Iota Chapter of Pi Lambda Theta, discovered it and adopted it as their ward. For some twenty-five or more years they nursed and cared for it, guiding its development, financing its sessions, and publishing and distributing its yearbooks.

Under their expert supervision and guidance the conference grew and developed; always, however, maintaining its original purpose: *the presentation and implementation of a more tenable idea concerning the nature of the reading process and of the ways in which that process serves mankind.*

A few years ago they were surprised and pleased to learn that this is the oldest conference in America that has consistently dealt with reading. They experienced even greater pleasure when Dr. William S. Gray, the dean of American students of reading, pointed out that this conference is the "only conference with a message." He amplified that statement by citing the conference theme and asserting its intrinsic validity.

In 1958 the conference held its final session under its old sponsorship. In that year it published the twenty-third volume of its distinguished yearbook series. It had successfully survived its infancy and adolescence and had now reached a status of "legal maturity." Hence, like sensible parents, its sponsors released it to seek its own associates and to direct its own course, hoping all the while that it would continue to grow and that it would attract worthy associates.

Since this is the first session following the untimely death of Dr. Gray, it seems appropriate that we turn to him with respect and appreciation, making use of another of his timely expressions. Some years ago he published a book

* REPRINTED by permission of the Claremont Reading Conference from the *Claremont College Reading Conference Yearbook*, Vol. 25, 1961, pp. 1–10.

with the title, "*On Their Own in Reading.*" That book was designed to describe the development of competency and independence on the part of readers. Today we are witnessing a dramatic illustration of that idea as applied to this conference.

Many of its former sponsors are gathered here within this large group of participants joyously witnessing their creation and former ward now "On Its Own in Reading." It would be difficult to express their feelings of gratification as they recognize their "baby" now on its own, but still holding true to the purpose for which it was created. The conference theme is still the same theme which has held together its founders and sponsors through the years.

Under the directorship of Dr. Malcolm Douglass and now under official sponsorship of Claremont College the conference shows every evidence of being fully developed, ready and equipped to serve. It has continued the publication of the yearbook series and it has taken constructive measures to increase the contacts with the instructional programs in the schools.

The special theme for this, the twenty-eighth annual session of the conference, is "*Meeting the Issues in Reading.*" In order to proceed constructively with the consideration of that theme there is need to establish some commonality of concern. For example, we need to make clear what the term "reading" is intended to denote. We need to identify the "issues," and we need to delimit the degree to which those issues are designed to be met.

Some years ago I was privileged to hear Dr. Robert Millikan discuss "*The Value of an Idea.*" I recall that he pointed out how tremendously important a good idea can be. He also made clear how devastating a poor idea may be if it is accepted and made the basis for human behavior. There is need to scrutinize ideas with great care.

This thought is illustrated and reinforced by an anecdote regarding Dr. Einstein. Someone asked Dr. Einstein how he accounted for his great and unique contributions to science. Without hesitation, Einstein replied, "*I challenged an axiom.*"

To be able to "challenge an axiom" and then successfully to demonstrate that the challenge was justified is the essence of good thinking. Too often there is a tendency to assume an idea as being valid and valuable without observing what it does when applied in human behavior.

There is a third statement similar to those cited above which has bearing upon our present consideration. It is, "*Beyond the Obvious Lies the Truth.*" That which is obvious is very likely to be superficial and symptomatic. *Truth* is not likely to be so readily discerned. It will be achieved only with greater effort.

With these ideas serving as a frame of reference let us approach the consideration of the conference theme, "Meeting the Issues in Reading." This conference series was initiated to "challenge an axiom," viz: *that reading is a special type of behavior which must be learned and which is utilized mainly in response to printed-word stimulation.*

That printed-words must be read in order that they may serve effectively the process of communication is self-evident, *i.e.*; axiomatic. But, that they constitute the whole or even a major portion of the stimulation which men must read is not a tenable corollary. Spoken-words, as vehicles for expression and communication, are comparable in every respect to written or printed-words and they surely must be sensed and interpreted, i.e. *read*, efficiently. Furthermore, words are merely symbols for ideas. The creation of the ideas to be symbolized is prerequisite to the use of words in any form for their expression.

This conference, throughout its existence, has presented the thesis that *"reading is the process of making discriminative responses."* The modifier, *discriminative*, expresses a very important aspect of the definition. Numerous synonyms, for that expression are in frequent use in educational literature, *e.g.*; "adaptive," "adjustive," "apt," fitting," "suitable," etc. The implication is that the response has been designed to serve the needs of the reader in the situation as the reader comprehends it.

A second important aspect of this concept is that it specifies no particular stimulus. Stimulation is implied, certainly, since response is indicated. However, the human body is equipped with many sense processes, *i.e.*; with many avenues of stimulation, and all of them must be read. There are important types of reading associated with each of our sensory processes. For example, we do visual-reading, aural-reading, tactile-reading, thermal-reading, olfactory-reading, kinesthetic-reading, etc.

This conference has pointed out that reading is an innate behavioral endowment. Reading is as native to human behavior as is digestion, respiration, or any other of the fundamental life processes. *THAT* one will read is assured by nature. But, *WHAT* one reads and *HOW WELL* the reading acts are performed are heavily affected by one's environment and one's experiencing.

To state that we begin to read at a certain age or at a specified stage of development makes about as much sense as to assert that, "Life Begins At Forty." Actually reading, like life, is operative prior to birth and serves continuously throughout the life span. However, there is also a sequential development of one's abilities with reading, and there is also shifting or redirecting of concern for what is important to be read with care. Among human beings there is no such person as a "non-reader." Everyone reads something. There is, however, a very considerable number of poor or inefficient readers as regards many of the important phases of our environment. Educational consideration for development "in and through reading" will be best achieved when it is directed toward particularized reading tasks. For example, Ann Bryan McCall pointed out that educational development consists in learning to read more effectively "oneself, other people, and things."

Given such a broad and demonstrably pertinent frame of reference for educational concern, one readily senses how inadequate is the restrictive concept that reading is merely a special type of behavior which is used mainly with printed-word stimulation. Printed-words are only one of multitudinous "things" which concern human behavior.

This conference has identified the reading process as being the act of sensing a stimulus situation, of interpreting that which is sensed, and performing an adaptive response which is designed adequately to cope with the sensed situation in a manner that is advantageous to the reader. For the facilitation of educational consideration the process may be conveniently structured into four sequential segments, each of which has its special characteristics and its corresponding educational problems.

The first or initial segment of the reading process is the *stimulus*. Actually the stimulus is peripheral to the reading act. It exists, very often, whether or not it is being sensed. For example, the printed-words exist in a book whether or not some one peruses them.

The second segment, and the first which is intrinsic with the reading process, is the act of stimulation or reception, *i.e. sensing*. There are many sense modalities thru which stimulation occurs. All are important for a proper consideration of reading behavior. There are characteristic types of reading associated with each of our sense modalities.

The third segment, and the heart of the reading process, is *perception*. Perception is the process of creating meaning and giving significance to that which is sensed. Edgar Dale has aptly characterized this stage of the reading process as "changing sensitivity into sensibility."

The fourth and final segment of a reading act may be identified as the *response* or *expression* phase. The *reading* has occurred during the preceding segment. During the response stage the reader is endeavoring to express by means of adaptive or adjustive behavior his understanding of the situation which he has sensed and interpreted. When the response behavior is aptly performed, it serves as a fair measure of the validity of the reading. However, when the behavior is inept, it is sometimes difficult to determine whether the deficiency is due to the reader's understanding or to his inability to perform as effectively as he perceives. Shakespeare put it very well when he wrote, "If to do were as easy as to know what were good to be done . . . ."

The reading process may be structurally pictured as follows:

STIMULUS	STIMULATION
Any thing which activates any sense receptor.	The activation of sense receptors. Transforming non-neural impulses into neural impulses.

PERCEPTION	EXPRESSION
Cognition, recognition, association, creating meaning, giving significance, formulating plan of action, activating and directing response mechanisms.	Performing the adaptive responses as directed, *e.g.*; orally expressing the words and word patterns as perceived under visual stimulation.

Of course, reading is a continuous behavior process. The response expressions are in turn read in association with the stimulus which provoked them. The response directives are what have been pertinently caled "Provisional Tries" for coping with the situations as sensed. If the response is aptly performed, and if it appears to meet the needs of the situation, it serves to confirm the reading. If, however, the response proves to be unsuited, it is necessary to determine whether the fault lies with the perception, *i.e.*, the reading aspect, or with the performance of the directive. Each reading act arises out of, emerges from, a preceding reading act, and merges into subsequent reading behavior.

Each of the structural segments of the reading process constitutes an area of special regard for us as educators. For example, since one's environment abounds with stimuli for reading, there is need to develop selectivity regarding *what* one will read with special care. Knowing *what to read* in any given situation is an important aspect of efficiency with reading. Comparably, arranging stimuli which are readily readable is a prominent factor in the facilitation of communication.

Among the "issues in reading" the problem of *what to read* needs careful consideration. The current concern for instruction in "phonics" or "phonetics" is a case in point. The "what-to-read" focus of such instruction is upon the "oral-aural cues inscribed within visual symbols." It is a "look-and-say" procedure altho, strangely enough, it purports to be opposed thereto. Oral-aural cues may facilitate the process of transforming visual word symbols into corresponding spoken-and-heard word symbols, but unless the reader can associate meaningful referents with the words when spoken or heard, communication does not occur. There is need to recognize that *words are merely symbols of ideas*. Therefore, attention needs to be centered upon the ideas and upon processes of ideating. In this connection it is well to point out how the restrictive definition of reading impedes this process.

Identifying reading as a special type of behavior for responding to printed-word stimulation excludes from the reading program the experiences requisite for creating the ideas which the printed-words symbolize. Without the ideas which they symbolize, words become counterfeit as media for communication. Educationally there is need to distinguish between *primary reading activity* and *secondary reading activity*. Primary reading consists in the direct experiencing of things in their concrete existence. This is the source of ideas which, for convenience, are symbolized. Secondary reading, on the other hand, deals with symbols to which meanings must be associated as the arrangement of the symbols is designed to map.

The second stage of the reading process has to do with the efficiency of the reception of the stimulation. Developmental instruction programs have been strangely remiss in their consideration of the receptive process. I notice with pleasure that this conference program has a section which is concerned with the processes of seeing and of hearing. That has been a consistent procedure with the sessions in the past. The yearbooks of the conference are rich as a reference source for discussions of the sensory processes. However, there is much still to be accomplished in that regard before we shall have effectively served this phase of reading behavior.

Since the term reading is so commonly associated with the process of visually sensing printed-words, it seems appropriate that we consider the process of visual reception, i.e., seeing, at this time. Comparable consideration should properly be given to the other sensory receptive processes if we treat of reading in its most tenable identification.

Sight is the process of sensing light waves and of transforming them into visual impulses. This transformation is accomplished by cells of the retina assisted by the other parts of the eye. Visual perception, commonly termed "vision," is a perceptive process which is performed by other areas of the central nervous system, particularly the brain.

A proper consideration of the processes of sight and of visual perception has been impeded by another of our "axiomatic" ideas, viz.; by accident, or other causes, sight or visual perception may be destroyed, hence care must be taken to prevent blindness and to conserve sight. Laudable and desirable as that idea is, it has tended to direct the reading of the visual process away from some of its extremely important characteristics. While sight and vision are gifts of nature, they are processes which are amenable to development. Some of the development consists in aiding the seeing process by means of optical instruments such as microscopes telescopes, and various devices for transforming non-visual stimuli into visible evidence, e.g., x-ray photography. Other forms of development have to do with learning how to see more effectively and how to perform visual perception more efficiently.

The defectiveness of our reading of the visual process is well illustrated by the fact that visual reception is commonly measured by a device which measures only monocular acuity and that at a distance of twenty feet. This seems unexplainable when even a casual observation reveals that printed-word reading is most frequently attempted with two eyes and at a distance of approximately fourteen inches. The differences between the monocular seeing of a single letter form at a distance of twenty feet and the binocular sensing of words and word patterns in a continuously changing sequence at a few inches are numerous and educationally important. For too long those differences have been ignored in our programs for developmental reading. Investigations have revealed that efficiency in seeing is an educational achievement which few persons accomplish but which can be attained thru educational assistance.

What has been pointed out concerning visual reception is equally true with regard to our other reception processes. One of the "issues in reading" is that of implementing and facilitating the sensory avenues thru which our reading is initiated. We need to be producers of sensory efficiency as well as consumers of sensory processes.

The third segment of the reading process is the one in which the actual reading is accomplished. This is the little understood but extremely important process of perception. During this segment sensory impulses are transformed into ideas and they in turn are transformed into neural impulses directing performance of our reacting mechanisms. The sensory impulses from all of the receptor organs which are activated are amalgamated, combined with the memory images which are recalled or "retrieved," given meaning and significance in the light of the perceiver's attitudinal biases and his goal purposes. This is the heart of the reading process and *it is always accomplished silently*. The two preceding stages and the final stages are in a very real sense peripheral but none the less important.

The process of making memory images readily recallable and of expediting their association with present sensory stimuli is one of great educational importance. To the extent that organic processes and general metabolism factor in the facilitation of recall, assistance from health services may be needed. However, educational development must accept responsibility for leading the educand to utilize the products of previous experiencing effectively to aid in giving meaningful significance to situations presently being sensed.

As this conference has repeatedly pointed out, restrictive definitions of areas of knowledge or of processes of behavior tend to impede the perceptive process. For example, when the consideration of phonics or phonetics is restricted to the identification of sound cues within printed-words, it fails to utilize the development of aural reading and of phonic expression which occurs with music, and with other applications of sound-reading. Recognizing that reading occurs with all sorts of stimuli and that it functions in all types of human behavior tends to facilitate the spread of learning and thereby to aid the process of giving meaning to presently sensed situations.

The final segment of a reading activity has to do with the performing of the response adjustment, *i.e.; with the expression of what was read*. When the expression takes the form of overt behavior, it can be read by other persons as well as by the performer of the response. To the degree that the response effectively expresses the reader's comprehension of what he has read, it may serve as a measure of the quality of his reading. However, when the act of responding presents aspects which interfere with the facile expression of the reader's ideas and purposes, it may well give a faulty impression of the true quality of the reading that was performed. For example, my ability to choose words and to arrange them in sequential order and then to express them with appropriate phonic emphasis may be inadequate to communicate to you the products of my thinking. If such is the case, the fault may lie with the expression segment of the reading process rather than with the perceptive segment. Of course, the perceptive segment may have been faulty also, but until it is adequately expressed there is no way of determining that.

The response or expression segment of a reading activity is almost as peripheral to the actual reading as is the stimulus segment. The reading has occurred prior to the expression or the adaptive responding. *All reading is done silently.* The term "reading out loud" is a semantic misnomer, since it refers to the expression of the reading which has been accomplished and which serves as a directive for the responding. The term "oral reading" may have educational values but it misrepresents the true nature of the activity. The words have been sensed and perceived previous to their being spoken. The speech is an expression of the reading and not the reading itself.

Each of the stages or segments of the reading process as they have been identified has educational significance. While they differ substantially as to their intrinsic natures, they are dynamically interrelated to such an extent that inadequacy in any stage affects the adequacy of the whole process. In like manner, each activity of reading occurs in sequential relationship with the acts which have preceded it and with those which follow. This condition naturally raises a question as to what constitutes *the* reading program of our schools.

This conference has presented reading as being synonymous with learning, with perceiving, and with the making of adaptive responses. Since the educational development of the individual needs to be balanced and to be equated with his needs, there are general phases of reading development and there are special phases as well.

The entire curriculum is the school's reading program. What one reads is the distinguishing feature which identifies the various areas of subject matter. *How* that reading may be most effectively accomplished is a proper concern for every instructional endeavor. Pointing out the WHAT and assisting with the HOW are the functions which are implied by the statement, "Every teacher is a teacher of reading."

Instruction *IN* reading may or may not be concerned directly with printed-words. It has to do with the developing of abilities to read more effectively the things of concern for a particular regard for reading. Instruction *THROUGH* reading is a different matter. While instruction THROUGH reading is not entirely disparate from instruction IN reading, the major emphasis is placed upon the achieving of knowledge about the things being read. Balance is important as regards these differing emphases in a developmental reading program.

Recently there appeared in the *Air Force Magazine* the following statement: "The World, for the first time in history, has been reduced to manageable size; and that means that sooner or later, by orderly process or by violence, someone will manage it; either a world democracy or a world dictator." (Van Zandt)

Instruction *in* reading will aid one to sense and to identify the words and word-patterns of the preceding statement, but it will be only *through* reading that the import and the importance of the word-map will be comprehended. Conceiving and then administering a program of developmental reading which will bring about, "by orderly process," a world democracy constitutes a challenge of the first magnitude. In order to accomplish such a goal we shall need a well balanced and highly productive program which has as its major concern the development of abilities effectively. to read ourselves, the other people on the Earth, and the things which affect human behavior.

In a program of such magnitude trivia have a place, but we must not become bogged down by them. We must think broadly and creatively. Ideas and ideals are matters of great importance. We must learn to "challenge axioms" and make them intellectually valid or discard them. We must read "beyond the obvious." We must utilize effectively all of our sensory avenues. We must provide a balanced intellectual diet as well as a balanced nutritional one. The entire curriculum is the school's reading program.

Chapter 2

READING POWER: WHAT KINDS?

Reading for different purposes or different kinds of satisfactions not only necessitates selecting different kinds of materials to read, it also requires different kinds of reading skills or reading powers.

In fact, reading may well be considered an expression of individual power. First of all, the individual, in choosing to read, exerts his own authority over the act of reading. He puts himself in the position of selecting the act of reading as an experience to be had.

Secondly, the individual, in deciding what he shall read, exerts his own jurisdiction over the content of materials to be read. Within that decision, he further selects the particular content of meaning to him.

Thirdly, the individual exerts command over the reading situation because he controls the decoding and translating of symbols. No one but he can perceive and conceptualize the material; in this way he experiences his reading.

Fourth, in exercising the ability to use his reading experience the individual must interpret it in terms of personal thought and behavior. In this sense, reading materials themselves exert no power, although some materials stimulate thought and imagination more profoundly than others. But the power inherent in materials lies dormant until a reader discovers it and draws it forth for personal use. Specialized vocabularies, concepts, and intricate, complex thoughts carry meanings only when the reader exerts his power to activate those meanings.

What emerges then is evidence of the personal nature of reading and the lack of any terminal point for development of reading powers. Not only must the individual gain power as a reader, he must also become aware of a need to gain power; he must become aware of the constancy and the range of his growing power in reading. At no time should material to be read become more important than the individual. Reading materials are only tools to enable the reader to achieve power. Appropriate reading matter for one child may not be appropriate for another child.

Being able to read may prove meaningless if the content of reading denies human growth or fails to increase intelligent behavior. Likewise, not being able to read may prove to be a denial of human growth and dreary acceptance of a static intelligence. Is it true that any reading experience is desirable? Or that to gain a narrow form of reading power is to have gained broad encompassing reading power? Are the goals and values of reading achieved through any one track of reading development?

How these questions are answered depend upon whether one chooses to view reading as an ongoing experience of developing powers inherent in the reader, or whether one chooses to believe that the recall of printed symbols of particular content is the sine qua non of reading achievement.

GREATER READING POWER
NEEDED TODAY *

Roma Gans

A NYONE who has even a slight acquaintance with today's children notices how up to date their interests are. Penetration of space, changing of car patterns and packaging of foods are topics with which they are at home. They are eager to explore new ideas and, if encouraged, ask for more. Many educators, parents and producers of materials for children recognize this learning readiness. As a result good schools are continually altering their programs to include more study of the fascinating world about us and are providing books, pamphlets, films and filmstrips which help the child to grow as an informed individual and as one who is motivated to keep up to date.

Emphasis is on continuing one's quest for information and pursuing reading as a regular way of learning. This emphasis is relatively new and absolutely essential if a child is to acquire reading habits and powers which will fit him for constructive living. According to test results of the past several decades, we have produced readers who do well on comprehension and relevant skills. But polls examining adult reading habits reveal the disturbing fact that we have failed to produce a truly reading public, adults who keep up with current affairs via newspapers and magazines and who read books of any kind. *Obviously we produce readers who can read, but too many who don't.* Therefore, along with a concern for developing real powers in reading must be a direct effort to create a continuing, self-propelling reader.

WHETTING APPETITE TO READ WIDELY

Many promising efforts in developing such readers can be found in schools. Carefully planned studies of problems and topics in science and social studies—through which children even in primary grades help select reference books, collect pertinent articles from books, papers, and magazines, and stay with one such study for several days and often for weeks—start many a youngster on the path of his continuing reading. He also discovers how much there is to know on almost every topic, a discovery which he might not make if taught in the short lesson-by-the-day manner. A reader whose appetite gets whetted to read about dinosaurs, the Lewis and Clark expedition or space

* REPRINTED by permission of Roma Gans and the Association for Childhood Education International, 3615 Wisconsin Avenue, N.W., Washington, D.C., from *Childhood Education*, Vol. 38, November, 1961, pp. 104–107. Copyright © 1961 by the Association.

explorations is tooling himself for perpetuating his education. Teachers and parents who help a child capture this eagerness to read have started him on a promising road of intelligent living.

There are other essential goals in today's reading programs which are proper for these times. In general, schools are eager to teach children to become comprehending critical and selective readers. The "reading-to-give-back" emphasis common in schools thirty or forty years ago may still be the major emphasis in some isolated spots, but in general schools have demonstrated genuine competence in giving broader and more adequate focus to reading programs. The expansion of library facilities in elementary and secondary schools is one form of evidence to support this observation. However, when we examine practices and materials now frequently determined in central administration or curriculum leaders' offices another question presents itself: Are the practices and materials we recommend consistent with our goals? In some (perhaps many) classrooms, yes. In thousands, no. The problem of unraveling the meaning of broadly stated goals in terms of what they imply in day-to-day classroom life has not been adequately met in either large or small school systems.

READING FOR DECISION-MAKING

A sketchy look at *power-in-reading* reveals that a reader must develop the abilities necessary to recognize words, to get at the author's meanings, to see the interrelationship of ideas from beginning to end of the story or article, to recall essential points and to make some personal reactions to them, such as "I like this," "Don't like this," "I believe it," "This is important," or "I am not sure of this." These aspects of power have been widely recognized and taught in our schools. With the provision of new texts and materials and some changes in method, these reading competencies have been developed. They go considerably beyond the reading-to-recall emphasis of earlier teaching.

However, the power which today's child needs must go beyond this stage. Its development cannot be achieved merely by purchasing new materials and altering some methods. Today's child faces a world in deep controversy. Most important matters on the international and national front are at issue. Not only are there pro and con positions but many variations in between. A conscientious citizen, the type we hope to be developing, takes decision-making seriously. Before he takes a stand on water chloridation, increase in sales taxes, the school bond issue, and increased aid to South America, he tries to gather data, weigh different points of view, and finally relates various proposals to his basic philosophy. To be unable to follow a process similar to this or to be unwilling to makes him either a pawn in the hands of others or an opinionated non-thinker. The use of reading in the decision-making process demands the application of abilities to think effectively. Schools in stressing critical reading have recognized the involvement of thinking, but proper help to teachers and leaders in the field on developing thinking is only at a beginning.

ATMOSPHERE CONDUCIVE TO THINKING

The critical reader who will be able to meet his desire to make competent choices in important matters must be schooled in the ability to think—not only to recognize and recall what he reads but also to grow in his ability to unravel complicated ideas, to analyze them in terms of relevance to the issue at point, to synthesize, to appreciate adequacy and inadequacy of data and ultimately to evaluate and come to a tentative or final conclusion. Such intellectual powers cannot be confined to a child's reading only but must be a part of the child's whole everyday environment. The classroom atmosphere must be conducive to thinking. It must be an atmosphere in which all youngsters feel at ease, are encouraged to think for themselves and to express their ideas even if divergent from others including the teacher's, and are able to accept correction and help in thinking better.

Central to the creation of such a thinking classroom is a thinking teacher—one who is free, encouraged and helped to develop a challenging intellectual classroom atmosphere. However, this is a professional need crying for attention. Crowded classrooms, congested time schedules and "required achievements" all too often minimize or blot out a teacher's concern for *time to think*. This observation alone should cause us to give serious attention to the quality of life which goes on in far too many schools today. Helpful books, pamphlets and reports of research on thinking are becoming increasingly available to reading program planners; and curriculum and reading specialists, along with teachers and school leaders, must face all changes in common procedures which will help meet this crucial need.

Along with the importance of the classroom atmosphere and the competence of the teacher is the quality of the curriculum with its implicit materials. Content areas that include both current and past important phases open up the interests and encourage the inquiries that aid the child in becoming an informed student. They also acquaint him with materials, various forms of writing, varied ways of presenting data as well as the substance out of which thought-provoking questions arise.

Techniques of discussion and skill in using them are also a part of the teacher's concern.

Well-guided discussion is an essential part of a program geared to develop high-powered reading. The hurried short-answer oral or written comprehension check meets many a classroom need; but its use to the exclusion of thoughtful discussion, sharing of divergent views, pausing to consider and reconsider the use of all the other ways of getting into the deeper understanding of an important learning will deny a child the right to develop as a thinker.

If one accepts points thus far presented, many common assumptions and practices need to be examined. Children need more opportunity and guidance in the selection of materials in school and public libraries. They also need to become selective buyers so that they continue as adults to be competent purchasers and subscribers. Much more opportunity is needed to discuss materials than the crowded schedule of today permits. More attention to authorship is long overdue, and for intermediate and upper grades such problems as ghostwriting, editorialized news and slanted writing are properly included to increase the child's competence in working his way through today's materials.

Changes in Evaluating Growth

The enhancement of reading power of the kind presented here will demand material changes in evaluating reading growth. Some essential reading skills can be assessed by current tests. Others, however, will require new tests and even year-round observations. Such questions as: Are youngsters growing in ability to act independently to material read? Are they selecting materials for a study with concern for relevance, date of publication, authorship and all the rest? Are they becoming more sensitive to subtle meanings? Do they ask about the author's purpose or motive? Answers to such questions and others must become a part of the assessment of reading growth.

Children are ready for this deeper concept of reading. It remains for administrators, teachers, curriculum and reading specialists to aid the steady progress toward the development of such reading power. To stop short of the inclusive changes required is to short-change today's child.

BUT—SKILLS ARE NOT ENOUGH *

A. Sterl Artley

It requires no argument to convince even a layman that a reading program could not long endure without attention to the development of skills. Much of the basic training for any type of work, a trade for example, is spent in acquiring skill in the use of tools and apparatus. So it is in reading, for one of the accepted goals of a sound program is the promotion of growth *in* reading as a process. To this end time and teaching effort go into the development of word attack skills, and of basic abilities in comprehension and interpretation. That these are skills indispensable to the reading act, goes without saying—but skills are not enough.

It would be salutary if one were to ask himself the simple question, "Why

* REPRINTED FROM the May, 1959, issue of *Education*. Copyright 1959 by the Bobbs-Merrill Company, Inc., Indianapolis, Indiana.

am I teaching reading?" In answer, considered thought would lead him to conclude that really the important goal is *what happens to the reader as a result of the skills he is applying.* This may be in terms of clearer insights and broadened understandings, heightened emotional responses, reinforced or changed attitudes, and modification in behavior,—in short, personal and social development. Growth *through* reading is the ultimate goal of instruction, while growth *in* reading is the means to that end. Unfortunately we seem to have gotten ourselves so ensnarled in issues relating to phonics, oral reading, and "self-selection," that we have lost sight of what happens, or should happen, to the reader. As Dr. Alstetter says in a recent article, ". . . we have confused the acquisition of skills and their creative use. We have called the skills reading when they are no more that than a book of recipes is cooking." (1)

It is to this point that David Russell writes in the recent proceedings of the International Reading Association, "High-level reading abilities are important . . . but the day has gone by when we can defend the place of reading in schools only on the basis of developing effective reading skills. In the years ahead, reading can keep its present place in the school curriculum only if it helps the individual in some of his important personal problems." (9:12) Russell then continues by showing how reading may provide the raw materials for thinking, the motivation for critical evaluation, and the basis of concepts and understandings about cultural values.

THE TYPE OF CONTENT IS IMPORTANT

If growth is to take place toward the attainment of accepted cultural patterns, of desirable attitudes with resultant modification in behavior, then it is obvious that the reading material itself must be rich in values. This does not mean that it must be "preachy" or obviously moralistic, but it should be rich in values and portray life realistically. One must be sure that what "brushes off" on the reader leaves him a better, richer person.

It is obvious that comics, series books, and lurid drugstore paper-backs can hardly suffice as a diet on which to promote mature growth. The teacher who made the comment in reference to the quality of material her children were reading, "What difference does it make, they're reading, aren't they?" had missed the point completely that there is more to reading than the practice of skills, that there is a residue, or, using a modern term, a "fall-out" from a book that may have lasting and pronounced effects.

The building of life values through story content begins early and continues throughout school and life. On the preprimer level understanding of human relationships begins as children read stories of home life and observe wholesome and desirable relationships between parents, brothers, and sisters. It continues as they see in well-written stories how a peer group shares fun, problems, and responsibilities. In the middle grades they note examples of good sportsmanship and responsible behavior from which they draw guiding principles for everyday living. On the level of the upper grades and junior high school their insights into human relations are carried to higher levels in stories that allow the child to recognize the inner resources of strength and ability that lie in themselves and others, to discover ways of handling handicaps and disappointments, and to recognize human qualities that lie behind an outward appearance. Story quality *is* important and no flimsy, whimsical tale, even though garbed about with clever illustrations, can be considered even a poor substitute.

Content Plus

But as interesting and well-written as materials may be and as many values as they may possess, these values are not necessarily transmitted to the reader through the sheer process of literal comprehension. They are extracted by a depth and quality of reading that has to be developed and stimulated. Regurgitating the facts, "knowing the story," preparing synopses, or answering questions about the details may have little or no influence on the reader in terms of his attitudes and behavior.

Some time ago a news article reported a case of vandalism in a junior high school. Desks were over-turned, windows were smashed, ink was thrown on the walls, and chalk boards were smashed. When the culprits were apprehended it was discovered that they were ninth grade pupils attending that school. What was not reported in the article was that in the ninth grade all the students "took" a course in civics or social living. It would not be too much to expect that the boys involved had been doing acceptable work in the course. They knew the answers, they even may have possessed certain skills of a good reader, but the facts were never translated into appropriate behavior.

Teaching reading so that desirable thought and behavior patterns eventuate becomes our primary problem. The process of making reading an integrative experience has been likened by Dr. Gray to placing a drop of bluing in a container of water. The bluing quickly loses its identity as such and becomes a part of the water. Chemically the water is changed, though the change may not be readily apparent to the viewer. This process is contrasted with one in which a hand-full of pebbles is dropped into a similar container. The pebbles remain pebbles, and the water is unchanged (7). In the case of the junior high boys above, the facts they had acquired, like the pebbles in the water, remained facts. As such, they could be tested and handed back to the teacher, but they were never integrated into desirable thought and action patterns. Insights, attitudes, and behavior are not changed by exhortation or verbal precept but by living—and reading should be an experience in living.

From evidence accumulated by research the process of integration appears to be closely allied with the ability of the reader to identify closely with the material being read. In a sense a mature reader is one who is able to lose himself in time and space and become an actual participant in the action taking place, whether it be a narrative account, a poem, or a historical episode.

In this sense, reading becomes an experience that has the quality of a first-hand experience.

The Place of Imagery

Making reading an experience through close identification with content may be promoted in several ways. Of these, two will be mentioned here. The first is that of helping the reader create imagery as he reads—imagery that involves sight, hearing, taste, smell, touch, and kinesthesis. Figuratively speaking, the reader creates through the stimuli of verbal symbols a motion picture in the mind's eye—in technicolor, with sound effects, and with added impressions of taste, touch, and smell.

Dr. Center (4) calls this, "third-dimensional reading" and comments on its importance as follows: "Unless he (the reader) forms a close partnership with the writer, thinking, imagining, feeling with him, the reader will not be affected by what he reads . . . . If the reader senses literature as human experience, no power can prevent his being stimulated by it." A well-written book, read by a creative reader, leaves its indelible imprint on the heart and mind.

"Third dimensional reading" is not innate or automatic, but needs to be developed the same as other reading abilities. This may be done through teacher questions deliberately designed to evoke different types of imagery. On the primary level a story titled, "Fun in the Snow" gave rise to such questions as, "How do you feel as you go swishing down a long hill on your sled? Describe what you see and hear. Can you feel the tug on the rope as you pull your sled back up the hill?"

On the upper grade level an exciting adventure story of two boys caught in a flooded building lends itself to such imagery evoking questions as these: "How did the opening sentences of the story describing the lightning and rain make you feel!" "What did you hear?" "What can you see as you look into the muddy water surrounding the building?" "How does it feel to be pulled into a hovering helicopter?" As young readers experience the excitement and tension of the story they thrill to the characters' ingenuity and come to appreciate that clear thinking, combined with an understanding of the scientific wonder of telegraphy made the difference between peril and safety.

Imagery is encouraged, not because it makes the reading more interesting, but because it creates an experience with the reader becoming a participant in the action of the story. In the words of Center, ". . . he forms a close partnership with the writer, thinking, feeling, imagining with him . . ." and thus is affected by the story.

The Place of Reaction

Close identification of reader with reading content may be brought about also by providing him an opportunity to react to the material critically or emotionally. When a child responds to such questions as, "If you had been Joe, would you have gone home without your dog?" or "Do you think it would have been a good idea for Tom to have put the baby squirrel in a cage and kept it for a pet?" he must for a few brief moments stand in the shoes of the story characters, face a problem situation, and make a response. As he reacts to events and episodes he makes generalizations and develops understandings that affect his attitudes, and thereby, his behavior.

The influence of reaction in changing attitudes and behavior was dramatically illustrated by Brady (3) in a report of the activities of the staff of the Intergroup Education in Cooperating Schools. This group made the discovery that if story content was to have any influence on existing attitudes, definite provisions had to be made to elicit pupil reactions. She writes, "Teachers learned how to conduct discussions which revealed what students thought, felt, or believed as a result of reading and in identifying what implications for behavior were present." As pupils became adept at projecting themselves into a situation they were able to read such a story as *Spotty*, the rabbit that was different in an all-white rabbit family, and see it as an instance of rejection. The children then concluded that, "it is not right to leave people out because 'their father does a different kind of work' or 'because they have a different religion.'" Hence, *Spotty* became more than an interesting animal story. It served as a mirror that reflected their own feelings and behavior. As they experienced in thought and feeling the action of the story their attitudes were modified accordingly.

Reading as a Social Experience

It should be pointed out that though changes taking place through reading are an individual matter, they can be brought about more effectively as children respond and react to each other over material that has been read as a common experience. Each reader's reactions trigger off reactions and feelings in others. The resultant is not one idea added to another, but one idea integrated with another. In this case, using Dr. Gray's analogy, the container of water becomes chemically different because drops of different colors along with their shades and tints are placed in it.

Summary

Reading should be used as a means of developing insights and understandings, of promoting growth toward pleasing and stable personalities. Through rich experiencing and close personal identification the child grows through reading. To this end skills are important and essential, but in Alstetter's words, "To stop with the teaching of the skills is downright cheating for that is only the beginning." (1)

SELECTED BIBLIOGRAPHY

1. Alstetter, Mabel. "How Full Is Full," *The Reading Teacher*, 12 (October, 1958), 14–18.

2. Arbuthnot, May Hill. "The Child and His Books," Ch. I, *Children and Books.* Chicago: Scott, Foresman, 1957.

3. Brady, Elizabeth Hall. "Promoting Maturity in Interpreting What Is Read: When the Purpose Is To Modify Attitudes and Behavior," 162–167, *Promoting Growth Toward Maturity in Interpreting What Is Read.* Supplementary Educational Monograph, No. 74. Chicago: University of Chicago Press, November, 1951.

4. Center, Stella. "Begin With the Best for the Young Reader," *Junior Libraries,* 1 (September 15, 1954), 8–10.

5. Cleary, Florence Damon. "Reading for Understanding and Values," Ch. 5, *Blueprints for Better Reading.* New York: H. W. Wilson Co., 1957.

6. Gray, William S. "Promoting Personal and Social Development Through Reading," *Promoting Personal and Social Growth Through Reading.* Supplementary Educational Monograph, No. 64. Chicago: University of Chicago Press, October, 1947.

7. ——, "Basic Competencies in Efficient Reading," *Reading in An Age of Mass Communication* (W. S. Gray, Editor). New York: Appleton-Century-Crofts, 1949.

8. Rosenblatt, Louise. "The Enriching Values of Reading," *Reading in An Age of Mass Communication* (W. S. Gray, Editor). New York: Appleton-Century-Crofts, 1949.

9. Russell, David. "Personal Values in Reading," *The Reading Teacher,* 12 (October, 1958), 3–9.

10. ——, "Reading for Effective Personal Living," *Reading for Effective Living,* pp. 12–17. International Reading Association Conference Proceedings Vol. III, 1958. New York: Scholastic Magazines.

11. Seegers, J. Conrad. "Some Aspects of Verbalism," *Elementary English,* 30 (November, 1953), 437–443.

12. Waples, Douglas, et al. *What Reading Does to People.* Chicago: University of Chicago Press, 1940.

TEACHING CRITICAL READING IN THE MIDDLE GRADES *

By Jeraldine Hill

One of the purposes in teaching children to read is that they may ultimately be able to think for themselves. A good reader is not only one who can read, but one who does read, enjoys reading and knows how to use what he has read. A search through literature on teaching reading reveals much written on

* REPRINTED with the permission of the National Council of Teachers of English and Jeraldine Hill, from *Elementary English,* Vol. 39, March, 1962, pp. 239–43.

teaching children to read and to enjoy reading. However, there is very little practical material available on teaching a child how to use what he has read, or, put another way, to do critical reading. Most of the material found has been written on teaching critical reading through the content areas above the elementary school level.

Spache [1] lists six skills necessary for critical reading:

1. Investigating sources
2. Recognizing author's purposes
3. Distinguishing opinion and fact
4. Making inferences
5. Forming judgments
6. Detecting propaganda devices.

These are separate from comprehension skills that require a lower level of inferences and interpretations. These are skills that go beyond the comprehension skills needed. Although you would not expect younger children to think as maturely as those in high school, this does not prove that middle graders cannot be taught to think critically. In fact, middle grade children are at the point in their development when they are questioning. They ask, "Can you prove it?" of their peers, their teachers and their parents. They are skeptical when proof is not available. Content areas can be used to teach critical reading to these children. Beyond this, the very books read for recreation or as part of an individualized reading program can also be used to teach the skills necessary to do critical reading.

One of the types of books that is of interest to children is biography and biographical fiction. A way to help children grow in their ability to do critical thinking is to compare various biographies and fictionalized stories about one famous person. For example, the life of Benjamin Franklin might be used. The child could read *Ben and Me* [2] and the one the D'Aulaire's wrote on Benjamin Franklin [3] and use some reference book's account of the life of Benjamin Franklin. The three accounts could be compared as to what phases of the person's life are covered, any bias shown by the author, what is historically true, what is perhaps legend and what perhaps is pure fiction. For the more able readers, adult versions and the children's versions of the biography of a famous person written by the same author can be used. The four-volume biography of Abraham Lincoln by Sandburg [4] and the book he wrote for children, *Abe Lincoln*,[5] or Esther Forbes' factual account of Paul Revere [6] and *Johnny*

[1] George Spache, *Toward Better Reading* (Champaign, Illinois; Garrard Press, 1961), Chapter 5.

[2] Robert Lawson, *Ben and Me* (Boston: Little Brown & Co., 1939).

[3] Ingri and Edgar P. D'Aulaire, *Benjamin Franklin* (Garden City, New York: Nelson, Doubleday, Inc., 1950).

[4] Carl Sandburg, *Abraham Lincoln* (4 Vols., New York: Harcourt, Brace and Co., 1928).

[5] Carl Sandburg, *Abe Lincoln, The Prairie Years* (New York: Harcourt, Brace & Co., 1928).

[6] Esther Forbes, *Paul Revere* (Boston: Houghton, Mifflin Co., 1942).

Tremain,[7] the fictionalized account of Paul Revere, can be studied for the author's different purposes in each book, variations in style between adult and children's versions, as well as distinguishing fact, legend and fiction.

Books about families are another kind of book of interest to the middle grade child. These include books such as, *The Moffats,*[8] *The All-of-Kind Family,*[9] the *Little House* [10] books. Children can discuss the different types of families, their homes, their standards of living, their ideas of discipline, etc. This helps to build the understandings of how families differ and yet are basically alike. Books such as *Elder Brother,*[11] *Thirty One Brothers and Sisters* [12] *Henner's Lydia* [13] and other De Angeli books give a picture of other cultures, ethnic and social groups and their type of family life. Books such as these also aid in developing more understandings of human interrelations.

Similar to the books about families are books about particular boys or girls. Such books as *Shen of the Sea,*[14] *The Courage of Sarah Noble,*[15] *Caddie Woodlawn,*[16] *Adam of the Road,*[17] *Isle of the Blue Dolphins,*[18] can be used to discuss the problems of the main character, his fears, his dreams and how he shows courage beyond his fears. The personality of the main character can be studied as to his strengths and weaknesses shown in the story, his values and judgments, and whether he is shown to have strong biases or prejudices. Children can consider what they would do under similar circumstances and project what would have happened if the children's suggestions were followed.

Puzzles are a challenge to middle grade children that they find hard to resist. A way to use books to stimulate puzzles is to have children write their version of how a book came to be written, or write how they would have ended a particular book if they had written it. Then the children can go even further and write to publishers and authors and ask about the story behind the books. This would also give children an opportunity to learn more about the publication of books and give them more knowledge of authors as real people. There is, of course, already published, *The Story Behind Modern Books,*[19] but it is

---

[7] Esther Forbes, *Johnny Tremain* (Boston: Houghton, Mifflin Co., 1943).

[8] Eleanor Estes, *The Moffats* (New York: Harcourt, Brace & Co., 1941).

[9] Sidney Taylor, *The All-of-a-Kind Family* (Chicago: Wilson & Follett Co., 1951).

[10] Laura Ingalls Wilder, *Little House* books (New Uniform Edition; New York: Harper & Bros., 1953).

[11] Evelyn S. Lampman, *Elder Brother* (Garden City, N.Y.: Doubleday, Inc., 1950).

[12] Reba P. Mirsky, *Thirty One Brothers and Sisters* (Chicago: Wilson & Follett, 1952).

[13] Marguerite De Angeli, *Henner's Lydia* (Garden City, N.Y.: Doubleday, Inc., 1936).

[14] Arthur Chrisman, *Shen of the Sea* (Garden City, N.Y.: E. P. Dutton, 1925).

[15] Alice Dalgliesh, *The Courage of Sarah Noble* (New York: Charles Scribner's Sons, 1954).

[16] Carol Brink, *Caddie Woodlawn* (New York: Macmillan Co., 1937).

[17] Elizabeth Janet Gray, *Adam of the Road* (New York: Viking Press, 1942).

[18] Scott O'Dell, *The Island of the Blue Dolphins* (Boston: Houghton, Mifflin Co., 1960).

[19] Elizabeth Montgomery, *The Story Behind Modern Books* (New York: Dodd, Mead & Co., 1949).

quite old. It might serve as a starting point to write about more current books.

Writing to publishers and authors can serve yet another purpose in teaching critical reading. A complete study can develop from writing to various publishers of books that are familiar and favorites of the children. This can take the form of a study of all of the books of a particular author or illustrator. This can lead to a discussion of a particular style of one author, expressions he uses in more than one of his books, similarity of characters or locales. It can be a study of the new books for the year that will be published by one company, their variety, the subject most popular for that year. Sometimes publishers will loan a school original manuscripts, galley sheets or original illustrations. This can lead to an appraisal of the field of publishing, the cost, the way books are advertised, the format, and so forth. The impact that publishers have on what is available for children to read can be discovered from such a study. The people who write books are of much interest to young readers. They enjoy trying to find out as much as they can about the authors' lives and families. *The Junior Book of Authors* [20] and magazines such as *Horn Book* and *Elementary English* can be of much help to them in seeking information about authors. Of course, writing to the author is always a way to learn how he lives, how he chooses his plots, his philosophy of writing, his family and his interests.

The pictures in books fascinate young children. As they grow older they still enjoy pictures, but their books have fewer and fewer illustrations. Children's picture books can be used by older readers for a different purpose. The different styles of various illustrators can be compared. The study of the style and media of one illustrator can be made by collecting as many books as possible and comparing the earlier books of an illustrator with his more recent books. One can never forget the change of style of Robert McCloskey from *Make Way for Ducklings* [21] to *Time of Wonder*.[22] It is very hard to believe that they were done by the same person. Another use of illustration is the comparison of media, color depth and the aesthetic aspects of illustrations. Older readers can appraise the part that the illustrations play in the stories in picture books. A more mature appraisal can be made by a consideration of how illustrators have affected the entire development of children's books.

Many of the basal reader series have a watered down version of famous children's books. Children can read the original books and compare the stories in the readers. They can evaluate the similarities and the differences of the two versions as to simplicity or difficulty, degrees of descriptive language, style and interest. Readers also have simplified versions of folk and fairy tales which can also be compared. Another comparison can be made between the original

[20] *Junior Book of Authors*, S. J. Kunitz & Howard Haycraft, ed. (2nd Revised Edition; New York: Wilson & Co., 1951).

[21] Robert McCloskey, *Make Way for Ducklings* (New York: Viking Press, 1941).

[22] Robert McCloskey, *A Time of Wonder* (New York: Viking Press, 1957).

versions of classics, such as, *Little Women*,[23] *Tom Sawyer*,[24] *Treasure Island*,[25] and series of these that are published in simpler and more attractive form by some book publishers. Don't be surprised if some children do not prefer the original! Studies such as these may include possible reasons for making more than one version, the job of editing, the place of illustrations, differences in cost, and so on.

Children can examine the advantages of various kinds of book clubs in learning how to build up their own personal libraries. Such clubs as the Junior Literary Guild, the Arrow Book Club, the Weekly Reader Book Club, will be good for this. Some readers may move into the adult Book-of-the-Month Club, the Literary Guild Book Club, *American Heritage*. Then there are the scientific types of monthly books, such as *Around the World Program, Know Your America, Nature Program, National Aviation*. The good periodicals for children should be introduced to them, also, for lighter and shorter reading periods. We build discriminating adult readers by helping children to be discriminating in their reading tastes.

One of the many of the mass media that can be used in the classroom to help children develop the ability to read critically is the newspaper. The accounts of important events can be compared in several newspapers. The newspaper can also be used as a spring board into the study of how news is gathered and reported, the effect that the printed word has on the children's lives. More advanced readers may be interested in the *New York Times*, the *Commercial Appeal*.

Poetry is one of the best ways to help children to read critically. For poetry is an abbreviated thought. The poet must leave so much to the reader's imagination. A keen interest in poetry is not developed in a short time. Poetry takes much tasting, much thinking, much time to assimilate the thoughts presented. But for these reasons it must not be neglected. Poetry, as all other reading, should be partly for enjoyment. It should never be presented to young children for analysis of structure, meter or rhyme. It should be presented for the beauty of the thought it brings, the release of emotion through verse. It can be used, without hindering any of these, to discuss and appraise the thought presented and its effect on the reader. Children should be encouraged to see that they, too, can write poetry. However, if we use poetry with children as we should, they will soon discover this for themselves.

There are many sources that a teacher can have in her classroom to help children develop an ability to use and learn more about books, authors and illustrators. Besides many and varied trade books, there are bibliographies put

---

[23] Louisa M. Alcott, *Little Women* (Boston: Little Brown & Co., 1934). (1868)

[24] Mark Twain (Samuel Clemens), *Tom Sawyer* (New York: Harper & Bros., 1917). (1876)

[25] Robert L. Stevenson, *Treasure Island* (New York: Charles Scribner's Sons, 1924). (1882)

out by the American Library Association, listing books of various age levels and subjects. There are bibliographies of adult books that young people will enjoy. This association also publishes *Libraries Bulletin*. The University of Chicago Children's Book Center publishes an excellent book list about books, their authors and illustrators. The *New York Times* Book Review Section and Supplement has valuable articles, also. The *Saturday Review* and the *Atlantic Monthly* magazines will be of interest to more mature readers. There are many more, but one of the best is a teacher or librarian who tells children of new books, shows them or reads from them to children. This personal appraisal means more to most children than a printed account, no matter how well done the printed account may be. Children, too, can be instrumental in encouraging others to read favorites by preparing bibliographies that they feel other children may enjoy.

The role of a school librarian in helping children grow in interest and ability with books is very important. The public librarian is also important. One who reads and tells stories to children and discusses their reading with them is invaluable. She is the spirit of the library to children. How she helps and guides children with books is one indication of how they will continue their use of libraries in the future. A good librarian will encourage children to feel at home in the library, to enjoy it. She will help children learn the aids the library can give. It is possible for even young children to become acquainted with the card catalog. As they grow older, the librarian can introduce the indexes that are available, and help them to discover aids to their own book needs. If teacher and librarian work together, the ways they can help children keep growing and stretching their abilities to use books are unlimited.

Any one of these suggestions may be used as a starting point to get children to thinking for themselves and interacting with the material that they are reading. There are, of course, many other ways in which this can be done. However, the first step is to begin. The questioning middle grade mind will take up from there. Children will begin to develop better ways to think about what they read if they have the training to do so. Then we have started them on the path toward becoming readers and thinkers who will not be fooled by the language of emotional persuasion. They will be able to recognize propaganda that, unless understood, can result in the enslavement of the minds and enslavement of the people themselves.

READING IN SUBJECT MATTER FIELDS *

Nila Banton Smith

The present social revolution and reading in the subject matter fields are mutually interactive. This revolution is ushering in new problems; reading is necessary in coping adequately with these problems.

The kind of reading, however, that will contribute to problem solution is not the kind that is done in pursuing sensational magazines, comic books, and news items on crime and casualty. It is the kind of reading used in delving deeply into social studies, science, mathematics and literature. We have a social, a political and a cultural responsibility in teaching children to read effectually in these fields.

READING IN SOCIAL STUDIES

At the present time, world events are having tremendous impacts upon our lives in the United States. For the average student or adult, the sources of information concerning these events are TV and radio, perhaps with the newspaper running as a poor third. Any interpretations that are given through these media represent the thinking of a commentator, reporter or editor.

We need to place more emphasis upon reading and thinking on the part of the individual, himself. It would be helpful if every family would take at least two newspapers, and would, themselves, compare and discuss differing accounts of the same event, in the presence of their children. When the children are old enough to read newspapers, parents should encourage them to read and compare, and join in the family discussion out of which may come generalizations and conclusions based upon family thinking and interpretation. This same procedure might well take place in classrooms with the use of newspapers and magazines brought in by the students.

Maps, globes and atlases have leapt into new significance in our rapidly changing world. Classrooms and living rooms should be well equipped with these locational references. Both teachers and parents would do well to refer to these facilities when a place has important mention on TV or in newspapers, with children "joining in" or looking up locations, themselves, when they are able to do so. Encouraging research to extend interest in social studies topics provides functional practice in the use of encyclopedias and other reference books as well as the use of library skills.

* REPRINTED with permission of the Association for Supervision and Curriculum Development and Nila Banton Smith, from *Educational Leadership*, Vol. 22, March, 1965, pp. 382–85. Copyright © 1965 by the Association for Supervision and Curriculum Development.

The cause and effect pattern of writing is characteristic of social studies content. Every event in history, every geographical change in the earth has had its cause which in turn has resulted in an effect. It is helpful to students if they are taught to identify this pattern when they encounter it. They may then read for the specific purpose of noting causes and effects, thus having an organizing platform on which to stand while gathering related information.

The ability to make comparisons is needed for effective reading in the social studies field. Much opportunity should be given for making comparisons while pupils are working with social studies.

All pupils, beginning with third grade, should be taught to recognize the basic propaganda tricks in printed materials. These tricks embody use of: bad (uncomplimentary) words, glad words, transfer, testimonial, bandwagon technique, plain folks concept, and stacking the cards. Children can be taught at home and in schools to recognize these tricks in advertisements, speeches of politicians, editorials, cartoons and comments of leaders in some of the foreign countries. It is extremely important that our young people should know when someone is trying to influence their thinking and behavior through printed materials.

READING IN SCIENCE

We are living in a highly scientific age. Increasing numbers of people will be working at jobs in science. All of us will be consumers of science and readers of materials involving science. It is of the utmost importance that children be taught special skills needed in the effective reading of content in this subject area. These skills have their roots in the textbooks of elementary school children but appear in increasingly difficult context in high school.

Specialized vocabulary is a significant factor in reading science material. The new words are long, difficult to pronounce and technical in concept. For teachers working with poor readers, it is suggested that they take a hint from procedures used in teaching reader stories, that is, to clear the way for study of new science content by providing vocabulary work before the students read, both in regard to pronunciation and meanings.

A unique pattern found in science textbooks is the kind of text needed in carrying out an experiment. This pattern usually consists of a set of directions. Every word in this set of directions must be recognized and every direction must be carried out exactly. Those children who have difficulty in reading and following directions should probably have temporary experience in reading the directions orally from the blackboard or book and telling *exactly* what they are going to do before actually following the directions in performing an experiment.

Another type of science text appearing at all levels falls into the *classification pattern* in which living things, objects, materials, elements, gases, liquids, forces, etc., are classified under a common heading which in turn deals with subdivisions. Students should not read this pattern as they would a story. If a child is taught to identify the classification pattern, he will be able to gear his reading procedure to obtaining the kind of information which is important in this particular pattern—that of grasping the subdivisions and the important characteristics of each.

Another pattern of writing which is particularly characteristic of science, and perhaps the most difficult one to read, is the explanation of a technical process, which usually is accompanied with diagrams necessitating very careful reading of text with continuous reference to diagrams, for example: "How Does the Telephone Work?" This kind of reading requires a doubling of techniques: reading the text and reading the diagram alternately as one feeds into the other. Students need help in learning how to read and understand diagrams, and guidance in adjusting from one to the other while pursuing an explanation.

Still another pattern frequently encountered in science textbooks but not entirely unique to science is the *detailed statement-of-facts pattern*. In this pattern the facts are dense, and they frequently embody a definition or a statement of a principle. In reading this pattern, the student is helped greatly if he is taught first of all to find the main idea in each paragraph, then to grasp the details as related to and clustering about this main idea—"as grapes grow out of and cluster about the main stem." Much oral discussion is necessary in developing this skill to a high level. After students have attained some proficiency in analyzing paragraph structure through oral discussion, they will find it helpful to outline science paragraphs heavy in detail.

READING IN MATHEMATICS

Mathematics, like science, is becoming increasingly important in our lives, partly because it is so closely integrated with science, and partly because mathematical concepts must be understood if we live intelligently in our rapidly expanding universe.

Mathematics text is unique in that it embraces types of reading content which differ markedly from narrative reading and from the text of geography, history, and science. It is more compact than text in any of these other fields. It is complicated also by having numerical symbols woven into the sentences along with word symbols.

The most highly specialized pattern of text in mathematics is the short paragraph setting forth a problem situation. Regardless of whether the text is in arithmetic, algebra, or geometry, problems are stated in this format: At the beginning the situation is given, or the condition under which the problem took place is stated; then follows a series of numbers or other mathematical values; and finally the reader is asked or told what to find.

The *reading* of most problems in mathematics involves four different processes: (a) reading the entire problem to grasp the situation as a whole; (b) concentrating on the question or statement at the end that asks or tells what to find; (c) deciding what processes or formulas to use in finding the answer; (d) pulling out the number facts or symbols presented for use in working the problem. After these *reading* activities accompanied with a high degree of reasoning have been completed, then the student is ready to compute the problem mentally or on paper. If a student is having difficulty in mathematics, it would be helpful to explain to him the importance of the *reading* activities which precede computation, and to provide him with special practice on the reading procedures involved, perhaps for a time without working the problems at all.

In addition to problems there are other reading situations in mathematics. At the elementary level pupils must be taught to read calendars, thermometers, time-tables, abbreviations, etc. In the secondary school, students must learn to read exponents, formulas, subscripts, equations, reference tables. The elementary teacher should teach reading as needed in arithmetical situations in the same ways that he teaches it in his basal reading instruction, and the secondary teacher of mathematics might obtain some very good hints from the elementary teacher.

READING LITERATURE

Interest in reading is the touchstone to all reading activities which contribute to our lives culturally, socially, informatively and recreationally. Development of interest in reading is of grave import at this time because of the competition of other mass communication agencies, and because of the present unsatisfactory status in the free reading both of students and adults. Literature is a content area which offers an excellent opportunity to develop interest in reading and discrimination in the choice of content.

Having a wide variety of materials available is one of the best ways of nurturing children's interests. Classrooms, libraries and homes should abound in collections of the best in books and magazines.

Parents need counseling about the purchase of books. They should be urged to take the child for whom books are being bought with them and to let him make selection in terms of his own interests. To avoid reading frustration, the parent should be advised to try the book out a little with the child to see whether it is easy enough for him to read. If not, then with his help another book may be selected which is of interest to him but still within the level of his reading maturity.

The enthusiasm of the teacher or parent for books is a strong factor in arousing child interest. Having periods of sharing may help. Supplementing literature with activities in the creative arts also contributes to interest.

At the secondary level different patterns of writing in literature become prominent. These are: the *story* (short story or novel); *essay; drama; biography; fable;* and *poetry* of many kinds (ballad, lyric, elegiac, epic, sonnet), some written in rhymed verse, some in free verse, some in blank verse and of many different meters.

Each of these patterns requires a different approach. A student should not read a story, an essay, and a drama in the same way. His purpose is different. He reads a story to enjoy plot, character and setting; an essay to get the slant of the author as he discusses some aspect of life; a drama to interpret the conversations of the characters involved. Drama is further differentiated in reading in that it is cast in a unique format. Biography and autobiography should be read not merely to follow separate chronological facts but to get a conclusive impression of the person writing it or being written about. Sometimes within the essay or biography the detailed statement-of-facts pattern appears, but this is very light as compared with this pattern which is characteristically used in science.

Interpretation is of the greatest significance in teaching literature. Students must continuously be encouraged to read between and behind the lines to get deeper meanings. Teachers of literature need to ask questions, and make remarks during discussion, and to formulate assignments for individual or group work, which will call forth such thinking activities as: speculating on what happened between events; anticipating what will happen next; making generalizations from details in text; detecting the significance of a statement, passage or selection; making comparisons of characters, events, locales; identifying the purpose of the writer or the motive of characters; associating personal experience with reading content; sensing visual images; and experiencing emotional reactions. Depth reading is an absolute necessity in full and satisfying appreciation.

THE ROLE OF READING IN THE SOCIAL STUDIES *

Paul A. Witty

During the past decade, there has been widespread criticism of reading methods and materials of instruction used in our schools. It has been shown that some of the criticisms are unjust. Children are, on the whole, reading better and more widely than ever before. However, some of the criticisms are valid and merit the serious consideration of teachers and administrators. It

* REPRINTED with the permission of the National Council of Teachers of English and Paul A. Witty, from *Elementary English*, Vol. 39, October, 1962, pp. 562–69+.

has been clearly shown, for example, that permanent interests in reading are *infrequently* developed in children and youth. Far too many people who *can* read do not choose to read books. They have failed to develop a strong interest in reading.

Not long ago, The American Institute of Public Opinion reported a poll in which six out of ten adults questioned stated that the last time they had read a book other than the Bible was a year or more ago. Moreover, one out of four college graduates had not read a book during the last twelve months.[1]

Lack of interest in reading has been demonstrated again and again in studies of children, young people and adults. And numerous speculations concerning the causes have been advanced.

It has been indicated, too, that there are unjustifiably large numbers of poor readers in our schools. Some studies do show large amounts of reading retardation. For example, in the South Side High School, Newark, New Jersey, of the 247 entering freshmen who were tested in September, 1952, more than 50 per cent tested at or below the sixth grade level.[2] This study reveals a higher frequency of poor reading than is generally reported in such investigations. Yet, other studies show that 15 to 20 percent of entering high school pupils in some schools read less well, according to test results, than the typical seventh grade pupil. It has been found that most of these pupils can be helped to read more effectively.

However, it should be noted that in most studies of entering high school pupils, *many* superior readers are reported. Such data should make us aware that in our zeal for helping students with reading problems we should not overlook the special needs of superior and gifted students. These pupils are frequently neglected or inadequately challenged. Such pupils are often potential leaders, much needed in the area of human relations. As Harry Passow states: "The daily press and professional journals alike are clamoring about shortages of scientists and engineers. . . . Perhaps our most frightening shortages are not in the general supply of scientists but in those rare persons with imagination, creativity, motivation, competence, and education who can contribute something fresh and basic to our understanding of man's relation with man." [3] To the development of such understanding, the role of reading in the social sciences is essential and unmistakably evident.

Dull Material Discourages Child

Some critics are convinced that certain teaching materials, especially primers and first grade readers, are unnatural and repetitious, and contribute vitally to inefficient instruction, and lack of interest in reading.

[1] *Reader's Digest*, March, 1956, p. 23.

[2] Vivian Zinkin, "A Staggering Reading Problem," *The Clearing House*, 28, November, 1953.

[3] Harry Passow, quoted in *Education Digest*, March, 1957.

Writers assert, too, that a concern for the interest factor should be shown not only in the primary grades but also at every level of instruction.[4] The desirability of this approach is emphasized by George Norvell who, after analyzing the selections taught in New York high schools, concluded that "To increase reading skill, promote the reading habit, and produce a generation of book lovers, there is no other factor so powerful as interest."[5]

The primary objective of a developmental reading program should be recognized clearly at all times: we should seek to help children to become skillful, self-reliant, and independent in using the library and other resources for satisfying interests and needs. This objective will be achieved only if students are enabled to enjoy the act of reading and the results.[6] The first part of this aim will be achieved through an efficient, systematic program of reading instruction. The second part will be realized by the association of reading with interests and needs. Accordingly, children and youth will become skillful readers and will probably continue to enrich their understandings and satisfactions all their lives.

FORMAL INSTRUCTION NECESSARY

Many school administrators and teachers will doubtless agree that a developmental reading program should be initiated throughout our schools. Instruction in reading today should not cease at the sixth grade level. Help and guidance should be given to all students in studying and reading efficiently the materials of each subject field.[7] Remedial instruction should be offered as a temporary expedient only.

There is a great need to extend opportunities in reading so that children's interests will be satisfied and their needs met judiciously through reading. Accordingly, a balanced reading program includes not only a variety of textbooks and practice books, but also an assortment of narratives, biographies, magazine articles, and factual presentations on many topics.[8] Such needs as the ability to understand oneself and to appreciate one's social environment

[4] Paul Witty, "The Role of Interest," Chap. VIII in *Development In and Through Reading*, the Sixtieth Yearbook of the National Society for the Study of Education, Pt.I, edited by Nelson B. Henry, 1961. Distributed by the University of Chicago Press, Chicago, Illinois.

[5] George W. Norvell, "Some Results of a Twelve-Year Study of Children's Reading Interests," The *English Journal*, Vol. 35, 1946, p. 531. See also George W. Norvell, *What Boys and Girls Like to Read*, Chicago: Silver Burdett, 1959.

[6] See Paul Witty, "Reading Instruction—A Forward Look," *Elementary English*, March 1961.

[7] Elizabeth Simpson, *Helping High School Students Read Better*, Chicago: Science Research Associates, 1954.

[8] Paul Witty, Chap. 2 in *Reading in the High School and College*, 47th Yearbook of the National Society for the Study of Education, W. S. Gray (Chm.) Chicago: University of Chicago Press, 1948. See also the discussions in Henry P. Smith and E. V. Dechant, *Psychology in Teaching Reading*. Englewood Cliffs, New Jersey: Prentice-Hall, 1961.

can be met to varying degrees through the use of printed materials. This approach recognizes the significance of using interesting, varied and individually suitable materials of instruction at every level. And it recognizes too the need for a definite program of instruction designed to apply and extend reading skills in the content fields.

To offer the most helpful guidance and instruction, the teacher requires considerably more information about each pupil's reading than that obtained from tests. For example, the teacher of social studies needs to know the nature and extent of the pupil's specialized vocabulary in this area. This appraisal is not always included in a standard test of reading. Nor do standard tests usually contain measures of the pupil's familiarity with, and ability to use, source materials. Moreover, most tests do not examine the ability to read critically.

To be an effective guide, the teacher needs also to know the pupil's rate of reading different kinds of materials. In addition, he should ascertain the nature and extent of each pupil's reading experience. It is clear, then, that to understand a pupil's status in reading, the teacher will employ data from standardized tests and will assemble additional information revealing the pupil's vocabulary, his ability to read and use various types of materials, and the amount and nature of his reading experience.

In offering reading instruction, the teacher requires not only facts about each pupil's reading, but also information pertaining to his interests and to his personal life and social adjustment. Some procedures such as the use of interest inventories, anecdotal records and various forms of observation are helpful in obtaining data of this type. Interest inventories (which include inquiries concerning play activities, hobbies, vocational preferences, wishes, etc.) may yield clues of value in understanding pupils' attitudes, problems, and adjustment.[9] An interest inventory may be used advantageously in studying groups as well as individuals. These data may be employed in association with others to afford a sound basis for planning appropriate and profitable reading experiences for a class or for an individual. Such data will reveal each pupil's readiness for reading at different levels of growth.

READING IN THE CONTENT FIELDS

In considering the role of reading in the content areas, W. S. Gray pointed out that various attitudes range from complete acceptance to total rejection of the idea that "every teacher is a teacher of reading." He also noted that this slogan, which appeared in the 36th Yearbook of the National Society for the

[9] See Witty-Kopel-Coomer Interest Inventories (Northwestern University). See also questionnaires used in A Study of the Interests of Children and Youths, a co-operative research based on a contract between Northwestern University and the Office of Education, U.S. Department of Health, Education and Welfare, Paul A. Witty, Ann Coomer, Robert Sizemore, and Paul Kinsella. 1959.

Study of Education, *The Teaching of Reading: A Second Report,* was unfortunate in that it designated responsibility without indicating reasons, goals, or methods to achieve objectives. What are the functions of the subject teacher insofar as reading is concerned? W. S. Gray states:

The basic view presented in this paper is that teachers of different curriculum fields become concerned about reading problems as reading assumes importance in attaining the aims of teaching in those fields. The three major duties of such teachers with respect to reading are to provide optimum conditions under which acquired reading ability may be used in attaining worthwhile goals, to promote growth in many aspects of reading which are unique to given fields, and to provide specific training in reading when for any reason they assign reading materials that are above the reading level of the pupils in their classes. The final level of reading competence attained by pupils in elementary and secondary schools is the product of the effort of all teachers. Whereas the reading teacher lays the foundation of good reading habits, the content teachers play a highly significant role in extending and refining the reading efficiency of pupils in specific areas.[10]

And we might add that special emphasis should be placed on flexibility and ready adaptation of reading skills in order to attain success in the subject fields. A. Sterl Artley states:

It is not enough to develop proficiency in specific abilities—to teach the child how to locate materials, to select material and evaluate in the light of the problem at hand, to read at various rates. We might say the job is half done when these abilities have been developed. The second half of the instructional job is that of teaching the child to recognize his particular reading needs and to adapt to those needs the necessary skills—developing the attitude that reading is not a static, inflexible activity, but a dynamic, modifiable activity that changes as conditions change.[11]

We have stressed the importance in a developmental program of the ability to read in the subject fields through effective application and extension of reading skills. Such applications result from emphasis on the ability to adapt reading skills readily to varied needs and purposes.

As a pupil proceeds in school, he encounters a wider and wider range of materials. In modern schools, reading of science and of social studies materials is often introduced in the primary grades. The pupil must learn how to read and to study such materials effectively. Soon he will have elementary books on these subjects to employ for varied purposes. He will increasingly utilize library resources in association with experience units and investigations of various kinds. In the intermediate grades, the program in the subject fields

---

[10] W. S. Gray, "Theme of the Conference," Chapter 1 in *Improving Reading in Content Fields,* Supplementary Educational Monograph, No. 62, compiled and edited by W. S. Gray. Chicago: University of Chicago Press, Jan. 1947, pp. 4–5.

[11] A. Sterl Artley, "Influence of the Field Studied on the Reading Attitudes and Skills Needed." Chapter V, in *Improving Reading in Content Fields,* op. cit., p. 42.

becomes intensified and greater demands are made on the pupil for the selection and application of varied reading skills. He must therefore develop flexibility in applying reading skills. It is clear that a good foundation in basic reading skills is one of the safeguards for successful reading in the content fields. However, beyond these basic skills, there are applications and extensions necessary in each field.[12]

It is worth noting that Guy Bond and Miles Tinker conclude: "The correlations between general reading tests and reading tests in the content fields range from about .30 to .50." Furthermore they state that there are many reading abilities (that operate) somewhat independent of each other.[13] A student may be competent in reading materials in one area and not in another. In the elementary school, there are four areas in which reading presents problems because of new vocabulary and concepts; readability obstacles traceable to style of writing, differences in typography, and so forth. The areas include social science, science, mathematics and literature.

One of the most valuable aids in the "teaching of essential study skills and the improvement of reading in the content areas" is the EDL *Study Skills Library* which is "planned as a sequential twelve-year program." The materials stress the skills of interpretation, evaluation, organization, and reference in the areas of science and social studies.[14] The use of these materials is especially valuable in providing the needed application and extension of reading skills in the content areas.

Bond and Tinker point out that within the social studies, difficulties are occasioned by factors such as the temporal sequence of events portrayed, unfamiliar content unassociated with present-day happenings and experience, and necessity for reading and interpreting maps, graphs, charts, etc. Similarly in geography, they indicate that understanding of reading material may depend on the possession of a special vocabulary based on conditions related to housing, food, or occupations; to physical features of the land; and to climate or agriculture in various, often unfamiliar places throughout the world. The interpretation of maps and "interrupted" reading involving reference to materials on various pages also require types of adjustment not previously emphasized. Mathematics presents other unique reading problems with its strong use of a technical vocabulary, symbols, diagrams, complex concepts, and verbally stated problems.[15]

[12] See David H. Russell, *Children Learn To Read*. (2nd edition) Boston: Ginn and Company, 1961.

[13] Guy Bond and Miles Tinker, *Reading Difficulties: Their Diagnosis and Correction*. New York: Appleton-Century-Crofts, Inc. 1957, p. 352. See also L. C. Fay, "What Research Has To Say About Reading in the Content Areas." *The Reading Teacher*, 1954, 8, pp. 68–72.

[14] *The EDL Study Skills Library*, Teacher's Guide, Levels 4–5–6, by H. Alan Robinson, Stanford E. Taylor, and Helen Frackenpohl. Huntington, New York: Educational Developmental Laboratories, 1961.

[15] Bond and Tinker, *op. cit.*

Responsibility for Developmental Reading Program

A developmental program requires the co-operation of administrators, supervisors, and teachers. A primary responsibility of the administrator in a secondary school is to encourage all-school participation in the work. The formation of a committee to study the total reading situation and to make plans for the development and maintenance of the program is a good initial step. This committee should include representatives from every subject field.

In the planning of extension of reading instruction in every area, certain conditions must be met. The reading demands or objectives of each subject should be set forth. We have chosen the social studies field for illustration. In this paper we shall limit our discussion to the following acquisitions: (1) vocabulary and concepts, (2) ability to see relationships between facts, (3) capacity to organize information, (4) tendency to read critically, and (5) ability to use source materials effectively.

Some Reading Proficiencies Essential in All Social Studies

The above list includes some of the skills essential for reading successfully in the social-studies area. In every subject, similar, more detailed lists may be assembled. This is perhaps the first step in embarking on a developmental program that stresses successful reading in the content fields. And it is a step which a teacher or a group representing each subject might follow. Lillian Gray and Dora Reese have discussed effectively and in detail such acquisitions for geography and history, the two social studies subjects commonly studied in elementary and secondary schools. For example, they have attempted to identify the varied skills needed for effective reading of geography content. They suggest that pupils be taught directly to:

1. Sense space relations. A thousand miles is a distance difficult for children to understand even though they can easily read the words. . . . To teach directions, children must be taught the location and significance of *north*, and not conceive of it, for example, as the 'top of the map.'
2. Understand how geography influences people and events.
3. Prepare detailed, well-organized reports for class discussion from materials read in different books.
4. Get the facts straight.
5. Sense cause and effect relationships.
6. Recognize generalities, such as the fact that increased altitude indicates a cooler climate.
7. Find the main ideas in an involved paragraph containing cross references and extraneous details.
8. Recognize supporting details.
9. Understand terminology. . . .

10. Classify geographical concepts according to basic human needs: food, shelter, clothing, occupations, recreation, communication, transportation, aesthetic appreciation, government, education, and religion.
11. Compare statements and draw accurate conclusions.
12. Read graphs, maps. . . .[16]

Although we recognize the need for detailed analyses and emphases such as that just given for geography, we shall in this paper limit our discussion to the five items previously cited.

1. *Vocabulary and Concepts*

One of the most important needs of pupils in successful endeavor in social studies is an understanding of the specialized vocabulary employed. The teacher should provide the background of experience and the related activities which help children to understand these words thoroughly and to have clear concepts of them.

This development should be planned with care. The teacher should be alert from the first to detect and correct misconceptions. Significant terms in each unit of instruction should be assembled, studied and discussed. The use of direct experience, photographs, filmstrips, and motion pictures will aid in building backgrounds essential for understanding many new words and phrases.

Discussion techniques may be used to advantage. By encouraging extensive reading, the teacher can help pupils obtain facts or illustrations upon which clear understanding of many terms depends.

The use of films and film readers is another way of providing a common background of experience for children. The phenomenal success of children employing film readers suggests their value in improving the efficiency of reading instruction, especially in clarifying the vocabulary employed and in fostering clear interpretation. Some teachers have reported considerable gains in fluency in silent reading and unprecedented gains in reading skill attending the use of the combined approach.[17] These results and indorsements will require validation by careful research. However, there already is clear evidence that the teacher will find the use of the film and the film reader an effective way to foster gains in reading skills.

2. *Ability to See Relationships Between Facts*

Pupils also need help in seeing the relationships between facts encountered in different contexts as well as in varied sources. Simple exercises such as the following may help somewhat in the acquisition of this skill. Dates and sig-

---

[16] Lillian Gray and Dora Reese, *Teaching Children to Read*, 28th edition, New York: The Ronald Press Company, 1957, pp. 379–380. Cited by Henry P. Smith and Emerald V. Dechant in *Psychology in Teaching Reading*. Englewood Cliffs, New Jersey: Prentice-Hall, Inc., 1961, pp. 360–361.

[17] Paul Witty and James Fitzwater, "An Experiment with Film, Film Readers, and the Magnetic Sound Track Projctor," *Elementary English*, April, 1953.

nificant events in an historical presentation may be arranged in two columns in mixed order. The pupils are asked to connect the associated items with lines. However, more important and subtle relationships should also be stressed. For example, the teacher may encourage the students to find the chief products of certain countries and to determine the amount and rate of production. Discussion and objective tests may be used to determine the accuracy of their conclusions. More complex relationships between such factors as resources and productivity or form of government and attitudes of different peoples may also be stressed.[18]

3. *Capacity to Organize Materials*

Some pupils appear to have little expectation that they will be required to do more than reproduce a few facts from the accounts they read. They give scant attention to the sequence of ideas and do not differentiate significant items from unimportant details. It is necessary, therefore, to encourage pupils to react more intensely to the content in social-studies presentations. Some pupils may be helped by practice in making outlines in which they differentiate main topics from subordinate themes. Practice in summarizing will also assist pupils to react to ideas as they read and to organize the information they acquire from reading. Since sources of information are so numerous and varied in worth, it is necessary for pupils to learn to evaluate presentations and to submit their findings in well-organized compact form.

4. *Tendency to Read Critically*

Charles B. Huelsman has summarized the critical reading skills that were mentioned in one or more of fifteen articles on the topic:

1. To define and delimit a problem
2. To formulate hypotheses
3. To locate information bearing on specific problems
4. To determine that a statement is important for a given purpose
5. To distinguish the difference between facts and opinions
6. To evaluate the dependability of data
7. To recognize the limitations of given data even when the items are assured to be dependable
8. To see elements common to several items of data
9. To make comparisons
10. To organize evidence that suggests relationships
11. To recognize prevailing tendencies or trends in the data
12. To judge the competency of a given author to make a valid statement on a given topic
13. To criticize data on the basis of its completeness and accuracy

[18] See also Guy Bond and E. B. Wagner, *Teaching the Child to Read.* New York: The Macmillan Company, 1960.

14. To criticize a presentation on the basis of the completeness and logic of its reasoning

15. To suspend judgment until all evidence is assembled and evaluated [19]

Several studies show that many elementary and secondary school pupils lack the ability to read critically. Pupils should be encouraged to study and to contrast the attitudes and points of view of various authors, as well as their sources of information. Attention should also be given to the extent to which authors are impartial and objective in drawing conclusions and in interpreting data.

In the development of "critical reading," specialized approaches have been devised by some teachers. For example, Spencer Brown employed "documentary techniques" to encourage pupils to seek accurate information on which to base their statements.[20] Pupils of varied nationalities and backgrounds visited the homes and neighborhoods of various "racial" groups found within a school district. After discussing their findings and observations, the facts which had been "documented" were utilized in writing a play entitled "America Is Only You and Me." Many elementary school teachers have found that this approach adds authenticity to information obtained from books and leads to a critical attitude toward the printed page. There are many other efforts to help pupils gain skill in critical reading as shown in booklets designed to aid junior and senior high school pupils improve their reading as well as in books designed to foster effective reading of the newspaper.[21]

5. Ability to Use Source Materials Effectively

Prevailing practice often neglects the wide range of reading abilities within classes. If a single textbook is prescribed for all pupils, little can be accomplished since a typical class contains pupils of widely differing abilities. In the upper grades of the elementary school the differences in ability between the poorest and the best pupil will probably equal a range of from four to five grades, according to test scores.

The following approach is being used by some teachers in recognition of the range of ability within classes. First, the teacher selects the topics or units

[19] Charles B. Huelsman, Jr., "Promoting Growth in Ability to Interpret when Reading Critically: In Grades Seven to Ten" in *Promoting Growth Toward Maturity in Interpreting What Is Read*, Supplementary Educational Monographs, No. 74, Chicago: University of Chicago Press, 1951, pp. 149–153, cited by H. P. Smith and E. V. Dechant, *op. cit.*, p. 358.

[20] Spencer Brown, *They See for Themselves*, Bureau of Intercultural Education Publication Series, Problems of Race and Culture in American Education, Vol. III, New York: Harper and Bros., 1945.

[21] (a) Paul Witty, *Streamline Your Reading*, Life Adjustment Booklet. Chicago: Science Research Associates, Inc., 1949. (b) Paul Witty and Harry Bricker, *You Can Read Better*. Junior Life Adjustment Booklet. Chicago: Science Research Associates, Inc., 1951. (c) Paul Witty and Edith Grotberg, *Improving Your Vocabulary*. Chicago: Science Research Associates, Inc., 1959. (d) Edgar Dale, *How to Read a Newspaper*. Chicago: Scott, Foresman and Company, 1941.

to be treated in the social-studies program. For each topic, varied source materials are assembled to meet the abilities within the class. The variety of materials includes factual accounts, biographies, story materials, magazine and newspaper articles, as well as reference sources such as encyclopedias, atlases, and almanacs. Fortunately, there is a substantial and growing amount of literature on every topic of significance in this field.[22]

CO-ORDINATING THE READING PROGRAM—A CONCLUDING STATEMENT

The foregoing concept of reading instruction differs, in some respects, from views previously held. We have seen that modern approaches to reading instruction include emphasis on the reading skills needed in the subject fields. The teacher of every subject has a responsibility for helping the child to read effectively the varied materials employed in instruction, for developing special vocabularies and for building concepts, for providing diversified materials so as to encourage growth for every pupil, for cultivating critical reading, and for fostering reading from varied sources.

When such practices are widely followed in our schools, co-ordination of the reading program will occur. Co-ordination will be facilitated further by the consideration on the part of all teachers of the interests and "developmental needs" of boys and girls and the selection of appropriate, related subject matter and experience.

These procedures are being followed with success in some schools. Not only are they leading to greater skill in reading, but they are helping students appreciate and enjoy the subject matter of the special fields. It is to be hoped that increased numbers of superintendents and supervisors will be led to initiate developmental reading programs in their schools. Certainly there appears to be a great need for stressing reading in the content fields in most schools. Moreover, efforts of this kind have proved abundantly rewarding.[23] This is an approach which when widely followed promises to increase greatly the efficiency of instruction in the modern school.

[22] The use of the *EDL Study Skills Library* previously described seems particularly appropriate to provide differentiated instruction within classes.

[23] K. B. Rudolph, *Effect of Reading Instruction on Achievement in Eighth Grade Social Studies*, New York: Teachers College Contribution to Education, No. 945, 1949. See also G. Bond and E. B. Wagner, *Teaching the Child to Read, op. cit.*

READING IN MATHEMATICS *

I. E. Aaron

Competences needed for successful reading of mathematical materials may be classified into two broad categories. The basal reading abilities, necessary for all types of reading, include the mechanics of word attack and comprehension. The reader of mathematics, in addition, must have the specialized reading skills unique to mathematics.

The mathematics teacher has five areas of responsibility in teaching the specialized reading skills and understandings of his subject. These responsibilities are to develop (1) the mathematical vocabulary, (2) the concept background necessary for understanding ideas presented in mathematics publications, (3) ability to select skills and rates appropriate for the materials being read, (4) proficiency in the special reading tasks of mathematics—reading word problems, equations, charts, graphs, and tables, and (5) skill in the interpretation of mathematical symbols and abbreviations.

Developing the Mathematical Vocabulary

Arithmetic, algebra and other areas of mathematics have their own technical vocabularies. To read mathematical materials with understanding, students must know the technical terms used in them. The teacher of mathematics—not the English, social studies, science, or reading teacher—has the responsibility for developing this special vocabulary. This vocabulary is at the heart of the subject and must be taught thoroughly.

Mathematics texts are filled with technical words. The student encounters such words as *addend, circumference, factors, decimal, diagonal, exponent, integer, isosceles, perimeter, perpendicular, quadrilateral, quinary, ratio, reciprocal, trapezoid,* and *volume*. A study of five consecutive pages in almost any mathematics text will reveal a heavy vocabulary load. Often several new words are introduced together because they are related to an operation being taught. This creates more difficulty for the student unless the teacher helps him before he reads to understand something about the meaning of the words. The length and intensity of the teacher's explanation should be governed by the clarity of the presentation in the text.

The reader's confusion is increased by the fact that some words already known are met again in mathematics, but this time with an entirely different

---

* REPRINTED with permission of Ira E. Aaron and the International Reading Association, from the *Journal of Reading*, No. 8, May, 1965, pp. 391-95+.

meaning. These include such words as *acute, axis, braces, chord, cone, cylinder, face, natural, primer, radius, rational, ray, scale, set,* and *square.*

Some students have trouble with difficult vocabulary in mathematics because explanations in the text or by the teacher assume incorrectly that they know the less complex vocabulary. The definition of *reciprocal,* for instance, may be presented as "multiplicative inverse." Interpreting this correctly depends on much knowledge, despite the inclusion of only two words in the definition. The newer textbooks often include reviews of the more elementary terms involved in the new word or operation, sometimes suggesting that the teacher review these concepts with the students before he introduces the more complex terms.

The student also meets many words not mathematical in nature but which are used to present problem situations. Word problems in arithmetic and algebra are cast in different settings. Those centering around banking use "bank vocabulary," as *teller, cashier, bank statement, check,* and *deposit.* Problems involving satellite flights include words such as *trajectory, astronaut, cosmonaut, jet stream,* and *capsule.* Words used in problems centered around the sale of flowers include *florist, bulbs, jonquil, tulips* and *camellias.* A discussion of the meanings of such words helps to enlarge the student's general vocabulary.

DEVELOPING CONCEPT BACKGROUND

What a reader takes with him to the printed page determines, in large measure, what he gets from the page. The more he knows about a subject, the more he can get from reading about it. One of the jobs of the mathematics teacher is to give the students some understanding to take with them to their reading of assignments in mathematics.

Relating the new topic to one previously studied helps to strengthen the background of understanding. The teacher may briefly review related units as a transition into the new material. When students are found to be deficient in the understandings basic to mastery of the new content, the teacher must take the necessary time for building the background before launching the new topic.

Some building of concepts will come before reading; some will come afterward. How much help the teacher gives before reading will depend upon the knowledge the students already have and how much explanation the text offers.

DEVELOPING ABILITY TO SELECT APPROPRIATE TECHNIQUES FOR READING MATHEMATICS MATERIALS

Reading mathematics, in most instances, is a slow and thorough process. Every word, every numeral, every symbol carries crucial meaning. Problems are "cut to the bone," with no wasted words. Mathematics calls for intense concentration. The reader must understand completely if he is to accomplish the mathematical task set up for him. His thought process is interrupted constantly as he moves from one brief exercise to another in a text. Seldom does he meet more than one page constructed around the same theme. Suddenly, in the middle of the page, word problems may change to computation problems. Rereading is often necessary.

The mathematics teacher needs to know these special problems inherent in mathematics materials, and he must prepare the student for meeting them. At the beginning of the year and at appropriate later times, how to read text materials effectively should be discussed with the students.

Many of the basic comprehension skills are employed in reading mathematics materials with understanding. Following directions, drawing inferences and generalizations, and evaluating critically are very important. As the student reads, he orders his thinking. He selects and discards in terms of the nature of the problem.

Though teachers work on following directions in many subjects, mathematics offers unusualy good opportunities for furthering the development of this basic comprehension skill. Almost every page contains at least one set of directions to be followed, and some pages contain several directions for the readers. Teachers must help students to develop exactness in following directions. Some students have developed an attitude of "If I come close to it, I've done the job." This attitude is fatal in mathematics. When students misinterpret directions, teachers have a tendency to correct them verbally because it is quicker and easier. Having such students re-read the directions and standing by to give just the bare amount of help needed is a much more effective way to teach. This places the burden where it should be—on the learner.

Developing Proficiency in the Special Reading Tasks in Mathematics

Students must be given help in reading word problems in arithmetic and in algebra. Most teacher's guidebooks offer ways of working problems. Though the words used and steps do not coincide exactly, the overall patterns are similar. They usually include the following:

1. Read the problem quickly to get an overview.
2. Re-read the problem, this time at a slower rate, to determine what facts are given.
3. Think of the specific question to be answered.
4. Think of the order in which the facts are to be used in answering the question raised in the problem.
5. Think of the operations required for solving the problem.
6. Estimate an answer that seems reasonable.

7. Work the problem by performing the appropriate operations.
8. Compare the answer with the estimated answer.
9. Go back to the first step if the answer seems unreasonable.

When a table, graph, chart, or other illustration is first included in text material, the teacher must teach students how to read it and give follow-up practice for permanent learning. He must also help the students to develop the habit of taking the necessary time to study these aids because they are vital parts of the reading matter and must be read.

The reading of equations is vitally important in mathematics. Students may easily memorize "meaning" instead of understanding. In elementary algebra, for example, the student may meet an equation such as $X + 5 = 7$. In solving this equation, the student who reasons that "you take the 5 across the equals sign and thus change it to a minus; therefore, the answer is 2" may get the correct answer, but he missed completely the meaning involved. When the teacher allows a device such as this to be used to the exclusion of what actually is happening, he is doing a disservice to the learner. He should insist upon understanding. Taking the time to think through "subtracting equals from equals" will assure comprehension of the concept.

Developing Skill in Interpreting Mathematical Symbols and Abbreviations

Symbols play an extremely important part in mathematics from the very beginning. The mathematics teacher is the person who has the responsibility of teaching the students in his classes to interpret these symbols correctly. As these symbols are encountered in mathematics, they should be explained thoroughly to students. Checks are necessary to insure thorough learning, and if testing or observation reveals that some students still do not know these symbols, re-teaching should occur. At the beginning of the year, the teacher may prepare a test on symbols taught at lower levels to be administered to the students. The teacher should then review those symbols not known.

Mathematics symbols sometimes involve understanding an operation. For instance, what we mean by adding is involved in the plus symbol; what we mean by subtraction is involved in the minus symbol. When a student encounters the Greek letter "pi" as a symbol representing one element in the circumference formula, the teacher may introduce this as an apparently arbitrary constant, or he may take the time to have the student measure, first the diameter, then the circumference, which is approximately three times the diameter. An explanation that precise measurement would show the circumference to be 3.1416 times the diameter would follow naturally. If such understanding has not been gained in the elementary school, the high school teacher must do the necessary remedial work.

The high school teacher may have to re-teach many abbreviations encountered in mathematics. Words such as *quart* and *miles* are usually spelled out in work problems and abbreviated in number problems. When abbreviations are not understood, the teacher should take the necessary time to teach them thoroughly.

Helping the Excellent and Poor Readers in Mathematics

In addition to teaching the special reading skills related to their subject, mathematics teachers also have another responsibility. Some students in the typical classroom are sufficiently disabled in reading to find the reading of texts on their grade level extremely difficult or almost impossible. Then there are some who find very little challenge in grade-level texts because they are such excellent readers and because they have excellent backgrounds in mathematics. The subject-matter teacher must be concerned with bringing these students into contact with mathematics materials that suit their varied reading levels.

The good reader who needs more challenge may be encouraged to build greater depth in the subject. More advanced treatments in other texts and use of reference materials are two possibilities for these students.

The poor readers present an entirely different problem. The teacher's challenge here is to locate material in mathematics—and on the topics being studied—that the student can read, if such materials are available. Students who are average and above in intelligence but are poor readers often can understand the mathematical concepts if they do not have to read about them. For these students, the teacher may depend less upon reading and more upon other avenues of learning. Word problems may be rewritten, or they may be read to the students. In addition to this help in mathematics classes, somewhere, somehow in the school day, somebody should devote some time to teaching these poor readers the basic skills they lack in reading. Poor readers cannot be expected to unravel word problems they meet in books if they cannot read well.

Summary

Teachers of mathematics must assume responsibility for teaching those special reading skills necessary for reading mathematics effectively. These reading needs, growing out of the nature of mathematics, must be met through teaching materials that are neither too difficult nor too easy for the students. Systematic attention to the development of the specialized reading skills in mathematics will result in better readers—and in higher achievement in mathematics.

READING SKILLS
IN TEACHING LITERATURE
IN THE ELEMENTARY SCHOOL *

William A. Jenkins

INTRODUCTION

Perhaps you will permit a non-expert in reading the luxury of beginning with a definition of terms. I do this because I believe that reading is the most complex of all language skills. It involves and is dependent on all the others. I hasten to add, however, that from my very biased vantage point, literature —the other part of my concern here—is the most important of the humanities. I take a cue from Edgar Dale who wrote in his *Newsletter* some time ago that the way we define reading will determine how we teach it.

EARLY READING

Perhaps it is significant that the first readers were called *spellers*, a nomenclature long ago discarded. We no longer view *reading* only as the act of translating visual symbol to sound. Unfortunately, vestiges of this narrow definition remain to haunt those who teach reading. But the ability to understand and ferret the structure of our language is one important element in reading, and this is what basal readers attempt to develop. Basal readers are built on the idea that during beginning reading oral language outstrips what children can elicit from the page. In a systematic fashion a child must be taught the act of translating. Criticisms of basal readers are based on the hunch that children can translate more than the systematic, restricted readers permit them to do at any given reading level. Not accepting the fact that a child can encounter *and then retain* only a limited number of new symbols, questioners ask why readers must be stripped of all literary content while emphasizing symbol translation. Some of the new readers and some of the new approaches to teaching reading assume that a child can elicit more from the page than we have hitherto believed.

INDIVIDUALIZED READING

One of the approaches is individualized reading, which as an organized, systematic instructional program goes back to the 1930's. In the last decade

---

* REPRINTED with the permission of the National Council of Teachers of English and William A. Jenkins, from *Elementary English*, Vol. 41, November, 1964, pp. 778–82.

it has enjoyed a Renaissance. Currently it is being tested, employed, and written about profusely, and it is working. Its use is dramatic recognition of the fact that basic reading programs are of greatest worth in the initial phases of reading instruction, and that reading from basal textbooks is intended to carry only part of the reading load that children will do. But the thing which troubles me about individualized reading is teachers' assumption that it is one thing. Actually it is many things, for it is individual guidance in reading. As such, it varies from teacher to teacher, from pupil to pupil.

LINGUISTICS AND READING

I began by indicating that reading is the most complicated of the communicative arts. Let me add here that we think we know more about it than we do the other language arts. At least the quantity of research which has been done on it and the volumes of writing about it would so indicate. But there are signs indicating that a great reassessment may be imperative in the near future. Harbingers of the new look are the oral language studies now being completed by such people as Loban and Strickland. Our notions about language development in children may well be reinforced if not replaced by radically different considerations. The work of the linguists on the nature of our language will eventually have great influence, too. Recently Creswell, a linguist, sounded such an alarm when he wrote this:

> Every reading program should be based (also) upon what we know about how children learn, upon a clear understanding of what children already know about language when we begin reading instruction, and upon what children typically learn about language from other sources and through other experiences while they are learning to read. It is extremely important to remember that learning to read does not take place in a linguistic vacuum. Beginning readers have already gained great control over spoken language and continue to develop skill in its use while they are learning to read.[1]

A DEFINITION OF READING

Now for a working definition. To me reading is the act of translating written symbols into oral units of expression and meaning. Reading is thinking. Reading is obtaining meaning from the structural elements of written language, finding meaning between the elements, and understanding at least part of what has been implied beyond the elements. The understanding between and beyond the lines comprises at least half of the meaning and so cannot be overlooked. Reading is getting meaning from the page by bringing meaning to the page. Reading is the mechanical act of translating symbol to sound,

[1] Thomas J. Creswell, "Remarks on B. Robert Tabachnick's Paper," in *Reading and the Language Arts*, edited by H. Alan Robinson. Chicago: The University of Chicago Press, 1963, p. 109.

and symbol to meaning. Reading is experiencing based on experiencing; it changes one, enhances one, reconstructs one. Reading is using concepts to increase our background of concepts. Reading is recognizing, using, and appreciating esthetic elements of language: figures, rhythm, and imagery. At its highest level reading is feeling, while thinking. But this is also literature—written material which makes one *feel* while he *thinks*. Let us look at literature for a moment.

A Definition of Literature

Like reading, literature is many things to many people. Most people are agreed that it epitomizes the expressive and receptive arts. Many would agree that it is writing which has been kept alive by beauty of style or thought. But there are serious questions about literature, even when one restricts himself to literature for children, questions which we will not attempt to answer here. Matters such as what literature, how much, and in what proportions the various types should be offered are vital and yet not definitively resolved. Perhaps Leland Jacobs' dictum that children should have some old and some new, some realistic and some fanciful, some prose and some poetry, is as good an answer to the questions as we can find. This, incidentally, is exactly what our NCTE committee has done with the area. Their report, which will comprise most of the May, 1964, issue of *Elementary English*, is titled simply, "Children's Literature—Old and New."

Perhaps a constructive approach here would be to look at what literature does for elementary school children—things which reading *may or may not do*, but which literature by definition *must* do.

What Literature Does

First of all literature presents a standard for judging language and experience. The best, the worst, the in-between, are open for inspection. Literature presents human nature, that great range of diffuse, diverse, and divergent ways in which we human beings have acted and thought and are capable of acting and thinking. Literature provides background which gives words their meaning. What does *run*, r-u-n, mean out of context? What are the possible dozens of contexts which can give it meaning? Literature can encompass the full range.

Literature has vocabulary, figures of speech, and sentence structure produced with artistry to delight the mind and the ear. Through history and biography, literature preserves cultures and civilizations. Literature holds forth an ideal, a set of values through such types as hero tales and myths. Good literature, according to May Hill Arbuthnot, gives children insights, satisfies curiosities, provides them with a zest for living, and imbues them with a reverence for life. These are unassailable reasons for teaching literature in the elementary school.

Stephen Dunning, co-director of the Project English center at Northwestern, has also offered reasons why we teach literature. He says:

1. Literature is taught so students will enjoy it.
2. Literature is taught so students will improve their taste and increase their capabilities as readers.
3. Literature is taught so students will have access to their literary heritage.[2]

Let me add a final, personal thought. Literature is that reading which *touches* a person, as he thinks, where he lives, and as he is. It's important to remember that no one book, or types of literature, or a single author can do this. Dr. Nila B. Smith has written in a study published by *Elementary English* in December, 1948, that in a group of elementary school pupils who indicated that their thinking and attitudes were changed or influenced by literature, with only one exception no child in any room mentioned the same book as other children. The effects and influences of a literary experience are highly subjective and personal.

READING AND LITERATURE UNEQUALLY EMPHASIZED

From what has been said so far, one might readily assume that in the elementary school, reading and literature are coequal partners in the language arts curriculum, complementing each other in developing literacy and appreciations. Unfortunately, this is not the case. The first groups of skills, the reading skills, are always undertaken in the elementary school. The second step, the application of these skills to literature, to broaden, refine, and reinforce reading, may or may not be taken. As my colleagues may attest, the reverse of this situation—emphasizing literature to the neglect of reading—is the usual situation in the high school, while the junior high school frequently assumes the characteristics of a no-man's land where neither literature nor reading is highlighted; where a stand has been taken, it is usually in favor of literature in the junior high school.

In my area of primary interest, the elementary school, reading and literature are not only viewed as separate entities, they are also unequal; literature is the lesser light. In their preparation, elementary teachers are greatly concerned that they know all they can about reading. Knowledge of literature frequently is a concern of secondary importance, if not neglected altogether. The natural relationship of the two concerns, the skill of reading and the content of literature, is lamentably ignored. Perhaps the current emphasis to capitalize on the interrelatedness of all of the language arts will change this situation. Unfortunately, literature for children is not considered one of the arts as are reading, spelling, and handwriting at the elementary level, or literature and composition at the senior high level.

[2] Stephen Dunning, "Some Reasons for Teaching Literature," *Bulletin* of the National Association of Secondary School Principals, 48 (February, 1964) 121–128.

SIMILAR SKILLS NEEDED

Why should this be so? Reading ability depends heavily on interest. Literature can provide for all types and ranges of interest. Reading depends on interest in as well as facility with language. Books of a literary type provide the means for creating an interest in language, for they interpret experiences of all ranges and types. Reading and literature have common purposes, symbols, and structures, and they involve common thinking processes. Yet they are still separated in far too many elementary classrooms.

When the concept *language arts* was advanced several decades ago it was felt that a breakaway from departmentalization had been achieved for the elementary school. The language arts, the skills, that is, were partly integrated, but the art of literature was kept apart. The condition, I submit, should no longer endure. Reading is vital because it is a basic skill. Reading is also an art. Literature, too, is an art. Even for young children it is, I postulate, a vital skill.

READING SKILLS IN LITERATURE

What are vital reading skills that must be entertained when teaching literature in the elementary school? I think the list is as comprehensive as our knowledge of reading. However, let me highlight some basic ones.

First of all, I believe that as he is learning to read and increasing his power in reading, a child must be taught to interpret life in varying degrees of seriousness, whether through skimming or through reflective reading. Just as the contexts of literature can be varied widely to teach him words and phrases, they can be varied widely for depicting man and his concerns.

A child should be taught that language has nuances, subtleties, and intricacies. He should learn to recognize these and to understand how they create differences in the author's intent and effect. Only wide and varied types of reading can fully accomplish this objective.

A child should be taught to interpret a wide range of vocabulary and discourse, even in dialect. Again, only a wide acquaintance with books, authors, themes, plots, and styles can accomplish this aim. Least effective are the readers set in middle-class or suburban environments with children who never cheat or steal, who do not have to fight for life, sustenance, and recognition; who are never frustrated, thwarted, or defeated; who never seemingly encounter parental tyranny, yellow, red, or black skins; who do not know poverty, squalor, hunger, or fatigue. They do know these—only they know them outside of their books. Out of school they frequently have experienced these and even more impressive facts of life—a younger sister dying of starvation, as recently happened in Kansas City to a child who was regularly given breakfast at school. When this happened, he could no longer eat. He lost his appetite! Or they know nothing but fathers who communicate only when in a drunken stupor, as Charlotte Brooks has vividly described in her pictures of the culturally disadvantaged in Washington, D.C.

A child needs to be taught to pursue a series of events in order of time. Stories should do this for him.

He must be taught to grasp the tone and mood of a reading selection. Again wide reading will provide the opportunities. This includes being read to, and reading aloud connected discourse.

A child must, of course, be taught comprehension of both the main idea and pertinent details. Practice in this is readily provided by stories which have a skeleton of plot that can be stripped away and to which details can be readily fastened and pegged.

In reading in the elementary school a child must be taught to use pictorial aids to meaning. Readers and trade books both afford opportunities for developing this skill, but in my experience teachers too seldom seize the chance or use it at its maximum.

A child must be taught to make generalizations from the specific instances he encounters in reading, and he must learn to become emotionally involved through characters and events which he encounters in his reading.

With limitations, a child must learn to recognize and understand the figures and other esthetic elements he encounters in his reading. I say with limitations, because here too our notions are being questioned. Many teachers at all levels have assumed that in his early reading of myths, folk tales, Bible stories, and so forth, a child builds a foundation of allusion upon which later literary experiences will rest. A study being conducted by Dr. James Squire, NCTE Executive Secretary, to be published some time this year, may change our position. Based on an analysis of fifty anthologies, Dr. Squire's study tentatively has found that upper grade children *do* need a background knowledge of the Greek myths (particularly the Trojan War); and of the Arthurian cycle. More allusions refer to Arthur and his Knights than to all other figures in British and American folklore combined. The study has found also that children need a knowledge of Bible stories of the Old Testament. Of less importance, according to this study, are the Norse myths, stories of the Far East, American folk tales, and English balladry.[3]

A final reading skill area in teaching literature in the elementary school must be vocabulary. In young children, vocabulary grows through finding the best word to share experience. Their language development evolves as they move from egocentric concerns to the group life of school and as their teacher takes them beyond themselves in both reading and non-reading activities. For older children, the quickest way to climb the reading vocabulary ladder is to read widely in books which are exciting or personally meaningful.

---

[3] James R. Squire, "Reading and the Language Arts: A Probe into the Future," in *Reading and the Language Arts*, edited by H. Alan Robinson. Chicago: The University of Chicago Press, 1963, pp. 204–212.

Conclusion

It has been said that whether a man writes with style and taste depends on the styles he has tasted. I think we can paraphrase that to say that how well and what a child reads depends on what he has read. No one honors a great poem until he has attempted to write one and then instead of a happy walk through field and meadow, writing a poem suddenly becomes a mountain to climb. I think we must teach children to climb mountains. Today, however, I only ask that we teach them to walk knowingly, appreciatively, and confidently through field and meadow. Reading literature can do this for them.

Chapter 3

CHILDREN'S READING NEEDS: PROBLEMS OR CHALLENGES?

As individuals grow in reading powers, they exhibit different kinds of needs. Some children experience rapid success in reading and need to be encouraged and stimulated with appropriate materials. Others experience difficulties in relating successfully to reading. These difficulties may result because of personal affairs—limited communication at home, unfamiliarity with the language, or emotional upsets or anxieties; because of physical conditions—poor eyesight or hearing, low energy levels, or other health factors; because of the school environment—lack of rapport with teachers, dull materials, dull learning experiences, or school failures; or because of all kinds of situations or various combinations.

Children are not alike and they do not have similar experiences in or out of school. The differences are a fact, not an assumption. Handicaps, limitations, deprivations, or peculiarities may be perceived either as problems to the school or as realities to be explored and, hopefully, changed. Whether differences are or are not accepted and enhanced in terms of individual growth depends in part upon society's goals. In a democratic society, individual differences are expected to contribute toward making the society stronger. As society grows increasingly complex, there is a greater demand for a diversity of talents and skills. The single standard of performance has no official sanction, any more than does an attitude of hopelessness or defeatism by any school or teacher toward any child in the society.

The school and the teacher have the choice of being viewed by the child as a helper in his need, as a source of support for his inevitable growth in reading; or they run the risk of being viewed as one more destructive force in his life.

In turn, the child may be viewed by the teacher and the school as a failure in reading, and hence, a failure in school; as someone who simply cannot fit in with the ongoing pattern of school life; or he may be seen as a child who can and will grow in reading power, who can and will meet success as a reader.

For the teacher who searches to understand the child as he must become, a fully functioning person, specialized reading needs are simply treated as an integral part of a grand design for reading power. Remedial teaching as a concept loses its meaning.

Shall children's needs in reading be counted as problems to be frightened away by being ignored; or shall children's reading needs be met by a creative reshaping of the learning environment? Is there any real choice?

CAUSES OF READING DIFFICULTY *

Thomas G. Devine

D URING the past years I have been associated in oné way or another with secondary school reading programs, as a remedial reading teacher, a clinician in a high school and college reading clinic, director of a secondary school reading clinic, and, more recently, a teacher of teachers of reading. During this time I have talked to hundreds of parents and teachers about the reading problems of children. I have discovered that no matter where I go and no matter to whom I talk the same questions keep recurring. Parents and teachers want to know: What are the causes of reading difficulty? "Why," I am asked, "has Johnny failed in reading? What is the cause of his trouble? Has he inherited some physical condition that retards him in reading? Is poor eyesight the cause of his trouble? Is he the victim of word blindness? Were we wrong to force him to use his right hand? Does he have an emotional block? Are the schools to blame? Do they teach enough phonics today? Are his teachers at fault?"

Answers to these questions exist. Enough work has been done in remedial reading classes and clinics during the past decades so that reading teachers and clinicians are able to respond to certain questions with some degree of assurance. Enough research has been completed in the universities and clinics so that we can at least recognize significant questions and point to possible answers. Unfortunately, a gap exists between what the researchers and clinicians know and the knowledge of reading shared by most parents and many teachers in the classrooms.

What do research and clinicial experience have to say about the causes of reading difficulties?

Will glasses help?" It seems obvious that a child who has trouble in seeing will have trouble in learning to read. It is less obvious, however, that visual deficiencies are the *cause* of reading difficulties. Investigators have failed to find either a cause-and-effect relationship between visual deficiencies and reading difficulties or any significant relationship between visual deficiencies and success and failure in reading. There is evidence, though, which suggests that certain binocular difficulties such as strabismus (the turning of one or both eyes from normal position) and certain refractive errors such as hyperopia (farsightedness) tend to contribute to lack of success in reading, but the evidence is not unequivocal. Most clinicians today recommend that retarded

* REPRINTED by permission of the publisher, from *The Clearing House*, Vol. 37, October, 1962, pp. 83–86.

readers be given an optometric examination in order to identify visual deficiencies which may contribute to reading disability, but few would agree that the correction of a visual defect is enough to remedy retardation. Most authorities recognize that reading disability is the result of many factors operating together in a complex pattern and that, consequently, the elimination of any single causal factor—such as a visual deficiency—is insufficient treatment.

"*Is he word-blind?*" In an effort to explain reading disability by means of a single cause, various writers through the years have suggested that some children fail to read because of "congenital word-blindness." This theory, first proposed in England more than forty years ago, is based upon the existence of a recognized condition known as *acquired* word-blindness. In acquired word-blindness, brain hemorrhage destroys sections of the visual area of the brain, causing the patient to lose memories of word forms. Because the reactions of children with severe reading disability often resemble the symptoms of adult patients with acquired word-blindness caused by cerebral lesions, some writers have suggested that these children were born word-blind. However, there is little clinical evidence to support the theory. Very few authorities today recognize the existence of congenital word-blindness, but the theory lingers on in the minds of enough parents and teachers to haunt clinicians.

"*Is crossed dominance the cause?*" One of the most controversial explanations of reading disability is that which attributes all difficulties to the child's failure to establish a consistent preference for using the muscles on one side of the body. Neurologists tell us that the right cerebral hemisphere of the brain controls movements of the left side of the body and the left hemisphere controls movements of the right side. They use the term "lateral dominance" to refer to the individual's consistent preference for using muscles on one side of the body. Most children establish very early a preference for the right hand and right eye or the left hand and left eye. These are our "righties" and "lefties."

During the 1930's, the American neurologist, Orton, attracted considerable attention by suggesting that reading disability was due to a child's failure to become either a "righty" or a "lefty." According to his theory, children who have difficulties in learning to read are children who have not established a consistent preference for using the muscles of either the right side or the left side of the body. Such children have "crossed dominance" (that is, they are right eyed, left handed or left eyed, right handed) or they are ambidextrous (they have established no preferential dominance at all). These children can be readily identified—according to Orton and his followers—by their tendency to read "was" for "saw" and "saw" for "was" and make other comparable reversals.

Since Orton's theory was first proposed, many studies of laterality have been made by neurologists and reading clinicians, but we still do not have enough evidence to accept or completely reject the theory. In a series of investigations made at Harvard in the thirties and forties, Professor Dearborn found a greater incidence of crossed dominance and lack of dominance among retarded readers than in successful readers. He also found that reading difficulties were often possessed by children who had been forced to change from the use of the left hand to the right hand. However, other investigators working with different children in other parts of the country found no evidence that lateral dominance anomalies exist in greater numbers among disabled readers than among unselected cases. To this date, the evidence is still insufficient to permit definite conclusions, but clinicians working with retarded readers usually operate on the following assumptions: first, that the dominance anomalies of good readers are overcome *when these anomalies are not accompanied by other handicaps,* and, second, that the anomalies among poor readers constitute only one of several handicapping conditions.

"Does he have an emotional block?" A very popular explanation of reading difficulties in certain circles is emotional maladjustment. The growth and glamour of the child guidance movement in the last decades has made teachers and parents sharply conscious of the personal and social adjustment of children, and, as a consequence, many teachers and parents tend to explain all learning problems in terms of social and personal adjustment. It has become fashionable to say that Johnny can't read because his Mommy doesn't love his Daddy or because neither of them love him. Some enthusiasts are inclined to recommend psychiatric counseling or play therapy when Johnny may actually need instruction in hearing initial consonants or in using structural and context clues.

There is evidence to support the view that emotional maladjustment is linked with reading disability. Teachers who have retarded readers in their classes have always noted that some of these children bite their nails, that some are excessively shy, and that others are overly aggressive. Remedial specialists are well aware that the children assigned to a reading clinic are under varying emotional stresses and that these children are often isolated, fearful, withdrawn, antagonistic, indecisive, or truant. That emotional maladjustment and reading disability are related seems evident, but whether the emotional maladjustment is the *cause* of the disability is questionable. Some authorities believe that the failure to learn to read is caused by various preschool experiences. The clinician, according to these authorities, is advised to identify the nature of the emotional maladjustment and arrange counseling and therapy before beginning remedial instruction. Other authorities, however, believe that emotional maladjustment is secondary rather than primary. One clinician, for example, analyzed the case histories of seventy-eight seriously retarded readers with records of emotional maladjustment and found only four children who had shown symptoms of maladjustment prior to the beginning of reading instruction in school. She concluded that emotional upsets were the result of failure in reading rather than the cause of it.

After a survey of the reported research and literature on reading and emotional maladjustment, it is possible to conclude that:

(1) Some children are emotionally maladjusted when they come to school. These are the children whose failure in reading can be attributed to emotional upsets.

(2) The emotional maladjustment that often accompanies reading disability is—in the great majority of cases—caused by the frustration from failure to learn to read. The child who cannot read as well as his friends and who is continually frustrated in his attempts to learn is going to be upset emotionally. It would take a remarkable child indeed who could meet failure everyday and still maintain his emotional equilibrium.

(3) In the cases of some children assigned to remedial clinics it may be said that emotional maladjustment is *both* a cause and an effect. The failure to learn to read produces emotional upsets which in turn act as a block in the way of subsequent efforts to learn to read.

"*Are the schools to blame?*" Remedial reading teachers and investigators in the university clinics agree that reading retardation is almost inevitably caused by a complex of related conditions. In the diagnoses that must precede treatment, they search for patterns of related factors which contribute to disability. They find that each pattern is unique and that correctional strategies must be structured individually. However, it has become increasingly evident that one factor seems involved in most causal patterns. In case after case, it appears that one of the major contributing conditions that affect reading disability is *ineffective teaching*. Sufficient clinical evidence has been accumulated to make the following conclusion possible: the great majority of children referred to reading clinics are the victims of ineffective teaching.

Reading is a highly complex process. In learning to read, children must acquire a variety of skills and develop several language abilities. Acquiring proficiency in these skills and abilities requires several years of learning and directed practice under the guidance of highly skilled teachers. In the early stages of beginning reading, children must be given practice in visual and auditory discrimination, in left-to-right eye movements, in recognizing familiar words. Later, they must become skilled in different word attack methods; they must learn to use phonics and to use structural and context clues. They have to learn to read for main ideas, for specific details, for sequence, for organizational patterns. They need guidance in developing the reading skills associated with elaborative, organizational, and critical reading. Complicating the teaching process is the fact that all children do not develop these skills and abilities in the same order or at the same rate. Some children learn basic skills readily and are soon prepared to move ahead to more advanced skills, while others need prolonged practice in basic skills.

It seems obvious that teachers who teach reading must be highly competent. Teaching children to read is an incredibly complicated task.

And now—it seems to me—we are approaching the heart of the matter. "Why," I am asked, "do children fail in reading?" One simple but reasonably valid answer seems to be that there are just not enough teachers who can guide children through the complexities of learning to read. Such teachers need to possess more than normal intelligence, considerable creativity, and certain specific professional competencies. Fortunately, great numbers of teachers at work in the schools are intelligent, creative, and competent to teach reading. This fact is attested to by the preponderance of students who have not only mastered basic reading skills but who have also developed many of the higher reading skills. That large numbers of boys and girls have reading difficulties which can be traced to ineffective teaching seems to indicate that many schools lack qualified personnel. Too many teachers without proper training in the teaching of reading and without the necessary intelligence and the necessary personality traits are going through the motions of teaching children to read.

EMOTIONS CAN IMPEDE
GROWTH IN READING *

Children Respond to Failure
With Aggression, Withdrawal

Clotile P. Glover

When a child doesn't learn to read, something has happened to him which has caused him to alter what might be called the usual pattern of growth in children, and learning to read comes to have a different meaning for him than that which it has for the normal child. All investigators and specialists in the field of reading agree that an emotional factor is evident in cases of reading disability. There is some disagreement as to whether emotional maladjustment causes reading disability or reading disability causes emotional maladjustment. Some maintain that emotional maladjustment is both the cause and the effect of reading disability. There is general agreement, however, that, regardless of whether emotional problems give rise to reading difficulties, failure in reading produces emotional problems.

Even if the child is emotionally well-adjusted when he enters school, continued failure in reading, that most important part of school work, is practically certain to have unfavorable effects on his personality and emotional structure. He soon becomes convinced that he is "dumb" or "stupid." When he is asked to read, the child is apt to become so tense and so emotionally upset that

* REPRINTED by permission of the *Illinois Schools Journal* and Clotile P. Glover, from the *Chicago Schools Journal*, January, 1963, pp. 179–82.

his performance is worse than it would be if he were relaxed and not in fear of the situation. As a result of repeated failure or inadequate performance, the child tends to develop a strong dislike (surely an emotional effect) for reading and soon comes to avoid reading whenever possible. The effects of this dislike and avoidance are cumulative. The child loses interest in much of his classwork and becomes inattentive during reading lessons.

FAILURE IN READING ALWAYS PRODUCES EMOTIONAL REACTIONS

Numerous studies have pointed out that, no matter what else happens as a result of failure in reading, emotional attitudes which work against subsequent success develop. Osburn [1] maintains that most children come to school hopeful of learning to read. Typically, the child who, for whatever reason, fails to learn to read is promoted to a higher grade at the end of the year, due to what Osburn calls the "mistaken notion" that membership in a certain fixed social group is all-important. The child is denied participation in the group in spite of his promotion—this because he cannot read. He is *in* his group, but not *of* it. His morale is damaged. He comes to dislike reading, sometimes taking the attitude, "I could read if I wanted to, but I don't like reading." Such children come to school each day with marked feelings of inferiority and insecurity already well established.

Psychologists who have studied the problem of reading disability have classified in various ways the kinds of emotional disturbances which result from failure to learn to read. Among the broad kinds of behavior most frequently observed are resistance to and aggressive dislike of reading; apathy and discouragement; a tendency to withdraw from life and from school situations; and a wide variety of mechanisms designed to compensate for the failure. Some of the specific manifestations of such emotional "solutions" for the problem of reading failure are worth listing. It is not to be assumed that the kinds of behavior listed can arise *only* from failure to learn to read, but numerous studies have revealed that these kinds of behavior can and do accompany problems in reading.

EMOTIONAL MALADJUSTMENT SHOWN IN MANY WAYS

Arthur I. Gates [2] has listed the symptoms of emotional maladjustment he observed in one hundred random cases of reading disability.

1. Nervous tension and habits such as stuttering, nailbiting, restlessness, insomnia, pathological illness.

---

[1] Worth J. Osburn, "Emotional Blocks in Reading," *Elementary School Journal*, September, 1951, pp. 23–30.

[2] Arthur I. Gates, "Role of Personality Maladjustment in Reading Disability," *Journal of Genetic Psychology*, 1941, pp. 77–83.

2. Putting on a bold front as a defense reaction, loud talk, defiant conduct, sullenness.
3. Retreat reactions such as withdrawal from ordinary associations, joining outside gangs, truancy.
4. Counterattack: mischief at school, playing practical jokes, thefts, destructiveness, cruelty, bullying.
5. Withdrawing reactions, including daydreaming.
6. Extreme self-consciousness: becoming easily injured; blushing; developing peculiar fads, frills, eccentricities; otherwise demonstrating inferiority feelings.
7. Give-up or submissive adjustment as shown by inattentiveness, indifference, apparent laziness.

Every teacher has, of course, observed all of the kinds of behavior listed above. Further, any one or a combination of these kinds of behavior can be observed in children who have experienced *no* difficulty in learning to read. Most researchers are agreed that the child with reading difficulties does not reveal a distinct, unique personality, different from those of his more successful classmates. The behavior traits found in a retarded reader can be found among average and better-than-average readers. What this evidence means is that children who have reading problems do not share a common personality structure. What they do have in common is a status in school, and frequently at home, which interferes with their feelings of security. Children who are successful at reading and who exhibit the kinds of behavior described above typically have other reasons for feeling insecure.

When a child learns to read with a minimum of difficulty, his feelings of security are not diminished in relation to his school work. Such a child, because of his feeling of security, can accept reproof with a minimum of frustration and anxiety. When he is criticized, annoyed, or even humiliated because of errors in reading, he rarely becomes debilitated and disorganized. Not so the child who experiences initial failure in learning to read. For him, reading becomes an area to be feared, for fear is associated with insecurity.

Home, School Fail To Develop Security

Frequently, neither the home nor the school, no matter how well-meaning are parents and teachers, gives the child the sense of security about reading that is essential to the avoidance of emotional complications and to the maintenance of emotional stability. Under such circumstances, the child is denied the opportunity to experience the sense of satisfaction which accompanies a degree of success at his own level.

Pressure from parents on the child to learn to read can very well produce the opposite effect. A growing child is so dependent on the love and approval of the adults in his home that every time one of them exhibits strong anxiety about his performance or criticizes him strongly he may experience extremely strong fear—fear that he will lose parental love and approval. Even if the parent tries to help by reading the basic reader with the child, there is the risk of showing up or "rubbing in" the child's difficulties and errors. Parents are perhaps properly anxious for their children's success in reading; as a result, many parents put pressure on their children. Unknowingly, they thus contribute to a failure in reading. Parents with a strong sense of the importance of success in reading can and do experience great disappointment when their child brings home a poor report card. Sometimes, unfortunately, they threaten and punish the child, intensifying his emotional difficulties and increasing his dislike for reading.

TEACHERS HAVE ROLE IN STRUCTURING EMOTIONS

Teachers, too, can become so emotionally involved in the failure of some children to learn to read that they unwittingly add to the pressure from which such children are frequently already suffering. Almost every child enters school with the impression that the biggest task before him is learning to read. If he learns, all is well. If he does not at first learn, emotional pressures may well make it impossible for him to do so later. If the classroom teacher is unduly anxious about the children's progress in reading, most of them will sense this anxiety. Those who become anxious, worried, tense, insecure, and afraid may fail to learn. Just as undue parental anxiety and pressure can lead to failure in reading so can similar attitudes on the part of teachers.

It is important for both parents and teachers to realize that continued reading failure tends to create frustrations which may, in turn, create mental blocks to reading. The child may react to failure by acts of agressiveness or withdrawal. Although their seems to be no single personality pattern characteristic of children who experience reading failure, and there is no proven one-to-one relationship between adjustment difficulties and various types of reading disability, still, both parents and teachers should be constantly alert to the fact that failure in reading can be both the effect of and the cause of emotional maladjustment.

SOLVING READING PROBLEM MAY EASE EMOTIONS

Even more important, perhaps, than the treatment of emotional disturbances once they have become apparent is the prevention of failure in reading. Paul Witty [3] has suggested that attention to both the teaching of reading and the atmosphere of home and school as reflected in the attitudes of parent and teacher may be the most successful method of preventing failure and subsequent emotional disturbance. He recommends the following:

1. Providing successful first experiences in reading by expert teachers.
2. Fostering enjoyment of the reading process as well as the results.

[3] Paul Witty, "Reading Success and Emotional Adjustment," *Elementary English*, May, 1950, Vol. XXVII, pp. 281–293.

3. Providing a desirable classroom atmosphere and sympathetic teacher-pupil relationship.
4. Providing a sympathetic parent-child relationship, by encouragement and affection.

If reading disability arises, it must be identified early and given systematic treatment. As the child matures, the reading problems become more difficult to reduce or eliminate and emotional disorders become more obstinate and deep-rooted.

Parental pressure, as the result of disappointment at the child's failure to learn to read, frequently makes the child more emotionally disturbed than he might otherwise be. The teacher's attitude and conduct toward the child having difficulty with reading can increase emotional tension and hence impede the learning process. If reading difficulties are the cause of emotional disabilities, skilled remedial work in reading may clear up rather easily a considerable number of these maladjustments. The more severe personality problems should be referred to psychologists for analysis and treatment.

EVALUATION OF SILENT READING *

Paul C. Burns

Shortly after school has begun, the more specific jobs of diagnosis and evaluation must be undertaken. It is suggested that silent reading diagnosis and evaluation would include: levels of reading achievement, both independent and instructional; comprehension; content materials; speed; literary appreciation; creative and critical reading. (Word recognition skills and vocabulary would be more easily gauged through oral reading.)

Of course, other more minor features may be observed as a pupil reads silently from a selection; vocalization (degree of lip movement, whispering, audible speech); finger pointing; head movements; signs of tenseness; posture, distractability; and other similar habits.

① LEVELS OF READING ACHIEVEMENT

Perhaps the single most valuable approach to help the teacher define his work with specific groups and individuals would be to provide some time early

* REPRINTED from the March, 1964 issue of *Education*. Copyright 1964 by The Bobbs-Merrill Company, Inc., Indianapolis, Indiana.

in the school year to check individually each pupil's reading in order to establish his *instructional level* (reading instruction under teacher guidance) and *independent reading level* (reading "on his own"). This procedure would require that pupils read short selections silently from sets of unfamiliar basal readers. The pupil reads at successively higher levels of readability until his instructional level is located.

When a pupil reaches the highest level where he comprehends approximately eighty to ninety per cent of the questions put to him, he has achieved roughly his instructional level. This is the level at which the teaching may effectively begin. If a pupil comprehends less than seventy per cent of the questions on the material, the level may be too advanced.

This procedure is merely "trying on" books until the one is found that best "fits." The independent level of reading would be indicated when the pupil can read the material with a comprehension above ninety per cent. The frustration level would be indicated at that point where there was fifty per cent or less comprehension.

Several authors have eased the teacher's work in this type of diagnosis by collecting and arranging selections which allow the teacher to measure levels in basal materials (1, 2).

On the other hand, the teacher may choose to make his own booklet for checking reading instructional level by cutting out specimen passages and developing comprehension questions about them. The types of silent comprehension check questions should include main idea, sequence, details, critical thinking, and drawing conclusions.

Another source helpful to the teacher in diagnosing and evaluating a child's silent reading needs may be found in the various types of exercises often included in workbooks that accompany the basal reader. For example, many such workbooks contain an index indicating the pages on which specific silent reading skills are emphasized. The teacher may devise a few sample illustrations for each of the particular skills and refer the pupil to the proper pages for suitable follow-up material.

A general standardized reading test may be administered to support the teacher's judgment if such a test has not been administered recently. A couple of the more widely used tests would include *Gates Reading Tests (Silent)* (3) and *Iowa Silent Reading Tests* (4).

Such a test would supplement the teacher's thinking and perhaps help to identify pupils who might require a follow-up check of a more exacting or specific nature.

② COMPREHENSION

After pupils read material silently, the recall of information is most frequently checked by oral questioning. The teacher may note the pupil's ability at drawing conclusions (What do you think Jim might do now?); interpreting characters and feelings (Do you think Bob was a responsible boy in this incident? How did he feel after the deed was done?); interpreting figurative language (How did you interpret the phrase "as numerous as the hands of the seas"?).

Does the pupil grasp the main and supporting ideas of a selection? Do the pupil's note-taking and outlining indicate a grasp of the author's organization of information? Can he follow precise directions given in print? Can he fuse ideas from various sources? These are the kinds of questions teachers will hold in mind in observing the comprehension power of pupils.

If more specific checking is indicated in the area of comprehension, one of the following tests might be used for this purpose: *Silent Reading Diagnostic Tests* (5) or *Gates Basic Reading Tests* (6).

③ CONTENT

The teacher should give considerable attention to the reading of material in the content fields. As pupils work in functional reading situations, the teacher can observe how they handle the jobs of locating, evaluating, and organizing information.

Study skills such as the establishment of purposes, use of the table of contents and index, location and use of basic reference materials, map and globe reading, use of dictionary, reading of tables, charts, and graphs may be diagnosed and evaluated directly in situations in which such materials are being used. Thoughtful examination of pupil notebooks and reports helps to reveal strengths and weaknesses in power of organization, summarization, outlining, and note-taking.

Many occasions occur in content instruction for observing the pupil at work: How does he attack reading tasks in social studies, mathematics, and science textbooks and trade books? Does he know how to find information in resource materials? Is he learning to read in different ways for different purposes?

Informal teacher-made tests could be used to supplement observations. In addition, there are several standardized tests which measure basic study skills, such as the *Iowa Test of Basic Skills* (7) or *The Stanford Achievement Test* (8).

④ SPEED

Questions which may help the teacher diagnose and evaluate the pupil's performance in speed of reading would include the following: What are the pupil's rates of speed in reading for various purposes? Is the speed appropriate to purposes and content? Does the pupil vary the rate according to the material? Does he insist upon comprehension of what he reads?

⑤ LITERARY APPRECIATION

Questions such as these should be in the mind of the teacher: Is the pupil eager to participate in reading activities? Is he interested in finding information in books? Does he use books in free-time periods? What are his favorite books, magazines, and newspapers? What titles is he checking out from the school and public libraries?

If a teacher wishes to read more about some important items to be considered in diagnosing and evaluating this particular area of the reading program, he will find in several professional books, such as the following, informal check lists that could help to direct his attention: *Foundations of Reading Instruction* by Betts (9) or *Improving Reading Instruction* by Durrell (10).

⑥ CREATIVE AND CRITICAL READING

Here the teacher is attempting to see if the pupil is looking below the surface, thinking as he reads. Is the pupil reacting to the material? Does he read for implied and inferred meanings, using given facts to derive fresh meanings? Does the pupil go beyond the stated facts? Does he sense what hidden meanings are there? Does he call sensory imagery into play and read with sensitivity and appreciation of the situation? Can he discover relationships? Can he use new ideas gained in other activities? Does he read critically, detecting the author's possible bias? Can he judge and compare materials critically, evaluating logic of the selection, and recognizing propaganda?

The teacher strives to make diagnosis and evaluation of such types of reading by asking pupils for sequence implied in a paragraph; by asking for an original inference (What do you think will happen next?). Frequently such question types as these are posed; "What do you think of this story?" "Why was _____ admired?" "What should we do about this?" "What similar illustrations of your own can you give?" "Can you suggest reasons why this might be the case?" "Were both sides of the issue given fair treatment?"

CONCLUSION

The best diagnosis and evaluation are useless unless they are used as a blueprint for instruction. The whole purpose of the teacher's observing and recording of individual strengths and weaknesses is to adjust instruction to detected needs. Diagnosis and evaluation in themselves have no salutary effect on performance.

Good teaching implies continuous diagnosis and evaluation. Under such an approach, patterns of errors become more apparent and their subsequent elimination more assured when necessary adjustments in the instructional program are made.

REFERENCES

1. Betts, Emmett A., *Handbook on Corrective Reading* (Chicago: Wheeler, 1956).
2. Smith, Nila B., *Graded Selections for Informal Reading Diagnosis* (New York: New York University Press, 1959).
3. Gates, Arthur I., *Gates Reading Tests* (*Silent*) (New York: Bureau of Publications, Teachers College, Columbia University, 1958).
4. Green, H. A., Jergenson, A. N., and Kelley, V. H. *Iowa Silent Reading Tests*, Revised (New York: Harcourt, Brace and World, Inc., 1956).
5. Bond, Guy L., Clymer, T. W., and Hoyt, C. J. *Silent Reading Diagnostic Tests* (Chicago: Lyons and Carnahan, 1955).
6. Gates, Arthur I., *Gates Basic Reading Tests* (New York: Bureau of Publications, Teachers College, Columbia University, 1958).
7. *Iowa Tests of Basic Skills*, Work-Study Skills (Boston: Houghton-Mifflin Co., 1955–1956).
8. *Stanford Achievement Test*, Study Skills (New York: Harcourt, Brace and World, Inc., 1954).
9. Betts, Emmett A. *Foundations of Reading Instruction* (New York: American Book Company, 1957), pp. 472–475.
10. Durrell, Donald D. *Improving Reading Instruction* (New York: Harcourt, Brace and World, Inc., 1956), pp. 67, 110, 122.

TEACHING LANGUAGE AND READING TO DISADVANTAGED NEGRO CHILDREN *

Allison Davis

A hopeful young teacher, trained in the theory and methods taught in our best colleges and universities, often has to *begin* her teaching in a school where the majority of the pupils come from disadvantaged Negro families. This is normal central-office procedure in most cities. New teachers are assigned to the schools in the lower socio-economic neighborhoods because most of the experienced teachers "transfer out" of these lower-class schools as soon as they may. Most of them have found it impossible to understand the pupils of the masses. They have been puzzled by the language of these pupils, by their attitudes toward school work and toward the *teacher*; by their indifference to the

* REPRINTED with the permission of the National Council of Teachers of English and Allison Davis, from *Elementary English*, Vol. 42, November, 1965, pp. 791–97.

curriculum—and in the later grades, by the pupils' sullen resentful behavior. If the experienced teacher flees from these schools, it is a mystery what the central offices *expect* to happen to the *beginning* teacher, who is given her first assignment in a school in a lower socio-economic area. We know what actually happens to most such new teachers. Going from her college classes on theory and from her sheltered practice teaching into these schools of the masses, the new teacher experiences a cultural shock, a trauma of fear, disillusionment, and frustration from which she only slowly, if ever, recovers. This initiation trauma of the inexperienced, middle-class teacher has been studied at the University of Chicago. The new teacher, who finds most of her colleges preparation useless in a classroom where her pupils appear to come from a different language world and a world of different values and goals, does actually suffer a period of deep anxiety, resulting from both moral and emotional shock.

In spite of his emotional spontaneity and expressiveness, the Negro child from the low socio-economic groups is likely to lack confidence in his ability and in his future. His parents usually do not encourage him to compete in school, so that he usually lacks the *drive to achievement*, the prime incentive which middle-class parents seek to teach their children.

Moreover, the school program itself, including the so-called (but incorrectly termed) reading-readiness tests, the educational-aptitude tests, the primers, readers, and the curriculum as a whole soon damage severely the confidence and the basic self-esteem of the Negro or white child from low socio-economic groups. Finally, his low place in society and that of his parents, friends, and neighbors tends to weaken his self-esteem. This self-depreciation is typical of all low-status groups, and is the result of their having been severely stigmatized in most relationships with dominant groups. It results in a poor self-image for the Negro child and adolescent and in hidden self-contempt beneath the facade of stupidity and resentment.

These children need, most of all, teachers who will encourage them to try, to hope, to believe in their futures, and to believe in themselves against the dead weight of the social and economic pressures which drive them down to self-depreciation and sullen resentment.

The chief obstacle to school-achievement by the Negro disadvantaged child is his *first-learned culture,* that language and way of life which he already has learned in his family. In school, the child is expected to change the behavior which his own father, mother, and peer group have taught him. He has to learn to speak and understand a new language, "standard" English, and to learn increasingly complex middle-class behavior, with respect to study habits, control of aggression, and sexual values.

For both white and Negro low-status groups, the school is one of the most powerful factors in changing their culture. But the schools and our whole educational system are operating at the level of only a half of their potential effectiveness in training these children.

We know, for instance, that a third of the white children of unskilled and semi-skilled families in a midwestern city already are retarded in grade-replacement by the time they are nine and ten years old.[1] By the time white children from these lowest occupational groups are in their tenth year, they are about one year behind the children from the top occupational families in reading, and ten points lower in I.Q. ratings. Negro children of the lowest economic group are about a year behind the white lowest economic group in reading, and six points lower in I.Q. at age ten.[2]

But both groups have improved markedly in the last generation. The average I.Q. of white children of unskilled and semi-skilled parents in Chicago is 102.3, actually above the national average for all children.[3] The average I.Q. of Negro children born in Philadelphia, New York, or Chicago is 97.[4] Klineberg and Lee have shown, moreover, that the I.Q.'s of Negro children born in the South improve steadily with length of residence in New York or Philadelphia.[5] This trend is statistically significant and continuous. Such improvement, in an overall measure of educational aptitude, indicates the great power of acculturation, both in the school and in the community, in changing language and cognitive skills.

We need, however, to accelerate the pace of acculturation of these groups in our schools. In presenting a tentative plan for such acceleration, I wish first to consider the relationship between the teacher and the disadvantaged Negro or white child.

It seems clear that the first thing we have to do, if we are to help students improve their attitudes toward themselves and toward the school work, is to *change our attitudes toward them*. If they are to develop hope for their futures and faith in their ability to achieve a useful life, we must have faith in them. No one does anything well in life unless he feels that someone has faith in him and in his ability to achieve.

But it is difficult for teachers to believe in culturally disadvantaged students who are loud and aggressive. These pupils, the teacher learns, are uninterested in the silly and dull primers, in social studies texts or in arithmetic problems unrelated to their lives.

To stimulate new learning in these pupils, we need first a new relationship between the teacher and the student. The teacher will have to initiate this new relationship by trying to understand the student and his strange, stigma-

[1] Kenneth Eells, Allison Davis, Robert J. Havinghurst, Virgil E. Herrick, and Ralph W. Tyler, under the chairmanship of Allison Davis, *Intelligence and Cultural Differences*. Chicago: University of Chicago Press, 1951, p. 112.

[2] Robert D. Hess, *An Experimental Culture-Fair Test of Mental Ability*, Unpublished doctoral dissertation, Committee on Human Development, the University of Chicago, 1950, p. 97.

[3] Ibid; p. 91.

[4] Everett S. Lee, "Negro Intelligence and Selective Migration," *American Sociological Review*, 16 (1951), 231; also Hess, *op. cit.*

[5] Otto Klineberg, *Negro Intelligence and Selective Migration*, New York: Columbia University Press, 1935, p. 59. Also E. S. Lee, *op. cit.*, pp. 231–232.

tized culture. The teacher must also remember that the processes by which human beings change their behavior (learn) are extremely complex, and are usually slow.

The major principles involved in the student's learning what the teacher has to teach may be stated as follows:

1. All learning is stimulated or hindered by the teacher's feelings toward the student. They must trust and have faith in each other.
2. All school learning is influenced by the cultural attitudes which the teacher has toward the student, and which the student experiences toward the teacher. Often in rejecting the student's cultural background, the teacher appears to reject the student himself, as a human being. In return, and as early as the first grade, the student may reject the culture of the school, and of the teacher. Both teacher and pupil must learn to *respect* the ability and position of the other.
3. All school-learning is influenced by the degree of interest and drive with respect to schoolwork which the student has learned in his family and peer-group.
4. All school learning is influenced by the presence, or absence, of intrinsic motivation in the curriculum itself. Neither the teacher nor the student can create interest in dull, unrealistic texts in reading, social studies, or arithmetic.

Suggestions for Improving the Teaching of Language and Other Cognitive Processes to Disadvantaged Negro Children

These proposals are designed both (1) to increase the familiarity of the child with cultural objects and symbols and, at the same time, (2) to increase the child's desire to learn in school.

(A) All authorities on this subject have agreed that the school behavior of children from the Negro or white lower economic groups is characterized by:

1. Their relative lack of attention to the problem as a whole, and its details. In research on an individual test of problem-solving ability conducted by Robert D. Hess and myself, we were struck by the fact that, *in the test situation*, the average six-year-old child from the Negro low economic groups looked out of the window or at the pictures on the wall, or sat passively, while the average middle-class child asked questions about what was expected of him, handled the toys and other test materials, and repeatedly asked whether he had made the correct response. The "lack of attention" by low economic groups is a cultural factor, and is related to their lack of identification with the school, its activities, and its teachers.

2. Their lack of apparent interest in and desire to learn the school activities and tasks.

3. Their lack of competitive drive and confidence with respect to achieving in the classroom, and

4. Their relatively poor work habits.

As stated in my reports of research in testing both low and middle socio-economic groups of white and Negro children, the lack of attention and of desire to learn and to compete in school, on the part of the low-income groups, result in part from their cultural handicap. They discover at the very beginning of their school life that they do not know many objects, words, pictures, and concepts which many of the other (middle class) children know.

An equally powerful deterrent to achievement, however, is their fear and distrust of the school and the teacher, which constitute an alien environment, and their failure to identify with the stranger (the teacher) and her behavior. The so-called "lack" of attention, "lack" of desire to learn, and "lack" of competitive drive in school are expressions of urgent realities: of fear and feelings of inadequacy, and the consequent resentment toward the teacher and the school tasks.

The primary emphasis in the kindergarten and the primary grades, therefore, should be placed upon the establishment of a strong relationship of trust and mutual acceptance between the teacher and pupil. The first step in education is to train the pupil to like the teacher. If he likes the teacher, he will later learn to *respect* the teacher and *will want to win her approval*. It is generally true that middle-class children have this positive feeling for the teacher (in spite of frequent parental criticism of their teachers). The feeling of liking for the teacher develops into respect and the desire to win her approval. It is just this step which is missing in the early school life of most Negro children from low socio-economic groups, and which must be built-in at the pre-school and primary level. Enjoyable informal activities, such as story-reading and games; the child's freedom to tell his *own stories* about his *own* life or fantasies, in whatever words he knows, together with songs, dances, and little plays can establish a bridge between the culture of the teacher and that of the low-status child.

Across this bridge the teacher can lead the child into new learning and new behavior, into a new world of letters, numbers, and writing which now become invested with the importance and the feeling which the child attaches to the teacher, and to *whatever she values*. From the good relationship with the teacher comes interest in the school, in the materials, and even in the workbooks. It is this spark, struck by the relationships with the teacher, which illuminates and enlivens the world of the mind even in the first grade. Therefore we need to bring the Negro and white child from low economic groups into a relationship with such a teacher as early as possible, and to structure this relationship as rewarding to both pupil and teacher.

(B) The courageous and effective teacher will shift from the so-called "basic reader" program. In this rigid program, the goals are simply (1) decoding these materials, and (2) doing so at a certain pace. The materials in these primers and readers, however, exert little or no intrinsic stimulation upon Negro or white children from culturally disadvantaged groups. These stories arouse neither imaginative nor dramatic interest. As we know, the pupils come to the first grade unprepared for the language environment of the classroom, and for most of the other cultural demands and activities of the school.

As a result, we find in the low-income schools and in the central city schools a conflict between the culturally alienated pupils, who can find nothing appealing, meaningful or exciting in the primers and readers, and the teacher who finds it impossible to succeed, or to maintain the required pace, using materials which inherently are lacking in fantasy, exciting action, emotional appeal, and the other qualities which children enjoy.

The problem, however, is not merely to replace one set of primers and readers with another, which merely change minor aspects of the pictures, and use the same uninteresting situations with the postman (who seldom has any letters for the slum family) or with the milkman (who never delivers milk to these homes since it costs three to four cents more a quart, when delivered).

The problem is, first, to help these children learn to speak and understand oral English in the kindergarten and the primary, so as to learn to understand the language of the teacher. To be effective, the teaching of reading must begin with the teaching of English vocabulary and usage, both in the kindergarten and primary. Teachers of reading and of kindergarten must learn to become teachers of speech. They should specialize in the field of children's speech, and have had some training in the use of the phonetic techniques and equipment familiar to teachers of speech, and of a foreign language.

The time is here when the obsession with reading in the first three grades—the reading of nonsense in the primers and readers—an obsession which has contributed to the retardation of Negro and other disadvantaged children by two whole years when they have been in school less than six years—has been recognized as a waste of time and money in vast amounts. Speaking and understanding spoken language come first. The basic language is the spoken language, as linguists agree. Kindergarten through third grade will increasingly emphasize the teaching of speech, which results in a much more rapid learning of both vocabulary and syntax.

Secondly, in addition to shifting the emphasis from the visual to the oral and auditory language in the first three grades, the kindergarten and primary must devote far more time to helping children learn to think, that is to guide cognitive (intellectual) development. Learning to think, as the great student of language, Edward Sapir, wrote, is a more basic process than learning to use language. *Thinking* precedes expression. Language is only the clothing of thought. Learning to think, as I pointed out in *Social-Class Influences upon Learning*, many years ago at Harvard, is the prime goal of early education. The child is in school, first of all, to learn how to think; that is to learn to observe, to perceive; to recognize relationships, differences and similarities between his observations; and to make inferences which we regard as reasonable.

The basic changes in the education of the disadvantaged Negro or white child, therefore, will be the same as those in good education generally. First, children have to learn to understand and to speak language before they can read it well or intelligently. Speech training and learning to understand speech will come before reading. Secondly, much more time will be given to learning to observe, to classify, to discriminate between observations, to reason, and to engage in expressive verbal activities than will be given to the rigid, outmoded textbook method. Elsewhere, the writer is publishing cognitive, emotional, and social criteria for the development of sequences, and materials in the field of speech and reading.

(C) With regard to methods for teaching language:

(a) Pictures, objects, stories, and television shows are to be used to develop interest on the part of the child in learning to identify and name objects, animals, groups, *etc.*, and to raise and explore problems. The teacher approves his interests and efforts, and supplies words to name objects or describes experiences, but she does not show him how to solve a problem unless he has exhausted his own approaches.

(b) With regard to the learning of language, objects, slides, and pictures should be used just as they are by good foreign-language teachers to make clear the meaning of a new word. The child's slum dialect word may be incomprehensible to the teacher. This makes no difference, for the child will learn the teacher's (standard English) word for it, when she gives him practice in naming the object as she does. This method will apply only to nouns and to those verbs, adverbs, and prepositions which may be illustrated by moving objects. The use of pictures and of slides also will help arouse the child's interest in identifying and naming objects, animals, and categories of people and of actions.

(c) After the child has a basic group of words and concepts, he is ready for narrative. By far the most powerful stimulus to his desire to learn concepts, experiences, and words is the story. The story enables him to extend his experience of nature and people vicariously, and gives him the language of action which is far more interesting to him at this age than the language of categories, description, or exposition.

Stories may be presented (1) through the teacher's telling (or reading) those appropriate to this development stage, (2) through the acting, singing, or dancing out of nursery rhymes and simple stories like "The Three Bears," or "The King and the Dairy Maid" by the children themselves, and (3) through "children's programs" on television, records, tapes, or radio. The use made of the stories, like that made of the identification of objects, models, and pictures, is in encouraging and stimulating the child to talk, to extend his vocabulary and his concepts, and to increase the complexity of his thinking and verbalization of relationships.

For the in-service education of teachers, I should suggest, in addition, the following steps:

(1) *Study of the school's community.* The young teacher, just out of college, usually knows nothing about the actual values, motives, and feelings of the lower socio-economic community. Teachers may learn these facts by individual case studies or by informal talks with the pupils in their classes. Or the faculty, as a whole, may cooperate in a study, using census data on the community, and questionnaires and interviews with parents and students.

(2) *In-service training of teachers.* All success in improving schools depends upon the willingness of teachers to learn from each other. To improve any aspect of teaching or learning in the school, the administration must provide for serious in-service training of teachers. Groups of teachers should analyze their own classroom experiences, the problems which they have met in their daily work. For any of the problems I have mentioned, there is no effective start toward a solution without the participation of the majority of the most influential teachers in prolonged in-service training programs.

(3) *Reading.* Here is an exciting opportunity for the sensitive, alert, and constructive teacher: (a) In learning the real interests and experiences of children and adolescents, and (b) in selecting stories and reading materials in the social studies and in psychology which will meet these interests. New reading materials of this realistic, exciting kind will not come usually from college and university professors. They will come chiefly from classroom teachers who are in daily contact with children and adolescents. Any alert teacher can find such stories or materials and test their value by use with her classes.

(4) *The curriculum.* What I have said of reading applies to the content of the rest of the curriculum. New materials in literature, the social studies, home economics, and even mathematics, which deal with both life and fantasy, as the pupils know it, are greatly needed, but I have seen few texts which have interest for students. Only school staffs who know children and adolescents, their interests and communities, can select these new curricular materials. Let us have the eyes to observe our students, the interest to use our observations in finding pertinent materials, and the courage to use them in experimental dittoed form, as a part of classroom work. We have had thirty years of talk about a new curriculum. Where is the new curriculum? We want to develop it, and write it—not talk about it.

(5) *Teaching method.* Discussion and participation: this is another field in which much has been said and little done. We need a method by which the students of all groups, and all socio-economic levels will be drawn into classroom discussions in each subject. At present, the teacher usually fears allowing the low-status students to talk freely; she is afraid of their English, or of the subjects they raise out of real life, or of her own reactions. But the best classes

I have seen in the hundreds of schools I have visited have been those in which there was free discussion.

The process of cultural learning which is raising the hopes and lifting the aspirations of the Negro masses in America cannot be stopped, although it is being impeded. Its working is inevitable. It is only in these terms of cultural change that one can begin to understand the tremendous efforts of Negro Americans, after nearly fourteen generations in America, for full participation in the educational, economic, political, and cultural life of the United States.

In this highly complex process of acculturation, which operates over decades and generations, some teachers and schools have labored hard, though at times blindly. Teachers have made sacrifices, have given their hearts to their work, but often have been discouraged. Looking at the results of their hard, nerve-wracking work in one class period, or one semester, or one year, they sometimes have felt that their lives have been wasted.

But the sacrifices have not been in vain. Time and work are telling. In just one generation, the I.Q. of Negro children in Philadelphia, New York, and Chicago has increased about ten points. Furthermore, as revealed by Special Monograph, No. 10, Volume 1, on Special Groups, by the Selective Service System (1953, Washington, D.C., Government Printing Office, p. 147) the Negroes drafted in Illinois and New York had a far lower rate of failure on the educational test used by Selective Services than did the whites in fifteen southern states.

What we, as teachers, must always remember is that man is a learner. No matter how handicapped he may be, he still possesses the highest of human capacities, the ability to improve himself by learning. Given the opportunity, he will learn his way up.

SOME PSYCHOSOCIAL ASPECTS
OF LEARNING IN THE DISADVANTAGED *

Martin Deutsch

It has long been known that some general relationship exists between the conditions of social, cultural, and economic deprivation and cognitive deficit. The environment having the highest rate of disease, crime, and social disorganization also has the highest rate of school retardation. Deficiencies in

---

* REPRINTED by permission of Martin Deutsch and the publisher, from *Teachers College Record*, January, 1966, pp. 260–65.

linguistic skills and reading are particularly striking. School dropout and failure, apart from what they represent in lost potential to the individual and his community, mean that, as adults, those who have failed or dropped out will be confined to the least skilled and least desirable jobs and will have almost no opportunity for upward social mobility.

A large body of empirical literature supports the assumption that certain environmental conditions may retard psychological processes, including intellectual development. This conclusion is borne out in research on both animals and human beings (12, 13). One of the most comprehensive reviews of the effects of environmental impoverishment on intellectual development, by Clarke and Clarke (7), presents data collected on adolescents and young adults who have experienced severe deprivation as a result of cruelty, neglect, or parental separation. Bruner (5) writes that "exposure to normally enriched environments makes the development of (cognitive) strategies possible by providing intervening opportunities for trial and error . . . that there is impairment under a deprived regimen seems . . . to be fairly evident." Although he does not refer specifically to the environment of the lower-class child, Bruner's remarks seem especially relevant here. The obvious implication is that disadvantaged children, who have a meager environmental basis for developing cognitive skills, are often unprepared to cope with the formal intellectual and learning demands of school.

Facilitating Growth

Nevertheless, a fostering environment for such children can facilitate intellectual development. Bruner (6), for example, suggests that certain environmental conditions increase the likelihood of learning cognitive strategies. And Clarke and Clarke (7) report striking increases in IQ in a deprived group during a six-year program aimed at reversing deprivation effects. That improved environmental conditions may have a positive impact on the intellectual development of children is also supported by the studies of the Iowa group (16, 17). Informal observation shows that, even in the most economically depressed areas, where school retardation rates are highest, some children manifest considerable school success and academic proficiency. If we assume a causal relationship between environmental conditions and cognitive development, then variation in such development could partially reflect variations within the environment. We can assume that no so-called under-privileged area is homogeneous: There are, indeed, considerable variations in the home environments of children from such areas—variations ranging from large fatherless families supported by public assistance to small intact families with inadequate but regular income.

Moreover, learning contexts are as heterogeneous as environmental backgrounds. Although the two contexts are not actually disparate, early socialization, mediated through home and neighborhood environments and mass media, requires responses different from those necessary for school learning and subject mastery. The formal learning processes carry well-defined criteria of failure and success not mediated through such behavioral indices as group leadership, influence, and the like, whereas the informal learning environment has not explicitly stated criteria or marking systems. In the latter, success may be more highly related to leadership, and failure to rejection or subordination by the group.

PSYCHOLOGICAL CONTEXTS

Even as his learning context changes when the child enters school, so does his psychological context for achievement. At this point the amount of continuity between the home environment and that of school can strongly influence the child's responses to the learning and achievement context of school. The discontinuity between the lower-class child's background and the school impairs his successful responses in the new situation.

The middle-class child is more likely to have been continuously prodded intellectually by his parents and rewarded for correct answers, whereas, in the main, the lower-class child's parents have seldom subjected him to the pressure of a formal adult-child learning situation. The middle-class child is likely to have experienced, in the behavior of adults in his environment, the essential ingredients implicit in the role of teacher. For the lower-class child, relating to the teacher and school officials requires a new kind of behavior, for which he has not necessarily been prepared.

School curricula and learning techniques usually imply an assumption that the child has had prior experience in the complex learning area, where there are logical assumptions as to appropriate behavior and where success is rewarded and failure is disapproved. The teacher, trained in our not-so-modern teacher-education institutions, assumes—probably consciously as well as unconsciously—that the school child is a quasi-passive recipient of knowledge, and that he clearly understands the teacher's educative and remedial functions. In this, the teacher is as likely to be as confused about the child's expectations as the child is confused about the school's expectations.

Lacking sufficient sociological sophistication, school authorities understandably tend to expect from children a level of comprehension and motivation that can only be built through positive experiences in the learning situation. Children who are used to a great deal of motor activity and who have certain environmentally determined deficiencies in learning to learn, often respond with an inappropriate academic orientation. Teachers meet this situation in several ways, most of which cause serious problems for the socially marginal child. Some teachers establish low expectations, anticipate failure, and, true to the Mertonian self-fulfilling prophecy, find an increasing rate of failure.

PROJECTION AND BLAME

Another reaction seems to be, "They can't learn; they don't care; their parents are not concerned." This projective device serves to relieve the professional of responsibility, since it does contain a grain of truth: Often older siblings and neighbors of the lower-class child have experienced so much failure and so much class and cultural arrogance as to generate a great apathy out of which none of them expects positive consequences from the school experience. This very apathy is sometimes reflected in the attitudes of the educational apparatus toward the lower-class community.

Still other teachers say, "It is all the environment-impoverishment, economic insecurity, segregation, second-class citizenship, historical chains. Of course, none of these things is the child's fault, but neither are they the school's fault." This approach has greater validity, invoking as it does social circumstances obviously crucial to the developing organism. Yet such a view often leads to negation not only of the essential responsibility of the school but also of the actual and potential strengths of the children. Most important, it induces an elaborate rationale for the further alienation of teachers from their primary function, teaching. The essential element, which is both professionally and psychologically threatening, is simply that, for the child inadequately equipped to handle what the school has to offer, it is up to the school to develop compensatory strategies through a program of stimulation appropriate to his capabilities. Essentially, the disadvantaged child is still further disadvantaged when the school, as the primary socializing and teaching agent, refuses to accept its own failure whenever any such child fails. For the school to assume its full responsibility requires constant self-criticism and self-evaluation; these have not been characteristic of educational systems, despite noteworthy exceptions.

To put it more bluntly, when teacher-training institutions and educational systems foster an atmosphere of critical evaluation of their procedures and establish high criteria for professional training and development, teachers will maintain a psychological connection with their children that today is often severed, especially when the teacher, with neither a theoretical nor a working model, must bridge social-class discontinuities. Were more of today's children succeeding in learning to read at grade level, we would be forced to reconstruct our theory considerably. They are not, and the total atmosphere in the majority of our urban schools having large groups of disadvantaged youngsters becomes less and less conducive not merely to the learning process but also to the positive child-teacher relationship that establishes motivation and gives rise to high standards of achievement.

REFLECTIONS OF FAILURE

Responsibility for this unfavorable learning situation is not the school's alone. It lies in a combination of social circumstances, historical apathy, economic exploitation, and a society that does not put its money where its explicit values are. Even so, the school most directly reflects society's failure: It is the one institution that has the opportunity directly to affect the situation.

In this total atmosphere, what are some of the additional handicaps that the disadvantaged child brings into school? If we expect the school to organize so as to meet the child on his own developmental level, then we must know a good deal about the specific intellectual sequelae likely to be associated more with economic impoverishment than with affluence. Further, we need simple and adequate ways of measuring the actual development of each child's abilities, because they are the foundation for the skills the school is to teach him. Such specific information will enable the teacher to teach him more adequately and to present him with the most appropriate stimuli. Moreover, the child's probable success will increase when the material presented is truly consistent with his developmental level, since engendering a sense of competence, in White's (19) terms, can sustain motivation, thereby facilitating learning.

The self-image is vital to learning. School experiences can either reinforce invidious self-concepts acquired from the environment, or help to develop—or even induce—a negative self-concept. Conversely, they can effect positive self-feelings by providing for concrete achievements and opportunities to function with competence, although initially these experiences must be in the most limited and restricted areas. The evidence leads us to the inescapable conclusion that, by the time they enter school, many disadvantaged children have developed negative self-images, which the school does little to mitigate.

Another significant element, usually ignored, probably helps shape the perception of himself that the child develops in school, namely, the use of time. Generally, time is inefficiently used, there is minimal individualized attention, and the child often spends much time in unproductive rote activities, while the teacher focuses her attention on remedial subgroups or the omnipresent paper work. Given the high pupil-teacher ratio, the critical need is for auto-instructional devices or preprogramed curriculum elements to which the child can turn. This is part of a situation where responsibility cannot be placed on the teacher, and the frequent use of this down-trodden professional as a scapegoat reflects chiefly only her position as the psychologically operative instrument in the education of the child.

In a sense, after passing through the whole of society's educational echelons, the buck stops with her (but not in her pocket). Nevertheless, this understanding does not improve the situation. Too often, the child is seriously understimulated, even with the best of teachers, and there is little over-all curriculum planning for the needs of disadvantaged children. Most important, society has furnished neither funds nor the educational leadership and training necessary for the new supplementary technologies that would enormously increase the effective use of time. These would, in turn, help the child develop a sense of purpose and belonging in the school context.

DECREASING ALIENATION

Autoinstructional and programed devices and methods might also give the child a sense of greater mastery over the unfamiliar school environment: They could reduce his passivity by giving him greater control over the timing of stimuli, thus minimizing cultural differences in time orientation. Further, in the self-corrective feedback of programed materials, the teacher's role of giving reward and disapproval would be shared; for a child unaccustomed to these as means of motivation for intellectual performance, it might help decrease his alienation from the school. If these hypotheses are valid, then the new educational techniques could socially facilitate the learning process.

The extent of the disadvantaged child's alienation as a crucial factor in handicapping his school performance and achievement has been emphasized. Much of this is structural, and much of the psychosocial problem lies in the interaction between the child and the school. However, cognitive variables which have been socially influenced or determined also contribute to the whole process of increasing the mutual alienation of the school and the child. Among these, one of the major difficulties is the often nonfunctional language system he brings to school. My colleagues and I have discussed this at length elsewhere (8, 9, 10, 11, 15).

LANGUAGE AND LEARNING

I would like to point out here that social-class determination of linguistic styles and habits is an effective deterrent to communication and understanding between child and teacher. To illustrate, the child is unaccustomed to both attending to, and being the object of, what are for him long, orderly, focused verbal sequences. Yet this is the primary scholastic teaching and discipline method. Further, because the disadvantaged child is less familiar with the syntactical regularities and normative frequencies of the language, he has difficulty in ordering its sequences and in both deriving meaning from, and putting it into, context. This is all the more disadvantageous for the lower-class child because he has a short attention span for the verbal material to which he is exposed in school. Consequently, he is likely to miss a great deal, even when he is trying to listen. For such a child it is extremely important to feel some mastery in handling at least receptive language. This is made more difficult by what Bernstein, the English sociologist (1, 2, 3, 4), has described as the different dialects spoken by lower- and middle-class people.

This discussion keeps returning to the need for helping the educator to develop a comprehensive consciousness of the psychological as well as the learning difficulties of the disadvantaged child; the real potential for change; the specifics involved in training children, for example, to ask questions, or to become aware of syntactical regularities, or to use autoinstructional materials; and the imperative need to maintain as high as possible the level of stimulation and relevancy in the classroom. Here the research and insights of the behavioral sciences should be able to contribute significantly, provided the educational albatross takes a few "risks" to accommodate social change.

REFERENCES

1. Bernstein, B. "Language and Social Class." *Brit. J. Sociol.*, 1960, *11*, 271–276.
2. ———, "Social Structure, Language and Learning." *Educ. Res.*, Vol. III, June 1961.
3. ———, "Linguistic Codes, Hesitation Phenomena and Intelligence." *Lang. and Speech*, 1962, 5, (1).
4. ———, "Social Class, Linguistic Codes and Grammatical Elements. *Lang. and Speech*, 1962, 5, (4).
5. Bruner, J. S. *The Process of Education.* Cambridge: Harvard Univer. Pr., 1960.
6. ———, "The Course of Cognitive Growth." *Amer. Psychol.*, 1964, *19*, 1–15.
7. Clarke, A. D. B., & Clarke, A. M. "Recovery From the Effects of Deprivation." *Acta Psychol.*, 1959, 16, 137–144.
8. Deutsch, M. Facilitating Development in the Pre-School Child: Social and Psychological Perspectives." *Merrill-Palmer Quart.*, 1964, *10*, 3, 249–263.
9. ———, "Training Programs as Preparation for Social Change." Paper read at Amer. Orthopsychiat. Assn., Chicago, March, 1964.
10. ———, "The Role of Social Class in Language Development and Cognition. *Amer. J. Orthopsychiat.*, 1965, 1, 78–88.
11. Deutsch, M.; Maliver, Alma; Brown, B., and Cherry, Estelle. "Communication of Information in the Elementary School Classroom." Washington, DC: Cooperative Research Project No. 908 of the Office of Education, US Department of Health, Education and Welfare, 1964.
12. Heb, D. O. *The Organization of Behavior.* New York: Wiley, 1949.
13. Hunt, J. McV. *Intelligence and Experience.* New York: Ronald, 1961.
14. ———, "The Psychological Basis for Using Pre-School Enrichment as an Antidote for Cultural Deprivation." *Merrill-Palmer Quart.*, 1964, *10*, 3, 209–243.
15. John, Vera P. "The Intellectual Development of Slum Children. Some preliminary findings." *Amer. J. Orthopsychiat.*, 1963, 5, 813–822.
16. Skeels, H. M., Updegraff, Ruth, Wellman, Beth L., & Williams, A. M. "A Study of Environmental Stimulation: An Orphanage Pre-School Project." *Univer. Iowa Stud. Child Welf.*, 1938, 15, no. 4.
17. Skodak, Marie, and Skeels, H. M. "A Final Follow-Up Study of One Hundred Adopted Children." *J. Genet. Psychol.*, 1949, 75, 85–125.
18. Wellman, Beth L. "Iowa Studies on the Effects of Schooling." *Yearb. Nat. Soc. Stud. Educ.*, 1940, 39, 377–399.
19. White, R. W. "Motivation Reconsidered: The Concept of Competence." *Psychol. Rev.*, 1959, 66, 297–333.

NEEDS OF SLOW-LEARNING PUPILS *

find their reading level, find their interests,

Paul A. Witty

Education is sometimes regarded as a process in which the greatest development of every child is sought, according to his unique nature and needs. One group, often neglected in our schools, is made up primarily of slow-learning children—pupils who are below average in ability, but not retarded enough to be considered mentally handicapped. These pupils are characterized, roughly, by IQ's ranging between 75 and 90. In many schools, these pupils constitute about 15 to 18 per cent of the class enrollment.

In our efforts to challenge average and superior students adequately, there is an ever-present threat that we shall overlook or neglect the slow-learning pupils. Because of the current emphasis on superior and gifted students, it is especially desirable for us to examine the extent to which slow-learning pupils are being recognized and challenged in every classroom today.

NATURE OF THE SLOW LEARNER

Studies show that the slow-learning pupil usually is not different from other pupils in his physical development, but he may have a slightly greater tendency toward instability. This tendency often is inevitable. The slow learner usually experiences disappointments and frustrations in school because he fails to comprehend materials fully and to make steady progress in learning. Indeed, his learning rate is so slow that, by the time he reaches the upper elementary grades, his educational status as shown by standard tests usually will be a year or more below the grade standard.

Recognition of these facts may have led Christine Ingram to state: "Satisfactory adjustment in life calls for self-confidence, self-reliance, and independence on the part of the individual. The mentally retarded, because of their inability to compete successfully with other children, tend to lack these essential qualities. It becomes, therefore, the responsibility of the school to provide experiences that will aid this group to become self-confident, self-reliant, independent workers at tasks commensurate with their learning abilities" (3).

Insecurities and anxieties often accompany the slow-learning pupil's growing recognition of his inferiority as he advances from grade to grade. However, the need for safeguarding him from needless anxiety and insecurity exists from the time he enters school. The attitudes of the slow-learning pupil may be

---

* REPRINTED from the February, 1961, issue of *Education*. Copyright 1961 by The Bobbs-Merrill Company, Inc., Indianapolis, Indiana.

influenced deeply by his experiences in the first grade in which his failures lead him to develop grave doubts concerning his own competence and acceptability.

Repeated failure may cause the slow-learning child to resort to compensatory mechanisms. Because of his insecurity, he may be led to exhibit one or a combination of the following reactions: withdrawal, aggression, indifference, lack of interest, nervousness, or marked anxiety. At home, he may reveal a lack of self-confidence and may resort to minor illnesses to receive attention or to avoid regular school attendance.

Care must be taken to insure reliability in appraising the ability of this pupil, since average and superior students who fail in school may exhibit similar behavior. Moreover, it is well to recall that learning rates for slow-learning pupils may vary because of motivational and environmental factors. Careful testing and observation are needed to justify designating pupils as "slow."

Because of the foregoing facts, it is essential at every level of the slow-learning pupil's education, for his goals to be attainable. It is essential also for his goals to be raised gradually in order for him to make steady progress.

BUILDING SKILLS

The educational attainment of the slow-learning pupil should be thoroughly appraised. He often needs help in acquiring the basic habits and skills in all areas, but the need for assistance in reading is usually great and persistent. Accordingly, his reading ability should be evaluated with utmost care. In the primary grades, special consideration should be given to readiness.

The results of standardized oral and silent reading tests may be used to ascertain the child's attainment. Later on, they may be employed to estimate his gains. Data obtained from diagnostic tests also may be helpful. In addition, the nature and amount of the child's reading in books and other sources may be investigated. Study of his rate of reading different types of material also may be pertinent and useful. With such information at hand, it will be possible for the teacher to offer the pupil an opportunity to read materials of appropriate difficulty and suitability.

STEADY READING GAINS POSSIBLE

If learning goals are adjusted to the slow-learning pupil's educational status and are geared to his rate of learning, the learner's progress usually will be steady. Recognizing his own continuous progress and relatively greater success in school also may contribute to his sense of security and may affect his general mental health favorably.

Within the regular classroom, provision may be made for the slow-learning pupils' acquisition of reading skills by use of multi-level materials. Special help in reading even may be provided throughout the junior and senior high school to satisfy the needs of slow-learning pupils, especially in the area of vocabulary growth.

STUDY OF INTERESTS

It is desirable for the teacher to study the interests of slow-learning pupils. Studies show that these pupils often have meager or narrow interests, in which cases, the crucial need is to encourage the development of new or more desirable patterns of interest through enrichment and extension of experience. Visits to near-by airports, farms, and other places of local importance will provide avenues for firsthand experiences which may engender interest.

Interest also may be cultivated through the use of films and filmstrips. The film readers, designed to accompany many films, may be employed successfully with slow-learning pupils, since the film supplies the background necessary for an understanding of each booklet. Experiences of these kinds often stimulate a strong interest in reading.

Observation of pupils during and following experiences of various kinds is one way of detecting worth-while interests or promising avenues for the development of interests. There are other more formal approaches for obtaining pertinent information about the nature and extent of children's interests.

Questionnaires recently have been developed and used in comprehensive studies of children and youth in a research project co-operatively undertaken by Northwestern University and the United States Office of Education, Department of Health, Education, and Welfare. The questionnaires included inquiries concerning the following areas of interest: TV, radio, and movies; play and recreation; reading and vocational and educational pursuits (4).

Interest inventories, designed to study play activities, fears, wishes, hobbies, preferences, and other or related interests, often yield clues of value in understanding pupils' attitudes and needs. The use of anecdotal records and similar approaches also may enable the teacher to gain further insight into pupil interest. Examination of personal or creative writing, too, may disclose needs.

The interests characteristic of the slow-learning pupil should be employed. He should be educated not in the shadow of average and superior pupils, but in terms of his own experiences, interests, and concerns. Some slow-learning pupils will be interested in particular vocations; others, in the people of various lands; and still others, in the exploits and discoveries in space. To satisfy these and other interests, the world of books offers a readily available avenue. In addition to factual presentations, there are narratives, poems, and biographies to satisfy almost every taste, hobby, or interest (6).

PUPIL NEEDS

We have indicated that, to offer effective instruction, the teacher should have available not only facts about each slow-learning pupil's reading, but also information pertaining to his interests. To help guide the pupil in attaining the most rewarding outcomes from reading, findings regarding each pupil's needs are also essential. The study of developmental needs differs somewhat from the study of interests, although similar techniques may be used in both cases. We are searching in our study of needs for evidence of the relative success of each pupil in his adjustment to recurring life demands and situations.

Needs are sometimes referred to as "developmental tasks." According to Robert Havighurst, a developmental task "arises at or about a certain period in the life of an individual, successful achievement of which leads to his happiness and to success with later tasks, while failure leads to unhappiness in the individual, disapproval by society and difficulty with later tasks . . ." (2)

The value of an approach to reading through a concern for need is gradually being acknowledged. This approach is particularly appropriate in the case of the slow-learning pupil because his needs are so frequently blocked or denied. His rehabilitation often appears to depend upon the extent to which his fundamental need for self-respect and self-esteem can be satisfied.

It is recognized, of course, that experience in reading in itself will not lead invariably to the fulfillment of needs. However, if reading is used in association with other activities, it may assist greatly. We must recognize, moreover, that many factors determine the impact of reading upon boys and girls. Thus David Russell wrote: "We must hypothesize that impact of reading is determined by the reader's expectations or set, by his overt purpose for reading, by his conscious or unconscious needs, by the personality traits or patterns which affect much of his conduct, and by combinations of these factors" (7).

It is generally acknowledged that research data on the impact of reading are inadequate and inconclusive. "From the research point of view, however, the effects of reading are an uncharted wasteland in an otherwise well-mapped territory" (7).

Nevertheless, there is, it seems, justification for recommending an approach to reading through a concern for the interests and needs of the slow-learning pupil. For case-studies do show that such reading often has a desirable effect upon the mental health and well-being of the pupil (9).

READING AND DEVELOPMENTAL NEEDS

In the Northwestern University Psycho-Educational Clinic, books have been employed for many years to aid children in making desirable personal and social adjustments.

A list of needs that characterize children at various levels has been drawn up, including, for example, understanding oneself better; adjusting to one's peers or associates; understanding and participating effectively in family life; achieving an understanding of, and an acceptable personal choice of, occupation and other needs. Books which may contribute to the fulfillment of each need often are suggested from a list of appropriate titles. Stories may be selected which provide the adolescent with an opportunity for appropriate identification and also with an opportunity to attain a better understanding of himself. Case-studies have revealed remarkable gains made by slow-learning pupils whose reading has been guided by this approach.

The clinic's list is only one of several such lists which have been compiled during the past decade. An excellent bibliography of this type was published as a supplement to the *Chicago Schools Journal* (5). This bibliography contains annotated references for books arranged under seventy-eight headings.

DEVELOPMENTAL READING AIMS

For the slow-learning pupil, a developmental reading program appears especially desirable. Such a program recognizes the value of continuous systematic instruction, utilization of interests, fulfillment of developmental needs, and the relationship of experience in reading to other types of worth-while activity. By this four-fold approach, steady growth in reading skills is made possible, and the attainment of basic human satisfactions is facilitated.

One aim of this program is to lead the slow learner to become like other pupils, independent in using the library and other resources for satisfying his interests and fulfilling his varied and changing needs. This objective will be achieved if the student is enabled to enjoy reading and the results of reading.

He usually will enjoy reading if he acquires a reasonable command of silent and oral reading skills. He can acquire this skill through an efficient, systematic program of reading instruction and guidance throughout the course of his education.

The slow-learning pupil will enjoy the results of reading when reading experience is associated with his interests and needs. Accordingly, slow-learning pupils may become skillful, independent readers on their own levels and may continue to extend their understandings and satisfactions throughout their lives by reading.

IMPORTANCE OF THE TEACHER

Perhaps the most significant single factor in determining the success of efforts with the slow-learning child is the teacher.

A major responsibility of the teacher of the slow-learning pupil is to provide a classroom atmosphere in which success, security, understanding, mutual respect, and opportunity to attain worthy educational goals are all pervading. In such an atmosphere the teacher will be prepared to direct children's development in such a way that their emotional life will yield the maximum of human satisfactions and values.

In all classrooms the mental health of the teacher is obviously a most important consideration (8). In a quest for mental health the teacher will find many sources of help, not the least of which will be the satisfactions derived from observing the growth and progress of all types of pupils. Especially great will be the satisfaction experienced by the teacher who observes, in the case of slow-learning pupils, conspicuous gains in self-confidence, self-respect, and general mental health as well as in academic attainment.

REFERENCES

1. Brooks, Alice R. "Integrating Books and Reading with Adolescent Tasks," *The School Review*, Vol. 43, pp. 211–219.
2. Havighurst, Robert J. *Developmental Tasks and Education* (Chicago: University of Chicago Press, 1948).
3. Ingram, Christine. *Education of the Slow-Learning Child* (2d. ed.; New York: The Ronald Press, 1953).
4. *The Interests of Children and Youth* (Washington, D. C., U. S. Office of Education, 1959).
5. LaPlante, Effie, and O'Donnell, Thelma. "Developmental Values through Books." *Supplement to Chicago Schools Journal* (March and April, 1950).
6. Larrick, Nancy. *A Teacher's Guide to Children's Books* (Columbus, Ohio: Charles E. Merrill Books, Inc., 1960).
7. Russell, David. "Some Research on the Impact of Reading," *The English Journal* (October, 1958).
8. Witty, Paul (Chairman). *Mental Health in Modern Education*, Fifty-fourth Yearbook, Part II, of the National Society for the Study of Education (Chicago: University of Chicago Press (Distributor), 1955).
9. ——, "Promoting Growth and Development through Reading," *Elementary English* (December, 1950).

CREATIVE READING AND THE GIFTED STUDENT * †

By John J. DeBoer

The term *creative reading* has had much currency in recent years. Is it a euphemism, intended to reinforce the impression of a modern classroom as a dynamic environment in which all emphasis is placed on stimulation as

* REPRINTED with permission of John J. DeBoer and the International Reading Association, from *The Reading Teacher*, Vol. 16, May, 1963, pp. 435–41.

† This article was adapted from a chapter by the author, "The Concept of Creativity in Reading," in *Perspectives on English: Essays to Honor W. Wilbur Hatfield*, edited by Robert C. Pooley (New York: Appleton-Century, Crofts, 1960), pp. 199–211.

opposed to lesson-learning? Or is it merely a faddish expression for plain "good reading"?

Traditionally, we have thought of the writer as the one who "creates," while the good reader enters the author's world and passively permits that world to act upon him. Thus the skills involved in increasing one's perception span, vocabulary, word recognition, speed, and recall have been taught in order to facilitate the process of efficient reception in reading. The purpose has been to provide the child with a new language, an indispensable, vast means of symbolic communication.

Certainly the factor of receptivity is essential to good reading. When the reader goes to the printed page with mind fixed, with views and emotions previously established dominating the reading, the author is powerless to communicate with him. The reader must let the author take the lead. He must give himself, at least temporarily, over to a "willing suspension of disbelief" as the author spins a tale, or he must follow obediently as the philosopher expounds his doctrines—not necessarily to accept, but to understand. Thus only can the child enter new worlds and let enchantment or excitement or surprise delight him.

But there is another side to the coin. For every action there is a reaction. All the skills enumerated in a previous paragraph call for selective effort on the part of the reader. In Emerson's phrase, one must be an inventor to read well. There can be no efficient receptivity in reading without active response. The good reader keeps supplying from his own experience. And in the discriminating evocation of personal experiences lies the source of true creativity in reading.

Thus effective reading shares with other types of creative effort one purpose: to combine and recombine the materials of language to achieve a meaningful result. This means that (1) the creative reader is an active agent, not merely a passive recipient; (2) he is a seeker and an experimenter; and (3) he is both a builder and a leveler.

Reading, of course, is inseparable from thinking. Creative thinking involves all the higher-order mental processes: perception, concept formation, seeing relationships, drawing conclusions, making comparisons, making applications. Teaching creative reading must therefore be accompanied by instruction in creative thinking, insofar as creativity is a thing that can be taught.

CREATIVITY IN THE GIFTED

In the sense in which we are employing the term, creativity is essential to reading growth from the earliest stages. The appeal to creativity must be made to learners of all levels of ability. But it is the cultivation of genuine creativity in the gifted pupil that provides probably the most difficult of all challenges to the teacher of reading. The creative act is always a unique response, personal to the individual.

Although the differences *among* gifted children are as great as those between the gifted and the average, we may reasonably expect that most gifted children have greater capacity for perceiving or educing relationships, greater originality in utilizing the fruits of past experiences, greater daring in drawing conclusions from data, greater hospitality to the new or unexpected, greater willingness to challenge authority. As in creative writing, the gifted student flourishes in an atmosphere of freedom, acceptance, and stimulation.

We may not assume, of course, that pupils of high potentiality necessarily display their talents in reading. It appears that the correlation between mental ability and reading comprehension is high, and it is reasonable to expect that the academically gifted boy or girl will do well in reading. We know, however, that many bright students are underachievers in reading. These are in just as great a need of systematic instruction and encouragement as are the retarded readers.

And what of those young people who score normal in reading tests (and sometimes below normal) who exhibit extraordinary talent in music, art, the dance, the mastery of quantitative concepts, or practical and mechanical operations? Since interests and creative abilities are usually associated, the teacher will make every effort to draw on the child's existing resources of creative interests to foster his growth in creative reading. A person's aptitudes may vary from one area of interest and competence to another, but human abilities are not generally highly compartmentalized. General intelligence, combined with such factors as experience, motivation, interest, and parental pressures, is commonly the basis for exceptional achievement in specific fields. Kirk illustrates the many categories of special aptitudes as the socially talented, the mechanically talented, the artistically talented, the musically talented, the physically talented, the linguistically talented, and the academically talented (1). The concepts and mental constructs developed in various categories of experience should be drawn upon in the reading process, which will in turn enrich and amplify the world of creative discovery and achievement outside of reading.

To avoid nebulous objectives in the cultivation of creative reading abilities, the teacher should learn to view creativity in its more specific manifestations. While creativity cannot be "taught," in any direct sense, it is possible for the teacher to help free the child from the roadblocks, emotional and technical, which impede his path to the unique expression of which he is capable. By seeing clearly some of the major tasks involved in creative reading, the young learner can assume attitudes toward the printed page which will effectively promote the kind of independence and active response that we seek in reading. Suggestive of these tasks are the following: (1) creative inquiry, (2) creative interpretation, (3) creative integration, (4) creative application, and (5) creative criticism. The list is by no means exhaustive, and the resourceful teacher will find additional specifics as she works with groups or individual children.

① Creative Inquiry

Modern schools have shifted their emphasis from mere subject-matter mastery and the retention of ready-made "learning products," in the Morrisonian sense, to the growth of a lively curiosity, a reaching-out for meaning, a re-examination of alternative "solutions" to old problems, and the discovery and definition of new problems. Under this new emphasis, the idea of communicating established principles, sometimes even by the lecture method, is not eliminated. But in all learning, the reader or listener is an active participant, and he learns only as he re-creates within himself the thing to be learned. The first step in such re-creation is the adventure of asking questions. In each problematic situation the versatility and individuality required of the learner take on the quality of creative thinking, or "creative" reading. Such creativity is called into play in reading at various levels.

The first task, then, is to learn how to ask the *right* questions.

At a simple level, the satisfaction of curiosity, the questions may be fairly obvious ones, such as, "What will happen next?" or "Why was Linda so quiet at Christmas dinner?" Questions may reveal a more mature kind of critical curiosity, as illustrated in a letter by a third grade boy written to an author in care of her publishers: "I've been reading your book at school called *Let's Take a Trip to the Firehouse*. Now what I'd like to know is why you call the aerial truck and the hook-and-ladder truck the same thing." He politely discusses the differences between the trucks and concludes by asking again why the author wrote as if they were the same (3).

Basic to this boy's capacity to make intelligent inquiry was the fact that he had had enriched experiences with toy fire equipment, had probably visited the fire station several times, and, perhaps most important, the fact that he was called upon to make comparisons among many books on the subject.

For older students, the questioning aroused by a very dramatic account of the detonation of the first atomic bomb presents a greater challenge. "It was the nearest thing to doomsday that one could possibly imagine. . . . But Laurence thought it might be the dawn of a new day for mankind, not doomsday at all. He shared the exuberance of the scientists, who leaped to their feet . . . shouting with joy."

In one class, such questions as these were raised after reading about the bomb: "What other inventions were motivated by defense and armament?" "How have such inventions affected the nation's economy?" "What peaceful uses could atomic energy serve?" "Was the discovery of atomic fission and fusion fortunate or unfortunate?" "Was Laurence right in thinking that atomic energy did not spell out doomsday but a great new hope for mankind?" "What steps could we as a nation take to reduce the danger of nuclear war?"

These questions were stimulated, but not demanded, by the story. They arose out of experience with previous reading and discussion, and out of the relationship between the passage and the day's news. It is in this perception of relationships and their formulation in words that the element of creativity is to be found.

Such an approach to creative inquiry, especially by talented children, has fundamental implications for the organization of the curriculum. Few questions that young people ask are limited to a single discipline. The answers must be drawn from a variety of subject fields. If the questions are worthwhile, they will concern situations and problems rather than neatly categorized items of information. The domain of reading is as broad as the world itself.

CREATIVE INTERPRETATION

Creative inquiry is a search for answers to questions which the reader asks to meet a need or satisfy curiosity; creative *interpretation* involves an intensive effort at reconstructing the author's precise meaning. Such reconstruction is not "free" creation, because it is sternly limited by the clues and symbols found in the reading matter. Nevertheless, interpretation at its best is a creative process because the ideas on the page must be built anew in the mind of each reader. Since minds of readers differ, and since some minds are both better informed and more creative than others, interpretations of literary materials may vary widely. Witness the conflicting interpretations of passages in the Bible or Shakespeare.

A familiar example of the need for creative interpretation is the expression found in newspapers almost daily, "the free world." In ascertaining the writers' intent when they use the word "free" in this context, a reader might examine the various classical definitions of "freedom," such as "absence of external restraint," or "power to choose and pursue a line of action," or "exemption from arbitrary domination." Some acquaintance, however, with the common use of the expression, "the free world," in America and Western Europe soon leads the perceptive reader to recognize that it refers to all the countries outside of the Communist orbit, except perhaps the uncommitted nations. The fact that these "free" countries include Franco's Spain, the dictatorships of Latin America, and the white supremacist Republic of South Africa, and that nations ground down by poverty and starvation cannot be considered really free, does not alter the true intent of the writer. "Freedom" in this sense may be a politically motivated euphemism, but to the sophisticated reader the writer's meaning is clear.

The understanding of metaphorical language, too, calls for a kind of creative interpretation. When Margaret Sidney writes, in *Five Little Peppers and How They Grew*, "It was just on the edge of twilight," she calls on the child to interpret the figure which borrows from space to describe time. Creative effort is involved in this simple translation, which the fluent reader almost unconsciously makes as he follows the sweep of the story. When an author calls his book, *Out of the Jaws of Victory*, the student must quickly supply the original metaphor and relate the inversion to the political analysis with which the book deals—Truman's election in 1948. This kind of interpretation, which calls for the formation and utilization of mental constructs on the part of the reader, is a creative activity, although on a relatively simple level.

CREATIVE INTEGRATION

We have seen that creativity in reading means putting things together—words, concepts, images—to create something new in the reader's mind. But this "putting together" extends also to the constituent factors in a remark, a situation, a plot, or the sayings and deeds of a character. The essential moments of insight in reading occur when the reader has perceived what the various factors "add up to." The "adding up to," however, is not a mere process of addition, but a perception, sometimes unexpected, of a central impact, a mood, a value, an attitude toward life.

To the creative reader, the "moment of insight" has value insofar as he is able to relate it to the body of his previous experience, his previous attitudes, his perception of reality, his outlook on life. *Integrating* what one reads (or hears on the radio, or sees on the stage or the television screen) with one's beliefs about self or others or the world or values is a process that must be unique to each individual, and is, therefore, in a true sense creative.

Let us take as an example the Biblical story of David and Goliath. The reader is moved by the story—the spectacle of a young man exhibiting great faith and courage, of the mighty defeated by the weak, of the arrogant brought low by the humble. But from this point on, each reader makes his own connections with past knowledge and experience—connections which heighten the emotional impact of the narrative, but which also give new meaning to a much broader cluster of events, issues, problems, goals, beliefs. Thus, one reader, following David as he ran forward to meet the giant, remembered that David was a pastoral poet, the "sweet singer of Israel," who was not merely a military hero but also one of the towering figures in the ancient and cultural tradition of the Jewish people. The reminder made him see in clearer perspective the nature of the barbaric mind which harbors anti-Semitism. The reaction was not one of free association; it was a creative transference from a single dramatic episode to a generalized insight or emotion. The task of the student is to build a structure fit for the cultivated mind to dwell in.

CREATIVE APPLICATION

One of the skills of reading frequently mentioned is the ability to apply what one reads. It is reasonable to question whether application is a proper part of reading itself. A closer examination of the mental processes involved in reading, however, will reveal that application is integral to creative reading. To construe what one reads, one must know what the reading matter *implies* for a variety of related situations.

The process of application may be illustrated by the simple examples of a housewife following a recipe and of a chess addict trying to solve a chess puzzle. In these instances, the reading is accompanied by other activities, but the reading itself is focused upon the ways in which the printed words are to be applied. Considering the relative simplicity of these examples, one might hesitate to use the term "creative" in this connection. No one, however, would dispute the creative quality of applications made when the reading material is abstract or when it calls for subtle distinctions of meaning.

To the extent that reading may affect one's thinking in general, or that an idea encountered on the printed page may reshape one's beliefs about related matters, whether they concern social organization or public health or penology, reading has brought about a kind of "application" that is truly creative.

CREATIVE CRITICISM

Discussions of critical reading have usually been concerned with the negative aspects of the process. They have stressed analysis rather than creation. If critical reading is essentially a process of acceptance and rejection, attention has been focused chiefly upon rejection. Thus, the reader has often been encouraged to look for pitfalls and errors, to beware of logical fallacies, of various propaganda devices, of stereotypes and emotionalized language. Critical reading has too often engendered mere skepticism and a purely defensive attitude.

While defense against the wiles of Madison Avenue experts and clever propagandists is important, it is not enough. Our youth must learn to seek a strategy of conquest, to develop philosophies of their own. Reading is a search for answers. The creative reader accepts, rejects, puts together, raises questions, draws inferences, and comes to (at least) tentative conclusions. He makes a declaration of independence of the author. He knows when he can draw independent conclusions, when he must suspend judgment, when he must trust the author.

The question of trust is crucial in creative criticism. The reader trusts the acknowledged expert with respect to facts. Without a degree of trust in the writer, very little learning could take place through reading. But always it must be guarded trust, a willingness to examine accompanied by a readiness to challenge.

Critical thinking and critical reading must lead to conclusions upon which one can act. Creative criticism does not result in a vacuum or intellectual stalemate. It is goal-oriented.

The creative reader comes to the printed page with a body of values and information against which he tests what he is reading. He revises his values and corrects his information if the material appears valid to him. For such a task, wide knowledge and experience and clear purposes are needed.

The elements of creative reading described in the foregoing paragraphs provide manageable targets for instruction, but in the reading process itself, they often operate simultaneously and interactively. The key is wide reading rather than single-textbook instruction, and frequent challenges by the teacher as to the reader's purposes and standards of judgment.

REFERENCES

1. Kirk, Samuel A. *Educating Exceptional Children*, p. 39. Boston: Houghton Mifflin, 1962.
2. Pooley, Robert C., and others. *All Around America*, p. 167. Chicago: Scott, Foresman.
3. Schatz, Esther E., Utterback, Roberta, Wilsberg, Mary E., and Frazier, Alexander. *Exploring Independent Reading in the Primary Grades*, pp. 66–67. Columbus, Ohio: Ohio State University.

A BALANCED READING PROGRAM
FOR THE GIFTED *

By Paul A. Witty

On the opening day of the school year six-year-old Bill arrived carrying under his arm a book—*All-About-Electricity*. At recess the principal of the school, who had noticed the book on Bill's desk, commented to the boy: "That's a good book. Are you enjoying the pictures?" "Yes, it is a good book," Bill answered. "I've read about two-thirds of it. I like the pictures too."

Bill's language development was really exceptional. Although he was barely six years of age, his vocabulary was outstanding. He was able to read and comprehend third or fourth grade materials readily. He had already completed a rather large number of children's books, and he was presently finding out all he could about electricity.

Bill could read before coming to school. He was not *taught* to read. He had learned, his mother said, by asking the names of the words he saw on signs and in newspapers, magazines, and books. Soon he was able to read phrases and short sentences.

* REPRINTED with permission of Paul A. Witty and the International Reading Association from *The Reading Teacher*, Vol. 16, May, 1963, pp. 418–24.

There is a considerable number of such very intelligent children. In Bill's own classroom in a suburban area there were two other pupils who on entering school were able to read primary grade materials successfully. In the second grade of the same school, there was Mary, who exceeded the average of pupils in the sixth grade on tests of reading ability.

These children are clearly to be classified as "gifted." There is of course no clear-cut line of distinction between the gifted and others, although educators have for many years been inclined to refer to children as gifted if their I.Q.'s were 130 or higher (12). At one time, such children were thought to comprise about 1 per cent of the elementary school population. Today, estimates are usually somewhat higher. For example, J. J. Gallagher indicates that 2–4 per cent of the general school population will have I.Q.'s of 132 and over and may be referred to as "gifted." In favorable socio-economic communities the percentage may be 6–12 (6).

CHARACTERISTICS OF THE GIFTED

One of the most noticeable characteristics of the gifted child is his remarkable language development. Thus, C. C. Miles states: "Approximately half of the California gifted children learned to read before starting to school. In Witty's group 38 per cent learned to read before the age of five; and of Terman's children, 20 per cent learn at this age, 6 per cent before three" (8).

Early precocity in vocabulary development continues in the typical gifted child. For example, one ten-year-old child studied by the writer said that *flaunt* mean "to show or display with intent to show"; *Mars* was defined as "a planet, God of War, also a verb."

Another characteristic of gifted children is the rapidity of their learning. They usually complete assignments in less than half the time allotted to them. On examinations such as the Stanford-Binet, they sometimes finish in a few seconds tests for which a minute is permitted.

By the time the typical child in the writer's early study was in the fourth grade, he had displayed knowledge and skills on tests which equalled the norms for children two grades above him (15). Many were the equals of pupils in grades three or four years above them.

The verbally superior child can be identified readily by the use of intelligence tests. There are other children, however, whose ability and promise are also outstanding who cannot be discovered in this way. These children, too, should be found and encouraged to make full use of their abilities. Perhaps it would be desirable to consider the gifted child as one whose performance in a potentially valuable line of human activity is consistently or repeatedly remarkable.

Educators must be concerned about all types of gifted and talented children, but attention will be given in the first part of this article to pupils of high abstract intelligence. There is evidence that this group is frequently neglected.

Moreover, such pupils are found in almost all classrooms. And every teacher can do much to enrich their experience and to encourage their full development. Perhaps the greatest possibility for enrichment lies in the field of reading and language development.

It is evident that guidance of gifted children should begin at home. Parents should read aloud to them and answer their numerous questions about the names of letters and words and phrases they see. Under such conditions and without formal instruction, some gifted children learn to read. Books on various topics should be made available to them, and they should be encouraged to read, without exploitation (1, 16).

It is important that the gifted child's ability and rate of learning be fully recognized when he starts school. Teachers, therefore, should have knowledge of the results of intelligence and aptitude tests. They should make an appraisal, too, of the child's reading status at the time he enters the first grade. If a gifted child who already can read is required to follow routine textbook assignments and is forced to "read highly repetitious and largely meaningless materials, he will often develop unfortunate attitudes and habits. From the first, reading materials should be made available which will challenge the gifted child's abilities, extend his interests, and present context in a meaningful way (17).

Although some gifted children learn to read before they start school, many others require instruction. In these cases it is essential for the teacher to recognize the rapidity of their learning. With such children it is usually desirable to begin with experience charts and then move rapidly into the reading of primers such as *Friskey the Goat* or *Peanuts the Pony* from Our Animal Story Book Series. There should be a correlated use of reading materials from such series as The True Books, I Want To Be Books, and others (10). Children's literature should be a part of a balanced reading program (7).

The provision of valuable experiences perhaps proceeds with fewer obstacles when grouping is practiced, as in Cleveland's Major Work Classes. Partial segregation, as followed in the Colfax Elementary School of Pittsburgh, is also highly successful in enabling the gifted child to advance rapidly in accord with his ability and interests. But how is the teacher in the typical heterogeneous class of the primary grades to offer such children appropriate opportunities and motivation? In the first grade the problem is especially perplexing and difficult. A crucial factor in determining the success of such a program resides in the availability of sufficient materials of instruction to satisfy the pupils' varied needs. Since a few gifted children will be able to read upon entering school, a wide assortment of books encompassing various topics and levels of difficulty should be provided. Children's encyclopedias, dictionaries, magazines, and weekly papers are also desirable. Plans should be made by the teacher for individual conferences with each child to offer the guidance many superior pupils require to gain skills in reading and develop resourcefulness and self-direction in selecting and using books.

To provide for skill development, standard tests of oral and silent reading may be administered to an entire class of primary grade pupils. Then the pupils may be assigned to small groups for the acquisition of needed skills. Appropriate practice materials or devices such as the Reading Laboratory may be used to offer the specific help some individuals may need, while the teacher gives additional help to other individuals encountering difficulties. If the gifted pupil needs little or no help in skill building, he may employ his time in independent reading or in other types of suitable, constructive endeavor to be shared later with his classmates (2, 5).

There are several kinds of group endeavor which are especially suitable for entire classes of pupils who vary widely in ability. Through suitable group endeavor the gifted pupil may receive appropriate attention. The writer has stressed the value of using certain films and their accompanying books in such efforts. For example, the film "Shep the Farm Dog" and others in the It's Fun to Find Out Series were shown and the books were read by pupils in second grade classes (18). Discussion followed, and opportunities were made for the pupils to explore each topic further in children's books.

The results of testing showed that under these conditions gifted pupils as well as others made significant gains in the acquisition of reading skills. Similar results have also been obtained in classrooms in which filmstrips such as "The Little House" have been shown and the text on the filmstrip has been followed in books.

The following type of grouping has also been employed successfully in attempts to meet the needs of the gifted in classes enrolling pupils of widely varying ability. Interest inventories are administered and the results are used to set up small flexible groups to explore each area of interest considered to be worthwhile and appealing. Reading materials related to each topic are then made available on varied levels of difficulty. In these interest groups the gifted child is able to participate and contribute from his own individually challenging reading. Such opportunities are not only profitable for the gifted pupil; they have been found of value in motivating other children to read books of greater difficulty than they ordinarily might be expected to read. This type of grouping is often effective in science and social studies.

As has already been indicated, the importance of interests should be fully recognized (4). Studies have shown that most gifted children have rich and varied interests. They often have a few strong interests, but usually are versatile. They may collect stamps or specimens of various kinds. They are often enthusiastic observers of birds, flowers, the stars, and animal life. But there are some whose home backgrounds are impoverished and in whom wholesome interests are few. To ascertain the extent and nature of the pupil's background and interests, it is desirable for the teacher to administer an interest inventory informally to each child. Worthy interests should then be identified and associated with reading materials whenever possible. In case interests are few or are deemed unsuitable, efforts should be made to create new patterns through direct experience, the use of films and filmstrips, and other activities. One of the chief responsibilities of the school is to provide for the gifted learner wide and suitable reading experience throughout the primary grades.

In the middle grades an effort should be made to provide a balanced program of reading according to the unique nature and needs of each child. Extensive reading in the subject fields is desirable for the gifted child, who should be encouraged to adjust his rate of reading according to his purposes and the type of subject matter.

Despite this promising picture, there are many gifted pupils who need greater help and guidance. In fact, each gifted child requires careful study to determine his particular nature and his needs. As L. M. Terman and M. H. Oden (13) have pointed out:

Gifted children do not fall into a single pattern but into an infinite variety of patterns. One can find within the group, individual examples of almost every type of personality defect, social maladjustment, behavior problem, and physical handicap; the only difference is that among gifted children the incidence of these deviations is, in varying degrees, lower than in the general population.

One problem teachers encounter in dealing with some gifted children is their tendency to concentrate too much reading in a single area, to become too specialized in their reading interests. This tendency sometimes appears in an area such as science, in which a gifted child may want to read to such an extent that his pattern of reading lacks balance. In this case, encouragement of wide reading is especially desirable, although special interests should be recognized. In many instances balance in reading is achieved when the teacher and the librarian work together in efforts to help gifted pupils become increasingly proficient in selecting and using books independently.

Some gifted pupils require assistance and guidance in acquiring reading skills. They should receive appropriate instruction geared to their needs. These children are sometimes regarded as "underachievers" and may display personality irregularities and emotional problems traceable to factors such as unfavorable home conditions and unfortunate previous school experience. Attention to these conditions should accompany reading instruction.

To engage successfully in encouraging the gifted child's reading, the teacher should have information about each child's ability and his status in silent and oral reading. The results of standard tests will be helpful. But the teacher should be able to employ other techniques of child study to obtain additional information. It has been pointed out that from interest inventories clues may be obtained which will help the teacher understand pupils' attitudes, problems, and needs (9). Similarly, anecdotal records and other forms of observation may yield data of value. Occasionally, such study will simply make it clear that the teacher's major problem is to help pupils develop more varied or worthwhile patterns of interest.

A balanced program provides the gifted pupil with opportunities to satisfy some of his personal and social needs through reading. An identification with a character in a story is sometimes beneficial. Thus, a gifted boy recovering from rheumatic fever experienced great personal satisfaction by reading Marguerite De Angeli's *Door in the Wall*, a narrative laid in seventeenth-century England, which portrays the ways in which Robin, the son of a nobleman, stricken on the eve of departure for the contests, overcame his affliction and won the king's recognition. Similarly, Eleanor Estes' *The Hundred Dresses* proved of value to an insecure girl through her discovery of the successful course followed by another girl in obtaining group sanction. Elizabeth Yates' *Amos Fortune: Free Man*, a story of a boy's rise above his environment, tells of the problems faced and overcome by an African prince sold into slavery. His devotion to the needy and his many sacrifices provide a heartening picture of what man can be at his best. This book has proved a source of inspiration to many boys.

In the excellent biographical literature now available, gifted pupils may find additional inspiration as well as a sound basis for the formation of an ideal of self that is in keeping with their outstanding abilities and promise. Regional books like Lois Lenski's *Strawberry Girl* and *Cotton in My Sack* and family stories such as Eleanor Estes' *Ginger Pye* may also help some gifted children understand people better. Many other books contain materials suitable for fulfilling varied needs.

Muriel Crosby has described a number of situations in which books have served admirably in enabling pupils to make wholesome indentifications(3). She states:

All children, like all adults, have problems. Books will not by themselves solve children's problems or adults' problems. But books may help. Books often tell of the problems children may sense but not fully recognize as their own. Books often bring to light a problem which a child cannot bring himself to talk about.

READING FOR THE CREATIVE STUDENT

Many of the foregoing suggestions concerning reading guidance apply not only to the verbally gifted, but also to pupils of outstanding promise in art, muisc, creative writing, and other fields. Such pupils may also be superior verbally. We cannot anticipate, however, that all gifted pupils will be located through the use of intelligence tests. In fact, E. P. Torrance states that "about 70 per cent of the top 20 per cent on measures of creativity would have been excluded from gifted groups which were selected on the basis of intelligence only" (14).

Since the coefficients of correlation between measures of verbal ability and proficiency in art, music, and other creative pursuits are relatively low, there will probably be found a considerably larger number of poor readers among creative pupils than among the verbally gifted. It is desirable, therefore, that creative students be identified and that a thorough appraisal be made of their reading ability and needs. Necessary skills should then be cultivated through the use of appropriate materials.[1]

In some talented children we may find reading limited to a narrow specialization, while in others there may be only a meager interest shown in reading. In still others, reading may be seldom engaged in because of unfortunate attitudes concerning its value. Attention to interest and motivation is essential if unfortunate habits and attitudes are to be altered. In this effort inventories may be employed to disclose interests that may often be profitably associated with reading experience. There is also the possibility of helping the creative child find suitable reading in the area of his talent.

That the need for guidance of the creative student is great may be seen by reference to the work of E. P. Torrance, who has pioneered in making suggestions for rewarding creative activity. In a provocative article on creative thinking (14) he states:

Many of the highly creative individuals are disturbing students in classroom groups in elementary schools. The problem of teachers and guidance workers resolves itself into one of helping highly creative individuals maintain those characteristics which seem essential to the development of creative talent and, at the same time, helping them acquire skills for avoiding, or reducing to a tolerable level, the peer sanctions.

Like the verbally gifted, the creative child often has a need for experience in reading that will enable him to meet personal and social problems and help him build an appropriate and individually suitable ideal of self. Reading for these purposes may prove even more effective for creative pupils, whose need for assistance appears to be so great. Of course, reading alone is not enough. But reading related to experience and accompanied by discussion may prove quite rewarding.

It will be noted that in this paper the suggested program in reading is essentially developmental in nature and may be recommended for all pupils. One of the great values of such an approach is the pleasure to be found by pupils in "the wonderful world of books." This statement certainly applies to gifted children who, when they have an opportunity to read materials of interest to them, turn joyfully to reading for information and recreation. Their lives will be enriched greatly as their satisfactions are enhanced through books.

REFERENCES

1. Abraham, Willard. *Common Sense about Gifted Children.* New York: Harper, 1958.
2. Barbe, Walter. *Educator's Guide to Personalized Reading Instruction.* Englewood Cliffs, N. J.: Prentice-Hall, 1961.
3. Crosby, Muriel. "Reading for Human Relations," *The Packet,* 16 (Winter 1961–62), 13.

[1] The Reading Laboratories of Science Research Associates and other skill-building materials may often be used independently by many of these pupils.

4. Darrow, Helen F., and Howes, Virgil M. *Approaches to Individualized Reading.* New York: Appleton-Century-Crofts, 1960.
5. Draper, Marcella K., and Schwietert, Louise H., revised and edited by May Lazar. *A Practical Guide to Individualized Reading.* New York: Board of Education, Publication No. 40, Oct. 1960.
6. Gallagher, James J. *Analysis of Research in the Education of Gifted Children.* State of Illinois: Office of the Superintendent of Public Instruction, 1960.
7. Larrick, Nancy. *A Teacher's Guide to Children's Books.* Columbus, Ohio: Charles E. Merrill, 1960.
8. Miles, Catherine Cox. "Gifted Children," Chapter 16 in *Manual of Child Psychology*, 2nd edition, edited by Leonard Carmichael. New York: John Wiley, 1954.
9. *Northwestern University Interest Inventories.* Evanston, Ill.: Northwestern University.
10. *Our Animal Story Books.* Boston: D. C. Heath. *The True Book Series.* Chicago: Children's Press. *I Want to Be Books.* Chicago: Children's Press. *The Walt Disney Story Books.* Boston: D. C. Heath.
11. Stauffer, Russell G. "Individualized and Group Directed Reading Instruction," *Elementary English*, 37 (Oct. 1960).
12. Terman, Lewis M., and Oden, Melita H. *The Gifted Child Grows Up.* Stanford, Calif.: Stanford University Press, 1947.
13. ——, "The Stanford Studies of the Gifted," in *The Gifted Child* (edited by Paul Witty), p. 25. Boston: D. C. Heath, 1951.
14. Torrance, E. P. "Exploration in Creative Thinking," *Education*, 81 (Dec. 1960).
15. Witty, Paul A. *A Study of 100 Gifted Children.* Lawrence, Kansas: University of Kansas Press, 1930.
16. ——, *Helping the Gifted Child.* Chicago: Science Research Associates, 1952.
17. ——, "Reading Instruction—A Forward Look," *Elementary English*, 38 (Mar. 1961).
18. Witty, Paul A., and Fitzwater, James P. "An Experiment with Films, Film Readers, and the Magnetic Sound Track," *Elementary English*, 32 (Apr. 1955).

Chapter 4

LEARNING TO READ:
EARLY OR LATE?

Virtually all will agree that reading power is on a continuum, but the question of when it begins brings forth different answers.

There are those who would say reading power begins in early infancy or even before, in the home where reading is a valued and practiced activity—where the infant is bombarded, so to speak, with print in his surroundings.

Others would say reading power starts as the young child listens to material being read, as he learns to turn the pages, and as he speaks to the pages. Or does reading power begin with rich oral language experiences some children have in contacts with others—the interaction of conversations, storytelling, describing excitements, and responding to inquiries and demands? Perhaps reading power begins as children see their talk written down by someone and as they begin to read the symbols that were made to express their talk.

Then there are those who would say true reading power begins with direct, formal instruction in word sounds, word recognition skills, and memorized sight vocabulary.

How one responds to the question of when reading power begins depends on one's point of view toward the child as a reader. And that response helps with the question: What kind of reading instruction should be given and when should it begin?

AN EARLIER START IN READING? *

Dolores Durkin

Today the subject of reading and the preschool child is attracting much attention. It is provoking controversy too—or at least differences of opinion. Reactions of kindergarten teachers, for example, tend to fall into three categories. Some spurn any kind of reading instruction for the five-year-old. Others seem too eager to rush to a workbook curriculum. Somewhere in the middle is another group that recognizes the inadequacy of typical kindergarten programs for some five-year-olds and does not interpret the asking of questions about these programs as a prelude to inevitable and unfriendly criticism.

Parents of young children show other differences in reaction. At one extreme are the Harvard-conscious parents who seriously believe that three years of age is none too soon to develop good study habits and at least a small amount of achievement in reading. At the other extreme are those parents who conscientiously heed educators who continue to maintain that preschool help with reading results in confusion and leads to problems when a child enters first grade.

Meanwhile, nationwide publicity is being given to the Denver schools as they attempt to develop TV programs on reading for parents of preschool children. Attention is also being focused on Omar Moore, at Yale University, who is using complicated machinery to introduce pre-first-grade children to written language. Whitby School in Connecticut, too, is attracting attention as it demonstrates the learnings of three- and four-year-olds when a Montessori curriculum is followed.

Many different groups, then, are examining, proposing, and opposing the idea that children start to learn to read before the age of six. Consequently, it becomes important to step outside the controversy to look carefully at the questions that are being raised and at those that ought to be raised.

Among the important questions, certainly, is that of the future value of an early start in reading. If a child gets a head start in reading, will he remain ahead? If a child enters first grade with the reading ability of an average second- or third-grader will he, over the years, continue to remain ahead of children who are of equal mental ability but could not read when they started first grade?

---

* REPRINTED from *The Elementary School Journal* (December, 1962, pp. 147–51) by Dolores Durkin, by permission of The University of Chicago Press. Copyright 1962 by The University of Chicago.

This article is directed to these questions. It is a report on one part of a longitudinal study of children who could read when they entered first grade.[1]

In September, 1958, all the beginning first-graders in a California public school system were individually tested to identify those who had learned to read at home.[2] From this group of 5,103 children, forty-nine were found to have some ability in reading. At the time of the first testing, their reading achievement ranged from 1.5 to 4.5, according to grade-level norms. The median grade level was 1.9. Intelligence quotients derived from the Revised Stanford-Binet Scale ranged from 91 to 161, with a median quotient of 121. The coefficient of correlation for intelligence and reading achievement was +0.40.

To examine the future value of an early start in reading, the plan was to compare, at the end of third grade, the reading achievement of the forty-nine early readers with the reading achievement of children who had started school with them, who had had the same teachers as they for the first three grades, and who were of comparable mental ability but who were not able to read when they started first grade. Mental ability was to be assessed in terms of intelligence quotients derived from the Kuhlmann-Anderson Intelligence test, which was administered by the school system when the children were in second grade.

As it turned out, even a cursory look at these intelligence quotients showed that they were anything but realistic. There was no apparent relationship, for example, between a child's intelligence, as measured by the Kuhlmann-Anderson Intelligence test, and his achievement score in reading.

For the children who were not early readers, the intelligence quotients hovered narrowly around 100. For the early readers the Kuhlmann-Anderson scores consistently underestimated the intelligence of the brighter children, as it had been measured by the Revised Stanford-Binet Scale.

It was decided, therefore, to include in the control group only those children who had been given the Revised Stanford-Binet Scale by a school psychometrist. This decision necessitated other changes and, in a sense, compromises in the research plan. These will be noted indirectly in the description of what finally constituted the experimental group and the control group.

The experimental group included twenty-five of the forty-nine early readers. The remaining twenty-four had either transferred to other schools or had been double-promoted during the three-year period. Although the experimental group was reduced to twenty-five children, the intelligence quotients based on results of the Revised Stanford-Binet Scale still ranged from 91 to 161. The median intelligence quotient for the group was 114.8. Reading scores based on

---

[1] This article is based on a paper read at a meeting of the American Educational Research Association in Atlantic City, February, 1962.

[2] Dolores Durkin. "Children Who Learned To Read at Home," *Elementary School Journal*, LXII (October, 1961), 15–18.

tests administered by the schools toward the end of Grade 3 showed grade levels ranging from 4.4 to 6.0, with a median of 5.0

The control group was made up of 201 children who had entered first grade with the twenty-five preschool readers but who could not read when they started school. They had remained in the same schools as these early readers for Grades 1, 2, and 3. They had also been given the Revised Stanford-Binet Scale. For this control group, intelligence quotients ranged from 70 to 191, with a median of 110.2. Reading achievement scores based on school-administered tests ranged from 2.0 to 6.0, with a median grade level of 4.3.

A scatter diagram, in which reading scores for both the experimental and the control groups were plotted, revealed the inadequacy of the school-administered reading tests in establishing upper limits of achievement for the brighter children.[3] Consequently, a twofold comparison was made between the achievement of the early readers and the achievement of children who were not early readers. The first comparison focused on children who had intelligence quotients of 120 or less. The second comparison considered children who had intelligence quotients of 121 or higher.

Of the children who were not early readers 129 had intelligence quotients of 120 or less. A first step in examining the value of a head start in reading was to calculate the coefficient of correlation between the intelligence as measured by the Revised Stanford-Binet Scale and the reading achievement of these children who were not early readers. The coefficient of correlation was found to be +0.61.

Next, the regression equation for predicting reading achievement on the basis of intelligence was formulated. The equation was then used to calculate predicted reading scores for each of the fifteen early readers who also had intelligence quotients of 120 or less.

When these predicted scores were calculated, it was found that for all the children who were early readers actual scores in reading were greater than would have been predicted for them on the basis of their intelligence, as measured by the Revised Stanford-Binet Scale. The greatest single difference, in terms of years of reading achievement, was 1.3. The smallest single difference was 0.2. Group differences, according to intelligence level, are shown in Table 1.

Because the groups were small, no statement can be made at this time about children who are early readers in general. Two observations can be made concerning these fifteen early readers who had intelligence quotients of 120 or less. First, they appear to have profited from their early start. Second, the lower the child's intelligence quotient, the greater seems to be the advantage of starting early.

What can be said about the children who had intelligence quotients higher

[3] A carefully planned testing procedure has been followed for all the forty-nine early readers. In this particular part of the study, data from school-administered reading tests had to be used because these were the only data available for the control group.

than 120? As I pointed out earlier, the school-administered reading tests were not difficult enough to establish the upper limits of achievement for the brighter children in either the control group or the experimental group. As a result, the coefficient of correlation between the intelligence quotients of the seventy-two children who were not early readers and their reading scores was only +0.17.

With such a low coefficient of correlation it is not too meaningful to ask: As derived from the relationship between reading achievement and intelligence, what would be the predicted reading score for each of the early readers who had intelligence quotients of 121 or more? Nonetheless the question was asked, and the answer appears in Table 1.

TABLE 1

Deviation of Achievement of Early Readers from Expected Achievement on the Basis of Intelligence Quotients

INTELLIGENCE QUOTIENT	NUMBER OF PUPILS	AVERAGE DEVIATION IN YEARS
91–100	5	+0.92
101–110	6	+0.68
111–120	4	+0.35
121–130	3	+0.30
131–140	4	−0.33
141–161	3	+0.43

Probably the most appropriate comment to make at this point is to express the hope that when more appropriate reading tests are used with the control and the experimental groups at the end of Grade 6, more meaningful and more significant findings will be available, especially for the brighter children in both groups.

Meanwhile, it seems appropriate to attempt some kind of summary of conclusions or, to be more accurate, some kind of summary of ideas and feelings that resulted from this longitudinal study of precocious readers.

Certainly, one persistent feeling is that many parents of preschool children are confused and uncertain about their role, or lack of it, in the matter of their child's learning to read. Frequent contacts with parents, through interviews and correspondence, repeatedly point to the need for home-school communication that gives parents, first, at least a general understanding of their role as educators of the preschool child and, second, specific help on how they, as parents, can advance the language skills of young children without putting uncomfortable pressures on them.

These same contacts with parents also suggest that educators have been encouraging parents, perhaps unintentionally, to put a child's questions about words into a do-not-touch category on the assumption that what a child learns about reading before he enters school interferes with subsequent school instruction. This study of early readers does not verify this assumption.

In fact, what is tentatively suggested is that children of relatively lower intelligence especially benefit from an early start. Should this finding be duplicated in a second study recently begun in another school system, it might well mean that slower children need contact with learning to read that is spread out over time. Instead of a postponement of reading instruction, they need an earlier start with it. This thinking, to be sure, is in contrast to much current thinking on reading readiness. But it is a possibility that deserves attention.

One final comment on kindergarten children and kindergarten programs. I urge that the schools pay some attention to the five-year-olds who are already reading and to those who are so close to it that even less than mediocre help would turn them into readers. If we really believe that good education begins where the child is, then kindergarten teachers ought to feel obligated to give certain children help with reading.

Out of this new concern might eventually come not only achievement in reading but, in addition, a really fresh approach to the teaching of beginning reading. It might well be that those of us who are interested in teaching methods and materials have for too long been greasing a squeaky wheel when we should have been looking for a genuinely new one.

READINESS IS BEING *

Ethelouise Carpenter

Readiness for anything is a state of being. It is a composite of many factors and must be measured in many ways. It is not a thing to be taught. It can neither be purchased in a box nor developed on paper. It is an individual state unresponsive to mass production. It is a part of life. A state of readiness manifests itself in many ways. Sometimes the outer appearances represent only a superficial readiness. Something vital must shine through. Manner, attitude, facial expression and expectancy are good indications of an inner

* REPRINTED by permission of Ethelouise Carpenter and the Association for Childhood Education International, 3615 Wisconsin Avenue, N.W., Washington, D.C., from *Childhood Education*, Vol. 38, November, 1961, pp. 114–16. Copyright © 1961 by the Association.

acceptance of what *is* in order to meet what *is to come*. It is a kind of reaching out which is recognizable to the skilled teacher as he works with children at any age level. It is a recognition which goes beyond the limits of testing.

Maturing Process

Children are constantly involved in different degrees of readiness. They are called to meals and they linger; they are put on their feet to walk and they plop down on the floor. There are signs for being ready and for not being ready. The state of readiness has not come about through practice of the things to come but through a maturing process fed by successions of related experiences. A child does not become ready for walking by walking. When all elements are perfectly coordinated he begins to walk and he perfects this skill over a long period of time.

Many people have come to look upon readiness as something that must happen to children during the spring preceding first grade! This readiness appears to be made possible through certain specific devices involving symbols. Visitors to kindergartens say, "When and how do you DO your readiness?" Has reading become so organized a *process* that even readiness for it must be dealt with mechanically, piece by piece? No wonder children in kindergarten think there are two kinds of reading—the kind you do in school and the kind you do for enjoyment! Many areas have instituted summer kindergartens which advertise the teaching of reading readiness!

Competencies Needed Now

Nursery schools and kindergartens are provided for what a child needs *now* and serve as a preparation for first grade only to the same degree that any experience supports a later one. Readiness evolves from practice with the environment, people and materials which promote the desire to look beyond the commonplace, beyond self-interest; to reach a level of physical maturity, of social competence, of emotional control and of mental alertness. Readiness for reading, as for anything else, is built on such experiences over a long period of time. In nursery school and kindergarten the child is helped to listen to others, to wait his turn, to do critical thinking, to take responsibility to the degree that he needs these competencies right now in order to be a contributing member of his present group. He is not taught to conduct himself in a particular way because "the first-grade teacher expects it." The plan of living in preschool groups makes possible a comfortable evolvement of self and readiness for what is and what will be. It is an environment of exploration, not of heated preparation.

In many schools reading has become such a huge Thing to be dealt with that all else is incidental. It often begins with dull experience charts which have grown out of equally dull and controlled trips. Children are still eager but often frightened, parents panic over grouping, discipline problems inconveniently appear, and everyone wonders what could have been done to *prepare* children better so that reading could move along more smoothly. Then eyes turn back to the kindergarten and administrators and others think they see the trouble in "too much play"! If children are moving around they cannot be learning. They must be sitting, producing on paper and quiet in order to learn and to work! Often the "solution" is the purchase of readiness materials for kindergarten. They can be ordered easily, they are paper, they *teach* readiness to all children alike. Reading is looked upon here as a cold process from which one can isolate the various steps and work on them. There are sheets and charts (many based on readiness tests!) for learning left-to-right eye movement, yet the child goes blithely on looking at life from right to left, up to down, in whatever way he finds best to read his environment. Children labor over marking the largest tree in a row, yet they have no difficulty finding the largest cookie on a plate!

CAN A PROGRAM BE PURCHASED?

Unfortunately schools which hire untrained preschool teachers think they can solve their problems of preparation by purchasing a program. Material falls into the hands of people least qualified to evaluate it; often no one knows how to use it, so it either explodes in their hands or is fed to children too limp with boredom to refuse it. Loud cries of protest are coming from well-trained and creative teachers upon whom this material is often forced. It is not merely a protest at the readiness materials but a protest at the complete disregard for all that has been gained in the child-development field!

During the preschool years children work with many materials and great varieties of ideas. They learn to manipulate their environment and to feel the worth of themselves and others. They find answers to questions by talking, moving freely, feeling, listening, looking. They grow in skills for finding out. They learn that books are sources of wonderful information and pleasure. They can challenge ideas and feel right about being different. They learn many ways of arriving at the same conclusions. They make fresh discoveries and use language which is delightful, colorful, imaginative and highly descriptive. They number and label as they feel the need; their own written symbols are a message to them but may be unintelligible to an adult. They become aware that certain combinations of letters on signs mean something to someone but for them it is enough to know that this is communication. There is time to live in the preschool atmosphere, and wider experiences and opportunities for exploration develop throughout the years. Boredom certainly is no sign of readiness to read but rather a clue to a stagnant program. In a good program children are developing the very skills which make later reading meaningful. These skills are not isolated bits of learning relegated to chopped-up pieces of clock time but are outgrowths of an environment of active participation.

The child whose teacher thinks readiness can be taught and practiced through devices and paper-pencil techniques should openly rebel, and many do! A few professional tears should be shed for the child whose readiness for moving on to the next delightful phase of life is measured by his ability to cross out a rabbit that doesn't look like other rabbits and to take left-hand mice to right-hand holes! *The time for being ready is short, but the time for getting there is long.* Readiness lies somewhere between wanting to and having to. It is the solid substance of growth, personality, imagination, self-realization. Let us work with it, take it out and examine and test it occasionally; but let us stop waving it around aimlessly. Certainly today's children deserve something better from progressively better-qualified teachers!

BUILDING ON CHILDREN'S EAGERNESS TO READ *

Lorene K. Fox

Certainly it is not the first-grade or even the kindergarten teacher who introduces children to reading. Even the youngest children come into classrooms today straight from an environment that is shot through with the printed word. Whether their homes provide a dearth or an abundance of good books and magazines, all children today are exposed to a constant and blatant barrage of written messages. Wherever children turn they find the printed word in use—in the corner drugstore, on the subway or bus, in the supermarket, on television, in the neon-lighted street or on the highway. At home advertisements and other appeals are left in the mailbox or shoved under the door. There is no escape. The vocabulary of our technological world is not confined to any economic or geographic group. Everywhere in the country school-age children and younger, as well as grownups, are responding every day of their lives to a welter of printed matter designed with the deliberate intent of catching the eye, of getting the message across.

Long before they come to school as kindergarteners or first-graders, children are well into their orientation to reading, or "reading readiness," as some spe-

* REPRINTED by permission of Lorene K. Fox and the Association for Childhood Education International, 3615 Wisconsin Avenue, N.W., Washington, D.C., from *Childhood Education*, Vol. 38, January, 1962, pp. 215–19. Copyright © 1962 by the Association.

cialists prefer to call it. They already know that reading is an important, convenient skill, that it can be useful to people—especially to people who like to hear stories, to watch television, to go shopping with Mother, to look at Brother's comics. Children in general come to school with positive if naive attitudes toward reading. They come to school eager to read.

As school people, let us build on this eagerness. Let's not stifle it with flat uninteresting workbooks or readiness exercises—or try to store it up until more formal introduction to reading at a later date. Let's make sure that the school environment also, from the first years through the last, is chock full of reading. Let's make sure there are all kinds of reading and writing opportunities, much more carefully screened and designed, of course, than those outside but just as interesting and varied and just as useful. Every child is entitled to and will respond to the excitement of being genuinely and successfully involved in the ongoing communication dynamics of his group.

Teachers are coming increasingly to realize what an individual or personal affair this business of reading really is, how much of the process simply has to go on inside the head of the person doing the reading. Therefore in order to make any sense in or out of school, reading skills must be viewed as individual behavior in the lives of the children reading. Skills must not be viewed as teacher-directed sequences of activities through which all children must be taken in systematic fashion as necessary steps in learning to read.

USING EXCITING, ATTRACTIVE BOOKS

This means that the school must provide an environment year after year in which children will need and use reading and writing in a wide variety of ways to meet their purposes. First and foremost in such an environment there will always be *books*—attractive, varied, challenging books that simply *invite* perusal and reading by children from first years on. Not the flat, dull, step-by-step, vocabulary-controlled, blandly illustrated books and workbooks of the reading specialists and commercial houses, so certainly eroding the eagerness to read of countless millions of our nation's children today! But selected rather from the unprecedented world of exciting and beautiful children's books that come from our ablest authors and illustrators every year! Experience shows that many important reading skills, including readiness, can be learned best when children have responsible access to a wide and varied selection of books —books that are changed from time to time to make sure that every child in the class can find those he can read and enjoy. The planning for use of these books and the kinds of help given will vary from room to room, as teachers resourcefully discover and devise ways which seem to work best for them with their particular children.

The careful, deliberate structuring of the classroom environment to provide for children's choice through *functional* use of the written communication skills in their day-to-day living is at the heart of an effective teacher's teaching of reading. The teacher is an essential factor in the environment he sets up—an environment so resourceful that children's learning can be *whole*. The very arrangement of the materials invites self-initiated, self-propelled learning. The teacher provides materials which are appropriate for children and, by so doing, can be alerted to their particular needs and ways of working as well as to plausible next steps.

READING SKILLS IN ACTION

Teachers learn to interpret the signals in children's behavior. Through their own sensitively developed ways of interpreting the signals they can tell when children are making headway with their learning, with their individual selecting and figuring out, and when and how they need help. Teachers can tell these things at whatever age level they teach if children are engaged in real live learning situations; e.g., reading situations when the research or the purpose is theirs and when the children are focusing on content:

- A child reading the recipe for making Jello for the first time
- A young child signing up for a piece of playground equipment on a class sign-up sheet
- Kindergarteners Judy and Michele selecting their name cards from those arranged on the table to tack them up on the bulletin board under the sign, *I am here today*
- Chucky and his friends trying to figure out if they have enough money to send, prepaid, for the roller skates they are ordering through the school supply catalogue
- Bonnie and Elizabeth reading a story to see if it will make a good class play for Book Week
- Several children at the reading table enjoying their own selections
- First-grader Rachel making her own book, *The Story of the Garden*, for her classmates
- Fifth-grader Herbert trying to reorganize his Table of Contents for the extensive book he is writing for the school library, *The Making of Aluminum*, his periodical and newspaper references laid out close at hand
- Three children planning and organizing a treasure hunt for their class party
- Two girls trying to figure out from directions how to use the new can of plastic spray on their carefully made gift coasters
- A trio of friends reading an article about Alan Shepard's historic flight into space
- Billy and Carlos consulting directions for putting Billy's model airplane together
- David and Timmy laying out their plans for a book on *What Young Historians Should Know About the Renaissance*

- Richie, Laura and Kaye at work writing their own individual newspapers
- Charles and Franklin getting out the latest issue of *The Space Club News*
- Jan and Barbara making a United Nations crossword puzzle to be duplicated for the class
- Suzanne and Curtis searching for information about the new dam their class will visit the following week, information they will need for making their trip booklet.

SENSING THE NEED FOR HELP

And so it goes. Resourceful teachers provide for and recognize the reading skills in action. They learn to know what these skills look like in the behavior of individual children at work—at work by themselves or in purposeful cooperation with others. They become increasingly competent in recognizing the cues as to when to stay out of the picture, when to proffer direct help, when to work along with a child or a group or the whole class. Teachers know when to offer a child a book with the comment, "I wonder if this would help," or "Have you seen this map of Africa? It's right up to date, you know—if one can be these days." It is in these real situations that teachers learn to interpret behavior that signals to them: "Am understanding—am making out all right," or "Am not making out—need help of some kind—now."

Being able to sense this *point of need for help* is most important to both teacher and child. It is at just this point that help can be of greatest worth. It is at just this point, in just this situation, where motivation and need are most sincere, that a child can incorporate the new learning with maximum meaning. Just the particular bit of help at the time it is most needed—from teacher, from neighbor, from some new piece of material—can help a child over the rough spot and open the gate, as it were. And this kind of help is worth more than any amount of systematic, repetitive drill apart from the point of real need. Once a child comprehends—by himself or with the needed help—once he "gets the hang," discovers the pattern, he is competent to move ahead on his own steam. It is then that the follow-up activities which the teacher provides individually or for the group will also be full of meaning. Practice will be based on insight and understanding rather than on repetitive drill or memorized rule.

PROVIDING CONDITIONS THAT TEACH

The teacher provides the conditions and gives direct help as needed to move children ahead comfortably in their learning. The teacher tells those children who need this any words they may ask as they read, to have them get the habit of focusing on the whole word and letting the context help to move them along. The teacher spells or writes difficult words a child cannot spell as he writes letters or stories or newspapers, so he will be accustomed to using properly spelled words and will not spend time writing words incorrectly. The teacher provides a writing table or desk with all the materials handy for choice and use. He provides lined Ditto sheets—a variety from which to choose—so children can write neatly and evenly within the margins without having to think about it; so they will be accustomed to writing and reading neat, attractively spaced pages instead of messy, crowded, ones. This is not to make life easier for children but to make it easier for them to write good interesting letters or good colorful chapters and thus develop better the skills of writing and reading.

Gearing Children's Choice Toward Learning the Skills

In a classroom deliberately and skillfully set up for gearing children's choice toward learning the skills, every child in the group is provided for. No child will ever reach the ceiling, as it were, will ever exhaust the challenges in his classroom because the teacher, planning with him in mind, will set out materials and set up situations accordingly. Similarly, a child who is restless and seems not to latch on will not be blamed but rather will lead the teacher to seek and try out other materials or ideas to challenge him. Thus every child in the group is challenged to select and reach out—to find his own kind of "giftedness," resources and growing skills—within a framework of good social living. In sum, in setting up an effective environment for reading, the teacher sensitively and continuously organizes materials, time and space and gives friendly help. All of this to invite the kind of group living that enhances—rather than levels off, ranks in order, or segregates—the unique and varying capabilities of all of the children!

TEACHING THE VERY YOUNG TO READ *

William D. Sheldon

Many reading and language arts specialists and others interested in the education of very young children are noting with interest and some alarm the experiments or demonstrations conducted by Dr. O. K. Moore (19) of Yale University and the staff of the Denver Public Schools (12), both of which are concerned with reading instruction for pre-school children.

* reprinted with permission of William D. Sheldon and the International Reading Association from *The Reading Teacher*, Vol. 16, December, 1962, pp. 163–69.

Newspaper and popular magazines have had a field day with early reports stemming from the Moore and Denver demonstrations and also from the reported studies of Dolores Durkin (7) and Nancy McCormick Rambusch (22).

The only common aspect of the work of Moore, Durkin, Rambusch and the Denver demonstration has been a mutual concern with the reading of very young children. The interest of the general public, the press and the great foundations in early reading instruction has forced educators to react to the drive to introduce reading to very young children.

Up to the present moment few educators have expressed opinions for or against the movement to teach two-, three-, and four-year-olds to read either in nursery schools or in the home by parents. A few have expressed negative reactions, however, to an ever increasing tendency of schools to introduce formal reading instruction in kindergarten (23).

THE VERY YOUNG READER

We have found at least one child in almost every kindergarten we have visited during the past twenty years who entered school able to identify a number of words, or in some instances able to read with some facility. These children have often been a source of despair to parents and kindergarten teachers. Faced with providing a flexible and relatively unstructured, informal program for thirty or more five-year-olds, most kindergarten teachers have been unable to cope with the simultaneous development of a structured sequential reading program for one or two precocious children.

Ordinarily in the past two things occurred in the kindergarten. Either the the early reader was ignored to a large extent and allowed to read on his own, or he was promoted to a first grade class for reading instruction alone or for his whole program. Occasionally the early reader and his parents relaxed, and by the end of the kindergarten year the child was one of six or seven others who had in some mysterious fashion begun to read on their own. These five or six children usually scored very high on readiness tests and often with some encouragement settled down to read during the post-kindergarten summer.

The studies of Terman (24) reported that at least 45 per cent of the children studied in his survey of genius read before the age of five. For many years the Terman studies seemed to indicate to some educators that it might be rather natural for the very able children to develop reading ability at an early age, either on their own or with slight encouragement from parents or other interested persons. It was often suggested that early reading was an ability reserved for the gifted and was unusual for average or above average children.

The report of Dolores Durkin has partially succeeded in modifying attitudes which might have derived from the Terman studies. Durkin located a number of preschool children who had begun to read and who represented the entire range of average and slightly above average intelligence. A significant aspect of the Durkin report was the fact that the children who read came from homes where there was a high regard for reading and where at least one adult or older child took an interest in the reading of the young child.

No evidence except casual comments from Oakland personnel has been offered to indicate whether or not the children in the Durkin study, who started to read at an early age, maintained their advantage over children of comparable intelligence who did not begin to read until the first grade.

The experiments of O. K. Moore are by far the most startling of the attempts to induce early reading. Fortunately for students of reading, Moore has recorded his experimental procedures in three reels of film entitled "Early Reading and Writing," which not only presents a step-by-step account of the procedures used in teaching two- and three-year-old children to read, but depicts the reaction of the children being taught. Moore's experiment accomplished startling results with his very young pupils through the use of an adapted electric typewriter and tachistoscopically presented words and phrases. There is no question about either the procedure or the immediate results. Moore succeeded in teaching several young children to recognize hundreds of words and to read and write with some competence.

Nancy M. Rambusch has presented an American approach to Montessori in the book *Learning How to Learn.* Mrs. Rambusch's book describes the methods of teaching originally developed by Madame Montessori as they are used with three-year-olds and older children in a private school in Whitby, Connecticut. Mrs. Rambusch discusses not only what is taking place at Whitby but depicts her ideal school of the next decade, a school "in which the arbitrary distinctions of pre-school versus 'real' school have disappeared, one in which children from age three until age eight are thought of as being in the first phase of learning." Rambusch goes on to describe the school—one with physical flexibility with children divided into two groups, the three to sixes and the fives to eights. The classrooms would be provided with a "wealth of structured teaching materials and teaching machines designed for both percept and concept acquisition." The teacher "would provide the dynamic link" between the children and the learning stimuli of their environment. Special teachers would be available at specific times to help children in the first group to acquire the skills of reading, writing, and mathematics as the academic portion of their learning.

One receives the impression from the Rambusch book that the pursuit of reading and writing is encouraged by the environment and facilitated by direct instruction after children have embarked on the pursuit of reading and writing themselves. One would have to observe the program directly, however, not to gain the same opinion as that of the reporter for the *Saturday Evening Post* who proclaimed that at Whitby three-year-olds were being taught to read (20).

In summary, very young children can and do learn to read, on their own or with more or less direction at home or in a specially oriented nursery school situation. The children do not have to be gifted to read at an early age, as Durkin revealed.

The unanswered questions, raised in particular by the Moore study, seem to be, "Is all the effort worthwhile in terms of a maintained advantage?" and perhaps more important, "Does early reading instruction, especially when it involves pressure and seemingly onerous drill, enhance or lessen future interest of the pupil in reading either for pleasure or profit?"

A Program for Parents

Mention in newspapers and magazines and a few rumors were the first heralds of a most interesting demonstration conducted by the Denver Public Schools. The writer has not yet found an authoritative statement of the demonstration, but has at hand what seems to be the first published work related to the Denver Project, entitled *Preparing Your Child for Reading*. In this booklet we find a series of sixteen lessons designed to prepare children for reading. The booklet contains lessons which are somewhat similar to those found in the typical first books of a basic reading series or in workbooks which present exclusive phonic lessons. The booklet is used by parents who are guided in their instruction by a television program. Parents are directed in teaching their own children the sixteen lessons of the booklet after being directed in each by the television lesson.

The lessons in the booklet focus on those prereading steps which help children to discriminate among sounds, relate sounds to letters, and utilize a combination of initial letter sounds and context to supply words in sentences. The material is learned through a series of well planned lessons which involve a friendly cooperation between parent and child. Some lessons require the addition of a neighbor child, such as the one learned through the game "Giant Steps."

The introduction of *Preparing Your Child for Reading* provides the rationale for the program. It states, "Many parents are eager to help the child become an independent reader as soon as possible. That is why it is important to teach him an economical and effective procedure to use in finding out all by himself what are given strange printed words." The introduction goes on to ask, "Would you like to help your child get ready to learn this procedure? It is the purpose of this guide to provide you with definite suggestions for doing just that."

We have no quarrel with the simple steps which are presented in *Preparing Your Child For Reading*. We shudder, however, at what can happen when thousands of eager parents, guided by television lessons and using this booklet, launch an attack on their young children. Obviously we cannot quarrel with the idea that parents should cooperate with their own children in such a venture. We can only express our deep concern about what may happen when relatively untutored parents begin to press very young children in the formal routine presented in this program. Perhaps the one-to-one relationship will be a key to success, and perhaps the magic of television and the very carefully developed lessons will do the trick, but we have serious doubts concerning this demonstration and its goals. Unfortunately it will take three or four years to evaluate the consequences of the demonstration, with the likelihood of a controlled experiment ruled out by the very nature of the activity.

Teaching Reading In the Kindergarten

In view of the above it seems rather absurd to express alarm at the growing tendency of kindergarten teachers to teach children to read, but absurd or not we feel concerned about the change which has taken place in the modern kindergarten.

The pressure to teach children to read in the kindergarten has come mainly from three sources: from parents of precocious children, from teachers in the first grade and some kindergarten teachers, and from commercial sources of materials made for use in the kindergarten. In a larger sense, the pressure might possibly be a part of our national anxiety over the technological advances of the Union of Soviet Socialist Republics.

It is ironical to study what is actually happening in Europe and, in particular, in Soviet kindergartens. Eunice Matthews (17) has described the Soviet kindergarten as it has developed during the past forty years. According to Matthews, the Soviet kindergarten child learns to classify, discriminate, compare, and designate what he sees in proper language and through discussion. The curriculum includes drawing, construction, and general language development. The teaching of reading and writing is not suggested as starting in the kindergarten; such teaching rather grows out of the language development program of the kindergarten, which features oral and pre-book learning. It is evident from the report that the Soviets look upon the kindergarten year as a time of informal learning with structure limited to the encouragement of language activities which precede reading.

A recent report from Great Britain by Vernon, O'Gorman, and McLellan (26) indicated that eight-year-old Scottish children who were taught to read at the age of five were not significantly more able in reading comprehension than a comparable group of English children whose reading instruction began at the age of six. Other reports suggested that at the age of fourteen, Scottish girls were better in reading comprehension than English girls, but that the Scottish boys were no better than the English boys. Girls apparently accepted early drilling better than boys and continued to profit from it, but the older boys seemed to resent the drilling and lost their initial advantage.

Vernon (25) has pointed out that while five-year-olds can be successful in visual discrimination activities, they have real problems in auditory discrimination. Vernon also asserts that the short attention span of young children has a negative effect on sequential learning.

Agnew (1) and Dolch and Bloomster (6) conclude from their studies that premature reading instruction, involving word analysis skills, often results in confusion and failure.

VISUAL PERCEPTION

It is generally suggested that before children are taught to read, they should be able to identify pictures of objects with which they are familiar. Studies by Binet (4), Miller (18), and Poston and Patrick (21) all revealed that young children encountered difficulty in associating meaning with picture.

More important than pictures is the problem of perception of two dimensional shapes. Here the research of Inhelder and Piaget (13) and Bender (2) is pertinent. Many studies indicate the difficulty of reproducing figures, perceiving figures accurately, noting small details, and perceiving differences in form. Vernon (25) reports that studies in perception of two dimensional shapes suggest, in reference to reading, that children are less likely to see words as wholes than as meaningless jumbles of details with no apparent relationships among them. Letters may perhaps be seen as unanalyzable wholes; hence there is difficulty in differentiating structure.

More pertinent to our problems are the studies of the role of visual perception in early reading. While it is evident that normal children of five and six, in terms of mental age, can perceive simple forms without great difficulty, it is less certain to what extent they can remember accurately small differences among a number of different shapes. Vernon cites the research of Gates (10), Kendall (14), Bender (2), and MacLatchy (16) in this regard.

Vernon's general conclusion, drawn from studies of form and word perception, is that children below a certain age are too immature to perceive and remember small details of shape with good accuracy. However, the normal child at the age of five or six learns rapidly, and in general the child who is learning to read is less likely to be handicapped by deficiency in visual perception of word shapes than by difficulty in auditory analysis of word sounds.

AUDITORY PERCEPTION

The research of Fletcher (8), Kennedy (15), Bennett (3), *Horn* (11), Agnew (1), Gates (10), and many others suggests that the auditory perception of word sounds and their association with printed shapes presents formidable difficulties to the young child. According to Vernon, children might not hear or enunciate words clearly and accurately. They may be uncertain of the precise meaning or range of meanings and may be incapable of using the words grammatically.

Children must learn to perceive and remember word sounds accurately as spoken in "standard English," which might call for accuracy of hearing and effort of attention beyond their capability. They must also realize that the sound of the word can be analyzed in phonetic units, associated with printed shapes of letters and letter groups. This often necessitates understanding the meaning of a word in a particular context.

It is probably due to this complex of sensory, intellectual, and experience-developed activities that children do not begin to profit from an analytic approach to reading much before they are seven years mentally, as Dolch and Bloomster (6) suggest. There is no doubt that children of lesser mentality can be taught in a drill-like manner to react in an automatic fashion to symbols. The problem is in the development of insight into meanings and an understanding of relationships which lead to later independence in word recognition.

There is obvious need for controlled experimentation in the teaching of reading to five-year-olds. To date we have rather inconclusive evidence of the effect of such instruction.

As far as reading instruction in the kindergarten is concerned, then, we have the task of determining how best to present the basic skills in reading with regard to the level of intellectual, social, and language development of children.

The work of Piaget and others related to the education of five-year-olds seems to indicate that at this stage in his life each child needs individual attention. Such attention cannot be given in a rigid atmosphere wherein children are grouped together for formal instruction. Instead, research would suggest that the five-year-old can best profit from learning in an atmosphere of leisure, with opportunity for discussion and comment about the things he encounters in his environment.

From the research which is pertinent from studies and observations of five-year-olds in a learning situation, and from the evidence of the later effect of early learning, there seems to be little or no justification for introducing reading into the curriculum at the kindergarten or five-year-old stage. To best develop Bruner's "spiral curriculum" (5) in language arts it would seem that the very young, and particularly the relatively immature five-year-old, would best profit from concept development and listening and speaking development in a comparatively unstructured environment.

REFERENCES

1. Agnew, Donald C. *The Effect of Varied Amounts of Phonetic Training in Primary Reading.* Duke University Research Studies in Education, No. 5. Durham, N.C.: Duke University Press, 1939.
2. Bender, Lauretta. *A Visual Motor Gestalt Test and Its Clinical Use.* American Orthopsychiatric Association, Research Monographs, No. 3. New York: The Association, 1938. P. 176.
3. Bennett, Chester C. *An Inquiry into the Genesis of Poor Reading.* Teachers College Contribution to Education, No. 755. New York: Teachers College, Columbia University, 1938. P. VII + 139.

4. Binet, Alfred. "Le Développement de l'Intélligence chez les Enfants." *L'Année Psychologique*, XIV (1908), 1–94.

5. Bruner, Jerome S. *The Process of Education.* Cambridge, Mass.: Harvard University Press, 1961.

6. Dolch, Edward W., and Bloomster, M. "Phonic Readiness." *Elementary School Journal*, XXXVIII (Nov. 1937), 201–05.

7. Durkin, Dolores. "Children Who Read Before Grade One." *The Reading Teacher*, XIV (Jan. 1961), 163–66.

8. Fletcher, Harvey. *Speech and Hearing in Communication.* New York: D. Van Nostrand, 1954. P. 461.

9. Gates, Arthur I. "A Further Evaluation of Reading Readiness Tests." *Elementary School Journal*, XL (Apr. 1940), 577–91.

10. ——. *The Psychology of Reading and Spelling with Special Reference to Disability.* Columbia University Contribution to Education, No. 129. New York: Teachers College, Columbia University, 1922. Pp. VII + 108.

11. Horn, Ernest. "Child's Early Experience With the Letter A." *Journal of Educational Psychology*, XX (1929), 161–68.

12. Hurd, Gwendolyn M., and Rimmel, Erma L. *Preparing Your Child for Reading.* Denver: Denver Public Schools, 1961.

13. Inhelder, Barbel, and Piaget, Jean. *The Growth of Logical Thinking.* New York: Basic Books, 1958. P. 356.

14. Kendall, B. S. "Note on the Relation of Retardation in Reading to Performance in a Memory for Designs Test." *Journal of Educational Psychology*, XXXIX (1948), 370–73.

15. Kennedy, Helen. "A Study of Children's Hearing as It Relates to Reading." *Journal of Experimental Education*, X, 238–51.

16. MacLatchy, Josephine. "Bexley Reading Study." *Educational Research Bulletin* (Ohio State University), XXV (Sept. 15, 1946), 141–68.

17. Matthews, Eunice. "What Is Expected of the Soviet Kindergarten?" *Harvard Educational Review*, XXIX (Mar. 1959), 43–53.

18. Miller, William A. "Reading With and Without Pictures." *Elementary School Journal*, XXXVIII (May 1938), 676–82.

19. Moore, Omar K. *Early Reading and Writing.* 16 mm. film in color. Basic Education Council, Guilford, Connecticut.

20. Morris, Joe Alex. "Can Our Children Learn Faster?" *Saturday Evening Post* (Sept. 23, 1961), 17–25.

21. Poston, F., and Patrick, J. R. "Evaluation of Word and Picture Tests for First and Second Grades." *Journal of Applied Psychology*, XXVIII (1944), 142–52.

22. Rambusch, Nancy McCormick. *Learning How to Learn: An American Approach to Montessori.* Baltimore: Helicon Press, 1962.

23. Sheldon, William D. "Reading . . . Where Do We Stand? Where Are We Going?" *Grade Teacher*, LXVIII (Apr. 1961), 40–41.

24. Terman, L. M., and Oden, Melita. *Genetic Studies of Genius, The Gifted Grows Up*, Vol. 4, Stanford, Calif.: Stanford University Press, 1947.

25. Vernon, M. D. *Backwardness in Reading.* New York: Cambridge University Press, 1958. P. 277.

26. Vernon, P. E., O'Gorman, M. B., and McClellan, T. "Comparative Study of Educational Attainments in England and Scotland." *British Journal of Educational Psychology*, XXV (1955), 195–203.

EARLY READING IS VERY RISKY BUSINESS *

James L. Hymes, Jr.

There is nothing wrong at all when individual children become accomplished readers at an early age, because they are fully ready for the achievement. But this is *not* what the current drive for early reading is all about.

Nor is there anything wrong when young children in groups—kindergarten youngsters, even children in nursery schools—have experiences with reading that are appropriate to their stage of development. But this, too, is *not* what the current drive for early reading is all about.

In today's early reading programs, individual differences are ignored. And while there is a plethora of new gimmicks—new phonetic approaches, a new alphabet, machines, TV, words in color, letters in sandpaper—the gimmicks are only skin deep variations on the old inappropriate formal workbook-textbook approaches. This kind of formal early reading has so many things wrong with it.

It makes learning to read a sterile un-intellectual act, with baby-like content.

It isolates reading from the ongoing life of a group, turning it into a functionless process.

It deranges the kindergarten program and turns kindergarten into a sit-down place.

It turns teachers into quizmasters, drillers.

But, most significant of all, formal early reading is a very risky business.

A child pressured into achievement before he is ready—a child manipulated by adults—a child straining—a child buying love and approval at the expense of his own developmental urges—runs the risk of becoming a less sturdy, a less sure, a less sound and healthy personality.

A child pressured into achievement before he is ready runs the risk of resisting and rejecting, when he is a free agent, the learning that has been forced on him.

---

* REPRINTED by permission of James L. Hymes, Jr. from *Grade Teacher*, Vol. 82, March, 1965, pp. 88+.

FRIGHTENING HAZARDS

These are two frightening hazards. Everyone loses if we produce early readers but in the process weaken humans. Everyone loses if we produce early readers but in the process kill the joy of reading.

The sad fact is that today's pressure for formal early reading is a re-hash of a pathetic old tale. Advocates of early reading programs cite their successes as if forced early achievement was news: "Eighteen-month-olds learn to read!" . . . "Two-year-olds learn to read!" . . . "Four- and five-year-olds learn to read!" Do they forget? Or did they never know? All through the years some mothers have always pushed for early achievement and "succeeded." Their children were weaned too early. They were toilet-trained too early. They were made to share too early, and to hold in their tears too early. They were made polite too early. The claim for this kind of "success" is ages old. Only the awareness of the degree of risk involved is new.

Today more and more mothers have become aware of the hazards of this "success" in infancy and in very early childhood. As professionals, we certainly ought to be aware of the dangers in the areas we guide.

Those who push early reading say: "The children love it." Doubtless some children do. Not every child is harmed, but every child is *exposed* to harm and it is difficult, if not impossible, to predict for sure on whom the blows will fall. But it is good at least to hear the claim that "the children love it." This is at least recognition of the need children have to accept learnings as their own, not imposed. Today the most authoritarian approaches use the sweetest words.

Why do we so blithely plunge into so risky a business? When there is such reason to believe that the real need is to take the heat off many of our Sixes, why do we pressure-cook our Fives?

The children may or may not really love formal early reading—but a great many adults do. Some have very dubious motives. Some parents love formal early reading because early reading is a new status symbol.

FOR THE WRONG REASONS

Some teachers love this reading in the kindergarten. The children sit—thank God! The children are more manageable. Through all the years there have been people who simply have never liked Fives in the public school. They have never liked Fives' noise and activity. They have never liked their imagination. They have taught Fives, but they have never felt comfortable setting a stage so that children could learn; they wanted to be the center of the stage themselves. They feel comfortable only when they hold all the right answers in their own hands.

These selfish adult reasons are a realistic part of the whole early-reading push. But other reasons also lead some to favor the idea. Formal early reading can look like the solution to some of the kindergarten's pressing problems. It is the wrong solution, or people have chosen the wrong problem.

In many an overcrowded kindergarten, movement and choice or activity or firsthand experiencing are impossible. A program of structured learning that keeps children seated can seem like the answer. But the basic problem isn't how to adjust ourselves or the children to the mess we are in. The real task is to reduce class size, to allow Fives to be up and about, in action.

The anxiety of many parents is another legitimate cause for concern. Parents are frightened today. They are frightened by the scarcity of colleges; they are frightened by the bombardment of scare magazine articles. Everyone with sensitivity will agree: no parent should have to suffer today's anxieties about whether his child will learn to read. A program of formal early reading can seem like a solution to these unpleasant worries. But giving in to anxiety is hardly a sound approach. Working with parents intensively is a much better alternative than working prematurely with children. Schools today have a wonderful chance to build on what Spock has already taught parents about individual differences, about readiness, about the developmental significance of stages of growth, about the wholeness of humans. We ought to be doing much more than any school is now doing to strengthen and deepen parent understanding. We do parents no favor, and their children no favor, when we turn to answers that stem from fear.

So Different?

Many people are persuaded that today's Five is different. He has looked at TV. He has been all around in the family car. He has had stories at home, and sometimes has been to nursery school. Youngsters today seem "brighter," so the reports go; they seem to "know so much more."

This observation has curriculum implications, but it does not necessarily lead specifically to programs of formal early reading. Do these childhood experiences actually speed up total maturation? Do they argue for less first-hand learning for today's children, or for more? Do they in any way change the basic style of a five-year-old: a social, active, talking, playing, imaginative youngster, immersed in the task of finding himself and finding for himself his way in this world? Kindergarten must be challenging, but there are alternatives more stimulating than sitting today's children down with a workbook.

Perhaps our lack of imagination about alternatives is the heart of the difficulty. We act as if we had only two choices: formal reading or no reading at all for Fives. We act as if we either had to wait . . . wait . . . wait until children are ready, doing nothing with reading in the meantime—or plunge into formal programs, ready or not.

The fact is, *children at all ages are always ready for significant experiences in reading.* Given decent class size—this we *do* have to work for—it is no superhuman task to create a kindergarten life that taps the varying readiness of a whole wide range of Fives.

Reading does not begin suddenly (in kindergarten now, or in first grade, or nowhere suddenly) once a book is put in a child's hand or once the child is sat in a circle.

Reading is no one single, isolated activity.

Reading involves no single skill alone.

Many of the old-fashioned experiences, truly beloved by Fives through all the years, teach reading. When a child has the chance to hear one good story after another, day after day, he is being taught to read. When his kindergarten year is a series of mind-stretching eye-filling trips, helping him know more solidly his world, he is being taught to read. When a child hears good adult language, and when he has the fullest freest chance to use his own language, he is being taught to read. When he creates with blocks, when he communicates with paint, when he uses his body freely as a means of expression, he is being taught to read. When a child stares, fascinated, at a picture—when he looks ever so carefully at the scale in his store or at the life in his aquarium, he is being taught to read. When he hammers ever so carefully at the workbench, fashioning his battleship, this too teaches him to read. When he uses his whole body—two eyes, two hands, two arms, two legs and knees and feet—to pull himself up a scary slanted climbing board, he is being taught to read.

You can build into all of this natural, vigorous child-life as many of the symbols associated with reading as any of the children can make use of. Labels can be written on their dramatic play construction: *Garage. . . . Firehouse. . . . Gas. . . . Grocery Store. . . .* Letters can be written in connection with trips, recipes can be written in connection with cooking, plans can be written in connection with construction. And the more that children do, the more there is that can be written down: stories, reports, humorous incidents. . . .

In the good kindergarten, life doesn't *stop* so that the children can be taught to read. The *life goes on so* that the children can be taught to read. The chance to read is ever-present, but never in a coercive or artificial or teacher-dominated way. The chance is always there, built into a total on-going program, for any child to become an accomplished reader at an early age, if he is fully ready for the achievement. The chance is always there, too, for every child to have those experiences with reading that are appropriate to his own stage in development.

There is an alternative to formal early reading programs that is not a risky business. The alternative suffers from having too simple a name: *Kindergarten . . . a place for Fives.* It has no gimmicks, but it does have life going on, with busy children engrossed in a variety of work, compelled by their interests rather than the teacher's commands. In such a setting each child is strengthened, regardless of where he is on a long developmental line of readiness. And learning is exciting—regardless of where the child is on the line of readiness. This is not only the safer alternative, it is the sound way of living with humans.

SHOULD JOHNNY READ
IN KINDERGARTEN? *

A Report on
the Denver Experiment

Joseph E. Brzeinski, M. Lucile Harrison, and Paul McKee

A study of 4,000 Denver schoolchildren sought to learn whether beginning reading could be taught effectively in kindergarten. The children, whom we followed from kindergarten through the fifth grade, were randomly assigned by their schools to comparable control groups (1,500 pupils) and experimental groups (2,500 pupils) for kindergarten instruction. The teaching of the two groups was similar except for one major difference: The children in the experimental groups were given special reading instruction for 20 minutes a day.

This instruction consisted of seven types of learning activities:

1. *Spoken context.* From sentences or short paragraphs read or spoken by the teacher, the pupils practiced using context to figure out several words that would make sense where the teacher had omitted a word. (Johnny drank his _____. milk, juice, water)

2. *Initial consonant sounds.* The children gained awareness of beginning consonant sounds by sorting objects according to the initial sounds of their names, by naming words that began with the same sounds as words spoken by the teacher, and so on.

3. *Forms of letters.* They learned to recognize capital and small letters by matching and naming them in games.

4. *Context and initial consonant sounds.* The pupils practiced using the context of a sentence or paragraph read or spoken by the teacher and a beginning consonant sound supplied by her to think of the correct missing word.

* REPRINTED by permission of the National Education Association and Joseph E. Brzeinski, M. Lucile Harrison, and Paul McKee from the *National Education Association Journal*, March, 1967, pp. 23–25. Research Project No. 5-0371 reported herein, *The Effectiveness of Teaching Reading in Kindergarten*, by McKee and Brzeinski, was supported by the Cooperative Research Program of the Office of Education, U.S. Department of Health, Education, and Welfare.

(Tom wants to cut a board in half. He needs a tool that begins with the same sound as *sit* and *sat*. He needs a _____. saw)

5. *Sounds and forms of letters.* The forms of letters were related to the sounds they make by grouping pictures of objects according to the beginning letters of their names, rearranging incorrectly placed picture cards in their proper groups, and so on.

6. *Context and displayed initial letter.* The children practiced using context and a viewed letter to figure out the missing word in a sentence or paragraph read or spoken by the teacher.

7. *Context and displayed word.* The teacher read or spoke a sentence or paragraph in which the word omitted was the only one that would make sense. At the same time she displayed the entire printed word on a card and asked the pupils to name the word.

The children in the control group followed the regular kindergarten program, typical of those in many parts of the country.

When the children entered first grade, both the experimental groups and the control groups were divided into two subgroups.

Group I—The Control Group (750 pupils)
- Regular program in kindergarten
- Regular program in the first and later grades

Group II—The Delayed-Experimental Group (750 pupils)
- Regular program in kindergarten
- Experimental program in early first grade
- Adjusted program in the first and later grades

Group III—The Short-Term Experimental Group (1,250 pupils)
- Experimental program in kindergarten
- Regular program in the first and later grades

Group IV—The Experimental Group (1,250 pupils)
- Experimental program in kindergarten
- Adjusted program in the first and later grades.

We followed the four groups through the fifth grade. Group I provided a base against which to compare other groups. Group II enabled us to compare groups who received the same instruction introduced at different times. Group III showed the effect on the children's performance of shifting to regular instruction after one year of experimental instruction. Group IV was the full-scale experimental group, having a teaching program adjusted to the children's level of achievement throughout the study.

The regular reading program was similar to those programs suggested in teachers' manuals of most basal texts.

We evaluated and analyzed the experimental and control groups from the standpoint of every relevant variable: chronological and mental age when the child is first taught reading; his sex, IQ, and family characteristics. We gave particular attention to the relationship between age when first taught reading and the other variables as it affected reading achievement.

The findings were:

1. Beginning reading can be effectively taught to large numbers of typical kindergarten pupils. The Denver children readily learned letter-sound associations for commonly used consonants and acquired skill in identifying new printed words by using context and beginning-letter-sound associations.

2. The gains made by the experimental group could be maintained only by following up the kindergarten year with an adjusted teaching program in the subsequent grades. The children who received the experimental instruction in kindergarten and who had an adjusted program in later grades (Group IV) registered the highest reading achievement. We found the adjustment to be vital if the advantages of early reading instruction were to be preserved beyond the second grade.

3. The experimental kindergarten group (Group IV) showed the greatest initial and long-range gains in both reading comprehension and reading vocabulary. They also did better in other areas that depended on reading proficiency.

4. The children in Group IV read with greater speed than any of the other groups when tested at the end of the third grade.

5. Those children who were given the experimental instruction in the first grade, rather than in the kindergarten, and then were given an adjusted program in subsequent grades (Group II), did second best in reading achievement.

6. No evidence was found that early instruction in beginning reading affected visual acuity, created problems of school adjustment, or caused dislike for reading.

A little girl in one of the experimental classes who came from a broken home and was living with her grandmother was emotionally disturbed and could not enter into most of the activities of the class. During a demonstration, the teacher advised the demonstrator not to ask for responses from that child. But shortly after the demonstration teaching began, the child showed interest and literally demanded to be heard.

She could and did respond to the program with more success than many others. When she found how well she was doing, she grinned from ear to ear for the first time in the new school. After a few more successful responses, she actually cried for joy. From that time on, her emotional problems began to disappear. She had found herself in this program.

This investigation gives reassuring evidence that early reading instruction need not be harmful to children. Instead, the evidence shows that it can have a positive, measurable, continuing effect. Undoubtedly, potential dangers do exist, but the experimental methodology we used has shown that they can be avoided through employing a proper procedure. The possible hazards do not constitute an excuse for opposing change or for inaction.

A surprising and most important aspect of the study is the finding that most *average* youngsters in a large city public school system can profit from beginning reading instruction in kindergarten. Advanced reading achievement was not limited to precocious, gifted children from high socioeconomic backgrounds. The children in this study had the wide range of abilities and representative backgrounds usually found in large urban schools.

No elaborate screening or readiness testing was used. However, teachers were advised to delay starting any child they felt to be too immature to begin the program with the whole group.

One teacher told us about a small boy who, she had decided, was not mature enough to begin with the group. She found other areas of interest for him to work in while she taught reading to the experimental group. It soon became obvious, however, that the boy kept listening to the teacher and was so interested in what was going on that he ignored the substitute program planned for him. Each day he edged a little closer to the experimental group until one day he saw an empty chair and joined the group. He soon caught up with the others, and eventually passed them in achievement.

The implications of the study seem clear. School systems must reevaluate the goals they have established for their kindergartens. Emerging psychological theory, recent research evidence, and the present study suggest that children profit from early educational stimulation. As a result of changes that have occurred in their environment, children today appear to have a greater aptitude for learning. Methods and materials of instruction are better.

Other school systems might well experiment with early introduction in language, writing, science, or number skills, to name but a few possibilities.

A COMMENT ON THE DENVER EXPERIMENT *

Kenneth D. Wann

I believe that a reading program such as the one in Denver, which teaches kindergarten children about meaning in spoken language and the relation of language sounds to the symbols that stand for them, merits careful consideration by those interested in developing modern kindergarten programs.

Those involved in the Denver study concluded that reading can and should be taught in kindergarten. The investigators came to their conclusion by carrying out a carefully designed program of beginning reading instruction

---

* REPRINTED by permission of the National Education Association and Kenneth D. Wann, from the *National Education Association Journal*, March, 1967, pp. 25–26.

starting in kindergarten or first grade, and matching it against the usual type of reading program used around the country.

To some educators, reading in kindergarten means a direct attack on printed symbols, using many of the materials now used in the primary grades—experience charts, workbooks, and preprimers. The designers of this study, however, have used an approach that is much more appropriate to the way five-year-olds learn. By emphasizing manipulative materials—objects and pictures to be sorted and named—they have kept the program from becoming a highly abstract, verbal approach to reading instruction.

At the same time they have shown a commendable sense of responsibility in recognizing the need to provide for a balanced kindergarten day and for individual differences among children in their experimental program. From the very beginning of the program they advised teachers to:

- Go at a rational pace and limit instruction to 20 minutes a day
- Be prepared to stop temporarily or to retrench if necessary
- Excuse from the experiment any child unable to handle the material
- Avoid pushing the children to get through the program by a given date.

These suggestions imply that some pupils can learn all that the activities aim to teach, that others can absorb some but not all of this learning, that still others can absorb little if anything, and that each pupil, without being pushed, should be given the chance to learn all that he can. These are pertinent observations and should be heeded by anyone planning to develop such a program beginning at the kindergarten level.

Several aspects of the program call for critical examination. First, while I admire the flexibility demonstrated by the researchers in their suggestions to teachers in the program, I am concerned at their recommendation that the pupils who could learn little, if anything, should be excused. Certainly, children must be free of pressure to participate beyond their ability, but to excuse them and not help them move into other carefully defined language learnings that they apparently need suggests that the program is too narrowly defined to serve the entire range of learners at the kindergarten level.

Second, the designers of the program apparently assumed that all kindergarten children have enough experience in listening and talking to build a spoken vocabulary adequate to enable them to begin converting it into a reading vocabulary.

This was not the case in Denver, and it will not be the case for many children in many areas of the country. Indeed, an assumption of this sort need not be made, nor any program predicated on it. Recent advances in structural linguistics suggest that the learning needs of each child can be charted so as to allow the school to begin teaching him reading when he has mastered earlier stages of language development. Members of any group of five-year-olds will reach this point at different times, but each of them will need help with some language learning at all times.

Programs such as the Denver one need to be integrated into a total program of language development to assure the best possible teaching for all kindergarten children, including those who are ready to read.

The Denver study has made a significant contribution by demonstrating that kindergarten children *can* be taught reading and that using letter-sound association, spoken context, and initial-letter sounds and forms is one good way of doing so.

Schools and school systems that wish to experiment with early reading programs should consider the Denver program. And they should heed the Denver finding that if the children's gains in reading are to be preserved they must be followed up with a properly adjusted program.

Planners also need to realize that reading must be only one part of a sound kindergarten program. To focus too narrowly on a reading program is to fail to recognize the great range of experiences five-year-olds need in order to meet their developmental tasks. They should have a sound program in the social studies, science, and the arts to help them learn to think, to conceptualize, and to attach meaning to the world of people and things. All of these ingredients contribute to the kind of kindergarten program appropriate for today's young children.

REACHING CHILDREN: WHICH APPROACHES?

There is no shortage of programs and procedures advocated for use in helping children reach their potential in reading power. Over the years, various reading methods have been practiced; some have persisted for a long time, others only a relatively short time. Others have enjoyed alternating peaks and drops of popularity with new positions and new combinations, added and subtracted over the years.

Every position has its proponents who feel strongly about the approach; every position has its critics. Every position seems to marshal its evidence and to elaborate upon its raison d'être; every position demonstrates its results. Almost every procedure has its advantages and its limitations.

The array of choices facing the teacher is formidable. Aside from selecting a method because it is currently popular, there are guidelines that can be used to clarify a choice:

1. *Which procedures best fit the child?* If the focus is upon the child's gains in reading power, it seems reasonable to determine the procedure in which the particular child finds success, as well as stimulation and encouragement. But what might be appropriate for one child might not prove so for another. What even seems to work with a certain group of children might not at all be suitable for many other groups.

2. *Which procedure develops the broadest possible range of reading powers?* If one is concerned with efficiency, it would seem obvious that the procedure that simultaneously stimulates a variety of reading growths would be preferable to those that stimulate only one or two. For example, the procedure that develops positive attitudes toward reading at the same time as it develops word recognition skills would be ahead of the procedure that simply focused upon word recognition skills; or the procedure that stressed the many kinds of word recognition skills would be more appropriate than the procedure that stressed only one.

3. *Which procedure seems most closely related to the achievement of general goals in education?* If one wishes to keep in mind, at all times, the major goals of education, it would seem obvious that the kind of pro-

cedure that promotes not only reading growth but all of the general goals of education would be preferred. If independence, self-direction, and self-actualization are recognized goals of learning, then a search must be made for those methods of teaching reading that best achieve not only reading goals but educational goals.

The final choice is best made when criteria such as these are developed and used in analyzing the various possibilities. The best answer seems to lie in careful, continuous study and evaluation by the teacher who seeks to meet specific needs of his situation.

WHAT DO WE KNOW ABOUT
THE TEACHING OF READING? *

Theodore Clymer

R ESEARCH in reading over the past fifty years has revealed a great deal, but in terms of the importance and immensity of the job, we have made just a beginning. In the space of this editorial only selected ideas about our state of knowledge in reading can be developed. The ideas which have been selected are judged by the author to be of the greatest importance to the classroom teacher.

The Teacher Is Important

One of the reasons that methods research in the teaching of reading has been relatively unsuccessful in providing viable answers is that teacher influence has been neglected in the research design. Characteristically we find in research studies that there are greater differences among classrooms than among the methods being tested. While a number of factors might explain this phenomenon, the teacher seems clearly to be the most important element.

Part of the teacher impact may come through a particular "style of teaching." It seems likely, also, that a great deal is dependent on the teacher's ability to relate to the children being taught. We do not expect the principles of learning to vary from classroom to classroom, but the important personal element in applying these principles cannot be neglected in judging the effectiveness of a program.

Variability Is Inescapable

The history of reading methods could be organized around a theme of attempts to eliminate variability among pupils. Thoughtful educators recognize that variability is inescapable when curriculum goals are limitless. Indeed, the only way to keep youngsters alike is not to teach them anything—for the minute we begin to teach, the capable will learn a great deal and the less capable will learn but somewhat less. The net result then from our instructional program is greater variability at the end of the instructional period than at the beginning.

* REPRINTED with permission of the Association for Supervision and Curriculum Development and Theodore Clymer from *Educational Leadership*, Vol. 24, February, 1967, pp. 389–91. Copyright © 1967, by the Association for Supervision and Curriculum Development.

Programs in reading which are successful are those which recognize that variability exists and that variability will increase through the grade levels. Good programs are designed to accommodate children of different levels of ability at the same age or grade level. Hopefully, educators have abandoned their search for a magic technique, formula or set of materials which will enable all children to reach an arbitrary standard. A thoughtful examination of the research shows clearly that variability is inevitable and that the good program makes provisions for this variability.

Reading Growth Is One Part of Language Development

While studies for some years have demonstrated the interrelationships among the language arts, it has been only recently that the need to look at total language development has become widely accepted. In the early years of reading instruction, it is impossible to separate the teaching of reading, language, spelling and composition.

Increasingly it is recognized that development of skill in any one of these areas serves to reinforce and extend the skills in the other areas. This increasing recognition of the interrelationship among the language arts explains in part the recent interest in programs for early reading instruction which are called "language arts" or "language experience" approaches.

Planned Instruction Produces Superior Results

Throughout the history of reading instruction in the United States there has been a constant concern with the problem of providing a direct planned program of instruction which at the same time provides for more indirect and spontaneous instruction. The achievement of children in a planned program seems clearly superior to that of children taught by an incidental or spontaneous program.

Unfortunately, some direct and planned programs become so inflexible that children, while developing reading skills, lose their taste for reading. The problem here is to develop an approach which provides a structure and a sequence and, at the same time, utilizes the opportunities that arise incidentally and one which also capitalizes on the interests of children. Such an approach obviously requires a sensitive and well prepared teacher who can determine instructional needs and who reacts sympathetically to children's interests and special problems.

Independent Application Is Essential

Reading programs which confine children to a set of experiences from textbooks cannot develop fully independent readers. While instruction with a planned program may be necessary to provide instruction in skills, the text can never provide sufficient practice to develop fully independent and efficient readers. Such reading comes only from a variety of experiences in which the child makes independent application of his growing skills.

The reading program which is confined to a set of instructional materials alone is a dull program, but, in addition, such a program robs the child of true independence in reading skills. The need for classroom collections and a professionally staffed central library for all pupils, elementary as well as secondary, is clearly dictated by this information.

THERE ARE NO SIMPLE ANSWERS

One clear finding from the research literature is the complexity of reading growth and the enormous number of factors which influence the full development of reading skills. If this understanding is applied to instructional programs, it can be clearly seen that simple solutions—for example, the use of a set of particular diagnostic exercises, a change in art work in the basal programs, or a library in which the children are free to read what their interests and ability dictate—will not be enough to provide an effective program.

A program which is truly effective must be broad in scope, must meet a range of ability levels and interest levels, must provide a structured and planned program, must carry the child to independent application and must take into account differences in background and rate of learning. These necessary characteristics, combined with the complexity of the human individual, clearly negate any simple program or simple solution for improving the teaching of reading.

NEW VENTURES IN THE TEACHING OF READING *

Theodore Clymer

Let me begin by saying that I have nothing revolutionary to report, nothing dramatic to reveal, no "Newton's Law" of reading instruction to divulge which might electrify the nation's educators. Unfortunately, many—although certainly not all—of the significant ventures in the teaching of reading are neither novel nor revolutionary. They represent, instead, new applications,

---

* REPRINTED by permission of the Department of Elementary School Principals from *The National Elementary Principal*, Vol. 43, pp. 26–30, February, 1964.

new emphases, and new insights into problems and procedures as old as education itself.

Today, with so many people seeking the new and novel, one sometimes
wonders whether the quest for a different way may have become a goal rather
than a means to an end. In a recent press interview, after lengthy questioning
in which I discussed many of the points covered in this article, the reporter
asked in exasperation, "Don't you have anything to say with real news appeal?"
At that point I wished—at least for the reporter's sake—that I had taken up
the cudgels for the Augmented Roman alphabet. That might have satisfied
him. What I had to talk about did not.

Although there is nothing particularly startling to report, there are some
significant trends and factors which encompass a good number of the new
ventures in reading. Many of these ventures represent quests to answer important educational problems. In the discussion that follows, each of several
questions will be treated in turn.

CAN WE ALTER THE SCHOOL'S ORGANIZATION TO AID IN THE TEACHING OF READING?

In framing this question, I was tempted to use the word "revive" because
we must acknowledge that most of the "new" plans currently being offered
are only modifications or slight variations of organizational patterns of twenty,
forty, or even fifty years ago. The current trend toward departmentalizing the
elementary grades is certainly not without precedent. A principal in a school
still using the platoon plan, which is not unlike the Dual Progress Plan, set
forth the situation clearly. He said, "If I can just hang on a few more years, I
will be out in front again."

It is, of course, beneficial at this time that school administrators and teachers
at both the elementary and secondary levels are critically evaluating current
school organizational plans. Questions that are being asked about the self-
contained classroom may yield important and beneficial changes in the elementary school curriculum. The special part-time ability groupings, such as
are suggested under the so-called Joplin Plan, may provide a partial answer
to the instructional problems of individual differences in reading, arithmetic,
spelling, and perhaps other skill areas. Our concepts of grade level, always
unwieldy and overgeneralized, are being questioned in the "ungraded" or
"non-graded" schools. We may find that these patterns of organization provide for greater pupil growth toward the academic and social personal goals of
the curriculum.

This serious appraisal of current school organizational plans is healthy, but
a number of cautions need to be observed. Many of the current proposals
should be recognized for what they are: ghosts disinterred from the educational graveyard. They may appear to be new simply because we have forgotten or have failed to study our history of education.

In spite of the fact that most of the plans for reorganization have been used in some form or another in the past, we should give them a careful and impartial hearing. Some plans we can reject on the basis of what we know about the characteristics of pupils and how they learn. Some plans will require a careful and thoughtful evaluation in limited school settings before we can answer questions about pupil achievement, cost, teacher attitude, and so forth. In all cases in which trials are made, systematic provision should be made for a critical evaluation of the results. Such tryouts are not easily made, but our claims to professional status rest on our ability to demonstrate the value of what we do.

A second major consideration in looking at school organization concerns the research literature, meager as it is, on the relationship of school organization to pupil achievement. A thoughtful reader of this research is led to a disquieting conclusion. Organization plans seemingly have little to do with pupil achievement when viewed in relation to the quality of the instructional program. In our zeal to improve the schools, we must not lose sight of the fact that what we do in *teaching* pupils is far more important than how or for how long we assign them to a classroom. Recently, in preparing a chapter for a yearbook of one of the professional societies, I suggested that some of the current plans of organization seem to be an attempt to reduce elementary school teachers to the status of secondary school teachers. The editor, a wise man, redpenciled my comments.

SHOULD WE BEGIN READING INSTRUCTION AT A DIFFERENT TIME?

At present, there are two major aspects of the question about earlier reading instruction. Increasingly, schools are asking if readiness should be systematically developed and taught in the kindergarten. Other schools are asking whether reading instruction of a more formal nature—with texts and trade books—should become a part of the kindergarten curriculum. In other words, should the initial stages of formal reading instruction be moved from the first grade to the kindergarten?

With the public's continuing concern over "easy" education and the school's realization that some children come to school with an abundant background of experiences with books, working in groups, etc., it seems natural that readiness instruction would find its way into the kindergarten. The Denver experiments with formal instruction in the kindergarten have done much to stimulate interest in this area of teaching. So, too, has McKee's material for a kindergarten readiness program which considers letter names and sounds as the essential content of prereading material.

In an attempt to assess opinions about reading readiness in the kindergarten and current practices, a national survey was conducted by the University of Minnesota. A random selection was made of approximately 180 communities with populations of 20,000 and above. Questionnaires were mailed to the directors of elementary education in each of these communities with the request that principals, kindergarten teachers, and first grade teachers, as well as elementary consultants and the elementary directors, complete and return questionnaires.

Approximately 70 per cent of the communities responded with one or more questionnaires. While the results undoubtedly reflect the thinking of better school personnel, the findings are informative and useful in determining the possible changes and emphases in the kindergarten program. The study is not yet completed, but the following statements summarize some of the findings.

1. Classroom teachers favor systematic instruction in readiness to a much greater degree than do supervisors and consultants.

2. Principals' attitudes toward readiness instruction in the kindergarten are more similar to the attitudes of teachers than to those of consultants or supervisors.

3. Most of the schools reporting have readiness instruction in the kindergarten.

4. Many kindergarten teachers tend to see readiness instruction as a class-wide activity, while first grade teachers tend to see it as instruction of small groups within the class.

5. Instructional materials in order of preference are: 1) teacher-prepared picture charts, 2) teacher-prepared games and recordings, 3) teacher-prepared single sheets, 4) commercially published picture charts, and 5) commercially published readiness books.

6. Skills considered important to the kindergarten readiness program in order of their importance are: 1) listening skills, 2) following directions, 3) language skills, 4) visual discrimination, and 5) auditory discrimination.

An interesting side aspect of the study was the attitudes many of the respondents expressed. While the questionnaire was neutral as far as we were concerned, many respondents regarded the inquiry as evidence that we wished to change established practice. This led some persons to be thankful that "at last someone was doing something," while others attacked us as lacking knowledge of child development. One superintendent returned the questionnaire with a letter explaining that the inquiry was so abhorrent to the educational philosophy of his district that he dared not ask his teachers to express an opinion!

Two articles appearing recently in the NEA Journal addressed themselves to questions of early instruction in reading.[1] Durkin suggests that the very young should have the opportunity to learn to read. Her opinions are in contrast to those of Sheldon who suggests that harmful results may occur from giving the very young instruction in reading.

It appears that we may be headed for another unfortunate "either/or" controversy in education. It is not simply a question of whether all should be given instruction or whether all should be denied instruction. Rather the

[1] "Should the Very Young Be Taught To Read?" NEA Journal 52:20, November 1963.

question centers on whether or not it is reasonable and profitable to provide certain advanced students with a more or less formal introduction to reading skills at the kindergarten level.

Should We Employ Different Emphases and Procedures In Our Word Recognition Program?

To anyone who visits the schools consistently it is no secret that there have been great changes over the past ten years in the teaching of word recognition skills—in the emphasis, the ordering of skills, and the timing of their introduction. The next five years promise even greater change. The current popularity of the many "phonics" systems indicates that schools are not finding the type of word recognition program they feel they need within the organization of the present basal reading programs. It also seems likely that some basal programs delay the teaching of skills in word recognition longer than necessary. It might also be asked whether or not current basal programs have become so integrated that neither the pupil nor the teacher is fully aware of the word skills program.

We cannot leave our question of different emphases and procedures in word recognition without speaking about the impact of the findings of linguistic scholars on the teaching of reading. Currently, no word seems to arouse so much positive feeling as "linguistics." Its positive valence may be due in part to the fact that many of us are unsure of what linguistics is and of how the field can contribute to reading instruction. Added to the problem of placing linguistics in its proper perspective is the tendency of some linguists to offer their expertise in all aspects of language—including the over-all reading curriculum, the beginning reading program, suitable reading goals for the eight-year-old, the psychology of learning, reading disability, and so forth.

While many facets of the science of language have possible implications for the teaching of reading, the phonological aspects of linguistics have held the major attention of persons interested in the teaching of reading—especially beginning reading. The major premise of most of the phonological approaches to beginning reading is the restriction of the early teaching to words which are "regular" in their letter-sound relationships, with a gradual introduction of "partially irregular" and finally "irregular" words.

This approach has an appeal. It has logic, system, and scientific respectability. Further, it coincides with the current emphasis upon programed instruction. However, a close examination of the phonological approach reveals some major problems. For example, the English language being what it is, the reading of many words of high frequency and utility must be postponed because these words are "partially irregular" or more likely "irregular." In addition, the repetition of certain word elements, such as "an," "at," "ah," results in content with little meaning (in the traditional sense) and probably with little interest for the elementary child.

More important, such an approach fails to capitalize on the reading and writing experiences the children have beyond the formal reading class. Most good first-grade programs involve a considerable amount of reading and writing in a more or less informal, unstructured "language arts" approach to language skills. Strict adherence to a one-to-one relationship between letter and sound for a brief part of the school day, with a wide ranging letter-sound dissonance through the remainder of the child's experience with language, may promote an instructional division which will be apparent to everyone but the child.

While there is no satisfactory research to resolve the differences of opinion on the value of a gradual introduction of a symbol and sound relationship, a program which strives to combine meaning and some of the important aspects of linguistics seems to be a reasonable compromise. To the author's knowledge, no controlled research has been published which substantiates the superiority of a program which uses a gradual introduction of symbol-sound relationships.

An interesting and carefully designed study was recently completed at the University of Minnesota under the direction of Guy L. Bond. The study evaluated the reading achievement at beginning fourth-grade level of two contrasted groups of students. Both groups of students had been taught from a widely used basal reading series, but in one group the students had been given a modified linguistic approach to word skills in place of the word recognition program of the basal program. The linguistic approach incorporated many of the ideas of Bloomfield.

The results showed the superiority of achievement of the group taught with the modified linguistic materials. The linguistic group excelled in word recognition skills and also in speed and flexibility of reading, as well as in many of the comprehension abilities. While there can be no question that the performance of the experimental group was significantly and practically superior to the control group, it is not possible on the basis of the design of the study to assign the results to any specific aspect of the linguistic materials. Three hypotheses can be set forth which may account for the difference.

It is possible that the students taught by a modified linguistic approach had acquired a technique of perceiving the structure of words and letter patterns which gave them greater skill in building words and in taking them apart. To state the matter another way, it may not have been so much the materials used as the technique developed. A second hypothesis concerning the superiority of the modified linguistic approach would attribute the differences of the two groups to the early learning of the names of the letters of the alphabet, their sequence, and the sounds they represent. Still a third hypothesis is concerned with the effect on the experimental group of a clearly defined and systematic application of the principles of learning in the linguistic word recognition program. In the linguistic program, the goals were clearly specified. Both pupils and teachers clearly recognized growth or lack of growth toward the objectives of the word recognition program.

We do not regard this recently completed study as definitive or conclusive. It does suggest, however, the possibility of combining both the structured approach of the linguist with an early introduction of a vocabulary of useful, although not necessarily regular, words.

Mention should also be made of the imaginative and energetic attempts of Sir James Pitman to reintroduce the concept of the Augmented Roman alphabet as a beginning reading medium. John Carroll of Harvard, in a typically objective and candid assessment, has written:

> The real danger that may ensue from the Pitman-Downing experiment, however, is that if it "succeeds" (as is likely), it may misdirect the attention of educators toward what Downing calls the "medium," i.e., the orthography, and away from other elements in reading instruction which may be more critical than orthography. The Pitman-Downing experiment makes its comparisons solely, for understandable reasons, with control groups that are receiving conventional kinds of instruction. This aspect of the design should not lead us to overlook the possibility that there are less drastic and costly means of improving reading instruction than the introduction of a new orthography. One such means, I believe, is to modify conventional instruction in the direction of more attention to the systematic arrangement and progression of the early steps in reading instruction in the light of an analysis of the phoneme-grapheme correspondences of conventional spelling.[2]

My own prejudices would suggest that improving the quality of the instruction in terms of meeting a) range of achievement, b) rates of learning, c) skill requirements, and d) interests may be more crucial than either of the approaches suggested by Pitman or Carroll. My view would not, of course, relegate their positions to unimportant priorities in initial instruction.

Are We Meeting the Needs Of the Culturally Deprived?

We do not yet know much about the culturally deprived child or the type of reading program or total school instructional program which will enable him to achieve his full academic potential. Indeed, we have not even specified clearly what we mean by a culturally deprived child. In actual fact, we are not dealing with culturally deprived children but simply with children whose culture is different from that which is congenial to the school. When these children exist in as great numbers as they do, it is perhaps not correct to call them culturally different—another term of popular circulation.

There can be no question that effective reading skills are essential to the incorporation of these children into the social fabric of self-supporting and contributing members of American culture. It may be well, however, to ask whether the lack of reading skills among these students is a cause of social problems in employment and in personal and social relations or whether poor

---

[2] Carroll, John B. Review of *To Be Or Not To Be* by John A. Downing. *Harvard Educational Review* 33:391–92; Summer 1963.

reading is only a symptom of a broader dissatisfaction with and dislocation within the cultural framework. The educational programs which seemingly have the greatest impact with this group of children are the programs which attempt to do a great deal more than promote reading ability. The successful program must encompass the total social environment of such students. Viewed from this point, the problem becomes much larger than the school setting. In many situations, the school is asking—quite correctly and logically it seems—if it has the facilities, the training, and the competence to carry out such a program without the careful cooperation of other social agencies.

This, perhaps, is also a place for a comment concerning the changing role of the school. This new role for the school was clearly illustrated by a cartoon in the *Christian Science Monitor* which showed two elementary school boys trudging home from school, one of them saying, "Sit-ins, strikes, demonstrations. Remember when school was just for reading and writing?"

How Can the Classroom Teacher's Instruction Be Made More Effective?

Very few of the current ventures in the teaching of reading have taken as a point of departure an attempt to enable the teacher to meet the individual needs of pupils under his direction. Yet meeting individual needs is a crucial —perhaps *the* crucial—aspect of effective instruction. Mary Austin's studies have revealed inadequacies in both pre-service and in-service preparation of elementary teachers to meet individual differences. High school teachers undoubtedly receive less help in these areas than their elementary counterparts. Several of the demonstration centers and curriculum centers of Project English are moving in the direction of assessing techniques and materials which will help provide a quality instructional program. More such ventures are needed.

Quality instructional programs in the teaching of reading are likely to attract little dramatic interest. Such programs require good in-service education, reasonable class size or pupil load, generous classroom collections of books, well-stocked, professionally staffed central libraries, adequate consultant and supervisory help, and a wealth of different types of instructional material.

A superintendent inaugurating such a program may not be lauded. He probably will not receive national publicity, foundation aid, or lush offers of positions in California or other exotic places. On the contrary, he may find himself in difficulty, for such programs are expensive and require a generous mill rate. Yet such a quality program may do more to promote good reading than many other dramatic approaches.

READING: THE APPROACHES WE USE*

Arthur V. Olson

Never before has there been such a profusion of materials for teaching reading. With the advent of the "space race" and the resulting emphasis upon education, the public has placed the entire educational system under careful scrutiny. Since reading skills are the key to knowledge, it is obvious why the public has such an interest in the way reading is taught and the outcomes of progress in that field.

Without the skill of reading, a child cannot make satisfactory progress in our schools. Not all of our children learn to read. We know that this is true, but the failure of some children is not easily explained. It may be because of low intelligence, emotional problems, poor teaching, physical problems, moving from town to town continuously without establishing roots, or poor home environment—any one or a combination of these factors. Because of the inability to point to a single factor for reading failure, many approaches and panaceas have been offered to educators within the last few years. As a result of the interest by the general public and the misunderstandings concerning the teaching of reading, it is important that those directly responsible for the curriculum be as informed as possible.

The reading controversy centers, not on any claim that we are not teaching the reading skills, but on the question of how we can teach the reading skills so that more children will be able to find success in school. Several approaches are in use. The most common is the basal reading approach; second is the basal reading approach used in conjunction with experience charts; third is phonics programs; fourth is reading programs based upon the language experience of the child.[1] These four approaches are the ones which have the greatest frequency of use in our public schools. Two others, however, are worth mentioning: the initial teaching alphabet and the linguistic approach.

THE BASAL READING APPROACH

This approach is the one most commonly used throughout the United States at the present time. There are several series of readers on the market, each of which provides textbook material, workbooks, and supplementary

---

* REPRINTED by permission of the publisher, from *The Clearing House*, Vol. 39, No. 5, January, 1965.

[1] Mary C. Austin and Coleman Marrison, *The First R*. New York: The Macmillan Company, 1963.

materials for the students, and manuals and guides for the teacher. Usually the basal readers provide instruction from reading readiness up through grade six, and in many cases through grade eight.

The vocabulary is carefully controlled from book to book, primarily in grades one through three, with careful development of a sequential program and balanced skills. Within the last few years the basal readers have come through many an extensive change. The vocabulary has been enriched in many cases to meet the individual needs, the content has been changed somewhat by the introduction of stories written by well-known children's authors and authors of adult material. Much supplementary material for classroom use has also been introduced.

The basal readers are used by thousands of teachers throughout the United States with a great deal of success. Until a new teacher becomes thoroughly acquainted with the reading program, it is inadvisable for her to try to develop a reading program on her own. The material which is in the basal reader has been developed through years of study and many years of experience by classroom teachers. Because most of the material has been experimented with in many types of situations, the teacher's guide provides a valuable resource for the teacher in providing interest and productive activities for her class. Even for the teacher who has a great many years of experience and a good grasp of the skills which make up reading, the basal reader still offers a valuable source of material for devising a skills program. The teacher may feel that she wants to use the material in a variety of ways. She may want it used as a part of an enrichment program or an individualized reading program, or to supplement other basal readers. In any case, it should be useful to the teacher as a guide for checking on the skill to be developed.

In some cases the basal reader has not been used as it was intended. The basal reader is not a total and complete program by itself. It is merely a part of the total program. It is impossible to teach through the basal reader all of the skills which are needed. Most of the content is story material. Since this is true, many of the skills that we teach, such as finding main ideas, organization, sequence, study skills, and others, must be taught in the content area as well. The basal reader, although it does have a number on the outside cover, is intended to meet the different instructional levels of all the children in every class. Because of the wide range of ability which we have in our classrooms, it is impossible to take care of all of the instructional needs through one book. A teacher must use other books within the same series for the children below and above the instructional level of the grade, or she may use a co-basal series.

Since reading is a sequential development of skills, there is no such thing as having children cover all pages in a certain reader by the end of the year. The statement has been made by some experts in the field of reading that as many as 30 per cent of our children are reading at the frustration level. If this is true, we are not doing our job.

The teacher's guide was never meant as a detailed prescription to be followed exactly in all aspects for all children. We know full well that some children are going to need more development in some skills than in others. There are also going to be some children who do not need the drills or some of the skills which are taught.

One of the most important criticisms that have come out of the basal reading program is directed against the teacher's use of the workbooks. If workbooks are used indiscriminately with all children, they have little value in developing needed skills. If the teacher fails to check the workbook activities with the children so they know the progress they are making and the errors they are making, the material is being grossly misused. The value of the material lies in the information it can give the teacher about the application of the skills. It has never been intended as a testing situation or as a busy-work activity.

In many of the activities involving the basal reader, directions must be given to the children. As this is to be a learning situation, the experience that a child is going to need to bring to the reading must be developed before, and the teacher's guidance through the material is mandatory.

The basal reading programs which are most commonly used in our public schools are as follows:

Alice and Jerry Basic Readers, Mabel O'Donnel, and others. New York: Harper & Row, Publishers.

Betts Basic Readers, Emmett Betts, and others. New York: American Book Co.

Developmental Reading Series, Guy Bond, and others. Chicago: Lyons and Carnahan.

Ginn Basic Readers, David Russell, and others. Boston: Ginn and Company.

Macmillan Readers, Arthur Gates, and others. New York: The Macmillan Company.

New Basic Readers, Curriculum Foundation Series, Marion Monroe, and others. Chicago: Scott, Foresman & Co.

Reading for Interest Series, Paul Witty, and others. Boston: D. C. Heath & Co.

Reading for Meaning Series, Paul McKee, and others. Boston: Houghton Mifflin Co.

Sheldon Basic Readers, William D. Sheldon, and others. Boston: Allyn and Bacon, Inc.

Winston Basic Readers, Russell G. Stauffer, and others. New York: Holt, Rinehart and Winston, Inc.

The Basal Reading Approach Used in Conjunction with Experience Charts

Charts based upon the real experiences of children provide available reading material for the beginning stages of reading instruction and for later development. The preparation of the charts involves very specific techniques which can be mastered easily by any interested teacher. The charts can usually be divided into two general categories: (1) charts made by the teacher from the dictation of the students, and (2) practice charts made by the children with the aid of the teacher.

The function of the first type of chart is to give the children the experience of seeing their own spoken words converted into printed symbols. The emphasis is not upon reading the chart but upon noticing the fact that words can be written down and the process by which we do write words—primarily left to right, return sweep to the next line, and left to right again.

There will be some children who have advanced in reading maturity and who will probably be able to read some of the words just from seeing the material written. There may be some children who will even want to learn to read the whole chart by themselves.

The second kind of chart, the practice chart, is prepared primarily to give actual practice in reading and writing. In developing this, the teacher will try to guide the children into making simple sentences, with the vocabulary load closely related to those they will find in their reading material. Because these charts will be ones in which the children have a direct and immediate interest, the material will often provide a welcome change from that which they find in their basal reader.

Even as the children progress through the grades, the experience charts will be of value in helping them to summarize their ideas of materials that they have read in the content areas. It will also afford them the opportunity of having more experiences with the vocabulary that they are trying to learn.

The Phonics Approach

Of all the issues in reading instruction, none has received more attention or aroused more discussion and misunderstanding than phonics. Not only are teachers interested in the role of phonics, but parents have looked upon it as an answer to all the reading problems.

The advocates of this approach believe that phonics (sounds as they apply to reading) should be introduced either before a sight vocabulary is established or on a parallel with the beginning basal reader. They reject the "whole word" approach, because they believe the child first sees the word as individual letters and then the larger unit of the word as a whole.

Among the proponents of the "phonics-first approach" there is little consensus of opinion regarding the proper method of teaching. Each approach establishes a step-by-step sequence which the authors warn must be followed if the child is to read. They emphasize that learning phonics is a memorization process that can only be mastered by repetitive drill. Their material consists of workbooks containing page after page of isolated words and phonic elements.

One phonic system calls for learning the names of all 26 letters of the alphabet on the first day of instruction. Another emphasizes a letter-by-letter approach to reading, with the emphasis upon the sound of each separate letter. Others teach all of the vowel sounds first (long and short), followed by the consonants, while some teach only the long or short vowel sounds first. The teaching of blends, vowels or consonant digraphs, and diphthongs varies to a greater extent even than some of the other elements in the various materials. In some cases, only selected elements are taught, and others are ignored. In most of the material, there is little, if any, effort to help children evolve or understand phonic principles or to aid them in arriving at useful generalizations.

There is no evidence as to the value of many of the phonics programs now available to our schools except the opinions and prejudices of their authors. There is little consensus of opinion as to appropriate methods in the phonics approach, and serious doubts should be raised about the use of most phonics materials either in isolation or in conjunction with basal readers.

If the school is pressured into using a phonics program, it should be used on a very limited basis, rather than school wide, and it should be evaluated under the best research conditions possible. Wholesale adoption can only result in confusion, more problems, and no indication as to the worth of the material.

THE LANGUAGE EXPERIENCE APPROACH [2]

The language experience approach was developed in San Diego County, California, under the direction of R. Van Allen, curriculum director for the county school system. This approach attempts to integrate the communication skills of speaking, writing, reading, and listening.

In simplest terms, the approach can be thought of in the following manner. What a child thinks about he can talk about; what he can talk about he can write, or the teacher can write for him. What he writes he can read; he can read what he writes and what others write. What he has to say and write is as important to him as what other people have written for him to read.

From the very beginning of the school year, the children are encouraged to express themselves through speaking, writing, painting, and so forth. The teacher works with individual children and with small groups of children, helping them to write down "talk." Reading skills are taught informally by

[2] Dorris May Lee and R. Van Allen, *Learning to Read Through Experience.* New York: Appleton-Century-Crofts, Inc., 1963.

the teacher's talking to the children about the words, names of letters, beginning sounds, ending sounds, sounds in between.

The language experience approach seems to have some merit for beginning reading instruction. It does seem to develop an interest in reading, there is an integration of the language arts and other communication skills, the children understand that reading is an important form of communication, and the approach does encourage creative expression.

Certain aspects of the approach are open to careful questioning. A teacher using this approach would have to be well aware of the development of reading skills, to be sure that the children were getting a balanced and sound program. There would be some danger of continual misspelling, poor expression, and punctuation errors if the teacher, fearing to hamper creativity, failed to correct errors. It is also possible that memorization of written material may be mistaken for reading.

THE INITIAL TEACHING ALPHABET [3]

The i/t/a was developed in England by Sir James Pitman for use in teaching beginning readers. In this alphabet, there are 44 symbols instead of our 26-letter alphabet. These symbols represent all of the sounds in the English language and are consistent in that a given symbol represents the same sound each time it is encountered. In traditional orthography, the 26 letters, individually or in combination, can represent upwards of 2,000 sounds.

The i/t/a, derived from the Augmented Roman Alphabet, is not designed as a continuing method. It is devised for use during the first 15 months of formal reading instruction. This method is in its fourth year of a five-year research study in England, with concurrent research projects in the United States. The largest of these involves 46 first grade classrooms in Bethlehem, Pennsylvania, and is sponsored by a research grant from the Ford Foundation and directed by Dr. Albert J. Mazurkiewicz of the i/t/a study center at Lehigh University.

Supporters of i/t/a claim that a child using it can learn to read in much less time than those using traditional orthography. The studies have not been in progress for a sufficient length of time, however, to determine if wholesale adoption is justified. There is still the unanswered question of transition to regular print after the initial teaching period and the possible effect upon later spelling and speed of reading.

Sir James Pitman is more than aware of these problems, and warns that the i/t/a method is only in the first stage of a long-term research investigation.

[3] John Downing, *The Initial Teaching Alphabet*. New York: The Macmillan Company, 1964.

THE LINGUISTICS APPROACH [4]

The science of linguistics has aroused much interest in the last few years as a possible aid in improving reading competencies. Linguistics, because it is a complicated science, has resulted in misunderstanding, confusion, and hastily constructed material when applied to reading. The fact remains, however, that its application to reading is evolving.

The contribution of the science of linguistics to reading has come primarily from the descriptive linguists. They believe that, in reading, the child must be able to respond to the language signals as represented by written symbols (words) in the same way that he responds to the patterns of auditory shapes. The key to an understanding of descriptive linguistics is in the concept of "pattern." It is argued that some of our reading failures are due to the obvious differences between the patterns of speech of children and the patterns we ask them to read. Much of the child's reading material is in a pattern that is unreal to him. It is imperative that a child have sentence sense, that is, that he should possess a knowledge of word arrangement and corresponding word function.

At the present time, there is some confusion regarding where to start beginning readers. Some would have the child begin with the smaller units in structural analysis, such as the phoneme (elemental speech sound), morpheme (the smallest unit with a meaning), word, and grapheme (letter symbol for a phoneme). Others would have us start with the simple sentence first. At the present time the concepts in linguistics, as they apply to the development of reading skills, are not well enough defined or established to arouse more than curiosity and a "wait and see" attitude.

SUMMARY

The approaches used in teaching reading are many, and the problem of selecting the approach that will be most successful with all of our children is still solved by an educated trial-and-error method. There is probably no one approach that meets the needs of all. For most students, the basal reader has to be supplemented with more work in study skills, word recognition skills, comprehension skills, or other skill development areas. None of the approaches mentioned solves all the reading problems. The one thing we are sure of, however, is that an eclectic approach, taught by an intelligent teacher, supported by knowledgeable administration, is a prerequisite to good reading instruction.

[4] Carl E. Lefevre, *Linguistics and the Teaching of Reading.* New York: McGraw-Hill Book Company, 1964.

TEACHER DIFFERENCES AND
READING METHOD *

Teaching, among other things, is a series of actions directed toward pupils (2), and the teacher is, first and foremost, a stimulator of pupils.

As a stimulator of pupils, the teacher is dabbling in technique or method. If he is teaching reading, he uses a certain method of teaching. In recent years the teacher has seen debates over method come and go, but from them all have emerged a few basic principles (1):

1. Most children learn to read regardless of the method used. Many different roads can and do eventually lead to reading proficiency.
2. The "best" method for *most* children has both an analytical *and* a synthetic emphasis.
3. Some teachers do not make use of the best that is available, but if the teacher is a good teacher, other factors often pale into insignificance.
4. There are methods or specific teaching approaches that make a world of difference for the individual child. Not all methods work equally well with each individual child.

Principle four suggests that each learner learns according to his own individuality. Education is not simply the pouring in of a glob of information. Education more correctly refers to the internal process of learning. Where the former description emphasizes the stimulus aspects of teaching, those things that the teacher does, the latter emphasizes the organizational aspects, those things that the pupil does. Thus learning always is an individual process. The learner is individual and the criteria for effective teaching vary from individual to individual.

Today's teacher's frame of reference encompasses many aspects, the most agreed upon of which surely is the fact that our teaching needs to be pupil-centered. From this pupil-centered view, it isn't the method *per se* that frequently is the crucial element in teaching. The method must be adapted to the pupil. Unless the method works with this given child, for him it has to be an ineffective method. The teacher must change his technique to fit the learner's response characteristics. He must provide for the development of each learner's unique constellation of characteristics.

---

* REPRINTED from the September, 1965, issue of *Education*. Copyright 1965 by The Bobbs-Merrill Company, Inc., Indianapolis, Indiana.

There is another factor, however, that is just as significant as the method of teaching or pupil differences. Teachers are variable. Differences among teachers are a crucial determinant of the pupil's success in learning to read. Let us look at four key differences.

Knowledge of the Pupil

The effectiveness of the teacher depends to a great degree on his understanding of the pupil whom he wants to teach. This differential in knowledge of the learner quite frequently accounts for the fact that one teacher is successful with a given method and another teacher fails.

Today, we no longer accept the proposition that the response is determined simply by the stimulus, or that reading achievement depends simply on the method. Learning closely parallels and is an expression of the forces of human development generally. Growth and development are variable and so are learning and the child's readiness for learning. A method may work with one child and not with another—and the reason for this has to be found in the differences between the two children, but it also may be found in the teacher's knowledge or awareness of these differences.

To learn to read, a child must be able to make certain responses regardless of the method used. But if the child, because of inadequate sensory or neuromuscular development, cannot make the responses necessary for learning, he cannot learn. A method of teaching reading is adequate only if the child's maturational, experiential, intellectual, neural, physical, social, emotional, motivational, language, and sensory development permit it to be adequate. And a method of teaching is adequate only if the teacher knows enough about the child so that he can adapt the method to the specific child.

Effective learning (and hence effective teaching) commonly does not occur unless the teacher understands the nature of those factors that make for individuality and unless he makes adjustments from them. It is one thing for children to be different and another thing for the teacher to know these differences. The discrepancy between teacher practice in the actual study of pupils as individuals and the potentialities that exist for such study is one of the grave incongruities in education today.

Teacher's Ability and Motivation

There is another variable apart from the learner and the teacher's understanding of the learner that determines the successfulness of a reading method and that differentiates the successful teacher from the unsuccessful one. A method works only if the teacher *can* and *is willing* to use it.

Teacher ability and motivational differences are a crucial factor in pupil success. It is a common experience that teachers with a "novel approach" to teaching reading claim to be unusually successful with their method. It is quite possible that these teachers work harder than the average teacher. They may be both more skillful and more motivated. They are perhaps more interested than the average teacher in the success of their method. They may give more time to their students.

Also, some of the teacher's enthusiasm may rub off on the student. The pupil may be a more motivated student if he perceives himself to be an integral part of an experiment designed to demonstrate that a given method of teaching is better.

The simple fact is that often other factors pale into insignificance when the teacher is an interesting and interested teacher. The pupil commonly does not give attention to a lecture that is "sound and fury signifying nothing" or to a teacher who doesn't have knowledge worthy of the pupil's attention.

ATTITUDE OF THE TEACHER

Experience has shown that a good teacher seems possessed of certain key attitudes. He is acceptant of the student, he respects the individuality of the pupil, he shows understanding and interest, and he has a deep faith in the improvableness of the pupil. In short, it frequently is the attitude of the teacher rather than his method of teaching that is the crucial element in good teaching.

Perhaps a key attitude is the teacher's willingness to change his method to fit the client's response characteristics. We don't give much credence to a physician who seeks to alleviate all ailments with aspirin. Is the aspirin man less scientific than the one-method man in teaching?

Each learner develops in the course of living a response set. Just as a monkey that likes both lettuce and bananas will reject lettuce if he is expecting bananas, so the pupil may reject the method used by the teacher.

Whether a method is the "best" depends not so much on the teacher as on the pupil. Only the pupil will ultimately determine whether the method was successful or not. The pupil is a prime determinant of how effective a given method is or can be. It would thus appear that genuinely pupil-centered teaching means the adaptation of the teaching method to the pupil rather than of the pupil to the method.

Any teacher who proceeds on the assumption that his or her method is the "best" method or the "only" method seems in violation of this principle. The ultimate test of the effectiveness of a method may well be whether or not it helps the pupil to become independent and self-directive in the learning process.

In trying to understand why some methods work with most pupils, it may be interesting to note that clients in counseling seem to conform to the terminology and the theories of the therapist. If the counselor values dreams, the counselee will dream. It may well be that pupils do a better job of adapting themselves to the teacher's methods than the teacher does in adapting the method to the pupil.

THE TEACHER'S MODE OF REACTION

It seems that there is another teacher variable that we have not examined sufficiently. The teacher's mode of reaction may be as significant as the method. Even two equally competent teachers may not be able to use the same method with equal effectiveness. It may be as significant in the education of future teachers that prospective teachers develop competency in method in line with their own experiences and their natural style of responding and communicating. Some teacher, because of his personal makeup, may be able to do a beautiful job with individualized reading; another, because of his personal characteristics, may almost be doomed to failure.

Another area of variability among teachers is the teacher's mode of rewarding correct responses by the pupil. Some teachers reward the pupil's learning by a pat on the shoulder, by giving a star, or by saying a kind word. Other teachers offer themselves as models for imitation.

It may well be that whether a child learns to read or not is not so much a matter of the method of teaching as it is the teacher's mode of "rewarding" the pupil's correct responses. Some pupils react better to a reinforcing teacher; others, to a teacher with whom they can identify and imitate. And some teachers may be more at home reinforcing; others may possess those characteristics that elicit identifying and imitative behavior on the part of the pupil.

Obviously, reading method is not a closed book. Not all of the successful methods have been identified. And, certainly, the individual teacher may not have identified the method that best fits his own response characteristics. Teachers are different and so will be their success with methods of various types.

REFERENCES

1. Dechant, Emerald. *Improving the Teaching of Reading* (Englewood Cliffs: Prentice-Hall, Inc., 1964).
2. Smith, B. Othanel. "A Concept of Teaching." *Teachers College Record*, Vol. 61 (February, 1960), pp. 229–241.

A COMPARISON OF TEN DIFFERENT BEGINNING READING PROGRAMS IN FIRST GRADE *

Emery P. Bliesmer and Betty H. Yarborough

The current reemphasis on the study of initial or beginning reading instruction, the recent revision of several established basal reading series, and the simultaneous publication of several new commercially prepared reading programs prompted the public schools of one Virginia school division to investigate, during the 1963–64 school session, the relative effectiveness of ten approaches to teaching reading in the first grade.

The ten approaches studied differed in numerous ways, such as in suggested teaching materials, instructional techniques, order in which types of word or sound elements were introduced, and administrative procedures (e.g., grouping practices). Nevertheless, analysis of the approaches revealed two basic underlying psychological-pedagogical theories represented among them: 1) Five programs were based upon the belief that the child should be taught whole words and then, through various analytic techniques, recognition of letters and the sounds they represent (hereafter referred to as the *analytic* method); 2) Five approaches were based upon the belief that the child should be taught certain letter-sound relationships or word elements before beginning to read and then be taught to *synthesize* word elements learned into whole words (hereafter referred to as the *synthetic* method).

Analyses of the data resulting from this study indicate that the programs of initial reading instruction based upon one of the methods were more effective in grade one than were those based upon the other.

The major purpose of this investigation was to study and to determine the relative effectiveness of each of ten different approaches or programs for the teaching of beginning reading. The null hypothesis tested was that, other variables being relatively controlled, there would be no differences in mean reading achievement scores of ten groups of first-grade children when each group had been introduced to reading instruction by a different approach.

The pupils involved in this study were from twenty classrooms in four of the twenty elementary schools in the public schools of a suburban Virginia city. A total of 22,227 students were enrolled in the elementary and the high schools of this system at the beginning of the 1963–64 school year. The first-grade enrollment was 2,415 pupils.

---

* REPRINTED by permission of the publisher from *Phi Delta Kappan*, June, 1965, pp. 500–504.

The four schools involved were selected from two adjacent boroughs of the city. The two schools in each borough represented what supervisory, research, and administrative personnel of the school division considered to be relatively comparable socioeconomic environments. Since the socioeconomic level in one borough was what might be considered somewhat typical middle class and the other tended toward a lower level, efforts were made to use each of the ten programs in one classroom in each of the two boroughs. These efforts were successful for nine of the ten programs. Both classes involved in a tenth program, however, were from the lower socioeconomic area.

All of the 596 pupils in twenty of the twenty-one first-grade classes in the four participating schools were initially included in the study. The pupils in each of the four schools were assigned randomly to classes, or teachers, according to the usual practice in those schools. Complete data were obtained for thirty-eight to fifty-four pupils in each program group, or for a total of 484 pupils (248 for the analytic programs, 236 for the synthetic programs). Because the population in the school area is relatively mobile, 112 pupils were lost from the study.

The mean chronological age of the experimental subjects was 79.4 months, with a range by classes of 76.4 to 84.7 months. The mean Language I.Q. (*California Test of Mental Maturity*) was 95.2, with a range by classes of 82.8 to 107.0 The mean Non-Language I.Q. was 98.9, with a range by classes of 92.3 to 107.4. The mean *Metropolitan Readiness Tests* score was 57.5, with a range by classes of 37.2 to 72.0.

No special selection or school placement of teachers was arranged for the study other than that efforts were made to have experimental group teachers who had received ratings of at least "average" from supervisory staff members the previous year and to have no beginning teachers. Because of circumstances beyond the control of school officials, one beginning teacher was included. This teacher, however, was fully qualified in regard to certification and recommendations (and received an "above average" rating from supervisory staff members during the year of the study). The years of teaching experience of the other nineteen teachers ranged from one and one-half to forty-three. All of the teachers were women.

One teacher left the system at the end of March, six weeks before the conclusion of the study. This teacher, however, continued to work in the classroom with her replacement until satisfactory orientation of the new teacher to the reading program in progress was effected.

Eight of the programs studied were the latest (new or revised) programs of various publishers, as follows:

1. (AM)[1]: *ABC Betts Basic Readers* (1963), American Book Company.
2. (EC): *Phonetic Keys to Reading* (1953), Economy Company.

[1] These code designations for specific programs will be used in the remainder of this paper and in Table I.

3. (GI): *Ginn Basic Readers*, Revised (1959), Ginn.

4. (HO): *Reading for Meaning Series*, Third Edition (1963), Houghton Mifflin.

5. (LI): *Basic Reading* (1963), J. B. Lippincott.

6. (MC): *Programmed Reading* (1963), Webster Division, McGraw-Hill.

7. (SC): *The New Basic Readers: Sixties Edition* (1962), Scott, Foresman.

8. (SI): *Structural Reading Series* (1963), L. W. Singer.

In addition to these eight programs, all of which involve commercially prepared materials, the following two programs or approaches were used:

9. (IN): A completely individualized or personalized approach in which many different books were used but no specific set of commercially prepared books or materials was followed.

10. (IS): An individualized approach supplemented with *Reading Laboratory Ia* and *Reading Laboratory I: Word Games*, published by Science Research Associates.

The complete programs of the first eight approaches were used, including *all* accompanying and supplementary materials such as readiness books, workbooks, flash cards, recordings, filmstrips, and the like. One program, SC, also included use of the publisher's entire language arts program for grade one.

Of the five programs representing the analytic method, three are widely used basal reader programs (AM, GI, and SC). Each of these programs helps the pupil develop a small sight vocabulary before individual letters or sounds in words are pointed out. The other two were individualized reading (Nos. 9 and 10 above). It should be pointed out again that the latter two approaches did not employ the use of commercially structured procedures. From the readiness period until the conclusion of the experiment, pupils were provided reading instruction based upon teacher-recognized individual needs. The transfer from the readiness period into formal reading was developed in most cases through each pupil dictating "stories" which were recorded by the teacher and then read by the pupil.

Among the five programs based upon the synthetic method was one widely used basal reader program (HO). One new basal reader program (LI) was also included. The remaining three (EC, MC, and SI) have not been generally regarded as basal reader programs because the materials involved are used primarily in a consumable way. The synthetic programs studied differ markedly as to the order in which the letter-sound relationships are introduced, and all but one of the programs (SI) provides for the teaching of a few sight words; but each program promotes independence in reading by having pupils attack most new words at each stage of development through the synthesizing of word elements previously taught.

The ten approaches differed in the administrative implementation suggested by their authors. Three of the conventional basal programs (AM, GI, and SC) recommend small-group instruction. Two of the analytic programs

(IN and IS) and one of the synthetic programs (MC) were based essentially upon individualized procedures that allow each pupil to progress at his own rate. Some small-group instruction for specific purposes was necessary, however. Four of the five synthetic programs (EC, HO, LI, and SI) encourage the use of whole-class instruction to the extent possible, especially in the pre-reading period during which letter-sound elements are taught. Each of these programs provides ultimately for small-group instruction, however, as the range of pupil achievement widens.

At the beginning of the 1964–65 school year, the principals of the four participating schools "drew" for the reading programs to be used in their respective schools. The teachers in each school were then randomly assigned one of the methods their principal had drawn.

The pupils in this study did not begin working with any of the actual programs until approximately October 1 of the school year. Although the first month of school was spent in developing the pupils' general readiness skills, no specific publisher's reading readiness program was carried out until the experimental programs were begun.

Two general in-service meetings were held in September to acquaint the twenty teachers with the purpose and structure of the study and to establish certain working principles. In addition, the two teachers for each program (except IN and IS) had special extended training or assistance by a consultant from the publisher of their materials. The four teachers using the IN and the IS approaches were assisted by one of the school division's supervisors. In addition, the two teachers using the IS program also met with a representative of Science Research Associates.

Each of the publishers from whom materials for the experiment were secured was invited to maintain consultant services during the course of the experiment. All publishers responded by sending consultants two or three times during the year.

Four elementary supervisors in the school system, the director of reading, and the director of research supervised instruction in the classrooms in which the study was in progress. Teachers were told that no child was to receive more than forty-five minutes of formal reading instruction per day. As far as supervisory personnel could determine, these instructions were followed.

The *Metropolitan Readiness Tests*, Form S, were administered to all experimental subjects in September; the *California Short-Form Test of Mental Maturity* (1957 Edition), Primary, in October; and the *Stanford Achievement Test*, Primary I, Form W, at the end of May.[2]

The criterion measures used to test the null hypothesis were the *Stanford Achievement Test* scores (grade equivalents) obtained for the pupils in May.

---

[2] William Koontz, director of research, Chesapeake Public Schools, assumed major responsibility for the planning of the testing program and the compiling and initial programing of data. Milton Jacobson, Division of Educational Research, University of Virginia, assisted with later analyses and further programing plans.

Scores for the following five subtests were used: Word Reading, Paragraph Meaning, Vocabulary, Spelling, and Word Study Skills.

Analyses of variance revealed significant differences in the control variables of chronological age, language I.Q., non-language I.Q., and total readiness score. Analysis of covariance procedures were then applied to adjust mean criterion scores. Analysis of variance procedures subsequently applied to adjusted criterion scores revealed significant F-ratios for each of the five criterion measures. Further tests of significance were then applied to determine which of possible pairs of treatments had yielded significantly different scores or results.[3]

This study was subject to many of the characteristic limitations of methods studies. The usual cautions with regard to interpreting results and to generalizing should be made. Desirably, this study would have been carried on through grade two and even grade three; but this was not possible for budgetary and administrative reasons which were known before the investigation began. While it is quite possible that differences found among groups at the end of grade one might no longer be found to obtain at the end of grade two or three, this does not invalidate the present results or findings, because it is also quite possible, of course, that differences at the end of grade one might continue to be found at the end of grades two and three.

The adjusted mean criterion scores of each program or treatment group and the differences between adjusted mean criterion scores of various pairs of program groups have been presented in Table I (p. 192). The various reading programs are designated along the top and at the left side of the table, with the code designations which were presented in a previous section. The order of listing of programs, which is the same as that used in initial studies of the data before statistical analyses were performed, happens to be such that the five synthetic program groups are listed first and the five analytic program groups are listed last. Inspection of data presented in Table I will suggest various comparisons and groupings of treatment groups and will reveal some fairly definite patterns or trends.

When the means of the synthetic program groups (HO, LI, SI, EC, MC) are compared with those of the analytic program groups (IN, IS, GI, AM, SC), a great preponderance of differences among means (ninety-two out of 125, or 74 per cent) is found to be significantly in favor of the synthetic group. In only three instances are the obtained differences in favor of the analytic group, and none of these differences is significant at the .01 level. Further study of Table I reveals no instances in which the obtained differences with respect to scores on Word Reading (WR), Word Study Skills (WS), or Spelling (SP) favor the analytic group.

A criticism frequently made of synthetic programs is that the rather close attention given to word elements may lead to inadequate development of

[3] See E. F. Lindquist, *Design and Analysis of Experiments in Psychology and Education.* Boston: Houghton Mifflin Co., 1953. pp. 90–96.

comprehension skills. In the present study, however, there was only one instance (out of twenty-five) in which mean Paragraph Meaning (PM) scores favored an analytic program; and this difference was not significant. Conversely, twenty comparisons reveal all significant differences in favor of synthetic programs. It would appear, therefore, that beginning reading programs which give attention to sound-symbol relationships prior to teaching of words, or which involve a synthetic approach initially (pupils actually building words from sounds), tend to be significantly more productive in terms of specific reading achievement in grade one (as measured by the criterion test) than do analytic reading programs which involve the more conventional approach of going directly from readiness procedures (using pictures) to the reading of whole words before either letter names or the sounds the letters represent are taught.

It is of further interest to note that among corresponding means of the first three synthetic programs (HO, LI, and SI) only one of the fifteen differences is significant, although one program begins with intensive instruction in consonant letter-sound relationships, one with short vowels being taught, and one with consonants and short vowel sounds being taught individually. This suggests that the order of introduction of letter sound elements and/or relationships may not be as important in the success of synthetic programs as that the number of letter-sound relationships taught be sufficient to equip pupils with means for independent decoding of words.

It may also be noted, from further study of Table I, that the differences among the criterion measures of the five analytic approaches were significant in only six instances (out of fifty possibilities). These six significant differences all favored the IN approach, which appears to be more effective than each of the other analytic approaches in developing comprehension skills measured by the Paragraph Reading subtest. There were no significant differences among the other analytic approaches. It would seem, therefore, that methodology, rather than specific programs or materials used, is the more decisive factor in the overall effectiveness of reading instruction in grade one.

The use of data presented in Table I affords many other possible comparisons, and a number of additional inferences may perhaps be made. The study here reported has offered a unique opportunity to compare and analyze "methods" rather than merely or only specific publishers' materials. While a study longer in range and scope would have been desirable, it should be kept in mind that the first grade year is still a really crucial one in the development of foundations for good reading skill and is regarded by many authorities as perhaps the most vital aspect of the entire reading program. Although programs for further analyses are being planned, the preliminary analyses done thus far have been relatively extensive. It is believed that the results obtained in this study have definite pertinence and significance with respect to effectiveness of various approaches to initial reading instruction and validity of theories of methodology represented by these approaches.

TABLE I

Adjusted Mean Criterion Scores, and Differences Among Means, of Various Treatment Groups

PROGRAM GROUPS **		ADJUSTED MEAN SCORES ***	DIFFERENCES AMONG PROGRAM GROUP MEANS								
			LI	SI	EC	MC	IN	IS	GI	AM	SC
(HO)	WR	1.89	−0.21	−0.07	0.19	0.08	0.22*	0.27*	0.43*	0.33*	0.44*
	PM	1.81	−0.17	−0.12	−0.11	−0.06	−0.03	0.21	0.19	0.39*	0.28*
	VO	2.47	0.30	0.54*	−0.10	0.54*	0.58*	0.67*	0.51*	0.72*	0.67*
	SP	2.48	0.17	0.23	0.35*	0.64*	0.74*	0.82*	1.10*	1.01*	0.87*
	WS	2.58	−0.06	−0.09	0.43	0.56*	0.72*	0.71*	0.95*	0.83*	1.11*
(LI)	WR	2.10		0.14	0.40*	0.29*	0.43*	0.48*	0.64*	0.54*	0.65*
	PM	1.98		0.05	0.06	0.11	0.14	0.38*	0.36*	0.56*	0.45*
	VO	2.17		0.24	−0.40*	0.24	0.28	0.37*	0.21	0.42*	0.37*
	SP	2.31		0.06	0.18	0.47*	0.57*	0.65*	0.93*	0.84*	0.70*
	WS	2.64		−0.03	0.49*	0.62*	0.78*	0.77*	1.01*	0.89*	1.17*
(SI)	WR	1.96			0.26*	0.15	0.29*	0.34*	0.50*	0.40*	0.51*
	PM	1.93			0.01	0.06	0.09	0.33*	0.31*	0.51*	0.40*
	VO	1.93			−0.64*	0.00	0.04	0.13	−0.03	0.18	0.13
	SP	2.25			0.12	0.41*	0.51*	0.59*	0.87*	0.78*	0.64*
	WS	2.67			0.52*	0.65*	0.81*	0.80*	1.04*	0.92*	1.20*
(EC)	WR	1.70				0.11	0.03	0.08	0.24*	0.14	0.25*
	PM	1.92				0.05	0.08	0.32*	0.30*	0.50*	0.39*
	VO	2.57				0.64*	0.68*	0.77*	0.61*	0.82*	0.77*
	SP	2.13				0.29	0.39*	0.47*	0.75*	0.66*	0.52*
	WS	2.15				0.13	0.29	0.28	0.52*	0.40	0.68*
(MC)	WR	1.81					0.14	0.19	0.35*	0.25*	0.36*
	PM	1.87					0.03	0.27*	0.25*	0.45*	0.34*
	VO	1.93					0.04	0.13	−0.03	0.18	0.13
	SP	1.84					0.10	0.18	0.46*	0.37*	0.23
	WS	2.02					0.16	0.15	0.39	0.27	0.55*

Program	Test	Mean	IS	GI	AM	SC
(IN)	WR	1.67	0.05	0.21	0.11	0.22*
	PM	1.84	0.24*	0.22*	0.42*	0.31*
	VO	1.89	0.09	-0.07	0.14	0.09
	SP	1.74	0.08	0.36*	0.27	0.13
	WS	1.86	0.01	0.23	0.11	0.39
(IS)	WR	1.62		0.16	0.06	0.17
	PM	1.60		-0.02	0.18	0.07
	VO	1.80		-0.16	0.05	0.00
	SP	1.66		0.28	0.19	0.05
	WS	1.87		0.24	0.12	0.40
(GI)	WR	1.46			-0.10	0.01
	PM	1.62			0.20	0.09
	VO	1.96			0.21	0.16
	SP	1.38			-0.09	-0.23
	WS	1.63			-0.12	0.16
(AM)	WR	1.56				0.11
	PM	1.42				-0.11
	VO	1.75				-0.05
	SP	1.47				-0.14
	WS	1.75				0.28
(SC)	WR	1.45				
	PM	1.53				
	VO	1.80				
	SP	1.61				
	WS	1.47				

** HO : Houghton Mifflin
LI : Lippincott
SI : Singer
EC : Economy
MC : McGraw-Hill
IN : Individualized Completely
IS : Individualized Supplemented
GI : Ginn
AM : American
SC : Scott, Foresman

* Significant at .01 level. Positive differences favor program at left.
*** Stanford Achievement Test Scores (Grade Equiv.)
WR : Word Reading
PM : Paragraph Meaning
VO : Vocabulary
SP : Spelling
WS : Word Study Skills

AN ECLECTIC APPROACH TO READING *

A. Sterl Artley

Not since the days of Flesch and his *Why Johnny Can't Read* has the profession faced an issue that has aroused so much discussion and controversy as individualized reading. Rare is an elementary education journal that has not carried at least several articles dealing with the problem, or a reading conference that has not given over at least one session to an evaluation of this approach to reading instruction. A bibliography of seventy-five recently written articles dealing with the individualized approach appeared in the April, 1960 issue of *The Reading Teacher* (15). Since this bibliography was published many additional articles have appeared. Several carefully prepared evaluations of the method have been printed in the literature (13, 19), while at least three monographs have been published recently dealing exclusively with individualized reading (5, 11, 18).

As one reads dispassionately articles describing the theory behind individualized reading he cannot help noting that a great deal of what is written represents acceptable psychology and pedagogy. Everyone would find acceptable the principle of individuation of growth and the need to have the type and rate of instruction based on the characteristics of the child. For years school people have been exploring methods of instruction and classroom organization that will enable each child to develop to his maximum. Everyone recognizes the potency of reading interest as a factor in motivation. Everyone agrees that children should have a wide variety of material from which to select. All texts in reading methods discuss procedures for organizing individual or small "help" or "needs" groups for children with particular problems or special interests.

THE BASIC ISSUE

What then is the issue? Why all the controversy? Essentially, it appears to be the context in which these accepted principles and practices are placed in individualized reading. They are set off within a framework that puts them in opposition and contradistinction to the manner in which they are applied in a program using basal materials with group instruction.

For example, Jeannette Veatch, a spokesman for individualized reading, shows in chart form what she calls the "salient techniques and principles of

* REPRINTED with the permission of the National Council of Teachers of English and A. Sterl Artley from *Elementary English*, Vol. 38, May, 1961, pp. 320–27.

individualized and ability-grouped reading programs" in respect to materials, classroom organization and procedure, and the effects on the child and his reading (18). In each case she attempts to show that individualized reading is in sharp contrast to an "ability-grouped" approach. She writes:

As can be seen these two methods are sharply divergent on matters of book selection, grouping practices, lesson planning, and teacher-pupil interaction. While some teachers may shift from one program to another at times, the basic philosophy of individualized and ability-grouped reading differ profoundly. The conditions of self-selection, individual conferences, and short-term grouping *must be operative in an individual reading program as here presented* . . . [italics mine] (18, p. 10)

May Lazar (9), a leading proponent of the individualized approach, contends that reading of this type is not synonymous with library, extensive, or recreational reading widely used by many teachers as an adjunct to their basal program. It is, rather, a distinct approach to reading instruction that depends on the child's free selection of a book he wishes to read in relation to his current interests, from which instruction in the competencies is provided on an individual basis as need for a given skill arises. Obviously it denies the place of a sequential program carried on through basal materials used in group situations to promote growth in and through reading.

In other words, individualized reading procedures should not be construed as part of, employed with, nor adapted to an already existing basal program. Theoretically there are no shades of gray between the black and white of individualized reading and a program using basal materials with group instruction. One must be committed to either one program or the other.

EXTREMES IN EDUCATIONAL PRACTICE

Extreme points of view in philosophy and method are not new to education, unfortunately. Pendulums have a characteristic way of swinging to extremes, but denied the motivating power of a mainspring, they eventually swing to a neutral (and more defensible) position. Within the professional lifetime of most of us we have witnessed the extremes of phonics vs. sight words, oral vs. silent reading, experience vs. teacher-directed approach. In each case the extremes were vigorously defended at the time, but eventually the best of each approach was combined into an instructional pattern more effective than either used solely.

What is badly needed at the present time is research that will give us some indication as to what the best features of each approach are and how they may be applied best. We also need to know whether certain features are more applicable to one segment of the school population than to another. Little is to be gained in trying to "prove" the merits of one approach over another by comparing the mean gain of an "experimental" group with that made by a control group following a "traditional" method. Literally any plan, procedure, or technique can be "proved" superior if the researcher and his co-workers are enthusiastic about it. The results of a particular procedure are more likely to be a function of the teacher than of the procedure, *per se*.

AN ECLECTIC APPROACH TO READING INSTRUCTION

The need for an eclectic approach to reading instruction has been stressed by a number of leaders in the profession. After discussing at length the advantages and limitations of various approaches including individualized reading, group basal instruction, as well as several other patterns of grouping for individual differences, the late Dr. William Gray concludes:

In my judgment progress lies not in the adoption of a so-called "single package" solution but in the development of a flexible pattern which utilizes the advantages of both group and individual instruction and the use of both common and diversified materials. (8)

Dr. Emmett Betts writes with respect to the need for a variable approach to individual differences in the light of teacher needs as follows:

. . . Because teachers vary significantly in their administrative abilities, they cannot be regimented into the use of any one plan. Furthermore, the adoption of any one plan does not insure pupil development of interests and skills required for successively higher levels of achievement. (2, p. 145)

Dr. Paul Witty comes to a similar decision with regard to various approaches to reading instruction after an exhaustive and objective analysis of the literature dealing with individualized reading. He concludes:

It seems that a defensible program in reading will combine the best features of both individual and group instruction in reading. The basal text will be used and adopted so as to offer a dependable guide and an efficient plan for insuring the acquisition of basic skills. . . . It is necessary . . . for teachers to select "basal materials" with care and to use them judiciously to meet individual and group needs. Beyond doubt there is a need also for more diverse materials in any worthwhile reading program. (19, p. 450) He continues:
A defensible reading program accordingly recognized the value of systematic instruction, utilization of interests, fulfillment of developmental needs, and the articulation of reading experience with other types of worthwhile activities. By this fourfold approach, steady growth in reading skill is made possible and the attainment of emotional satisfaction may be assured. [19, p. 450]

Dr. Arthur Gates likewise stresses the need for both individual and group procedures in reading instruction. He writes in *The Reading Teacher:*

An open-minded survey of research and of the experience of teachers who have used basal reading programs and the better types of "individualized reading" procedures will enable one to see that the best teaching will combine the good features of both methods. The best work with basal books embodies individualized teaching, and the best "individualized teaching" includes whole class and subgroup activities and the use of materials taken from, or identical in principle with, basal readers and workbooks. . . . We must undertake to discern the good features of each and attempt to embody them into what should be a better system than either. (6)

RESEARCH POINTS THE DIRECTION

Not only do the opinions of respected authorities in the field stress the need for an eclectic approach to reading instruction, but research, as well, points to the same idea. Possibly one of the most carefully controlled studies that has been done in comparing individual and group procedures is that reported by Sartain (14). Five of ten classes of second graders were taught for fifty-six school days by means of an individualized approach, while the other five classes were taught by a program incorporating basal readers as well as an extensive program of voluntary reading. At the end of the first period the teachers who had taught individualized reading changed to the basal program and vice versa. Evaluations of progress were made by means of standardized tests, and appraisals of strengths and weaknesses of the individualized program were secured through teacher judgments.

Sartain's analysis of his findings shows "that the individualized method does not produce better reading gains than a strong basal program. . . ." He found, too, that capable students made approximately the same gains in reading under both methods. He says, however, that because of the efficiency of instruction and provision made through basal materials for systematic growth, both basic and supplementary materials should be retained for the capable as well as the slower pupils.

Sartain also found that one of the strong features of the individual program was the individual conferences with the pupils, developing, as they did, a strong personal relationship between teacher and child. Consequently, he recommends the incorporation of this feature into the basal program. He suggests that the pupils in the top reading groups may be able to acquire the competencies of reading through basal materials used in the morning reading period with individualized reading used in the afternoon. Hence, we see from this carefully controlled study that the basic recommendation is that certain features characteristic of the individualized approach should be incorporated into the structure of a basal reading program.

In a descriptive account of the procedures used in the second grade of one elementary school in Los Angeles, Sharpe (16) found that a combined individualized-basal reading program worked effectively. In order to secure the advantages of a systematic program of reading growth, basal readers were used for part of the week's instruction while an individualized program to promote individual interests was employed for the remainder. In the former program the children worked in groups on word attack, vocabulary building, location and organization skills, comprehension, and critical reading. On the individualized days each child read in a book of his own choice at his own interest and reading level, following the procedures ascribed to this type of program. Although Sharpe is rightly cautious in interpreting the achievement data which she presents as part of the description of her procedure, she does feel that combining opportunities for systematic instruction with free reading and reporting did work well in this particular situation. The literature describes the practices of a number of other teachers who have used an eclectic approach. Quite universally these teachers feel that there are advantages in combining the two approaches so as to capitalize on the best features of each.

Likewise, Stauffer (17) in discussing individualized and group-type directed reading instruction, emphasizes the need to specify the conditions under which both types of programs may operate so that they will complement each other rather than contradict. Stauffer suggests that both procedures be combined in such a way as to allow about half of the time for each. This might be done, he suggests, by using the group approach with basal readers for a week or two, followed by the self-selection approach for a similar period. Whether this is the desirable plan, or whether certain features of the two approaches should be combined within the structure of the existing developmental reading lesson remains to be seen.

Values of Group Basal Instruction

Though research does not give us a definitive answer as to the types of reading growth each procedure best promotes there are some straws in the wind that give some general indications. Dr. Gray in a scholarly analysis of the relative merits of group and individualized teaching, points out with regard to group basal instruction that:

It promotes the development of attitudes and skills which are common to the various reading activities in which children do and should engage in and out of school. It promotes a common background on which teachers can build in promoting added growth in and through reading in all school activities. It utilizes to distinct advantage group dynamics in stimulating interests and motives for reading among pupils who have not yet discovered that reading is a rewarding activity. It promotes breadth and depth of interpretation through discussions in which pupils compare their responses to stimulating problems and pool judgments in reaching sound conclusions (7).

In addition, Gray emphasizes the fact that group basal instruction provides for carefully planned learning experiences in various aspects of reading which are repeated and expanded as the learner progresses from grade to grade. Moreover, these experiences are arranged in such a manner that each builds on previous learnings as well as goes beyond to develop higher levels of skills and broader and deeper understandings. There seems to be little doubt among the authorities that the feature of planned, systematic sequences of learning stand out as one of the preeminent features of a basal program.

Another feature of group instruction that seemingly makes a valuable contribution to reading growth is the opportunity for interaction and reaction over material that the group has read as a common activity. This feature is particularly significant as one goes beyond the skills side of reading and shows concern with reading as a means of promoting changes in attitudes and behavior.

An extensive study of the value of reading experiences in effecting such changes was reported by Brady (4) in a paper presented before one of the University of Chicago Reading Conferences. She found that the ability to derive the author's meaning, to prepare oral and written synopses, and to make reproductions of the author's own words made little contribution to changes in attitudes. However, when the children were given an opportunity to discuss the story with other members of the group under the direction of a discerning teacher; when they were given an opportunity to reveal what they thought, felt, or believed, and to react to the ideas and feelings of others in the group, they began to see implications for their behavior and to give objective evidence of behavior changes. The give and take of ideas among the children seemed to make the difference between knowing about and being affected by. Brady concludes her paper by saying, ". . . every provision should be made in reading programs to assess what students believe, feel, and think. . . ." Certainly this admonition is a potent argument for as much discussion, informal writing, argument, analysis, and problem-solving as possible. It argues, too, for a classroom atmosphere where creative interpretation is welcomed ". . . and where real interest is shown in each person's ideas and opinions." Regardless of the validity of the claim for an individual approach as a means of promoting growth in skills, the fact cannot be ignored that if a reading program is responsible for promoting growth through reading, we must give the reader an opportunity to express his ideas and feelings and to challenge and be challenged by those of others. This kind of activity can take place best within the context of a group situation.

There are indications, too, that pupils of different levels of capacity and ability may profit from different amounts of group and individual instruction. As early as 1925, Zirbes, Keelor, and Miner (20) reported a study carried on in two second grade classes where one group engaged in a program of basal instruction while the other was instructed through a program that today would have many aspects of individualized reading. Though the study reports that the average growth was practically the same for both groups, an analysis of the results according to levels of reading ability showed that above-average readers who were exposed to the program of intensive individual silent reading made more progress than the upper half of the grouping having group instruction. In contrast, the lower half of the group having the informal program made less progress than the pupils in the lower half having systematic instruction.

Sartain's study (14), referred to earlier, confirmed in some degree that of Zirbes. He found that the slower pupils tended to make better gains in vocabulary where the basal materials were employed. Capable students, he found, made approximately the same gains under both methods. These two studies as well as others not referred to here give promising leads to fruitful areas of research.

VALUES OF INDIVIDUAL INSTRUCTION

On the other hand, Gray (7) pointed out that individualized instruction has certain desirable features. It makes possible the application of word-attack and comprehension skills on an independent basis. It gives the reader an opportunity to select materials in terms of his own interests. "It thus utilizes the personal motives of each child for reading, capitalizes on inner drives and reinforces the idea that reading is a rewarding activity." Gray added that through individual activity the teacher is afforded an opportunity to study the reading interests and habits of each child, and to provide immediate help if needed. At other times, he adds, the teacher should "confer at length with individuals to help identify their problems or difficulties more fully, to stimulate deeper interests in reading, and to encourage reading in areas previously neglected."

TEACHER-PUPIL INTERACTION

The feature of teacher-pupil interaction referred to by Dr. Gray above seems to be a highly important feature of reading instruction. Through conferences the teacher has the opportunity to assess the child's attitude toward reading, to note whether it is eager, defensive, or bored. Through tests, sociometric appraisals, and parent conferences she is better able to understand his ambitions, his feelings, and his frustrations. Both the teacher and the pupil come to know each other as persons, and to establish an understanding and a feeling of rapport, factors that are coming to be recognized more and more as extremely conducive to school learning. In fact, careful research might well show that the close teacher-pupil relationship making for feelings of self-worth, importance, and success is one of the major features contributing to the success of individualized reading.

Suggestions of this as a possibility are found in several studies showing a direct relation between a teacher's understanding of a pupil's behavior, and his academic achievement and school behavior. The first is a study of Ojemann and Wilkinson (12) who found that children comprising an experimental group in which the teacher had made a comprehensive study of their attitudes, motives, and environmental conditions, thereby coming to know them better as people, made significantly higher academic achievement over children comprising a control group. Moreover, this gain accrued even though the teachers were unaware of the fact that academic achievement was to be used as a measure of comparison.

The second study was reported by Martin (10) who attempted to show the effectiveness of certain types of guidance activities on the adjustment and achievement of fifth-grade children. In one of his experimental groups considerable time was given to small-group and individual counseling sessions. Stimulus stories were used as a basis for discussing attitudes and feelings. The teacher and counselor came to know these children better as individuals and to understand the factors that motivated their behavior. After ten weeks of this type of activity the experimental group showed gains over those made by a control group of 4.2 months in reading, 7.2 months in language, and 8.7 months in arithmetic. Particularly striking, too, is the fact that these academic gains were made even though the teacher made no basic change in her teaching procedure, nor was aware during the time the study was in progress that academic achievement was to be considered in the final evaluation.

Both of these studies seem to indicate that as teachers came to know their pupils better as individual personalities, they became more effective guides to learning; and as the children themselves increased in personal-social adjustment there was a concomitant increase in academic achievement. Though these studies relate only indirectly to the individualized *vs.* group teaching controversy, the implication remains that over-all achievement appears to increase as teachers come to understand their children better. Again it should be pointed out that improved understandings growing out of a closer pupil-teacher relationship are not the exclusive outcome of an individualized approach. Individual and small-group conferences may be just as much a part of a program using basal readers and group procedures as one using trade books and individualized procedures.

Sartain (14) makes this same point in discussing the results of the Roseville experiment. He feels also that the individual conference establishes a valuable relationship between teacher and pupil which contributes to better adjustment and achievement. He recommends that it be incorporated as part of the technique of sharing and reading supplementary materials. He says, ". . . There is no reason to forfeit the advantages of a well-planned basic system. Instead, the benefits of the individual conferences should be obtained by their addition to the basic reader plan."

Conclusion

On the basis of the judgment and opinion of qualified leaders in the field, along with the findings of a growing body of research, there seems to be no valid reason for concluding that one must make a choice between individualized reading and a group approach using basal materials. Rather, the wise procedure would be to combine and adapt the best features of each into a pattern that adequately serves the needs of the learner. At times this will involve group procedures, at other times, individual.

BIBLIOGRAPHY

1. Bartky, John, "The Nature of Teaching Method," *The Elementary School Journal*, 58:199–203, Jan., 1958.
2. Betts, Emmett A., "The Place of Basic Reading Instruction in Relation to the Total Curriculum," in *New Frontiers in Reading* (J. Allen Figurel, ed.) Conference Proceedings of International Reading Association, N. Y.: Scholastic Magazines, 1960.
3. Bohnhorst, Ben, and Sophia Sellars, "Individual Reading vs. Textbook Instruction," *Elementary English*, 36:185–190, 202, March, 1959.
4. Brady, Elizabeth, "Problems of Interpretation When the Purpose Is to Modify Attitudes and Behavior," in *Promoting Growth Toward Maturity in Interpreting What To Read* (W. S. Gray, ed.) Supplementary Educational Monographs, No. 74, Chicago: University of Chicago Press, 1951.
5. Darrow, Helen, and Virgil Howes, *Approaches to Individualized Reading*, N. Y.: Appleton-Century-Crofts, 1960.
6. Gates, Arthur I., "Improvements in Reading in the Near Future," *The Reading Teacher*, 12:83–88, December, 1958.
7. Gray, William S., "Role of Group and Individualized Teaching in a Sound Reading Program," *The Reading Teacher*, 11:99–104, December, 1957.
8. ——, "The Role of Group and Individual Instruction in Reading," in *Meeting Individual Needs Through Reading*, Proceedings of The Third Annual Conference Sacramento State College Council IRA, Sacramento: Sacramento State College Council, IRA, 1958.
9. Lazar, May, "Individualized Reading: A Dynamic Approach," *The Reading Teacher*, 11:95–98, December, 1957.
10. Martin, Lynn, *A Study of the Effect of Selected Guidance Activities Upon Elementary School Children*, Unpublished Doctoral Dissertation, University of Missouri, 1959.
11. Miel, Alice, ed. *Individualized Reading Practices*, Practical Suggestions for Teaching, No. 14. N. Y.: Teachers College, Columbia University, 1958.
12. Ojemann, Ralph, and Frances Wilkinson, "The Effect on Pupil Growth of an Increase in Teacher's Understanding of Pupil Behavior," *The Child: A Book of Readings* (Jerome Seidman, ed.) N. Y.: Rinehart, 1958.
13. Robinson, Helen, "News and Comment: Individualized Reading," *The Elementary School Journal*, 60:411–420, May, 1960.
14. Sartain, Harry, "The Roseville Experiment with Individualized Reading," *The Reading Teacher*, 13:277–281, April, 1960.
15. ——, "A Bibliography on Individualized Reading," *The Reading Teacher*, 13:262–265, 270, April, 1960.
16. Sharpe, Maida, "An Individualized Reading Program," *Elementary English*, 35:507–512, December, 1958.

17. Stauffer, Russell, "Individualized and Group Type Directed Reading Instruction," *Elementary English*, 37:375–382, October, 1960.
18. Veatch, Jeannette, *Individualizing Your Reading Program*, N. Y.: Putnam's Sons, 1959.
19. Witty, Paul, "Individualized Reading—A Summary and Evaluation," *Elementary English*, 36:401–412, 450, October, 1959.
20. Zirbes, Laura, Katherine Keelor, and Pauline Miner, *Practice Exercises and Checks on Silent Reading in the Primary Grades*, N. Y.: Lincoln School of Teachers College, Columbia University, 1925.

A. Individualized Reading

A PERSONALIZED READING PROGRAM *

Walter B. Barbe

The teaching of reading is far different today from what it was only a few years ago. Public awareness of the importance of education and government support have contributed to more and better materials, a wider variety of methods of teaching reading, and more careful attention to the outcomes of instruction (1). Disagreement over how reading should be taught no longer is directed primarily toward which method, rather than upon such factors as when to begin and to what degree the methods should be used.

Personalized reading (2) is a classroom organizational pattern which allows a creative teacher the flexibility to use those techniques and materials which are needed at any particular time. The personalized program differs from individualized reading in that the rigid rules applied by some in individualized reading need not be followed. For example, basal readers may be used in the personalized program for the specific purpose of teaching a particular skill, although it is not likely that children will methodically go through a basal reader page by page, and attention will be given to sequential development of skills both in small groups and in total class group instruction.

A personalized reading program incorporates the conference technique, used successfully in many individualized programs, without abandoning the gains made by the use of grouping in order to teach particular skills. The basic premise of the developmental program, that children are provided with interesting material and are taught at their level, is not violated in the per-

---

* REPRINTED from the September, 1966, issue of *Education*. Copyright 1966 by The Bobbs-Merrill Company, Inc., Indianapolis, Indiana.

sonalized program. As a classroom organizational pattern, the personalized program offers the teacher the opportunity to utilize the techniques which she feels are most helpful to each individual child. The language experience approach operates in the personalized program most effectively.

PHILOSOPHY OF PERSONALIZED READING

The essential part of the personalized reading program is that it allows for flexibility. Rather than state that every child must cover certain materials, or learn certain skills, a personalized program establishes no such rigid goals of learning. The key to a successful program is the teacher, not the method.

The personalized program allows the teacher great enough flexibility so that she can use those skills which she knows in order to teach reading most effectively. But at the same time the program is flexible enough to allow her to change methods and materials, and even to shift goals, if during the school year any one child or group of children is not making progress.

The elements of self-selection and self-pacing are essential to a personalized program. Opportunity is offered in the personalized program for the child to select for himself those materials from which he will learn. There are times when for a specific reason a teacher will assign particular material, but such an assignment is never made for a prolonged period so that the children become classified by the book from which they are reading. Self-pacing allows for goals to be set individually, rather than by some preconceived notion that each child should "finish the book" by the end of the year.

The goal of reading instruction in any program, of course, is to develop permanent interest and skills in reading. Only if our program succeeds in developing within children the desire to continue reading, and provides them with the skills to become ever better readers, can it be called successful. A personalized program, as all other programs, has intermediary goals, but the final goal of developing permanent interests and skills is more easily remembered when rigid intermediary goals are not established.

As Witty has stated, "Our aim should be to help pupils become skillful, self-reliant, and independent readers who will continue to enrich their understandings and satisfactions throughout their lives by reading" (3).

CLASSROOM ORGANIZATION

A personalized reading program can best be initiated at the beginning of the first grade. There is mounting evidence that the program is equally applicable to the junior and senior high schools.

Beginning with a language-experience approach in the first grade (4) the program moves from the experience charts and stories developed by the children to printed material in children's magazines and books. Materials such as the *Little Owl Series* (5) are effective at this level. The children select the material for themselves from a classroom library, which in no way replaces the need for a school library but, instead, enhances the children's interest in reading and in the use of the central library.

Beginning in the first grade with very short periods of time, and becoming longer and somewhat more formally organized in the higher elementary grades, conferences are scheduled and held with each child. At the time of the conference the teacher discusses with the child material which he has been selecting, gives direction if he has been choosing material of too difficult a level or material which is too easy, and checks his comprehension and skill development

The conference period in the personalized program is not used for instruction in skills, other than in an incidental way. Formal, sequential skill development is planned in a personalized program. Skills are taught generally in small groups, in total class groups or to individuals, at times other than the conference time. This instruction may be from material in the basal reader or any other source.

The teacher keeps a record of the materials which the child has read. The personalized program, as the individualized program, can become overly burdened with teacher-kept records. Having the children keep a record of the books which they have read, and showing them to a teacher at the time of each conference, eliminates much of this problem. The use of some kind of skills check list (6) also makes it possible for the teacher to more easily keep track of skill development, as well as be reminded of the sequence of skill learning so that it is not overlooked.

EVALUATION OF PROGRAMS

Sartain (7) has summarized the research on individualized reading. He concluded that individualized reading:

1. Can be somewhat successful under certain circumstances.
2. Successful teaching in individualized reading requires especially competent teachers.
3. Less capable pupils are less likely to achieve success in the individualized situation.
4. Children read more books under the plan of self-selection with individualized instruction.
5. The personal conference between the pupil and the teacher is of particular value.
6. Individualized reading does not allow adequate time for the setting of thought-provoking purposes for reading, nor for the introduction of new vocabulary.
7. The lack of a planned sequential skills program makes teachers uneasy about a wholly individualized organization.
8. Teachers using a wholly individualized approach are constantly pressed for time to provide the conferences that pupils need.

A personalized reading program suffers from many of these same problems, as indeed so does the basal program, but by being more flexible in terms of materials which can be used (i.e. basal texts and children's magazines, as well as library material) and providing for a sequential skills program, some of the problems of the individualized program may be overcome. Clearly, children do read more books under the individualized and personalized program, like reading better, and the teacher is freer to do those things which she knows will be helpful to individual children.

As has been stated: "We should encourage every teacher to become the best teacher she can be. The methods which she uses should free her to do the best possible job, rather than limit her effectiveness" (1). A personalized reading program offers a classroom organization which allows the well-trained and dedicated teacher the flexibility necessary to provide effective reading instruction for each child.

REFERENCES

1. Editorial, "Is There a Best Method for Teaching Reading?" *Highlights for Teachers*, No. 1 (Sept., 1965), pp. 1–3.
2. Barbe, Walter B., *Educator's Guide to Personalized Reading Instruction* (Englewood Cliffs, N.J.: Prentice-Hall, Inc., 1961).
3. Witty, Paul A., "Individualized Reading: A Postscript," *Elementary English*, Vol. 41, No. 3 (March, 1964), p. 217.
4. Lee, Dorris M. and Allen, R. V., *Learning to Read Through Experience* (2nd ed.) (New York: Appleton-Century-Crofts, 1963).
5. Martin, Bill, Jr. (editor), *Little Owl Series* (New York: Holt, Rinehart and Winston, Inc., 1964–65).
6. *Reading Skills Check Lists* (3124 Harriett Road, Cuyahoga Falls, Ohio).
7. Sartain, Harry W., "Research on Individualized Reading," *Education*, Vol. 81, No. 9 (May, 1961), pp. 515–20, reprinted in Walter B. Barbe (editor), *Teaching Reading: Selected Materials* (Oxford University Press, 1965), pp. 378–83.

INDIVIDUALIZED READING—A SYMBOL
FOR CHANGE *

Edith H. Grotberg

Continued interest in individualized reading is impressive, especially since three facts tend to refute it as a system. (1) Research findings consistently fail to demonstrate any definitive advantage of individualized reading in

* REPRINTED from the September, 1966, issue of *Education*. Copyright 1966 by The Bobbs-Merrill Company, Inc., Indianapolis, Indiana.

terms of reading gains made by pupils. (2) Agreement has not been reached by advocates of individualized reading as to what the system is or which method is to be used for teaching it. And (3) the assumptions basic to the individualized reading system or philosophy are untenable in light of available knowledge.

Since some teachers continue to adopt individualized reading and defend the system strongly, it is particularly important to look to the teacher as a major factor in determining why an apparently indefensible system is adopted.

The present article attempts to discuss the three facts and to explore what evidence there is which may shed light on why some teachers are interested in and committed to individualized reading.

RESEARCH FINDINGS NOT SIGNIFICANT

The proving ground for the claims of any reading system must be the classroom. Do children learn to read better in one system as compared to another? Research evidence for individualized reading is generally nonsupportive of the notion that children learn to read better in this system.

Outstanding persons in the reading field began to ask for research evidence as soon as individualized reading appeared as a system in the mid-fifties. In 1958 William S. Gray stated that because of "the recent development and limited use of individualized reading programs a corresponding body of evidence has not yet accumulated concerning its success" (5, p. 5). In 1959 Paul A. Witty observed that "available experimental data do not justify the recommendation of sole dependence on individualized reading" (19, p. 412). In 1960 Harry W. Sartain concluded that since carefully controlled studies show "the individualized method does not produce better reading gains than a strong basal program, there is no reason to forfeit the advantages of a well-planned basal system" (16, p. 277).

In 1962 Edith H. Grotberg stated, "The individualized reading program has yet to demonstrate its superiority over the basal reading program or the developmental reading program" (7, p. 24). Again, in 1962, Yvonne M. Lofthouse stated, after an examination of significant research, "Sufficient research data are definitely not yet available to warrant the changing of school systems from the traditional to the individualized reading approach" (12, p. 37).

Patrick Groff (6), in 1964, presented brief abstracts of thirty-two studies involving individualized reading, twenty-two of which compared individualized reading with ability grouping approaches to teaching reading. While the studies were largely for master or doctor degree requirements, the pattern of findings was clear: a few studies provided evidence that children make greater gains in reading in the individualized approach; a few studies support the ability grouping approach; the vast majority of cases, however, indicated no significant differences in reading gains when comparing the individualized and the ability grouping approaches.

Obviously we cannot look to research evidence to explain the extensive interest in and enthusiasm for individualized reading. The system produces no better results than other systems, and it produces no worse results than other systems.

MANY MEANINGS AND METHODS

What is individualized reading? Is it a basic reading program? Does it have a consistent methodology? Advocates of individualized reading have difficulty defining their special way of teaching in the classroom.

May Lazar, for example, stated, "Individualized reading is not subordinate to or an adjunct of the basic reading program—*it is the basic program*" (11, p. 198). Other supporters of individualized reading, however, have found combining a basal reading program with individualized reading is preferable (3, 10, 14, 17).

There is confusion in methodology, too. Jeannette Veatch suggests that specific methods which characterize all individualized reading include:

1. Self-selection of material by pupils for their own instruction
2. Individual conferences between each pupil and teacher
3. Groups organized for other than reasons of ability or proficiency in reading (18, p. ix).

However, Leland Jacobs states:

In the first place, "individualized reading" is not a single method with predetermined steps in procedure to be followed. It is not possible to say that every teacher who would individualize guidance in reading must do this or that. It is not feasible or desirable to present a simple, single methodological formulation of what is right in "individualized reading" which every teacher shall follow (9, p. 167).

Further, Albert Harris (8) suggested a carefully controlled sequence of books for early reading and Ruth Crossley and Mildred Kniley (2) recommended grouping when class size becomes large.

Again, a divergence of opinion exists among advocates of individualized reading on methods of teaching it.

UNTENABLE BASIC ASSUMPTIONS

Seeking, self-selection, and pacing are basic characteristics of individualized reading. In addition, teacher-pupil conferences, flexible grouping, teacher and pupil record keeping are found in most individualized reading programs. These characteristics and their underlying assumptions need examination.

Veatch makes the following claim for the traits of seeking, self-selection, and pacing:

The traits of seeking, self-selection, and pacing are inborn characteristics of men and animals. When creatures explore their surroundings they exhibit seeking behavior. When they take something from that environment to promote their own growth, they show the process of self-selection. When they use whatever has been selected, they pace the consumption at the proper rate for their own development. Examples of these traits can be cited at any level of the animal world (18, p. 7.)

These claims stem from Willard Olson's (13) principles of seeking, self-selection, and pacing. The only research evidence for such behavior is at a physiological food intake level for animals and human infants. There is some evidence that animals and human infants will select the proper food for their physical survival. To leap from this physiological behavioral phenomenon to the intellectual, emotional, social as well as physiological behavior involved in learning to read, requires an incredible kind of mental gymnastics that is completely unsubstantiated by research or, indeed, that is logically defensible.

One significant piece of research has been conducted by Robert Emans to determine the ability of trained teachers to "individualize" or "tailor-make" reading programs from needs of pupils determined during teacher-pupil conferences. He consistently found that teachers could not determine these needs as well as a diagnostic test could and, further, that the teachers "had some predetermined bias which influenced their judgments of the skills on which their pupils needed help" (4, p. 260).

No significant gains have been reported in the literature as a result of any special as compared to traditional type of grouping. Clearly, the basic characteristics of individualized reading and their underlying assumptions cannot be defended by research or present knowledge; rather, they are generally refuted.

LOOK TO THE TEACHER

In spite of the limitations and ambiguities of individualized reading, some teachers continue to adopt it as a desirable philosophy and method. It seems necessary, therefore, to look to the teacher to explain such approval and adoption.

No systematic study has appeared concerning the attitudes of teachers toward individualized reading. However, Witty (20, p. 211) observed the sense of freedom teachers feel who adopt individualized reading as compared to a basal program, and Sartain (15, p. 263) noted the enthusiasm teachers feel for the experimental approach of individualized reading. The appeal of individualized reading may well be a teacher appeal rather than a pupil appeal. Yet little attention is given to the teacher when reading systems are designed or tested. Even the present national study, financed by the U.S. Office of Education and directed by Guy Bond, compared reading systems only and neglected the important interaction between a teacher and a system as such interaction affects children's learning.

Examining more closely the appeal to some teachers of individualized reading, the factor of change seems important. Many teachers wish to bring about changes in their teaching as they feel such changes may improve pupil learning. Most school systems, however, have restrictions on change if it disturbs academic articulation from grade to grade or if it alters the overall educational goals of the school system.

Individualized reading lends itself admirably to effecting changes in the classroom without requiring special permission from the administration. No special materials are needed and no special equipment must be purchased.

Henry Brickell (1), reporting on an exhaustive study of agents for educational change, stressed the fact that while administrators are agents for educational change of major scope, the classroom teacher, so long as he remains inside his classroom, exerts almost total control. His control permits him to make changes in classroom practice and in relocating existing curriculum content.

Summary

In summary, then, individualized reading appeals to some teachers who wish to make changes in classroom practice and who, by nature of their extensive control within the classroom, are able to adopt individualized reading without requiring permission.

Lack of research support, lack of agreement on what individualized reading is or what method is used for teaching it, and lack of evidence to justify the underlying assumptions of the system, do not seem to detract greatly from the adoption of individualized reading by some teachers. These very lacks and inconsistencies may help to highlight the appeal of individualized reading.

The appeal seems to be in the area of change. Many teachers desire changes in the teacher-learning interaction. Under the umbrella of individualized reading various changes may take place without requiring major changes in the school system.

REFERENCES

1. Brickell, Henry, *Organizing New York State for Educational Change* (Albany, New York: State Department of Education, 1961).
2. Crossley, Ruth and Mildred Kniley, "An Individualized Reading Program," *Elementary English*, Vol. 36 (January, 1959), pp. 16–20.
3. Daniel, Mary Ann, "You Can Individualize Your Reading Program, Too," *Elementary English*, Vol. 33 (November, 1956), pp. 444–446.
4. Emas, Robert. "Teacher Evaluations of Reading Skills and Individualized Reading," *Elementary English*, Vol. 42 (March, 1965), pp. 258–260.
5. Gray, William S. "The Role of Group and Individual Instruction in Reading," *Third Annual Reading Conference Proceedings*, Sacramento, California: Sacramento State College Council, International Reading Association 1 (March 1, 1958).
6. Groff, Patrick. "Comparisons of Individualized and Ability Grouping Approaches to Teaching Reading: A Supplement," *Elementary English*, Vol. 41 (March, 1964), pp. 238–241.

7. Grotberg, Edith H. "Individualized Reading—What the Literature Says," Chicago Area Reading Association of the International Reading Association, *Report of Proceedings*, May 19, 1962, pp. 13–36.

8. Harris, Albert J. *How to Increase Reading Ability* (New York: Longmans, Green, 1956), pp. 116–121.

9. Jacobs, Leland. "Individualized Reading Is Not a Thing," in *Individualized Reading Practices*, edited by Alice Miel (New York: Bureau of Publications, Teachers College, Columbia University, 1958).

10. Kirby, M. "Tête-à tête Lessons Develop Independent Readers," *Elementary English*, Vol. 34 (May, 1957), pp. 302–303.

11. Lazar, May. "Individualized Reading: A Program of Seeking, Self-Selections, & Pacing," Chapter 15 in Jeannette Veatch, *Individualizing Your Reading Program* (New York: G. P. Putnam's Sons, 1959).

12. Lofthouse, Yvonne M. "Individualized Reading: Significant Research," *The Reading Teacher*, Vol. 16 (September, 1962), pp. 35–37, 47.

13. Olson, Willard C. "Seeking, Self-Selection and Pacing in Use of Books by Children," *The Packet* (Boston: D. C. Heath and Company, Spring, 1952), pp. 3–10.

14. Row, Ruth and Esther Aoomhoefer. "Individualized Reading," *Childhood Education*, Vol. 34 (November, 1957), pp. 118–122.

15. Sartain, Harry W. "A Bibliography on Individualized Reading," *The Reading Teacher*, Vol. 13 (April, 1960), pp. 262–265, 270.

16. ——, "The Roseville Experiment with Individualized Reading," *The Reading Teacher*, Vol. 13 (April, 1960), pp. 277–281.

17. Sharpe, Maida Wood. "An Individualized Reading Program," *Elementary English*, Vol. 35 (December, 1958), 507–512.

18. Veatch Jeannette. *Individualizing Your Reading Program* (New York: G. P. Putnam's Sons, 1959).

19. Witty, Paul. "Individualized Reading—A Summary and Evaluation," *Elementary English*, Vol. 36 (October, 1959), pp. 401–412, 450.

20. ——, "Individualized Reading: A Postscript," *Elementary English*, Vol. 41 (March, 1964), pp. 211–217.

STRUCTURE IN THE READING PROGRAM [*]

Jeannette Veatch

The instructional reading program must, above all, enable each pupil to adapt his reading to his own purposes, his own ability, his own speed. No matter how different the teaching styles of this teacher or that teacher, there

[*] REPRINTED with the permission of the National Council of Teachers of English and Jeannette Veatch, from *Elementary English*, Vol. 44, No. 3, pp. 252–56, March, 1967.

are certain characteristics, or certain operations, that must occur or the instruction will not allow for this essential individuality. These central characteristics, again regardless of teaching style differences, seem to me to include at least the following:

1. Self-choice of the majority of instructional materials.
2. The central role of children's normal speech patterns.
3. The central role of a variety of genuinely literary materials, particularly trade books.
4. The meeting of individual differences, purposes, and interests through individual conferences.
5. Efficient classroom management through groups organized upon identified tasks.

These are the elements, I submit, that give structure to the reading program. They certainly give structure to this reading program that I am about to describe. Without these salient elements, there would be little or no individuality possible.

What, then, do these five points do to guarantee that individual differences are truly met? In what way do they operate? Let us begin with the first, Pupil Choice of Material.

PUPIL CHOICE OF MATERIAL

Self-selection of material, or free choice on the part of the student as to what he is to read for his instructional program eliminates or markedly reduces four major problems commonly found in traditional reading programs; namely:

1. The problem of motivation.
2. The problem of reading readiness.
3. The problem of individual difference—regardless of degree.
4. The problem of skill teaching.

Looking at these, one at a time, we can see how such a practice eases the teachers' problems.

MOTIVATION

Self-selection, with rare exception, is a guarantee of a royal road to reading interest. Given enough books, homemade or published commercially, children need little incentive to read. Fitting a supply of books to a given class is a simple enough operation, and the fit is what guarantees that the pupils devour the pages therein. No need for the teacher to spend ten to fifteen minutes "developing interest." As the teacher has not decided what it is that each child is to read, there is no need for the teacher to persuade the pupils to be interested in whatever they are to read.

Most teachers welcome the peace and quiet of the library period. Such periods are quiet and peaceful because the children choose their own materials. This can happen every day during the regular reading period and independent work time.

READINESS

When children choose their own books, and are frequently checked on those choices, there is little need to worry about whether or not they are ready for what they have chosen. The current vast emphasis on reading readiness is unnecessary when the element of choice acts as a safeguard, as it moves to have each child find the right book *for him* at the right time.

On the contrary, when teachers do all the choosing of the instructional material, they must, of necessity, be vitally concerned with guessing about readiness. When the child chooses from a wide *enough* range of books to meet the ability spread, and the personal interest of all the children of the given class, they choose that for which they are ready.

INDIVIDUAL DIFFERENCES

When each child is reading a different book for his reading time, individual differences are met even if one is reading a second-grade book, and another a tenth-grade book. This is not to say that there are not times when several children might choose to read the same story, with encouragement, even assistance from their teacher, but this does not change the picture. Which children would choose to read together? Probably those that had a common interest in the story—or in a project connected to the material. I recall three boys who were three full grades apart as to reading level, working on an electro-magnet, following directions. They all read—and when stuck, the best one took over.

It seems to me that the uproar about separating children on ability bases, with what must undoubtedly be vicious psychological results, is made unnecessary. Children know who are the best readers. But it is not harmful knowledge. There are groups, as I will describe. But they are useful, healthy groups. The structure of a reading program must have groups.

Most important of all, though, is that the practice of each child reading his own book provides sensible justification for an individual conference. There is no substitute for one-to-one relationship in a teaching situation. Mark Hopkins on the end of the log may be an exaggerated myth, but it is marvelous education. If we are to accept the proven fact that each one of us is different, then we must accept the fact that the best way to meet differences is to teach them individually.

SKILL TEACHING

The sins committed in the name of skill teaching are legion, as we all know. This is so because children have not committed themselves to whatever it is they are reading—but have allowed themselves to be committed, to be made interested in what they are reading, by their teacher. Under these conditions children make more mistakes than if they had done their own choosing. We all know that when we are not "sold" on something we must do, the task becomes a long, hard chore. Of course, some school teachers are convinced that children will come to no good end unless they are made to do something *hard*—something distasteful—something *painful*—every morning at 9:30 a.m. This is the old Puritan ethic and it is nonsense. Long ago psychologists found that pain is so distasteful that a living organism forgets it—and then goes about making the same mistake over again. We remember pleasure—not pain.

When children are reading what they themselves have personally chosen, the meaning of the story brings the use of context into its full glory. Children do not need to examine every word, in all those numbers of ways described in reading texts. There are skills to be taught in reading, to be sure. But self-selection vastly reduces them. More importantly, it places the word analysis skills where they should have been all the time—in the field of written composition.

The central issue of structure, as I see it, is what Arthur Heileman calls the ego involvement of the learner. Do children learn to read earlier, easier, faster, and better when their own lives, emotions, feelings, and experiences are used in the teaching? Or do children learn to read best from materials unrelated to their own personal individual existence, however simplified, systematized, and presented?

There is a loose progression in learning to read, of course. But this progression is within each child. I cannot believe it to be in a set of inanimate materials. Teachers must be aware of general development and know the symptoms or signals of forward motion. Teachers must know what to do when delays and regressions occur. Teachers must fit a variety of activities to a variety of children. For teachers to depend on directions in a manual is to deny the obvious fact that the manual has no knowledge of the children in any specific class.

The elements of these progressions, then, are structure. Children must know when they know. They must recognize when they know it. Personally, I feel that such structure can be described, in package form, perhaps, by beginning with something like Sylvia Ashton-Warner's Key Vocabulary, with a bit of the John Day Company's *Urban Studies* and Holt, Rinehart and Winston's *Little Owls* mixed in, plus a big dose of Lee and Van Allen's ideas on the language experience approach, and on into the more advanced levels of reading on the practices commonly assigned to the label "individualized reading."

BEGINNING TO READ

Sylvia Ashton-Warner [1] starts her Maori Infant Reading with what she calls the Key Vocabulary, really sight vocabulary of the children's own words that they say. (One American teacher that I know calls them "said" words.) They are powerfully important to the child who says them. As the length of word has no relation to its power content, she has given us a unique practice not to be found in any text on the teaching of reading in this country.

Shades of sight vocabulary that, we have thought, must be learned by drill, reward, and punishment! Shades of "come," "look," and "see" and "here," "down," "up." One Master's project at Jersey City State College revealed that "come," "look," and "see" occurred only 48 times out of 4,862 words when one month's *spontaneous* writing of first graders was analyzed.[2]

I have tried the Key Vocabulary process many times. In demonstrations in California, Maryland, New Jersey, and even bilingual Quebec Province, I have invariably been given "ghost," "monster," and "gorilla." Child after child will want, as his favorite word, the name of his kitten, or his dog, or something he wants very much. One wanted (age 5) the words "first grade." These and many more are printed on large tough cards, as suggested by Ashton-Warner. Never have I had to repeat such words to the child who gave them. "One-look" words. No Drill. No reinforcement. The reward is in the child's own mind. He is consumed with unnameable fears. He enjoys highly nameable loves. This process of using personal words is an element of structure. Such words are the simplest, most easily learned, of all sight vocabulary.

Lee and Van Allen [3] work also to provide an element for the continuum of reading instruction. They say in part:

1. What a child thinks about he can talk about.
2. What he can talk about can be expressed in painting, writing, or some other form.
3. Anything he writes can be read (*i.e.*, by some one).
4. He can read what he writes and what other people write, *etc.*

There are some publishers who are providing instructional materials that aid teachers in all of this. Among the best, I believe, are the magnificent picture books of the *Urban Studies* [4] that, with at least one group of disadvantaged

---

[1] *Teacher.* New York: Simon and Schuster, 1964, p. 42.
[2] Lynn Bruzaitis, *A Comparison of Words from Daily Independent Writing of First Grade Children to Those Found in Dolch's Basic Sight List.*
[3] *Learning to Read Through Experience.* New York: Appleton-Century-Crofts, 1963.
[4] Elizabeth Wright, *Urban Studies.* New York: John Day, 1965.

and educationally wrecked children, help teachers get conversation going so that children's language is available for reading instruction. Another unique publisher contribution, and I also believe, destined to be a coming pattern of instructional book publication in the near future, is that collection of books known as *Little Owls*.[5] These ably interrelate the spontaneous language of children and the printed page. In that sense they are truly "linguistic" in contra-distinction to certain other publications inaccurately called "linguistic." The latter are merely a new form of old fashioned "phonics."

THE READING PERIOD ITSELF [6]

Classroom management must develop its own structure if the characteristics of a good reading program are to be realized. If we would chart a reading period for a class moving predominantly into book reading, the flow of action provides a further continuum.

THE INDEPENDENT WORK PERIOD

Children's Responsibilities Planned with the Teacher.

1. *First Activity:* Silent reading of a self-chosen book (and listing it in his notebook).
2. *Second Activity:* Making a decision as to what to do with that book.
    a. Prepare it to present to his teacher in an individual conference; or,
    b. Developing a project about it.
3. *Subsequent Activity:*
    a. Perfecting a skill in another curriculum area; or,
    b. Developing projects in other curriculum areas.

This is structure for learning for the child. What is it for the teacher? It involves individual conferences and group teaching.

THE INDIVIDUAL CONFERENCE

When each child presents himself to his teacher for an individual conference, the teacher must structure it to explore four major areas.

1. The mechanical skills of the child as to word analysis.
2. The ability to read the selected piece critically and evaluate it.
3. The child's awareness of his personal interest in what he has selected.
4. His ability to read aloud to hold his audience.

[5] New York: Holt, Rinehart and Winston.
[6] See also Association for Childhood Education International, *Individualizing Education*. Washington, D.C., 1964.

GROUP TEACHING

The structure of teaching groups depends upon 1) identification of need, 2) categorizing needs, 3) organization and instruction of group, and 4) follow-up if considered necessary.

Contrast these steps to those of the directed reading lesson, if the differences of the philosophies of these two approaches are to be realized. On the one hand the materials supply the sequence. On the other each child's growth and development dictate the patterns. Materials are not missing in the latter; but they only serve. They do not dominate.

READING AND WRITING

One of the most crucial areas for structure in a reading program is that of word analysis. While textbooks for years have noted the relationship of reading and spelling, they usually miss the point. Word analysis *cannot* be a reading skill as its action is to break a word apart, letter by letter, phoneme by phoneme, syllable by syllable.

On the other hand, word perception *is* a reading skill. Now this is not to say that the need to analyze words does not occur in reading, or that the need to perceive words or "see if it looks right" does not occur in writing (or spelling). But it is to say that the basic skills of word analysis *must* be *introduced* and *taught* in writing. Similarly the basic skills of seeing words *must* be taught as reading.

Put another way, I must insist that children learn to read by talking, giving dictation, and then writing down what was said. We learn to read by writing. We learn to write from reading.

Phonics, then, must become the province of written language. Sounds of letters are taught when children need to know how to spell the ideas they wish to record. Again, children are taught to hear and identify the first letters of phonemes of words—simply because the left side of the word is the first phoneme articulated. Lists from texts, readers, or workbooks are not needed.

Reading, then, in the skill building sense, must come from skills of perception, in the sense of crystallizing the seeing of wholes, recognizing, as rapidly as possible, the symbols that trigger the mind into understanding the written language presented. Writing, in the skill building sense, comes from word analysis.

The fallacy of basal systems lies in their insistence of a sacred sequence built into reading material intended for all.

The strength of a program that depends upon books of literary merit, selected by children on the basis of their pulling power, and upon frequent teacher-pupil conferences on a one-to-one basis, upon the spontaneous language of the pupils themselves, is the strength of ten, like Sir Galahad, because its educational purposes are pure. It develops from the stuff of life overflowing in the children.

BIBLIOGRAPHY

1. Ashton-Warner, Sylvia, *Teacher*. New York: Simon and Schuster, 1964.
2. Guggenheim, E., and C. Guggenheim (eds.), *New Frontiers in Education*. New York: Grune and Stratton, 1966.
3. Martin, William, Jr. (ed.), *Little Owls*. New York: Holt, Rinehart and Winston.
4. Lee, D. M., and R. Van Allen, *Learning to Read Thru Experience*. New York: Appleton-Century-Crofts, 1963.
5. Rasmussen, Margaret (ed.), *Individualizing Education*. Washington, D. C.: Association for Childhood Education International, 1964.
6. Veatch, Jeannette, *Individualizing Your Reading Program*. New York: G. P. Putnam, 1959.
7. ———, *Reading in the Elementary School*. New York: Ronald Press, 1966.
8. Wright, Elizabeth, *Urban Studies*. New York: John Day, 1965.

HELPING TEACHERS BEGIN
INDIVIDUALIZED READING *

Patrick J. Groff

Individualized reading is a subject of growing discussion in the professional literature. This development parallels, in a sense, an increase in the number of teachers who are seeking to adopt an individualized reading program. As a result, it is becoming more and more likely that elementary school principals will be asked by their teachers to evaluate this approach to the teaching of reading and to give guidance on its use in the classroom.

On the surface, individualized reading appears simple. But all of the experts in individualized reading agree that it is not something to be taken lightly or gone into frivolously. The seemingly uncomplicated nature of the approach is deceptive. No type of reading program can degenerate more quickly if misunderstood or misapplied. To rush headlong into individualized teaching of reading without careful study and preparation is to court certain failure and a consequent disillusionment about the value of the approach. It is far better to begin deliberately and gradually.

* REPRINTED by permission of the Department of Elementary School Principals, from *The National Elementary Principal*, Vol. 43, February, 1964, pp. 47–50.

On the other hand, there is no doubt that individualized reading can be successful under the proper conditions and with the use of appropriate procedures. The objection that children taught through this kind of program will fail to learn to read is not substantiated by the research. Evidence continues to mount that with individualized reading, normal or above normal gains in reading vocabulary and comprehension can be expected, along with greater—although less measurable—advances in creative and critical reading, in positive attitudes toward and appreciation of books, and in the self-direction and self-control of the reading situation. All of these gains are improbable, nevertheless, if the prerequisites for the success of the approach are overlooked in planning for its use.

There are many questions about individualized reading that must be considered if the teacher would insure both his success and satisfaction in using this approach. Through individual or group conferences, the principal should make sure that his teachers are aware of the problems in successfully using individualized reading. He should take the initiative in seeing that teachers are prepared to explain the program to parents and should be sure that the school patrons understand the purpose of individualized reading.

The following twelve questions and comments indicate the kind of information and procedures which will help both teachers and principals in planning and initiating a program of individualized reading.

Teachers should be led to ask themselves:

1. Do I understand the purposes and techniques of individualized reading? For example, what are the five essential parts of the program? (Planning; individual silent reading and oral reading with partners; pupil-teacher conferences; sharing what has been read; and cooperative evaluation of these procedures. Details about each of these aspects of individualized reading may be found in the references below.)

2. Will it be possible for me to see individualized reading in action? Will at least two teachers in our school be using it so we can exchange visits and ideas?

The principal can be instrumental in encouraging teachers to work in teams on individualized programs. The support and encouragement teachers can give each other will help a great deal in making the program successful. If no other arrangements can be made, the principal might take over a teacher's class so he can observe in another classroom. If possible, provisions should be made for teachers to see individualized reading in action in other schools.

3. Do my principal and supervisors understand individualized reading?

The principal of any school in which an individualized reading program is contemplated should be familiar with the theories and practices of individualized reading as described in the references below. Knowledgeable supervision of a constructively critical nature is crucial to this approach.

4. Does my school have available the professional literature from which I can learn the details of individualized reading?

The following are some of the primary sources that both the teacher and the principal should consult. They should all be readily available in the professional library of the school that uses individualized reading.

Barbe, Walter B. *Educator's Guide to Personalized Reading Instruction.* Englewood Cliffs, New Jersey: Prentice-Hall, 1961. 241 pp.

Brogan, Peggy, and Fox, Lorene K. *Helping Children Read.* New York: Holt, Rinehart & Winston, 1961. 330 pp.

Darrow, Helen F., and Howes, Virgil M. *Approaches to Individualized Reading.* New York: Appleton-Century-Crofts, 1960. 102 pp.

Draper, Marcella K.; Schwietert, Louise H.; and Lazar, May. *Practical Guide to Individualized Reading.* New York: Board of Education, 1960. 158 pp.

Duker, Sam. *Bibliography on Individualized Reading.* Brooklyn College, 1962.

Groff, Patrick. *Annotated list of comparisons of individualized reading with ability grouping.* National Council of Teachers of English (508 South Sixth Street, Champaign, Illinois), 1962.

Jacobs, Leland B., Miel, Alice, and others. *Individualizing Reading Practices.* New York: Teachers College, Columbia University. 1958. 91 pp.

Lee, Dorris, and Van Allen, Roach. *Learning to Read Through Experience.* Second edition. New York: Appleton-Century-Crofts, 1963.

Robinson, Ruth. *Why They Love to Learn.* Charlotte, North Carolina: Heritage, 1960. 172 pp.

Veatch, Jeannette. *Individualizing Your Reading Program.* New York: G. P. Putnam's Sons, 1959. 242 pp.

Articles on individualizing reading in *Elementary English* and *Reading Teacher* for the past few years.

5. Can my school provide enough books for me to make individualized reading work effectively?

Jeanette Veatch, in the book cited above, states that there must be a minimum of three books per pupil in the classroom library for an individualized reading program to work successfully. The number of books available will be greater if teachers teamed together in using the approach can pool their books in a commonly accessible place. Children can bring in personal books, library books, magazines and other reading materials. Many other suggestions about book collections are given in the references above.

6. Do I know enough about children's books to use individualized reading? Does my school have sources from which I can learn about children's literature?

The school's professional library should include at least the following books on children's literature. Of course, nothing can supplant a good college course in children's literature.

Arbuthnot, May Hill. *Children and Books.* Chicago: Scott, Foresman & Co., 1957. 684 pp.

Huck, Charlotte S., and Young, Doris A. *Children's Literature in the Elementary School.* New York: Holt, Rinehart & Winston, 1961. 522 pp.

Larrick, Nancy. *A Teacher's Guide to Children's Books.* Columbus, Ohio: Charles E. Merrill Books, 1960. 316 pp.

Tooze, Ruth A., and Krone, B. P. *Literature and Music as Resources for Social Studies.* Englewood Cliffs, New Jersey: Prentice-Hall, 1955. 456 pp.

7. Do I know where to find the right book for the right child at tht right time? Does my school have references which will assist in this search?

The teacher using individualized reading must be especially concerned with seeing that the books brought into the classroom meet both the children's interests and their reading abilities. Analyses of the pupils' interests and abilities should be made frequently to guide the use of the following book selection aids.

Basic Book Collection for Elementary Grades. Seventh edition. Compiled by Miriam S. Mathes. Chicago: American Library Association. (paper.)

Best Books for Children. Fifth edition. Compiled by Patricia H. Allen. New York: R. R. Bowker Co. (paper.)

Bibliography of Books for Children. Washington, D. C.: Association for Childhood Education, 1960.

Children's Catalog. Tenth edition. New York: H. W. Wilson Co., 1961 with supplements.

Dawson, Mildred A., and Pfeiffer, Louise. *Treasury of Books for the Primary Grades.* San Francisco: Howard Chandler, 1959.

Eakin, Mary K. *Good Books for Children.* Revised edition. University of Chicago, 1962.

Groff, Patrick. *Recent Easy Books for First Grade Children.* San Diego State College: the author, 1963. (25 cents.)

Recommended Children's Books. New York: School Libraries Journal.

8. Do I know enough about the techniques of teaching reading to use individualized reading? Can I teach reading without guidance from a teacher's manual?

With individualized reading, the teacher does not depend on the teacher's manual for direct guidance as he does when using a textbook for reading instruction. Consequently, he must know in detail at least the following aspects of reading methodology: word analysis and recognition; comprehension and study skills; flexibility of speed; oral reading; and appropriate independent review. Teachers need to self-evaluate frankly whether or not they will be able to develop these skills in an individualized reading program.

9. Can I find the time necessary to make an individualized reading program a success in a class of normal size?

There are many time-consuming aspects to individualized reading: for example, holding conferences, record keeping, directing sharing sessions, and teaching needed skills in groups. A well-organized time schedule should be developed. Further, in almost all cases it is better to begin by individualizing the reading of a small subgroup composed of dependable, industrious children. The amount of time needed for conducting individualized reading can be determined at this point.

10. Am I psychologically suited for this type of teaching? Is my personality such that I would feel a great loss of security if I could not depend on the teacher's manual for day-by-day directions?

Each individual teacher must judge for himself in the light of his experience, education, and personal characteristics whether or not he is suited to use individualized reading. The principal should, of course, be able to provide certain professional insights into this intricate and subtle problem.

11. Will I be able to explain the individualized reading program to parents?

Teachers, as well as principals, should be able to explain the advantages of an individualized reading program over ability grouping in terms of: pupil achievement; provisions for individual differences; pupils' attitudes toward reading; pupils' self-direction and control; and long-range effects. Teachers and principals should also be prepared to explain how the program differs from simple "free" reading.

If the teacher reads carefully in the above references, he should be able to explain these points to the satisfaction of most parents. The bibliography from the National Council of Teachers of English by this writer can be especially valuable in providing evidence that individualized reading does, in fact, develop reading skills.

12. Can I answer the objections that have been made to individualized reading?

The faculty of any school using individualized reading should be prepared to answer the various charges that have been made against this approach. Among the objections which are made are these:

• Individualized reading procedures are too disorganized, irregular, and time consuming for the average teacher.

• Individualized reading is too unsystematic to allow for sequential learning.

• Individualized reading does not develop children's reading tastes and interests.

• Parents do not want their children to use individualized reading.

• Reading achievement is low. Reading skills are neglected and faulty word recognition habits and weak study skills result.

• There is no possibility for group learning with individualized reading.

• Most teachers do not have the personality or the knowledge of books, children, and reading procedures to use individualized reading.

• Most authorities are opposed to individualized reading; therefore, it must be wrong.

• "Flexible grouping" will adequately take care of individual differences.

• There is not enough control or repetition of vocabulary. The reading level of tradebooks (not textbooks) is unknown. There is no provision for reading readiness.

• Discipline problems develop with individualized reading. Most children do not have the self-direction or control to work under this approach. They are inattentive and develop slovenly work habits.

• Most classes are too large for individualized reading to be used effectively

• There are not enough books in most schools to make individualized reading work.

• Individualized reading will not work with slow learners.

• Individualized reading will not work in the primary grades, especially the first grade.

The scope of this discussion precludes an adequate answer to these objections. Again, the teacher and principal should refer to the above references for help. Most of the questions are pertinent and reasonable; a few are misguided or obstructionist. In any case, the teacher using such an unconventional approach as individualized reading must be prepared to defend his heterodox procedures against such charges.

INDIVIDUALIZED READING:
TEACHING SKILLS *

Lyman C. Hunt, Jr.

They say it couldn't be done. They say it isn't being done. Yet teachers are doing it. Teachers are teaching children in the reading program as individuals, and they are teaching them needed skills. It is exciting to watch teachers who are trying to work out their own particular approach to teaching skills to individual children.

These venturesome teachers use every resource for improving skills. The textbook manual is a reference, not a heavily beaten path from which they

---

* REPRINTED from the May, 1961, issue of *Education*. Copyright 1961 by The Bobbs-Merrill Company, Inc., Indianapolis, Indiana.

cannot depart. While it may be true that the constant use of the manual gives greater security, it is not necessarily the best way to help each individual child learn skills. The days when the teacher, manual in her lap, herds her three ability groups through various exercises in revolving-door fashion are waning.

Many teachers say, "I want to try individualized reading, but will my children learn skills?" It is a sobering idea for the teacher to "go it alone." Undertaking an individualized program requires courage, vision and know-how.

Advocates of the basal-reader program say that teachers neglect skills if they try to individualize their reading instruction. There may be some truth in this contention. But what about controlled vocabulary? What about sacred sequences? What about organized structure? Have they been successful?

It is becoming increasingly clear to many teachers that many children do not learn reading skills according to the organized sequences and structures of the textbook manuals. The theory upon which the prescribed patterns are based may be sound; unfortunately, though, many children just don't grow according to the pattern.

Successful teachers are finding ways to identify skills needed by each individual child. Successful teachers are finding ways of developing those skills with individual children. Successful teachers are finding ways of organizing children into temporary groups for the purpose of studying skills needed by the groups and for the purpose of giving individual children help at the moment of need. Successful teachers are finding ways of showing children how to help themselves with skills. Successful teachers are accomplishing this in programs where every child is reading a book of his own choice at a pace consistent with his purpose.

Four Major Skill Areas

Important skills lie in four areas: (1) sight-recognition vocabulary; (2) word study; (3) oral-reading fluency; and (4) silent-reading efficiency.

Careful study will reveal that success must be built on the first step. Without an adequate sight-recognition vocabulary and without assurance of constant accumulation of words into the sight-recognition vocabulary, the child will stumble and falter. He will not gain the foundation needed to uphold the other three skill areas.

Word study is an important skill area primarily because it enables the child to help himself. It is always subordinate to accumulating a sight-recognition vocabulary, however.

Oral-reading performance is closely linked to a sight-recognition vocabulary. We often err by expecting fluent oral reading when the child has not truly accomplished the first step; he simply does not have sufficient skill in sight recognition to read well orally.

Sight recognition is a bond between the relatively separate processes of oral and silent reading. We unrealistically expect a child to read silently when his sight-recognition vocabulary is insufficient for the vocabulary included in a particular selection.

It is evident that skill development is intricate and complex. Neverthless, we are becoming increasingly aware of the variety of individual patterns through which children learn skills in each area. It will help to keep our focus on truly important skills and to avoid overemphasis on lesser skills. It is easy to become lost in a maze of minor skills.

ARE THE SEQUENCES SACRED?

The advocates of the basal-reader program claim that only through a controlled-vocabulary approach can the child successfully acquire sight-recognition skills. The proponents say that the scientifically worked-out sequences and structures for related skills development are so well defined that every child can succeed.

Let's examine the theory. The basal-reader program has a dual approach to word recognition. First, and rightly so, it begins with building a sight-recognition vocabulary which rests on predetermined sequences of words, arranged story by story, book by book, grade by grade, for the total program.

Once accumulation of a sight-recognition vocabulary is off to a good start, and even though there is an increasing number of words to be accumulated with each new story, a second skill task is introduced. This new element, word study, confronts the child with structures and sequences related to phonic development, to variations in word forms, and to syllable sensitivity.

There is a dual approach, too, to the silent- and oral-reading steps. With each story, provision is made for directed silent reading of the material to realize some teacher-designated purpose.

Following silent reading comes each child's opportunity to read orally or, at least, to listen as one of his groupmates reads orally. In this sequence of silent-followed-by-oral reading, each child is given roughly equal time and consideration. In the individualized reading program, with each child reading a selection of his own choice, silent reading far exceeds oral reading in time and emphasis. Yet neither is neglected.

WHAT IS THE ISSUE?

The critical issue lies within this complex of sequences. The system which prescribes that particular words are to be learned for each particular book during each particular year by every child must be carefully considered by the teacher. Is this a sequence of controlled vocabulary or overcontrolled vocabulary? Prescribing the particular time for learning particular words is too brittle and too rigid a system for many children and for many teachers. This system lacks flexibility.

The result of over-attention to a prescribed order for learning words can be disastrous for both the able and the unable. If the child does not assimilate the designated words into his recognition vocabulary at the particular time they are introduced (with the number of allowed repetitions) then this vast, but fragile, superstructure can fall all about him. This condition of accumulating specified words at a specified time in order to be successful can serve as a handicap and a hindrance to many children even though it may be beneficial to others. The able child bursts out of the structure; the slow child struggles unsuccessfully to maintain the pace.

When teachers have realized this fact and certain other basic facts about words, they do not necessarily need to become entangled with their children in this vast system in order to help children accumulate an adequate sight-recognition vocabulary.

IMPORTANT FACTS ABOUT WORDS

Fact: A word means something. When teachers try to teach children to recognize words for which meaning is inadequate or lacking, they violate a basic principle about words and how children should learn to recognize them.

Fact: Each word looks different from every other word. With minor exceptions, no two words look alike; each word has its unique, individual appearance. While it is true that many words have brothers and sisters of close resemblance (*wake, fake*) and while there are a few identical twins, (*read, read*) these latter are the rare exceptions. Words most alike in appearance are frequently most difficult for children to learn to recognize. It is only through a slow, laborious process that some children come to respond to subtle differences in appearances. True sight recognition involves responding to differences in appearance in total word forms.

Fact: A word can have variations in form. Word appearances are modified slightly by adding common endings or common beginnings or by combining one word to form a compound word. Slight changes affect appearances markedly. Some children find it difficult to respond to these minor variations in word appearances.

Fact: A word is made of letters combined together, and the letters represent sounds. We can study word forms by examining letter-sound blends. Some people proclaim this to be the primary fact about words, but blending letter sounds is no substitute for responding to differences in appearances on sight.

When teachers know these facts about words and when teachers can base teaching practices on these facts, they can help youngsters to develop skills. Approaches to sequences and structures can be worked out in a more flexible manner. Instruction with respect to accumulating recognition vocabulary and studying words can be tailor-made to children's needs. Instruction in skills need not consume every one's time as it often does when we try to fit groups into the previously prepared patterns.

What about Phonics?

Most teachers are not sufficiently sensitive to the most important fact about phonics. One system is based on the fact that words are composed of letters which stand for sounds and which, when combined, form words. When the letter sounds are known, word forms automatically emerge. This is an unwarranted assumption.

As stated previously, even though each word appears to be different in its total form from every other word, there are many brothers and sisters among words and many dozens of aunts, uncles, and cousins. This means that a part or parts of any particular word may be common to a part or parts of many other words. As we study these parts, we can see the relationships that exist among them.

Relationship phonics, the second system, is the study of these similar parts. A very well-defined sequence supports such study. We start with the most obvious relationship, words that rhyme. Rhyming words must be perceived prior to recognizing the second relationship, words which start with the same initial letter. We continue by developing the relationship emerging from the fact that many words end with the same letter; then we move on to the more complex relationship based on words which begin or end with double and triple consonants. Next come relationships built around vowels, both long and short, and finally the relationships built on the syllable structure of words.

This five-part sequence underlying relationship phonics is delicately balanced. We err by attempting to teach an advanced step when children are barely managing some of the preliminary steps. We err because our manuals tell us to develop a complex relationship even though the child needs to learn a more elementary step. When we attempt to teach vowel relationships while the child is still confused by changes in initial or final consonants, we are guilty of this error. Critics say we err in phonics because we do not teach letter-sound blend phonics. This is nonsense. We err by trying to teach the wrong relationship to the wrong children at the wrong time.

Common Ways to Word Recognition

Any teacher who is endeavoring to help youngsters build an adequate sight-recognition vocabulary, any teacher endeavoring to help children learn ways to help themselves study words must have instant command of the seven common ways of helping children gain acquaintance with word forms.

1. *Word form with pronunciation.* Ordinary consideration is given to the word form, its pronunciation, and, if needed, its meaning.

2. *Visual scrutiny.* The child is asked to exercise extreme effort to study word appearance visually and to construct mental images of word forms.

3. *Contextual meaning.* Words are recognized through their stress on meaning.

4. *Word structure.* Attention is paid to changes in word forms which result from adding beginnings and endings, or from combining words.

5. *Configuration or outline.* Notice is given to lengths, shapes, and outlines of word forms.

6. *Relationship or letter-sound blend phonics.*

7. *Syllables.* Studying syllables as subparts of word forms.

The secret of success, discovered by teachers teaching skills to individual children, can be revealed. Success comes from combining several of the seven ways of recognizing words according to the child's needs and according to his present mastery of skills. Teachers can learn to utilize proper combinations effectively.

Teachers should sense the balanced relationships within the four skill areas and the major subdivisions thereof. They should be able to detect individual patterns of accumulation of sight-recognition vocabulary, to manage the two phonic systems, and to command the seven ways of knowing words. Then skills can be taught individually.

How Do Teachers Do It?

How do teachers detect the needs of each child when they have thirty to thirty-five children? Each teacher has her own individual approach, but a common practice is to maintain some kind of check sheet on which the basic skill areas are listed as major headings. This list may take the form of a graph or a notebook page for each child; the teacher, through individual conferences or through work in skill groups, notes the child's accomplishment and records needed work.

Sometimes teachers have children keep their own records with respect to performance in sight-recognition vocabulary, word study, oral reading, and silent reading. Children can work out word lists for self study.

A variety of ways for independent word study exists. While most skills teaching is accomplished with the individual during conferences, many teachers form groups to work on skills, according to needs of children within the group. Sometimes teachers will announce to the class which skill element will be developed and the children themselves volunteer to participate in that group. If a child is not sufficiently aware of his need for working with the group, the teacher will counsel with him. He can learn to recognize his own need for attending the group which has been formed to work on double-consonant beginnings, if that happens to be a point of weakness for him.

Word examples taken from the reading of one child might be used to teach a particular skill to the group. Word examples taken from another child's reading might be used in teaching another skill. Many times the teacher, sufficiently skilled, can determine whether the children in this group need to work to perfect recognition of the·difficult *wh* words. This can be done through a game-motivating approach.

Appraising progress again rests on the ingenuity of the teacher. While record-keeping is primarily the responsibility of the teacher, valuable assistance can come from the children. A teacher must be able to discern and record when any particular child is making great strides in accumulating a sight vocabulary; when he is barely crawling up the steep incline; when he is perhaps stalled or even gradually slipping backwards.

She must be able to discern and record the approach most frequently used by the child as he tries to study out words for himself. She must teach students to look within the word, to cover up endings, to use meaning, and/or to use the seven common ways to help themselves.

She must be able to discern and record whether oral reading is becoming more fluent, more enjoyable, more presentable to herself and to the group. She must be able to discern whether silent reading is becoming truly effective. She must help children to concentrate on meanings when they read to themselves. She must constantly try to transfer to the child her know-how in all the skill areas so she can help him to help himself.

WHAT DIRECTION DO WE TAKE?

It is most important to realize that many teachers are ready, willing, and able to put the manual aside and venture forth on their own in teaching skills. There is an urgent need to stop giving teachers recipe books which prescribe steps. Rather, teachers need to have a clear command of major skill areas, and need to utilize this source.

A great deal of our present word-study program as developed in manuals of the basal-reader program is repeated and duplicated in the spelling program. We should do more reading of an individual type during so-called reading class and place more emphasis on the word-study program in connection with writing where spelling fits naturally.

We should have, above all, faith that we as teachers can learn to know important reading skills and transmit to the children the ways of mastering skills on an individual basis. The happy result will be that all children may be engaged in reading books of their own choosing at their own rate of speed during reading class.

SELF-SELECTION IN READING:
REPORT OF A
LONGITUDINAL STUDY *

Frances V. Cyrog

For nearly ten years, the Whittier Schools have used an approach to reading variously called self-selective, independent, or individualized reading. The program began in 1952–53, when a few teachers in several schools began experimenting with individualized reading as an outgrowth of a series of in-service programs arranged by consultants from the Los Angeles County School Office. This spring, almost ten years later, the Superintendent of the Whittier Schools reported to his school board that 75 per cent of the district teachers were using this approach to teaching printed-word reading. Obviously, with such a large percentage of the teachers involved in this reading program, continuous evaluations must be made.

The purpose of this paper is to review briefly the history of individualized or self-selection reading as used in the Whittier Schools, outline the kinds of evaluations which have been made, and present some of the results.

I

In the fall of 1952, following the in-service programs in individualized reading, a number of teachers at each grade level began experimentations. Some used individualized reading for a full year, some for part of a year; some involved all children, others only part of a class, and still others used a modified approach combining the basic text and self-selective reading on an alternate day basis. In several schools these trials were carefully checked. Standardized group tests in reading were given at the beginning and at the end of the year, and other assessments were made of less tangible aspects of growth in reading ability, such as teacher and pupil acceptance of the new program, interest in reading, etc. Results of these more or less informal surveys and of the standard test data were encouraging enough to cause the curriculum department to recommend the continued use of individualized reading at any grade level where the teacher wished to do so and where adequate professional preparation was evidenced.

A teachers' handbook on individualized reading was also developed by the

* REPRINTED by permission of the Claremont Reading Conference from the *Claremont College Reading Conference Yearbook*, Vol. 26, 1962, pp. 106–13.

curriculum department during this first year of experimentation. It contained descriptions of good practices in use in various classrooms in the city, an outline of procedures for a teacher interested in using this approach to teaching reading, and three articles explaining the philosophy behind the approach. These articles pointed out the major differences between an individualized or self-selective approach to teaching printed-word reading and the basal reader approach and the reactions of students who had been introduced to individualized reading.[1]

Individualized or self-selection reading, as defined in these articles, was the approach used entirely in the classrooms which are included in the study reported here. This approach was not a combined or partial program including some type of basic textbook work during part of the time. Instead, each child selected his own reading material from a large assortment of pre-selected books, read at his own pace, and met periodically with his teacher concerning his book and his progress in reading. The teacher kept records of each student's reading growth and needs and provided the materials and atmosphere which, as Olson put it, "expected from each child only what he could yield at his stage of maturity."

II

It is the pupils who began individualized reading in the first grade between the years 1954 and 1956 on whom the study reported here was focused. During the 1959–60 and 1960–61 school years, it was possible to identify each of the children in four schools who had been taught continuously through this approach to reading. Systematic assessments of reading progress were then made for all of these children who were then in grades three through six.

Obviously, a comprehensive study of progress in reading would include many facets such as interest in reading, the quality and number of books read, points of difficulty, oral reading abilities, comprehension, and speed in silent reading. However, this report is limited to an analysis of standardized test scores of these children whose reading program had been consistently a self-selective or individualized one from the time they entered the first grade. The fundamental question for which answers were sought here was this:

Do the children who had individualized reading for all their years in the elementary grades show progress on reading achievement tests consistent with district and national norms and with their own tested mental maturity expectancies?

---

[1] The articles were: Willard C. Olson, "Seeking, Self-Selection, and Pacing in the Use of Books by Children," The Packet, Boston: D. C. Heath and Company, Spring, 1952. Delores Cooper Palmer, "To Determine the Reaction of a Fourth Grade to a Program of Self-Selection Reading Materials," Unpublished Master's Thesis, Salt Lake City: University of Utah, 1953. Jeannette Veatch, "Individualized Reading—for Success in the Classroom," *The Educational Trend*, No. 654, 1954.

III

Data for the study were secured from the regular city-wide testing surveys given between 1953 and 1960. The surveys included the California Tests of Achievement in Reading and the California Mental Maturity Tests. The population for the study was derived from four schools within the district. Within these schools, all pupils who had been taught consistently within the framework of an individualized or self-selective reading program as defined above were identified. Some data were also gathered concerning the teachers of these pupils over the six year period, such as their educational background, professional experience, and teaching record as evaluated by district administrative personnel. Since all teachers were encouraged to begin the program if they wished, it should be obvious that no effort was made to allow only those teachers believed to be specially competent to teach reading on an individualized basis to begin the program. The teachers who had children in their classes who were included in this study were, therefore, characteristic of *all* teachers in the district, numbering among them the same percentage of those rated excellent, good, or poor as would be true of the district as a whole.

Seven hundred twenty-six pupils from grades three through six comprised the population of this study. They contributed 955 different sets of reading Achievement and Mental Maturity test scores. The disparity between numbers of pupils and scores on tests arises from the fact that 229 of the 726 children tested during the 1959–60 school year were subsequently re-tested one year later, *i.e.*, while they were enrolled during 1960–61.

The community from which this population was drawn is an older one which has not experienced the rapid and tumultuous growth so common in western urban areas. The relatively low number of pupil transfers to other schools provided a more stable population than one might normally find in Southern California.

To establish a check-point against which test scores of children who experienced an individualized reading program might be compared, district norms for reading achievement during the five year period immediately preceding the launching of the experimental program were established. Table I presents these norms for the 1949–54 period.

This table shows that students were, on the average, above the norm in intelligence and their expectancy scores in reading were correspondingly above national norms. The "expectancy score," or the anticipated achievement score is presented in terms of grade placement and is derived from the California Test Bureau's extension of the Horn formula, correlating IQ, grade placement, and chronological age for all tests used in this study. Achievement scores were obtained from the yearly district reading survey made each October. The test used in this survey was the California Achievement Test in Reading for primary and intermediate grades. Different forms of the test were given each year.

Table I also indicates that achievement was generally lower than expected at all grade levels. This was most evident in grades five and six where achievement was .7 and .5 of a year respectively below expected scores.

TABLE I

Norms Derived from Five Year Averages of Achievement and Expectancy, 1949–54 Whittier Elementary Schools, Whittier, California *

	IQ	EXPECTED SCORE, READING	ACTUAL SCORE, READING ACHIEVEMENT		
			VOCABULARY	COMPREHENSION	TOTAL READING
GRADE 3	107	3.5	3.4	3.0	3.2
GRADE 4	107	4.6	4.5	4.2	4.4
GRADE 5	110	5.8	5.0	5.2	5.1
GRADE 6	108	6.6	6.1	5.9	6.1

* Based upon approximately 2,000 cases.

Expectancy scores were also computed for the children who were included in the individualized or self-selection reading program. The pupils represented in these data were drawn from four of the twelve schools in the district. Table II show these scores.

Obviously, the group scores shown in Table II are not directly comparable. From these data we can only say that the group included in the study reported here varied little in expectancy from the general population of the school district during a prior period—a period in which no individualized or self-selection reading instruction was being used in the district.

TABLE II

A Comparison of Expected Scores of Reading Achievement: District Norms 1949– 54 and Individualized Reading Group Expectancy Norms 1959–61

	TOTAL DISTRICT *		INDIVIDUALIZED READING **	
	IQ	EXPECTED READING SCORE	IQ	EXPECTED READING SCORE
GRADE 3	107	3.5	108	3.6
GRADE 4	107	4.6	107	4.6
GRADE 5	110	5.8	108	5.6
GRADE 6	108	6.6	109	6.7

* N equals approximately 2,000 cases
** N equals approximately 955 cases

Table III presents the results of the reading achievement tests for all pupils in grades three through six who had had individualized reading instruction for all their previous years in school.

TABLE III

Individualized Reading Group Test Scores for 1959 and 1960 in Relation to
Expected Achievement (Combined Scores)

	IQ	EXPECTED †	RV *	RC *	TR *
GRADE 3	108	3.6	4.0	3.8	3.9
GRADE 4	107	4.6	5.9	5.7	5.7
GRADE 5	108	5.6	6.8	6.6	6.7
GRADE 6	109	6.7	8.1	7.9	8.0

N equals 955 (derived from 726 pupils)
† See Table II
* California Achievement Test in Reading consists of two sections: Reading Vocabulary (RV)
and Reading Comprehension (RC) and an average of these two scores. Total Reading (TR).
All averages are reported in terms of grade placement.

This table shows that the achievement averages for the individualized reading groups in the four grades were higher than their expected scores. Pupils at the beginning of third, fourth, fifth, and sixth grades were averaging, respectively, .3, 1.1, 1.1 and 1.3 grades above their expected scores derived from tests administered in 1960 and 1961.

Table IV shows achievement of the individualized reading groups in direct comparison with district norms in each of the subdivisions of the test of reading ability.

TABLE IV

Individualized Reading Group Test Scores for 1959 and 1960 *
Compared with District Norms, 1949–54 † (Combined Scores)

	IQ		EXP.		RV		RC		TR	
	D **	I **	D	I	D	I	D	I	D	I
GRADE 3	107	108	3.5	3.6	3.4	4.0	3.0	3.8	3.2	3.9
GRADE 4	107	107	4.6	4.6	4.5	5.9	4.2	5.7	4.4	5.7
GRADE 5	110	108	5.8	5.6	5.0	6.8	5.2	6.6	5.1	6.7
GRADE 6	108	109	6.6	6.7	6.1	8.1	5.9	7.9	6.1	8.0

 * N equals 955 (derived from 726 pupils)
 † N equals approximately 2,000 pupils
** D stands for district norms; I stands for those pupils taught reading through the individualized or self-selective program of instruction.

There are some indications in this table and the preceding one that the longer the children received individualized reading instruction the more rapid did their achievement in reading accelerate.

A survey of the effect of the individualized reading program on district reading achievement is presented in Table V. In 1954, individualized reading was being introduced to pupils by a few teachers in several schools in the district. By 1961, seventy-five per cent of the teachers were using it in their classrooms. This table shows the growth in reading achievement for the remaining eight schools not included in this study.

TABLE V

Annual Achievement Test Results in Reading (1954–61)
for the Eight Schools in the District not in the Study *

GRADES	3	4	5	6
1954	3.1	4.3	4.5	5.7
1955	3.2	4.2	4.5	5.7
1956	3.5	4.2	5.0	6.1
1957	3.1	4.0	5.0	6.1
1958	3.6	4.9	5.8	7.0
1959	3.6	4.4	5.8	6.5
1960	3.6	5.0	5.9	6.9
1961	3.8	5.0	6.1	7.1
Total Reading Ach. Scores, Individualized Reading Groups, 1960–61 **	3.9	5.7	6.7	8.0
District Norms 1949–54 **	3.2	4.4	5.1	6.1

* N equals approximately 1,200 pupils
** N equals approximately 2,000 pupils
*** N equals 955 scores (derived from 726 pupils)

Reading achievement at each grade level for the eight schools not in the study shows consistent and continuous improvement during the seven year period. Compared with district norms derived from achievement throughout the district during the period 1949–54, the overall reading ability of the children appears to have improved notably. Except for one grade level (3rd), achievement in eight schools still is markedly behind that of the children who had been taught through an individualized reading program since entering the first grade.

IV

In sum, evidence was gathered in this study to find out whether pupils who were taught reading through an individualized approach continuously upon entering the first grade would show progress on reading achievement tests consistent with district and national norms and their expectancies as measured by standardized mental maturity tests. The results have indicated that the group of pupils studied made conspicuously higher achievement scores than the district as a whole had made during the period 1949–54 when the conventional basic-text approach was the dominant pattern of instruction. Expectancies for both groups were, nevertheless, approximately the same.

This, then, has been a brief and condensed picture of an extensive and detailed study of one district's evaluation of the teaching of reading through an individualized approach. It was the opinion of teachers and school administrative personnel that all the evidence strongly supported continuing and extending the program at all grade levels and for all children in the district.

THE DEVELOPMENTAL APPROACH
IN READING *

Laura Zirbes

Newborn infants are almost wholly dependent on human nurture, but they nevertheless have unlearned ways of responding to experience and nurture. Their efforts to get or increase satisfactions from experience are forward adjustments in which unlearned ways are modified or extended. Thus, they learn by experience in the very process of experiencing. This is the nature of functional learning or learning by doing. There is nothing casual about this type of learning. It is not merely incidental or opportunistic. It is purposeful and wholehearted. It is integrative and organismic. It is experimental, adaptive, and creative. The capacity to learn functionally is a creative capacity which has lifelong value. It should be cultivated. It is the capacity that enables infants, children, and adults who are not rigid and habit bound to function spontaneously and to meet challenges for which habits do not provide.

In the continuity of language development, new learnings draw upon earlier backgrounds and prior learnings. Participation in spontaneous conversation is satisfying even in its earliest stages and makes for increasing fluency and adequacy of oral communication. Natural inflections are learned functionally in this process. Sensitivity to sounds and shades of meaning is developed without recourse to didactic training when developmental guidance fosters it functionally. In the same way, familiarity with phrase and sentence structure is carried forward as a background for later language learnings and reading readiness, while reading itself must be deferred until maturation has readied the neural mechanisms for the coordinated functioning which reading requires. Meanwhile, direct experiences provide material for dramatic play and con-

---

* REPRINTED by permission of the International Reading Association from *The Reading Teacher*, Vol. 16, March, 1962, pp. 347–52.

current speech. Stories can be heard and enjoyed in various ways which contribute to reading readiness. Pictures and picture books can hold attention, and concurrent conversation can encourage associations with direct experience.

The child who asks what picture legends, signs, and labels say is associating visual symbols with oral language and giving signs of readiness for reading.

At this point it is possible to catch the oral language that recounts some vivid shared experience and set it down clearly in large print or script in visual language. The visual language becomes reconvertible into talk. The actual experience backgrounds and personal involvement challenge recall and association of meaningful statements, phrases, names, and ideas in their contexts in the visual account.

Almost immediately there occurs the threefold association of the flow of events in a direct experience, with the oral recounting of the experience and the visual account reinforcing the challenge to locate and identify the correspondence of the sequence of events with the sequential visual account. If the story has been composed and set down cooperatively, sequential and positional cues may suffice to set off the location and identification of whole statements that "tell" something. Quotations of things said and the names of persons who said them are readily identified in context by reference to such cues as quotation marks and prior familiarity with names or initials. It is significant to note the variety of cues children discover when they are free to rise to the challenge of identification. It is also interesting to note how *one* child's discovery becomes a challenge to others, and how this contributes to intelligent inference, satisfaction, and confidence. An encouraging word and a smile may suffice to spur lagging effort, and thus do more good than a stern admonition.

Developmental guidance helps the child as he moves from the concrete and particular toward the conceptual and the abstract. Such guidance does not assume the adult prerogative of starting with a logical presentation of abstractions and directives. Insightful developmental guidance not only counts on the satisfactions and associations of the initial effort, but reinforces these concomitants before expecting much more in the way of recognition.

There are many creative ways of reinforcing the early satisfactions and associations so that they make a firmer foundation for further effort and encourage responsiveness to more demanding challenges. The values and concerns of these creative ways can be clarified and projected, but they cannot be reduced to a "pat" formula or set of directives to be followed in uncreative fashion.

Creative guidance is not a skill but an *art* that is oriented in the basic human sciences. Rote learning, for example, has practically no carry-over value. To "read" a selection by rote is not really reading at all. It is memorization, which simulates reading but does not develop the ability to read at sight. "How" lessons in the formalities of letter writing are "dead-end" unless they are carried over into flexible use in actual letter writing. Functional learning can develop flexible skills without formal lessons.

The stereotyped routines followed in formal reading lessons are "dead-end" because they do not develop or encourage self-directed purposeful reading. They do not lead on to flexible forward adjustments and life-related uses of reading. The child who is "processed" through a presumptively directive approach achieves proficiency in the directed materials, but at the expense of a more integrative conception of reading. A method which subordinates everything to powers of recognition distorts a child's concept of what is expected from him in reading. A method which relies on prior training in which the "new words" are added to the sight vocabulary leads to some fluency in successive selections used as lesson material, but it does so at the expense of sight reading and carry-over. Any approach which is prematurely concerned with fine discrimination and analytical perception not only makes reading needlessly laborious; it also puts an undesirable and unnecessary strain on the still immature visual mechanisms on which reading and other close work depend. Furthermore, the overanalytical approach discourages the use of contextual cues and marginal vision, on which the widening of the perceptual span and fluency and smoothness depend.

Insightful guidance notes indicative behavior, and developmental insights are the bases for sensitivity to indicative behavior.

The child who frowns and shows anxiety is having difficulty and needs immediate aid and encouragement. The child who does not enter into the process may be bored.

The child who uses the table of contents of his own book to locate material independently is showing readiness for self selection and self direction in a wider array of books.

The rhythmic behavior of the eyes which characterizes fluent reading is indicative of the coordinated functioning of the sensory, motor, mental, and neural mechanisms involved.

Creative developmental guidance differs from the methodical instruction in several significant ways. It will be noted that creative guidance uses insights into child development and creative learning as sources of suggestion. It cues in flexibly and spontaneously on the actual responses and efforts of children in a particular ongoing learning situation. It does not proceed to put children through the predetermined steps in a "method" and expect them to submit and adjust. It does not depend on particular materials and specific directions for their use. It makes the most of the immediate satisfaction to be gained from successfully meeting the challenges of learning, and it reduces the chances of failure and discouragement. It does not resort to extrinsic motivation or pressure, because it realizes that neither is conducive to the wholehearted involvement which makes for carry-over, or to the autonomy which creative learning fosters. It does not oversimplify the process of learning to read so that the beginner gets a narrowed or skewed concept of what is involved. It meets the child where he is, using his prior language learnings as a resource and accepting his psychological immaturity as a challenge to guidance.

The very useful common words of the English language will occur and recur in almost any account of experience, but they will be imbedded in the context, in association with less common key words that identify the particular experience and tell *who* was involved, *where* things took place, and *what* it was all about. The importance of these key words is quite distinct from the importance of words emphasized in preprimers.

Whereas the preprimer is usually designed to use and emphasize the content words in a particular primer, the experience approach is designed to reach *back* and bring *forward* backgrounds of experience and oral language for use and support in the first attempts to interpret visual language. The first steps in this challenging creative process require more courage than skill. Insightful devolopmental guidance not only counts on the satisfactions and associations of this initial effort but reinforces them and builds on them as it proceeds.

The response to challenge and the flexibility of response so characteristic of infancy and early childhood are all too often diminished or lost by early stereotyping and training which put a premium on conformity. Overemphasis on the "fixing" of knowledge and skill, techniques, and routines discourages spontaneity and creative learning. Formal training assumes that habits and skills are flexible and that they can be drawn upon in meeting new situations, but it too often lacks the very qualities which are conducive to flexibility and carry-over. When skills are not acquired in the course of use, and are not carried forward into free use, they are dead-end learnings which actually block creative potential. It is easy to illustrate the difference between formal, dead-end learnings, on the one hand, and learnings which are truly developmental and conducive to further learning, on the other. The stilted sentences in primers which overdo vocabulary development make reading boresome. Words that are essential to an account of experience may not even appear in primers or first readers, but if they function as key words in their context they belong in the approach. Beginning reading material should not be so narrowly conceived that it prepares only for one book; it should serve as a developmental general introduction to reading and as an extension of prior language backgrounds.

The uses made of accounts of direct experience in a developmental approach should not be narrowly conceived. They should contribute to favorable attitudes and to a wholehearted involvement in all the child's learning activities. The nonreading activities provide content for experience stories, news bulletins, and notices, which are introductions to functional social uses of reading. Parts of the story can be acted out. The experience stories themselves can be duplicated or cut into strips to be used as titles for large original illustrations. These and other uses of the story introduce enough variation to discourage memorization and rote reading. Many uses keep interest from sagging and provide new contexts and settings for many of the words as they become familiar. Typed copies of pages or sentences can be duplicated and illustrated so that each child can become the illustrator of his own copy of the assembled pages in booklet form.

When the children cooperate in the planning and projection of these activities, guidance can find numerous opportunities to challenge attention and encourage intelligent inferences and discriminating perception. The child who is *"looking* for the place where it tells" what *he* said, or the line that tells "how many there were" is on the way to purposeful reading. He gets satisfaction from success *or* attends to helpful suggestions in his attempt to find what he is looking for. The child who says "Three lines start the same way" helps others to discover and look for the similarities and differences which are cues to recognition and to the direct relationships between sounds and visual symbols. Gross differences and gross cues are likely to be noted first in a developmental approach because they are less abstract and more meaningful. Gross cues also serve to develop responsiveness to similarities and differences that lead to finer discrimination and to generalization. The child who says, "I knew it was going to say Bobby, because it was Bobby who said that," is not as far along as the one who replies, saying, "Yes, and then too, all those B's in Bobby would help if you *didn't* know who said it." Such comments challenge others to note similarities and differences that set off recognition without sacrificing meaning. Occasionally a teacher can foster this kind of observation by asking a child how he knew.

The process should not be formal. By encouraging inferences and associations which serve as cues, the teacher can put children on the way to functional awareness of phonetic cues, common prefixes and endings, punctuation and other matters that supplement contextual inference and recognition at sight. To limit children to some one arbitrary method may be more systematic, but it is less developmental because it shuts off the child's initiative and the normal exploratory *use* of associations suggested by prior language learning.

Before a printed book is used for reading instruction, beginners also need to *hear* stories that are not accounts of their own firsthand experience. In the use of such stories guidance is not concerned with recognition of reading skills, but with the cultivation of interest in vicarious experience or curiosity about what happened to others, encouraging the anticipation of events or ideas, cultivating an eagerness to find out, lengthening attention span, the building of awareness of what reading opens up for free use, and fostering the aspiration to learn to read and to read independently. These purposes shape creative guidance and suggest the pauses for talk which encourage anticipation and the informal dramatizations which enrich experience. Teachers should provide a variety of easy books to which children can have free access for browsing and for selection of stories they want to hear again, and want to read as soon as they can! Since such books are usually illustrated, they become sources of enjoyment, challenges, and means of anticipation in the "reading" of illustrations. Furthermore, pictures contribute to emotional identification with the vicarious experience even before actual reading of the accompanying printed matter is attempted. Identification is associated with the popularity of comic books, but it has real developmental possibilities with the resources of children's literature, and is something to be encouraged on that account.

If more children could be given the advantage of an individualized developmental approach to reading there would certainly be less retardation and less need for remedial instruction. There would also be far greater likelihood of carry-over and abiding interest in reading. Children should have the satisfaction of reading more books of their own selection independently, each at his own level. At the same time they should experience challenging group guidance in the maturing of their reading tastes and reading abilities. They should also be guided to fuller use of reading for information and for purposeful study in every phase of the curriculum. One book is not enough for any phase of the curriculum in our day. Reliance on a single text fosters unthinking assimilation. Broader orientation is essential for personality development.

Only by *using* reading freely and purposefully will children develop into functionally literate citizens. Times like ours call for forward adjustments in education. We need vital teaching and a fuller use of today's abundance of good reading material. We need to abandon class centered reading instruction, with its deadening effects on the ablest and its failure to serve the developmental needs of the least able, if we are to lead children to a lifetime use of reading for personal satisfaction and social orientation.

EVALUATING DIFFERENTIATION OF LEARNING IN READING INSTRUCTION *

Jeannette Veatch

A noticeable trend in the teaching of reading is the declining influence of the traditional basal reading programs. As a result, there is a veritable explosion of all types and varieties of materials moving into the deepening vacuum. Some of these phenomena exist as materials alone, while others insist that they are a full blown program.

The best of curriculum workers, through the years, have worked to fit teaching to the learning of each child. Differentiation of learning for a class of children, nevertheless, has, like the weather, had much said about it, and

* REPRINTED with permission of the Association for Supervision and Curriculum Development and Jeannette Veatch from *Educational Leadership*, Vol. 22, March, 1965, pp. 408–11. Copyright 1965 by the Association for Supervision and Curriculum Development.

little done about it. The most notable push of practical classroom help in this direction began about 1952 and continues with a spate of writing and research around the practice called, however inadequately, "individualized reading." Hindsight shows a groundswell was in existence, as other curricular areas (for example, mathematics and science) responded in the direction of similar methodology for independent, individualistic education.

Differentiated learning is most easily a fact when the learners are the ones that choose the material by which they are taught to read. This factor of pupil choice, sometimes called self-selection or free-choice, is crucial. The uniqueness of every human being has been substantiated too fundamentally to allow contrary argument. There is no sameness between individuals' personality development, their needs, their interests. We differ, and we have a right to differ. How does this apply to a reading program?

Sylvia Ashton-Warner [1] describes how she develops what she calls "key vocabulary" or what we would call "sight vocabulary." In this activity, each one of her five year olds is free to tell her any word that has a personal, dynamic attraction to him. It does not matter if the word is "ghost" or "house." Each child has his own words. Miss Warner teaches the necessary reading and writing skills with whatever words are said. She accepts these pupil offerings. There is clear, unmistakable free choice and, therefore, differentiated learning.

Were a teacher to use this "key vocabulary" of children to develop a permanent list intended for all children, it would be as Ashton-Warner said, a dead vocabulary. Words must come "bubbling hot" each day to each child, and be recorded for the use of that child only. To the degree that teachers allow true freedom of choice, to that degree do we meet our criteria of individual differences.

In the same vein, the "language-experience" approach, as notably described by Lee and Van Allen,[2] lends itself to gradations of differentiated teaching. Teachers take dictation from the class (or group or child) and record what is said on large paper or on the chalkboard. If teachers maintain the children's own expressions as carefully as possible, to that extent do children see their own language in written form.

Our guideline is that of pupil choice. When each child recognizes his own spoken language in writing, to that degree he has chosen the path to reading through his own unique ideas. The problem, of course, lies in the size of classes. Taking dictation from all children every day is a formidable task. Short cuts must be found, and grouping for dictation is common.

Yet there is another danger that must be mentioned. Many are mistakenly concerned that pupils will "miss something" unless they read the preprimers before they read the primer, and the primer before the first reader, etc., etc.

---

[1] Sylvia Ashton-Warner. *Teacher*. New York: Simon and Schuster, 1963.

[2] Dorris M. Lee and R. Van Allen. *Learning To Read Through Experience*. New York: Appleton-Century-Crofts, 1963.

Such teachers thus corrupt the process of pupil choice if they use pupil dicta-tion to teach the sight vocabulary of the coming preprimers or primers. The intention is that all children will eventually be reading the same books. This is a clear denial of individual differences, even though the paths through many experience charts and stories could and do provide variety along the way.

To continue, there are many programs called "phonics" that need evalu-ating with our yardstick of pupil choice. Unfortunately, they largely fail to measure up. There are none that teach letter sounds with the use of children's own words or language to initiate understanding of phonics. One or two sys-tems bring in children's own words after early initiation to reinforce phonic learnings. But all, without exception, as far as this writer has been able to ascertain, are based upon lists of words without regard for their origin in a given class's spoken or written language.

The current teaching of phonics, therefore, fails on this criterion, whatever its success on others.

Before passing on to another guideline, the matter of programed materials, as far as pupil choice is concerned, must be mentioned. Whatever else may be said about programing, and there is a lot else, there is no doubt that the pupil has a great deal of choice in what he will read.

He may choose to skip around. He may choose to "cheat" on answering the questions that are supposed to test what he has learned from the material. But whether or not he follows the program as he is supposed to, the right of choice is a feature of programed materials. To that extent, programing is differenti-ated in character.

One of the best known programs built almost entirely upon the principle of self-choice is Montessori. While there are serious deficiencies in its pre-reading activities, the freedom with which children choose those activities available is to be commended on this basis.

The best known practice of this concept of free choice, or self-selection, came to prominence with Willard Olson's now famous article called, "Seek-ing, Self-Selection and Pacing." [3] In this reading program, each child chooses a book or piece of material with which he is taught to read. Each child has his own book. At frequent intervals he brings a book of his choice to the teacher for an individual conference during which matters of individual needs are recognized. These are dealt with on the spot, or handled in a group situa-tion with those other pupils having the same difficulties.

In such an approach as this, heterogeneous grouping comes into its own. In a fourth grade, for example, with an adequate book supply, children reading from first grade levels to eighth grade levels can be handled without crucifying the slow or holding back the able. The differences that exist and that are noticed are not hurtful to anyone.

[3] Willard Olson, "Seeking, Self-Selection and Pacing." *The Packet.* Vol. 7, No. 1; Spring 1952.

INDEPENDENT WRITING

Pupil choice or self-selection comes into its own when independent writing is part of the reading instruction program. If the writing is *not* independent and is the result of assignment in a workbook, or upon a specified teacher-thought-up theme or topic, then individual differences are less well met. The criterion of pupil choice is a major one when looking at an approach that encourages, *as part of the reading program*, the writing of independently developed ideas.

Sylvia Ashton-Warner's work, the language experience approach, and to some degree activities found in the i/t/a Manual [4] are along these lines. The reliability of the symbol-sound relationship in the last approach is demonstrably pushing the use of writing in connection with reading. Similarly, Durrell [5] recognized the importance of writing when he stated that "word analysis is best done . . . in the spelling period."

The use of independent writing to teach reading is an excellent bench mark in assaying whether or not a reading program allows for differentiated learning.

PACING OR RATE OF READING

The capacity of reading approaches to differentiate learning must, among others, be judged on the criteria of pacing or rate of reading. This is not meant as the actual speed of reading, although this is related. Rate, or pacing, refers to the amount to be read at a given daily sitting. One page a day? One story a day? As far as a pupil may go? All read the same? All read at their own pace or rate?

In the traditional basal systems the amount of reading is governed by the manuals. Children are not asked to read ahead on the theory that they will miss some aspect of skill development, supposedly, and without any research proof, imbedded in a given piece of material. Because of this discouragement of self-pacing, there can be little differentiation of teaching. All must follow the preset, predeveloped lesson. Yet basal authors insist that individual differences are met through the device of ability grouping, or of recreational reading.

The most extreme example of ability, or homogeneous grouping, is that called the Joplin Plan. Inherently this plan puts children together on similarities rather than differences. The plan, in effect, makes it difficult for a teacher to differentiate the learning. With a room full of pupils at the allegedly same level of ability, the teacher teaches in the same way, from the same books and other materials. That there is yet no well-designed research that proves the effectiveness of such an approach is probably no accident. This approach certainly does not make individualization easy.

[4] A. J. Mazurkiewicz and H. J. Tanyzer. *Teacher's Manual and Key. Book I, Ready for Reading*. New York: i/t/a Publications.

[5] D. D. Durrell. *Improving Reading Instruction*. New York: World Book, 1956. p. 267.

In general, whether or not a reading approach meets individual differences well, depends upon the way it suggests the grouping of pupils. Grouping on test results is grouping upon generalized bases.[6] Grouping is more suited to individual needs when it is accomplished on more specific, task oriented, day-to-day, this-is-what-I-don't-know bases.

PERSONAL IDENTIFICATION

Reading instruction cannot meet individual differences if it ignores the personality characteristics of the pupils involved. Imbedded in any proper approach to teaching reading must be some practice that *uses* the personal experiences, interests, needs, fears, concerns of the learner.

The practices that come off best in this aspect of evaluation are those programs that start with children's own language for instruction. The language-experience approach has already been mentioned.

Similarly, any approach that allows self-choice and self-pacing must, inherently, be based upon the bibliotherapeutic criterion of personal identification. Children choose the books that they *like*. Personal identification differentiates what is read.

Classroom practices that enable a teacher to teach pupils on an individual basis are the best practices for meeting individual differences. There is simply no substitute for an individual conference. Even teachers who are shaky as to how to proceed in a one-to-one or a one-to-two conference, fall into a helpful line as they talk with each child. This is not usually the problem. Rather the problem is the rest of the class.

It is notable that there is no program of reading instruction aside from that called "individualized reading" that encourages and plans for a teacher-pupil individual conference.

The art of good conferencing is largely dependent upon an effective independent work period.[7] When a class is busy at constructive and absorbing tasks, a teacher is freed to pursue individual and group teaching.

Some materials, notably the SRA *Individualized Reading*, are set up in such a way as to encourage such a conference. But this, and other programs like it, are more appropriately described as programed materials. The degree of differentiation depends upon the material to be covered, not upon the teacher's analysis of what needs to be learned.

In summary, then, reading programs that meet the criteria of differentiating teaching and learning stand or fall upon the guidelines of: pupil choice of

---

[6] See the writer's article, "Grouping Is the Function and Process of Content," *Educational Leadership* 18: 425–28, April 1961.

Also Carleton W. Washburne, "Adjusting the Program to the Child," *Educational Leadership* 11: 138; December 1963.

[7] One of the best references for teachers for "seatwork" is: Darrow and Allen. *Independent Activities for Creative Learning*. New York: Bureau of Publications, Teachers College, Columbia University, 1961.

material, independent writing, pacing or rate of reading, personal identification, and individual conferences.

Reading instruction can be evaluated upon other criteria, but these are submitted as crucial if the evaluation is to be that of meeting individual differences.

B. Language Experience

EARLY WRITING AS AN AID TO READING *

Gertrude Hildreth

Learning to read is reinforced by simultaneous experience in writing, judging from observations of primary school pupils and facts about the interrelationships between the two processes. Reading and writing are both forms of language expressed with a common graphic symbol system representing the spoken language; in the case of English, the ABC's. The word units of reading material have already been composed; in writing the writer, with a knowledge of the ABC's and spelling, proceeds to construct words. In reading, the task is to identify words or parts within words for clues to meaning; in writing, the pupil must think of the letters that represent the sounds in the words he wants to write and reproduce them. Whether a child is reading or spelling, he is dealing with the same set of phonic elements represented with the same graphic symbols.

It is rare to find a child who can express ideas in writing, however simple, who cannot read. Those who are unable to read can scarcely write their names or spell the simplest words. Older slow readers tend to be semi-literates, retarded in all phases of written expression. A fourth grade teacher of a slow class says few of the children can write the ABC's beyond M, N, O, P, and they cannot read. Twelve-year-old Billy has had a history of reading backwardness in spite of an average I.Q. At present his reading is barely up to second grade, he has made scarcely a beginning in spelling, and can do no independent writing.

A view widely held is that children should not begin practicing writing until

* REPRINTED with the permission of the National Council of Teachers of English and Gertrude Hildreth from *Elementary English*, Vol. 40, June, 1963, pp. 15–20.

they have learned to read the words they will write and spell. The assumption is that early practice in writing is inimical to the formation of good reading habits, a hazard in word study; that early writing interferes with whole-word recognition and prevents the development of fluent silent reading. A teacher reported that in her school no writing is permitted until the primer, "Fun with Dick and Jane," is completed toward the latter part of the first grade.

The tendency to keep reading and writing apart in beginning reading instruction is unfortunate because of the mutual relationship between the two processes. Pushing reading far ahead of writing means that the two skills cannot be mutually reinforcing to the fullest extent; and that writing, in contrast to reading, will seem to be a tedious, difficult task. Abroad, the practice of teaching beginning reading and writing simultaneouly is far more common than here in the United States.

Today, in our concern over the improvement of reading, the tendency is to lengthen the daily reading time, step up word drills, and require more extensive use of texts and workbooks. It may be more productive in the long run to introduce writing earlier, and to relate writing closely to the initial reading experiences. Some of the drills included in reading might better be shifted to writing and spelling, resulting in gains for both reading and writing.

How many primary teachers or instructors of slow learners suggest that their pupils *write* the difficult reading words as a means of fixing them in mind and recognizing the letter parts composing the sounds the words contain?

In the controversy over the whole-word, Look-and-Say approach to beginning reading *versus* phonics and the ABC's, the intermediary role of writing has been overlooked. Writing serves as a bridge between the parts and the wholes. In writing, the beginners gain practice in observing the separate letters, thinking of the sounds they represent and recording whole words beginning with the parts, *e.g.*, h-o-u-s-e. Then the children read the words and sentences they have written.

In the initial stages of learning to read any experience with writing benefits reading, no matter what methods are used in reading instruction. With more emphasis on writing paralleling the reading experience fewer children would reach an early plateau in reading and be unable to learn at a normal rate.

One reason that follow-up studies have failed to show any permanent differences in reading achievement when groups of children are instructed initially by look-and-say or by phonics, is that by the time the middle grades are reached the common writing and spelling experience has evened up the groups taught by different methods.

The key to writing as an aid to reading in the early stages lies in the use of manuscript-style writing. Manuscript-style more closely resembles the type of the printed page and typewritten material than cursive-style writing, as these samples indicate:

Beautiful   **Beautiful**   Beautiful   *Beautiful*

Cursive-style writing has less carry-over to beginning reading both because the letter forms differ from print and are usually slanted; also because cursive style takes longer to learn in order to achieve a practical script for expressive writing. With manuscript writing the child begins at once using writing to record his familiar language patterns. Throughout this paper all reference to "writing" is to manuscript style unjoined letter forms.

Early Beginnings in Handwriting

Evidence of children's early interest in writing is proof of readiness by beginning school age. The typical school beginner is apt to have shown some interest in writing before entering school. He may be able to write his first name and print other letters of the alphabet and some numbers. An alert five-year-old industriously copies graphic symbols commonly observed, WABC, JIF, STOP, OR-72, 195, etc. He asks to be shown how to make an A, a G, or the number 3. This becomes an absorbing task along with exploring the mysteries of chalk, crayons, pencils, and scrap paper. This early interest in writing reflects the young child's eagerness to imitate adult accomplishments.

When young children play school they are more apt to think of school work as writing and spelling than reading or other school activities. Ira, a bright school boy, says that at the age of four his favorite game was playing school with his friend and his older sister as teacher. The first day they showed up with note books and pencils ready to *learn to write!* By kindergarten, Ira could do a little writing and had also made good progress in reading.

Four-year-olds in the Brooklyn College Early Childhood Center made valentines which they decorated and on which they "wrote" messages and their names with colored felt marking pens. A few of the children could make the individual letters of their first names and write simple words with the teacher's help. All this was great fun; not a writing lesson at all. A bright five-year-old after seeing a children's holiday movie wrote about the experience in legible print, "I SAW SNO WHITE."

How Early Writing Benefits Beginning Reading

The advantages of early writing as an aid to reading may be summarized as follows:

Writing, an Active Motor Response

Writing is an active motor-muscular response which produces word patterns that are perceived visually. The motor response aids memory of the letter forms and words. The young writer must observe how each word and the separate elements in each word are formed. To write the separate letters, to copy short words, to print his name are comparatively simple tasks that give a beginner the satisfaction of seeing tangible results.

Restless young boys whose attention wanders during reading, who can't find the page or keep the place, who lose interest in the little stories that are foreign to their background and interests, may be able to give attention to copying and writing experiences which entail overt activity and relate to themselves. Passive children and those lacking self-confidence, who seem overwhelmed by a page of print, may be able to concentrate on a bit of writing.

Learning the ABC's

Learning to write acquaints the beginners with the ABC's. Instead of merely looking at the letters and naming them or trying to spot them in printed words, the child in writing must construct the letters from memory or actively copy them. Here is one of the surest ways of fixing the 26 letter forms in mind and learning their names.

Word Recognition and Discrimination

No writing can be done without recalling the letter forms and their standard arrangement in common words. Writing and copying words forces the young writer to pay attention to the details in words, to likenesses and differences, peculiarities or unusual features. Writing helps the beginner catch on to the make-up of a word, to get hold of a word such as *between* or *circus* or *party*.

In writing his name, or *Love to Mother*, or *Santa Claus* the beginner must name the separate letters, trying to recall them in order within the words, to say and see the word parts in orderly progression. This process of building up the words, though exactly the opposite of reading, reinforces memory for the distinctive features of a word, *e.g., apple, ready*. On completion of the writing the learner perceives a whole word with all its parts assembled, *e.g., because.*

Discrimination of similar appearing words is sharpened by the writing-spelling experience: *who-how, where-when, this-that, farther-father, brook-broke.*

A child who found words such as *funny* or *start* difficult to sound out in reading enjoyed copying them on cards, letter by letter, saying over the letters, then pronouncing the words.

Writing is a means of recognizing and concentrating on phonetically irregular words, their appearance and distinctive features, *e.g., knife, through, tough, many.*

Reversals and other confusions straighten out as the children practice writing the confusing words and then pronouncing them, *e.g., was-saw, bread-bear, help-play*, etc.

"Spelling-out" is objectionable in reading because it slows down word recognition and interferes with thought getting. In writing, on the contrary, spelling-out is essential in building up the separate words.

As the child writes and spells he can see the need of matching letters to sounds. "What sounds do I hear in the word I want to write? *fed, fill, feet, foot*," etc. In writing words from memory the child must think of the succession of sounds within words, and try to call up a visual impression of the word parts, all valuable aids in reading.

Written spelling sharpens perception of cognates, that is, words related by a common root or stem, *e.g., set, settle, settling, upset,* etc. Writing the word *smiles* or *smiling* focuses the pupil's attention on the changes made in the root word *smile,* furnishing practice in one of the commonest skills employed in reading.

Word-building, for example, adding *s* for plural form, or *ed* for past tense can be understood best in the spelling-writing lesson where changes and additions in word forms must be made for correct forms of expression.

Writing as an Aid to Learning Phonics

Teachers have expressed surprise at the difficulty children experience in detecting the initial sounds and component parts within printed words, *e.g.,* the *s* in *song, say, see;* the *m* in *mother, my, most,* etc. Composing words by their sounds as in written spelling forces the child to say and see the parts in words. One way to reinforce memory for the initial consonant sounds, *e.g., d* as in *dog, do, did; th* in *thing, this, them* is to practice writing these words.

Teaching children to write and copy simple words might well supplant much of the meaningless practice in sounding the separate letters and letter combinations in reading lessons. Whether or not the child actually vocalizes the sounds in writing a word, he tends to think of the series of sounds as he writes, *e.g., pen-cil.* Writing out words, *before, singing, perhaps, around, tomorrow,* helps form the habit of sounding through the parts in words in order from left to right, and in saying words through by syllables.

Fixing Words in Mind

In the course of writing, the pupil thinks about individual words, their appearance and construction. As a result, he steadily builds up a store of easily recognized words.

A school beginner who was uncertain of *from* in reading had no further difficulty after he printed valentine messages for all the class, using the word *from* and then signing his name to each one. A boy who could never seem to remember the word *until* in his reading got hold of it by writing the word and using it in sentences.

An older boy mastered *your* and *friend* after writing the expression on thirty cards for his classmates. A young lady in the fifth grade was sure of *secretary* after having been appointed class secretary because she made a label for her desk and wrote the word on reports after signing her name.

Self-Constructed Reading Material

In writing familiar language patterns the young writer creates material to read, extending the amount of reading material that is easy to understand because it reflects the child's own ideas, vocabulary, and modes of expression. Writing a greeting, a message, or a one-sentence story is certain to enhance reading because of children's interest in reading what they have written, for example, a valentine greeting,

> I love you, Mother
> Jimmy

or an account of a trip:

> We went to the Zoo.
> Grade I
> (List of pupils' names)

Reading back these sentences is done with ease and interest because every word is already known and understood.

Writing furnishes practice in using words in meaningful sentences, strengthening the association between word forms and their meanings, and increasing the child's familiarity with sentence patterns. The pupil begins to recognize the different kinds of sentences used in expression, and the conventional punctuation of sentences required in writing, all of which contributes to reading comprehension. The value of sentence punctuation for reading becomes more obvious as the children themselves learn to punctuate the sentences they write.

Left-to-Right Direction

Another value of writing is that it accustoms the young learner to move across the lines in a left-to-right direction, returning to the left side for the beginning of each new line. Thus eye-hand coordination in writing helps train the eye-movements required in reading.

Various Writing Tools

The writing tools need not be limited to chalk or bulky pencils. The beginner may find more satisfaction in "writing" with brush and water colors; he will enjoy using a felt marker or printing the letters with finger paints.

Another form of "writing" that interests beginners is shaping the letters with small sticks or other small objects. In foreign schools children copy letters and words with hard white beans or small sticks.

Still another form of "writing" school beginners enjoy is playing with anagrams—the capital and small letters printed on small blocks or cards available as "cut outs" to be used in spelling out words. A felt board provides a holder for cardboard letters. This convenient brand of "writing" is fun to do and easy for the teacher to check.

A comparatively new development in the writing approach to reading is the introduction to the ABC's and spelling *via* the typewriter. Recent experiments have focused attention on the use of the electric typewriter as a means of acquainting young children with the alphabet, with spelling, and sentence composition, as a basis for beginning reading. No doubt, schools of the future will experiment extensively with a simplified typewriter as an aid in teaching literacy.

The advantage of the typewriter is that the letters are already formed, needing only to be recognized to construct words; the letter forms resemble book page print and the child can observe the correct sequence of print as the words take shape from left to right.

As for tracing dotted lines for letters and numbers, this has questionable value unless the practice is related to meaning and the child's purposes.

Some Conclusions and Recommendations

In view of children's early interest and experience with imitative writing, the ease of learning manuscript writing, and the close tie between reading and writing, teachers are advised to provide informal writing experiences for children early in the first grade, devoting as much time to writing as to reading in beginning instruction.

Writing practice is too often identified with penmanship drills, push-and-pull exercises, with mechanical aspects that have no relation to linguistic experience. Actually, there is no real writing apart from "writing something," words to spell or sentences that need to be written. The recommendation is to make writing a functional skill, serving the child's real purposes of communication from the beginning.

Working with words and items that are meaningful is more interesting to children than drill on meaningless details. When children begin to sense the purposes writing serves, they will see the reasons for practicing to produce legible script.

Five- and six-year-olds in the Brooklyn College Early Childhood Center told what they did during Christmas vacation, then wrote the stories with help from the teacher, and illustrated them.

> Peter and Johanna went ice-skating.
> Scott saw a rocket at the museum.
> Danny saw a boat and a train.

Paul was busy copying over and over a sentence he enjoyed:

> Paul has a papa.

A six-year-old, Robin, wrote sentences:

> Robin has a cat.
> Robin has a dog.

then read them back to the teacher.

In beginning stages the children learn about writing by watching as the teacher writes on the board, or the child's paper, or makes a chart. The simple letter forms of manuscript writing enable the beginner to use writing for communication immediately, without a long series of preparatory drills on letter strokes and movements.

The beginner learns to write by copying words and simple text, by helping the teacher write, by writing from oral dictation, and by independent attempts to write and label. Children who are too immature to spell words independently can do partial writing by helping the teacher complete words:

co-coat
sh-shoes
Sun-Sunday

Using the ABC's to write or copy meaningful words has more bearing on reading than exercises such as: Mark the letter that is unlike the others in each group:

k o k   m n m   c d d

Let the pupils take plenty of time for beginning writing; they will need time to explore the letters, to get acquainted with writing tools, to discover the possibilities of ordering the ABC's in readable words.

Do not expect too much in the child's first efforts to copy his name or to write words and numbers independently.

Allow ample paper space for early writing, inch wide rulings, folded paper with ample creases, or no markings at all. Keep work periods short.

Although children in the age range five to seven are developing rapidly in visual perception, eye-hand coordination and motor-manual controls, some are slow developers in these aspects of growth.

In the normal course of events reading will soon outdistance writing, both because of the nature of the process and difficulties with English spelling. But the rapid gains in reading will be due in part to the early experience with writing.

These conclusions and recommendations have special significance for slow learners, non-English speaking children learning literacy, illiterate adults learning to read and write, and for students learning to read foreign languages.

Adult literacy programs would benefit from adopting a program combining practice in reading and functional writing, all related to oral expression used in daily living. For this work, the use of manuscript style writing with simple, unjoined letter forms is recommended. An elderly woman, an illiterate refugee, learned to read chiefly through mastering print-style writing, learning to spell a vocabulary of common words, and writing simple sentences.

Studies of the relation of reading and writing provide a promising area for research. Experiments should be set up to explore the possibilities of early writing experience as an aid to reading through the link with oral expression.

BEGINNING READING—
A PERSONAL AFFAIR *

Esther Levin

After several weeks of close observation, I found that thirteen children in my "heterogeneous" first-grade class of twenty-three were not ready to read. All thirteen came from educationally and economically deprived areas. Three of the thirteen were almost eight years old and were attending school for the first time. They had spent the first seven years of their lives in isolated farm or mining areas, where apparently there had been no pressure to enroll young children in school.

All thirteen children had at least one of the following characteristics: fearfulness, excessive shyness, submissiveness, high distractibility, and short attention span. Most of the children were inarticulate. They spoke in monosyllables. Their speech patterns were poor: they constantly slurred and mispronounced words. Many of them could not use verbs and articles. The children were interested in learning to read, but they were so bewildered, so inarticulate, so fearful, and so unable to listen that the idea of reading may have seemed awesome to them.

If I concentrated on the readiness skills, this group would soon be ready for beginning reading. Or so I thought until I discovered that the children lacked not only skills that are ordinarily learned before school age but also skills essential to a readiness program.

The children were confused about the meaning of *top* and *bottom*, *up* and *down*, *above* and *below*. *Left* and *right* meant nothing to them. Numbers, letters, words, and sounds were all one big jumble. Directions brought no response. Listening to directions was, I suppose, like listening to commercials on TV: just bear with them, and they will soon go away.

The ability to distinguish likenesses and differences had to be developed from an almost primitive level. The children had no comprehension of the

* REPRINTED from *The Elementary School Journal* (November, 1966, pp. 67–71) by Esther Levin by permission of The University of Chicago Press. Copyright 1966 by The University of Chicago.

meaning of the words *shape, form, different, alike, same, first, last, row,* and *line.* Just remembering what to look for was a problem, and the problem of recall was compounded by ineptness with crayons, pencils, chalk, and paint.

Search for a Solution

Stories were read to the children and told and retold to encourage them to speak; however, their impoverished vocabularies blocked any but the most meager verbal response. Rhyming games were played, but from one second to the next the children forgot the rhyming words. Visual recall games were also unsuccessful. The children seemed to have no conception of what a word was. To them words seemed to be a conglomeration of sounds.

At the children's hesitant dictation chart stories were written, but these group experiences were soon discarded because of the continuous struggle to muster words. Stories the teacher made up were also unsuccessful; they failed to hold the children's attention. A completely different approach was needed, but what was it to be?

I considered an extended readiness program, but decided against the idea. A more rapid approach seemed necessary to keep these children interested in learning to read. A structured program had to be found—one that emphasized the language arts and used the children's unique backgrounds. With such a program, perhaps, I could find a key to unlock the door to their dormant abilities.

Obviously each child needed individual attention. Yet it seemed desirable to teach these children in a group, since the rest of the class and the rest of the curriculum could not be neglected. Besides, in a group the children would learn from one another; each could act as a catalyst, and they would profit from one another's mistakes, achievements, and experiences. The children worked in a group of six or seven.

By stressing each child's name, I hoped to enhance his self-image and his self-confidence, and establish for him a beginning association between the spoken and the written word. Each child was given a name card with his name in large black manuscript writing. All the names were listed on a large chart, each name in a different color. Each child then matched the name on his card with his name on the chart. Almost immediately afterward, each child was able to find his name without his name card, using only the color cue. Soon the configuration of the name alone was sufficient, and the color cue was discarded.

As each child found his name on the chart, he was shown how to use his right hand in a left-to-right movement under his name. Special attention was called to names with the same beginning sounds. A great to-do was made about each name—the way it sounded, its configuration, the tall letters, the short letters, the tail letters, the hump letters, and the names that were on "one track." As might be expected, talking about names seemed to give the children a feeling of importance and satisfaction, and seemed to release vague and unexpressed thoughts about themselves and their families.

PICTURES AND STORIES

At the same time that the children were learning to read their names, they were being encouraged to speak in complete sentences. A collection of large colorful pictures of classic fairy tales was used to motivate the children to talk. One of these pictures was displayed as the teacher told the story. She deliberately made mistakes to test the children. They were quick to make corrections, and they began to speak more freely and in complete sentences. Another device used during story time was to ask some outlandish question about the story to stimulate the children to react and to respond.

In time, the children began to take an active part in the story-telling. Later, dramatization was used. The teacher or one of the more able children acted as narrator while other children acted out the various parts and supplied the necessary dialogue.

After the children had learned to recognize their names and had participated in story-telling, large colorful picture alphabet cards were adapted by the teacher for the children's use. Each letter of the alphabet was represented by a picture. The teacher wrote the name of the object pictured at the bottom of the card and always used her right hand in a left-to-right motion under the word as she said it or helped each child use this motion as he called the word. As the children identified and discussed each picture, they learned to look at words from left to right. They did not learn to read the words under these pictures until weeks later, but they did become aware of the fact that things—like children—have names and that these names can be written as words.

One day the children were talking about themselves and their families, and were expressing complete thoughts. It seemed a propitious time to let the children see their thoughts in print. Here is the conversation that took place that day:

TEACHER: Listen to what I say. I'm going to tell you something, and then I am going to write what I say on this paper (*indicating large chart paper*). The words that come out of my mouth are going to be written here. Listen and then watch me write, "I am a teacher." (*Writes:* "Mrs. Levin said, 'I am a teacher.'" *Repeats sentence and uses left-to-right motion. Then looks at the first child.*) Now, Susan, you tell me something, and I will write what you say on this paper. The words that come out of your mouth I will write here. They will be your words—only yours.

SUSAN (*after a great deal of thought*): I'se a girl.

TEACHER (*rightly or wrongly*): I am a girl.

SUSAN: I'se am a girl.

TEACHER (*writes and repeats*): Susan said, "I am a girl." That's fine, Susan. These are your words. They came out of your mouth. (*Susan is mute but beaming with pride.*)

TEACHER (*looks at Lisa*): Now, you tell me something you want to say, and I will write it down here. They will be your words—only yours.

LISA: Hello, Mrs. Levin.

TEACHER (*writes and reads*): Lisa said, "Hello, Mrs. Levin." Very, very good, Lisa. (*Now many hands were waving. The other children wanted to see their names in print and their thoughts on paper.*)

JANE: Hi, Mrs. Levin.

HENRY: Howdy, Mrs. Levin.

MAGGIE: Goodbye, Mrs. Levin.

LARRY: Bye, bye, Mrs. Levin.

As each child spoke, his name was written on the chart, and what he said was set off by quotation marks. It was then quite simple for each child to frame and read what he or she said. This was the children's first attempt to read a sentence. Success was theirs to cherish. The chart held a precious personalized thought from each of them. Interest was maintained because they were eager to repeat what they had said. They were fascinated by the fact that what they had said was written in black and white on the chart.

Several thought-charts along these lines were made. Popeye and the Three Stooges were among the subjects the children chose. Always I emphasized the fact that each sentence belonged to a particular person. This personal involvement in the sentences plus the interest inspired by familiar subjects helped maintain the children's interest in learning to read. My fortuitous reading of the book *Spinster* [1] gave further impetus to this personalized approach to reading.

On a later occasion, I introduced another technique through which the children learned to read their own personal words. Each child was told to think of a word he would like to learn to read. The word was to be written on a card five inches by eight inches and given to the child as his very own. Each child was asked to think carefully, to choose a word that was important to him. Here are the first seven words the children wanted to read: *lunch, telephone, lamp, television, bald-headed baby, monkey,* and *peaches.* Each child dictated his word and watched to see how it was written. Then each child was asked to tell why he wanted that word. Here are some of the reasons:

Ma telephone's not workin'.
Ma mother's lamp's pretty.
Telebision set's new.
Duane's ma ball-head baby. He ma doll
    baby [her brother].
Monkeys they's funny.
Ah hates peaches.

The cards were kept in individual brown envelopes with the children's names on them and were given to the children only at reading time or on

---

[1] Sylvia Ashton-Warner, *Spinster.* New York: Simon and Schuster, 1958.

special occasions. Each day one additional word was written for each child. The same procedure was followed each time: the child thought of the word, he watched it being written, and he told why he wanted that word. After a child had three or four words in his envelope, any words that he repeatedly misread were discarded. Few words had to be eliminated.

Mounting Pride

As the words accumulated, so did the children's excitement. They pleaded to read their word cards to one another, to the school secretary, to the principal, to other teachers, and to their parents. Praise and encouragement were constant and came from all quarters: from the teacher, from children in the group, from other members of the class, and from the staff. Fear vanished as the children's feeling of security and power grew.

After each child had accumulated seven to ten words, another procedure was used for reinforcement. Words were taken from the cards at random and written on a chart. The children then identified and read their words and illustrated them whenever possible. Later, each child was given a notebook. The children dictated simple sentences to the teacher, who wrote them in the notebooks for the children to illustrate. This device, though successful, proved too cumbersome and too time-consuming, and was discarded.

Before long the children began to ask for the vocabulary from the basic textbooks used by the other children in the regular reading program. Soon all the first preprimer words were among their word cards. Words with the same beginnings were emphasized. When the children themselves began to find similarities in word beginings, it became a great source of pride to them and a signal to the teacher that progress was truly being made.

Mounting Confidence

Now that the children had overcome their fear of the unknown and had gained confidence in themselves, they were eager to read books. Their enjoyment of their first book was full, and their success complete. As they progressed in a regular reading program, more phonics skills were introduced and there was less emphasis on sight recognition of words. The word cards continued to interest the children and were not entirely forgotten. The children's main interest, however, turned more and more to books.

By the end of the year, eight of the thirteen children had read three preprimers, one junior primer, one primer, and halfway through a first reader. One child left the school; the other four had read three preprimers, one junior primer, and halfway through a primer.

The experience was rewarding for the teacher and hopefully for the children as well. The personalized approach seemed to release unplumbed depths of interest, ability, and individuality. Having a set of word cards of his own gave cach child the feeling of possession and a personal involvement that made reading something of unique importance. The teacher gained many insights into the children's backgrounds, problems, and personalities that would not have been possible otherwise.

Reading became an exciting adventure. Learning to read *monkey, peaches,* and *bald-headed baby* was far more exciting than reading *come, look,* or *see.* The phrase *bald-headed baby* had a zip to it that could never compare with "*Look, Baby, look,*" especially when the bald-headed baby was someone's own "doll baby" of a brother. The word *monkey* had far more personality than any little old stuffed bear. And the word *peaches.* How could you forget it when you "hates peaches!" To the children these words express love, laughter, and hate. These words have interest, color, and vitality. They are personal, positive, picturesque, and using them helped the children learn to read.

LURING THE NONREADER *

By Bernice H. Moss

Every year, everywhere, teachers are faced with the problem of children who have resisted all attempts to teach them to read. In spite of sound instructional techniques and varied materials, they withdraw further and further from learning experiences. The longer these children have been in school, the more sensitive and defensive they become. The reasons are many, and we know little about them except that they are complex.

Last year this situation was brought to my attention rather forcibly by a bit of drama. On the second day of school, I prepared to decide the placement of the three children in the low group. They came, dispiritedly but obediently, to the reading table. While I was at the cupboard selecting materials, they were talking together. As I sat down, Edwin reported rather solemnly, "Jane's going to kill herself. Lou's going to kill herself, too."

My startled expression must have affected them, because they grinned sheepishly and said they guessed they wouldn't kill themselves but they didn't like to read.

Subsequent lessons proved their point. No amount of motivation aroused much interest, enthusiasm, or progress. Indifference to the printed word colored all their responses to reading experiences. As a result, I was prompted to take my courage in hand and attempt an experiment that had its inception in a speech I had heard William Sheldon make at the Corning [New York] Council of the International Reading Association.

---

* REPRINTED by permission of the National Education Association and Bernice H. Moss from the *National Education Association Journal*, Vol. 50, January, 1961, pp. 14–16.

He had spoken most provocatively about the importance of recognizing the limitations of a child's background when trying to develop concepts in reading. He had suggested that teachers read *Spinster* by Sylvia Ashton-Warner. This story is about Anna Vorontosov, a school teacher among the Maori people of New Zealand. Fiction though it may be, this story rings true as it portrays Anna's warmth and wholehearted attempts to understand the needs and fears of the children in her care.

The impact of Anna's philosophy can best be observed in the comparison of the content of the basal reader material from the States with the original experience material developed by Anna. Maori children took four months to learn the basal-reader vocabulary words that had no meaning in the life they knew. These same children took four minutes to learn words in the material that Anna set down for them because the key vocabulary was rich in concept for them and recorded experiences familiar to them.

As Anna thoughtfully expressed it: "Vocabularies developed through their own need for communication resulted in an attentive, teachable group. The teachings and learnings are in their own hands, mixed up with all the natural concomitants of relationships."

With this philosophy and much apprehension, I approached the three youngsters with the suggestion that we write our own book. This was greeted with either apathy or alarm. Edwin and Louise couldn't have cared less. Jane reacted immediately with despair in her voice, "I can't write stories."

It seemed at first as though fear of failure had blocked every avenue to the world of words, but my suggestion of a title, *Our Family*, and the making of the title page sparked a bit of interest. Jane was pleased to have her name appearing there, with the middle initial included. Edwin offered his middle name as the surname of "Our Family." Francis, named for Louise's father, established our first character.

Thus, we became the LeRoys. Edwin wanted the father to work in a junk yard, but the girls overruled him in favor of the local glass works. Each day a new character and a new page were added. It was uphill work at first, but soon the children became delighted with their ability to read the pages of our book.

With the completion of each day's work, the children chose words with which they needed special help. I made flash cards showing these words. Phrase cards followed. Practice in the basic skills developed as the children became more aware of words.

On colored construction paper I printed word families and words illustrating beginning sounds and displayed them where they could be used every day. As the struggle for meaning grew, it soon became apparent that these children needed much more practice in using words, especially pronouns, in sentences.

Each day, I placed on the board exercises based on their special needs. Inevitably, the speech patterns of poor readers reflect their lack of comprehension of the written and spoken word, and these children were no exception. Their stories revealed the need for specific practice. They often said *walk* for *walked*, *look* for *looked*.

We worked on this type of exercise with various words:

Walk, Walks, Walking, Walked
1. Louise likes to . . . . . . to school.
2. We were . . . . to the library when the fire bell rang.
3. Edwin always . . . . slowly in the hall.
4. Yesterday Jane . . . . to school with Louise.

Similar practice was given by putting other troublesome words into sentences depicting the children's everyday activities. Pronouns presented a special challenge as the children had no idea where to begin in using words like *him, her,* or *that*. I had to proceed cautiously, because if I went too fast or made the work too difficult, my pupils wilted.

Gradually, as the stories evolved, interest and enthusiasm developed. Jane, who had rebelled at the thought of writing stories, became the most voluble of the group. She suggested that a pet be added to the LeRoy household; Butch, the dog, was her choice. The story, "Trouble for Butch," initiated the first bit of real fun. In this story Butch liked to visit the LeRoys' neighbor, the Russells, much to the annoyance of Mrs. Russell, but to the delight of the little Russells, who always let him in.

The children enjoyed reading their story aloud. When Butch got into trouble at the Russells' house, Mrs. Russell queried in a raucous voice, "Who let Butch in?" Her son Lyle fairly snarled his reply, "I did." We became quite hilarious at times. It should be noted, perhaps, that the youngsters seemed to take special delight in having Lyle reply in this defiant tone.

They became proud of their knowledge of new words such as *machine, condition, polishes*. They liked to watch the total grow on the board, where we kept count.

They made definite progress, but whenever I became overconfident about the gains, I was brought to earth by that most dependable leveler—the plateau of learning. One day, for example, feeling rather elated over their success in some comprehension exercises we had worked on together, I felt it was time for them to try to answer some questions on their own. I prepared the questions and we read them together. Then hopefully, I sent them off in the corner to work independently on the book about the LeRoys.

There didn't seem to be the rewarding sense of accomplishment I had anticipated. Before long, Edwin appeared at my side and whispered dejectedly, "Jane's going home. Lou's going home, too." I was dismayed, but at least it was a step up—they weren't going to commit suicide.

Soon, I began to consider what to do next, since it was apparent that we couldn't go on forever in the LeRoy book. I decided to try to write some stories using the vocabulary we had developed, plus the Dolch list as a guide. For interest, the characters would be the children themselves.

When I passed out the booklet, *More About the LeRoys*, complete with worksheets, the children received it with pleasure and read it fluently and with interest. Of course, they required plenty of encouragement, and the worksheets contained in the booklet had to be done under careful guidance. But they became much more skillful in recognizing words in context.

To obtain an audience reaction, they read the stories to the rest of the class. Then they asked questions about the stories. Their confidence and pleasure in this showed in their voices and posture.

Supplementary lessons were planned to pave the way for a return to the basal reader. Each time I attempted to go back to the reader, however, the interest of the group dropped. The defeatist attitude returned: grim faces, sighs, shuffling feet, all signs of a definite aversion to books. They read because I was bigger than they were! Even to me the material seemed dull, and flat compared to our current vocabulary. When we finished *More About the LeRoys*, we still needed additional stories based on their background.

As they advanced, their needs pointed the way to the next step. The day came when I felt they must be given experience in something besides purely personal material. Yet the new subject matter, I sensed, could not be very far afield.

So the next booklet, *Of Many Things*, contained descriptions of familiar objects in the classroom, such as our terrarium and explanations of games they like to play. With their experience and gradually increasing vocabulary, they could read this new material with understanding and personal satisfaction.

This experiment has been valuable. For me, it has meant new insight. I have learned that when the philosophy "Teach them where they are" fails, "Teach them where they live" may succeed. For the children, it has meant progress—in reading ability, reading interest, and in classroom behavior.

And finally we come to the place where the rewards are immeasurable. For the first time now, there is a *request*. Louise says, "When we finish *Of Many Things*, let's read in one of the *real* books."

HOW A LANGUAGE-EXPERIENCE PROGRAM WORKS *

Roach Van Allen

What Is a Language-Experience Approach?

A language-experience approach to instruction in beginning reading is one that makes no distinction between the development of reading skills and the

* REPRINTED by permission of R. Van Allen from an address at the International Reading Association Conference, Seattle, Washington, May, 1967.

development of listening, speaking, spelling, and writing skills. All are considered to be essential in the instructional program and are viewed by teachers as providing reciprocal reinforcement. All facets of language are used as experiences related to the reconstruction of printed materials. All experiences of a child which he can express, especially in oral language, are included as the raw material out of which reading refinement grows. During the instructional program he conceptualizes:

- What I can think about, I can talk about
- What I can say, I can write (or someone can write for me)
- What I can write, I can read
- I can read what others write for me to read.

A language-experience approach recognizes in daily practice that the oral-language background of each child is a basic ingredient in word recognition. As implemented in most programs:

- The thinking of each child is valued, regardless of how limited _____ which leads to
- Encouraging each child to express his thinking in many forms, but especially in oral language _____ which can be
- Represented in written form by a teacher or by the child _____ which can be reconstructed (read) by the author and others _____ which leads to
- Reading the written language of others from a variety of sources _____ which should
- Influence the thinking and oral language of the reader so that his spelling, writing, and reading improve.

Each Child Becomes Increasingly Sensitive to His Environment

The basis of children's oral and written expression is their sensitivity to their environment, especially their language environment, both within the classroom and in the world at large. The continuing responsibility of the teacher is to help children at all levels of ability become increasingly aware of the world in which they live—to "talk" about it in many media and to relate their observations and impressions to their own experiences. They should learn through repeated experiences that our heritage of literature, art, music, and science are the products of men and women who viewed the world with sensitive eyes and ears. For this reason there is a continuing program in a language-experience approach that urges every teacher to

- Read something of children's literature each day
- Provide a place for children to express their ideas with art media throughout the school day

- Discuss topics of interest with children
- Provide a time and place for children to record in writing and in illustrations what they see, hear, discover, taste, smell, feel, imagine
- Tell stories from real experiences
- Author books which record the real and imaginary experiences of the children in the class.

Children Succeed Through a Variety of Experiences

Children's communication skills, including word-recognition skills, are promoted through the use of numerous activities, experiences, and devices. A major goal is that of increasing the chances of success for more children and to do this it is expected that every teacher will know multiple ways of working with individuals. Positive attitudes which result from repeated success are viewed as being as significant as any method or material which might be employed.

The classroom is operated as a language laboratory that extends throughout the day. Language skills are extended and ideas are refined as children listen to stories and recordings, view films and filmstrips, make individual and class books, dictate stories to each other, study words, develop flexibility in using the letters of the alphabet to serve their spelling needs, and begin to record their ideas in writing of their own. They view filmstrips and provide the commentary before listening to the accompanying recording. They view motion picture films with the sound track turned off and discuss their own meanings and interpretations prior to hearing the commentary. They build confidence in the use of their own ability to use language at the same time that they are making progress in recognizing the language of other people—people who are not present but whose ideas have been recorded with writing.

Children have frequent opportunities to read their own writing to the entire class, to small groups within the class, and to other groups in the school. The child who is reading his own writing is using material with a meaning load of zero. Thus, he devotes his energies in oral reading to clarity of expression, effectiveness of presentation, interpretation of punctuation, and other necessary details that make listening to oral reading a pleasure.

Motivation for improving language form and usage comes as children's writing is read by others. Pride in "published" work stimulates the young author to seek language forms that will be understood by others. They are also influenced by what they read and what they hear read to them from hundreds of authors.

As children study the English language—its alphabet, its spelling, its sentence patterns, and the flexibility of meaning in English words—they come to realize that other people use words very much like their own to express ideas. The study of words of high frequency in English to the point of mastering them at sight correctly spelled becomes a meaningful experience.

As children express their own ideas, they are interested in finding out, through reading, what other people think and say about topics of interest to them. Wide reading, in turn, stimulates individual authorship, which is handled in the classroom through a variety of publishing procedures.

Understanding the nature and flexibility of the English language to a degree that one can look at printed symbols and reproduce the language of another person is considered to be a lifelong process. These understandings do not always result from "exercises" in reworking other people's language. They are more likely to develop as a child works with and reworks his own language. As he writes to say something important or interesting to him he is dealing with the language letter-by-letter, word-by-word, and sentence-by-sentence. It is when he has been helped to improve his own language—that which he has constructed—that he makes significant gains in understanding the strengths and weaknesses of that language. Repeated success in this process of writing and refining language gives the child confidence to view reading materials as another person's language. He can approach the act of reading with an attitude of "being able to reproduce the talk of someone who is not present."

BASIC FRAMEWORK OF A LANGUAGE-EXPERIENCE APPROACH

Through numerous studies, including the San Diego County Reading Study Project (1958–1967), researchers have identified twenty language experiences which contribute to the balanced development of language skills, including reading skills. These twenty language experiences are grouped in three categories as an aid in helping teachers select activities and materials. In well-planned programs some activities are selected from each category each day and during the progress of several weeks the teacher is careful to choose activities which will extend the learnings in all twenty experiences.

The three major categories with their emphases are:

Group One: Extending experiences to include words—through oral and written sharing of personal experiences, discussing selected topics, listening to and telling stories, writing independently, and making and reading individual books.

Group Two: Studying the English language—through developing an understanding of speaking, writing, and reading relationships, expanding vocabularies, improving personal expression, studying words, and gaining some awareness of the nature of the use of high frequency words and sentence patterns.

Group Three: Relating ideas of authors to personal experiences—through reading whole stories and books, learning to use a variety of printed resources, summarizing, outlining, reading for specific purposes, and determining the validity and reliability of statements found in print.

Resource books for teachers using this basic framework to insure that all three categories are dealt with frequently and that all twenty language experiences are extended through the elementary grades are now available.[1]

FLEXIBLE ORGANIZATION IS VITAL

Learning situations must be designed so that each child can view himself as worthy and able to succeed in reading tasks of increasing difficulty. How a child feels about himself and his relations to others—his family, his teacher, and other members of the class—will determine to a great extent what he is able to say, write and read.

School practices that make reading achievement the measure of success in the early grades, such as grouping techniques that highlight lack of this success, may destroy the child's self-image rather than improve his reading skills. Ability grouping for daily reading instruction can negate any positive attitudes that may be developed in other language experiences. Since every child individualizes his reading whether the teacher wants him to or not, the sensible attitude toward building good learning situations is one that emphasizes each child's success and provides for flexible groupings.

A language-experience approach allows great flexibility in organization and scheduling. The activities are selected to help the teacher use three basic patterns of classroom organization, singly or in combination, depending upon the nature of the work of the day.

1. The teacher works with the entire class. This arrangement works well for:

    • reading aloud to children
    • children reading their stories or compositions aloud
    • children composing stories orally
    • class discussions on topics of interest
    • extending experiences through films, filmstrips, field trips
    • introducing and playing games
    • singing and rhythms
    • conducting seminars on the development of various skills

2. The teacher works with small groups:

    • completing activities initiated in the large group
    • taking dictation from one while others observe

[1] Allen, R. V., and Claryce Allen, "Language Experiences in Reading," *Teacher's Resource Book*, Level I, Level II, and Level III. Encyclopaedia Britannica Educational Corp., Chicago.

- letting children read their own books as well as those of others
- giving special instruction in skills to some children identified as needing them
- playing games to practice skills
- practicing effective oral reading
- choosing appropriate books

3. The teacher serves as a resource person for individual and independent activities:

- suggesting ideas for individual books
- helping with spelling
- furnishing words for independent readers
- helping children choose and organize an independent activity
- conferring about reading and writing progress.

Some Advantages of a Language-Experience Approach

Whether a language-experience approach is used as the major reading program or whether it is used in conjunction with other programs, it has inherent in it certain advantages. Some are:

1. It does not require standard English as a basis for success in the beginning stages. Children whose language is greatly divergent from standard English are not placed at a severe disadvantage. Children who enter school with great fluency do not experience a period of language regression while they take time to develop a small sight vocabulary and learn a few word-recognition skills.

2. It does not require, nor does it recommend ability grouping in the class. Teachers can proceed without administering readiness tests or using valuable time placing children in ability groups which serve a questionable purpose in over-all language development.

3. Materials already available can be used effectively. There is no need for large expenditures for special materials to try to solve reading problems for special groups of children. Basal readers, supplementary readers, recordings, films, filmstrips, trade books, picture sets, children's newspapers, reference materials, and word-study progress can be used to advantage within the basic framework.

4. Children can begin reading using a sight vocabulary which has been developing in their homes and community environment—brand names, labels, signs, and other words seen often on television. To this vocabulary can be added words of high frequency which most children do not develop independently.

5. It allows for the effective use of aides to the teacher-semi-professionals, older children in the school, interested parents, and other volunteers.

6. Team teaching arrangements can be used to great advantage. A division of activities into large and small groups continues through most of the day, thus making maximum use of all team members and their ideas.

7. It is ungraded in the sense that much of the direct language teaching is done with material produced by the children. Each child produces at a level which he can understand and thus he learns to recognize words at his own level. Frustration is avoided. Also, children are helped to choose their own stories and books for independent reading from the beginning. They spend little, if any, time keeping the place while another child reads something which might be too easy or too challenging.

8. Children learn to spell the words of highest frequency at the same time that they learn to recognize them as sight words.

9. Phonics is an integral part of the daily program. Children learn and practice the relationships of sounds they make when they talk and the symbols used to represent the sounds in writing. They view phonics as a natural, normal language experience. They experience the flexibility of sound-symbol relationships in English as a challenge in self-expression. Teachers who wish to reinforce and extend phonics learnings with a more structured program can do so and still use a language-experience approach.

10. Children develop a level of independence in making choices in the daily program which is seldom observed among those who study with highly structured reading programs.

11. The programs require that all children participate in a variety of expressive activities. What appears to be additional time scheduled for language study includes art, music, dramatization, and rhythmic activities as essential for self-expression of ideas which might later be written and used for reading development.

12. Children choose writing as an independent, recreational activity as often as they choose reading. Self-expression is as important to them as is contact with the ideas and language of other people.

Children who live in a classroom with three major emphases in language development DO have an advantage! They develop desire and resources for self expression; they learn how to study the English language as a lifelong pursuit; they are influenced in their own thinking and their own language by the ideas and language of thousands of authors whom they view as friends.

C. The Initial Teaching Alphabet

ɑi	ch	au	œ	æ	h	ie	ee	au	wh	th	ʃ
ɑi	ch	au	œ	æ	h	ie	ee	au	wh	th	ʒ
ʃh	w	e	r	t	y	u	i	o	p	a	"
ʃh	w	e	r	t	y	u	i	o	p	a	–
a	s	d	f	g	h	j	k	l	ω	ω	/
a	s	d	f	g	h	j	k	l	ŋ	ω	?
z	œ	c	v	b	n	m	r	.	'		
z	œ	c	v	b	n	m	,	.	_		

this is printed in an augmented ræman alfabet, the purpos
ov which is not, as miet bee suppœsd, tω reform aur spelling,
but tω imprωv the lerning ov reeding. it is intended that
when the beginner has acheevd the inishial sucsess ov flωensy
in this speshially eesy form, his fuetuer progress shωd bee
confiend tω reeding in the present alfabets and spellings ov
them œnly.

i/t/a HELPS JOHNNY LEARN TO READ *

Frank Zeitz

The Initial Teaching Alphabet is England's answer to "Why Johnny can't read." i/t/a is Sir James Pitman's simplification of the spelling of the words in the English language.

Phonetic in nature, it avoids many of the complexities that presently exist in our written language. Simplicity. Simplicity is the keynote, the essence of the Initial Teaching Alphabet.

In the i/t/a, simplicity is found in the symbols. There are 44 symbols, each representing a sound, representing all the sounds found in the English language.

There exists an almost absolute one-to-one correspondence between symbol

---

* REPRINTED by permission of the publisher from *School and Community*, Vol. 51, May, 1965, pp. 28+.

and sound. Words are phonetically decoded and encoded. There is no mystery, no silent letters, no rules to memorize.

The reader reads exactly what is written. The writer writes exactly what he hears.

i/t/a simplifies reading. Each symbol has a "sound" name. The name of the symbol is the exact sound that the symbol, with very few exceptions, elicits.

Once a child learns the sounds of the symbols, he is ready to read any word written with the symbols. Coming upon an unfamiliar word, being unable to read, to say the word, the child merely "spells" the word. In the "spelling" operation, he pronounces every sound in the word.

In effect, he says the word in "slow-motion." If this fails to bring about his correctly pronouncing the word, a speeding-up of the spelling, the "sounding-out" of the word, results in his pronouncing the word.

i/t/a simplifies spelling. Once the 44 symbols have been mastered, the child can encode, write any word he can say. He simply mentally verbalizes the word to be encoded.

Saying the word slowly, he merely writes down the sounds that he hears. As can be imagined, this is extremly conducive to creative writing.

Fear of the failure of misspelling words vanishes. It gives way to the secure feeling that any word that can be said can be written. This results in profuse amounts of original stories.

Of the 44 sound-symbols, 24 are the same in appearance as their counterparts in the traditional, standard alphabet. These are: (Italicized symbols are i/t/a.)

b (bat), *c* (candy), *d* (dig), *f* (fish), *g* (good), *h* (hate), *j* (jack), *k* (kite), *l* (lite), *m* (men), *n* (nice), *p* (pipe), *r* (rich), *s* (sink), *t* (tent), *v* (vine), *w* (will), *y* (yard), *z* (zipper), *a* (at), *e* (elephant), *i* (it), *o* (octopus), *u* (up).

Long vowel sound-symbols are created by simply adding what appears to be an "e" to the short forms.

æ (ate), Œ (eat), ie (ice), œ (open), ue (use).

Eight are simple combinations, whose counterparts in the traditional alphabet are easily recognized.

ᴡʜ(when), ᴄʜ(church), ∫ʜ(shirt), ᵗʰ(this), ᵗʰ(thought), ᵑ (ring), ᴀᴜ(out), ᴏᵢ(oil).

Seven remain. Of the 44 sound-symbols in i/t/a there are only seven that could be considered strange or foreign to the reader. They are:

ω (look), ω (moon), ᴀᴜ(ought), ɑ(far), ʒ(edge), ʃ(his), ʌ .

The ʌ , the controlled ʌ , alone needs explanation. Following *i* (first), *e* (her), and *u* (fur), the ʌ in combination with the short vowel that controls it has the sound of the *r*.

Once these "foreign" symbols are mastered, the average teacher is well on his or her way to reading, to writing, to teaching with the Initial Teaching Alphabet.

Simplification. i/t/a brings simplicity to the non-reader. The traditional, the standard is extremely complicated.

Consider this list of 17 words: ruby, rule, do, move, fruit, bruise, group, through, noon, wooed, rheumatism, loose, blue, maneuver, grew, canoe, two. What sound do they have in common?

i/t/a in its simplicity overcomes this confusion, this chaos, with the sound-symbol, (ω)(moon), which is the sound shared by this list of 17.

Until a few years ago i/t/a was used only in England's Infant Schools, where children between the ages of four and one-half and five were successfully taught to read.

Brought to the United States by men like Dr. Albert Mazurkiewicz, the Initial Teaching Alphabet is causing results here that have spread its use from Pennsylvania to California, and in Missouri, to school districts like University City and Ferguson-Florissant, St. Louis County.

Used in kindergarten and first grade, i/t/a produces equally satisfactory results in remedial work in higher grades.

The scientifically gathered results in the reading performance of children exposed to i/t/a indicates that the Initial Teaching Alphabet is a breakthrough in the technique of teaching reading.

WHAT'S WRONG WITH i.t.a.? *

John Downing

Isn't there anything wrong with i.t.a.?" is the question William B. Gillooly is alleged to have asked an Initial Teaching Alphabet Publications, Inc. sales representative, according to a recent issue of the PHI DELTA KAPPAN.[1] That unanswered question, plus Gillooly's [2] valuable critical analysis of some American i.t.a. researches, prompt this attempt to tell what is wrong with i.t.a. If the following criticisms of i.t.a. are to be constructive and to lead to correction, there is an important distinction which must be made in reference to i.t.a. On the one hand, these criticisms will be concerned with the essential stuff of i.t.a.—its basic reality—the i.t.a. characters and the way they are used to represent the sounds and words of English. On the other hand, we should

---

* REPRINTED by permission of the publisher, from *Phi Delta Kappan*, Vol. 48, No. 6, February, 1967, pp. 262–66.

[1] Theodore B. Dolmatch, "Comments on Mr. Gillooly's Review," PHI DELTA KAPPAN, June, 1966, pp. 550–51.

[2] William B. Gillooly, "The Promise of i.t.a. Is a Delusion," PHI DELTA KAPPAN, June, 1966, pp. 545–50.

distinguish and set apart from the essence of i.t.a. the quite separate issue of i.t.a.'s accretions, i.e., materials in i.t.a., teaching methods in i.t.a. classes, propaganda used to sell i.t.a., investment and profit from i.t.a. publishing, etc. There will be criticisms of these aspects of the i.t.a. scene, but let us be clear from the outset that they are not essential to our judgment of the basic principles of the i.t.a. idea.

WHAT'S WRONG WITH i.t.a. SYSTEM

A great deal of confusion has been created by the failure of some educators to grasp precisely what is the basic essence of i.t.a. Linguistic science has a descriptive category into which i.t.a. fits and which gives i.t.a. a clear definition. In linguistic terminology, i.t.a. is a writing-system. This does not necessarily mean a system for teaching writing. What it does mean is a system of ink marks on paper to represent the primary system of sounds in air which is the spoken language. Of course, methods of teaching and the design of materials may ultimately be influenced by a change of writing-systems such as i.t.a., but it is vital to understand that i.t.a. is just a writing system—not a teaching method.

i.t.a. belongs to a special class of writing-systems. In contrast with the more complex and irregular traditional orthography (t.o.) writing-system, i.t.a. is one of a number of simplified and regularized writing-systems (s.r.w.s.) which have been devised for printing or writing English over the past 400 years. Examples of other s.r.w.s.'s currently being advocated are "English the New Way," [3] "Diacritical Marking System," [4] "Regularized English," [5] "Unifon," [6] "Words in Colour," [7] and "Phonetic Colour." [8] A complete description of the i.t.a. writing-system has been provided in several publications of the Reading Research Unit, University of London.[9]

Is there anything wrong with the i.t.a. writing-system itself? The British report on five years of extensive research on i.t.a. in beginners' classes suggests that there *is*, and that the next step in research should be to improve on the

[3] R. Cortright, "Another Simplified Spelling," *Reading Teacher*, Vol. 19 (1966), pp. 508–11.

[4] E. B. Fry, "First Grade Reading Instruction Using Diacritical Marking System, Initial Teaching Alphabet and Basal Reading System," *Reading Teacher*, Vol. 19 (1966), pp. 666–69.

[5] A Wijk, *Regularized English*. Stockholm: Wiksell, 1958.

[6] F. Zeitz, "Uniform—The Sound Alphabet," *School and Community*, April, 1966, p. 23.

[7] C. Gattegno, "Words in Colour," *Forward Trends*, Vol. 8 (1964), pp. 141–44.

[8] J. K. Jones, "Colour as an Aid to Visual Perception in Early Reading," *British Journal of Educational Psychology*, Vol. 35 (1965), pp. 21–27.

[9] J. A. Downing, *The Initial Teaching Alphabet Explained and Illustrated*, New York: Macmillan, 1965; F. McBride, *Teacher's Course in Writing with the Initial Teaching Alphabet*. London: Reading Research Unit, University of London Institute of Education, 1965, J. Mountford, *i.t.a. as a Grading Device*. London: Reading Research Unit, University of London Institute of Education, 1965.

original i.t.a. writing-system. Before giving more details, perhaps the context of this finding should be provided in a summary of the three main conclusions of the British i.t.a. research report: [10]

1. t.o. is a serious cause of difficulty in the early stages of learning to read and write. Thus English spelling is a severe handicap to teachers and children in the English-speaking countries of the world.

2. i.t.a. generally leads to superior t.o. reading and t.o. spelling by the end of the third year in school. In word recognition the average i.t.a. student is five or six months advanced in reading t.o.

3. This success of i.t.a. in improving t.o. literacy skills comes only after a *plateau or even regression in the growth of such skills at the stage of transition from i.t.a. to t.o.*

The success of i.t.a. ought not to be belittled.

The difference between the i.t.a. reading of i.t.a. students and the t.o. reading of t.o. students up till the middle of the second year of school is truly remarkable. For instance, the average i.t.a. student just before mid-second year reads two and a half times as many i.t.a. test words as the average t.o. pupil can read in t.o. on the same test sample of the English language. During the usual time of transition for most children (end of second or beginning of third year) the average achievements in t.o. reading of the i.t.a. students are not worse than those of the t.o. pupils, and by the end of third year the average i.t.a. pupil has regained a lead over the average t.o. student.

These are encouraging results, but are they good enough? No. The plateau or regression effect at the transition stage suggests that attempts should be made to reduce this loss. Improvements in teaching methods and materials may help, but what is urgently needed now is a reappraisal of the i.t.a. writing-system itself. In the British experiments, i.t.a. has been used only as one example of the s.r.w.s. principle in contrast to t.o. Now that the s.r.w.s. principle has been shown to be valid and important, it should be followed through logically by a series of researches designed to approach closer to the ideal s.r.w.s. for English. The goal of this new research should not be confined to improving the transitional aspect of i.t.a. It should also determine whether the residue of complexity and irreguglarity in i.t.a. can be still further reduced, e.g., *c* and *k* for the same sound adds to the child's learning load and is a source of mystification to him.

[10] National Foundation for Educational Research in England and Wales, *The i.t.a. Symposium.* Slough, Bucks, England: The Foundation, 1967. Contains "Report on the British i.t.a. Experiment," by J. A. Downing, and reviews of the research report by A. S. Artley, University of Missouri; Cyril Burt; H. Diack, University of Nottingham; R. Gulliford, University of Birmingham; James Hemming; Jack Holmes, University of California; A. R. MacKinnon, Simon Fraser University, British Columbia; Marie Neale, University of Sydney; M. Procter and A. H. Morgan, Inner London Education Authority; J. F. Reid, Godfrey Thomson Unit for Educational Research, Edinburgh; and M. D. Vernon, University of Reading. The foreword is by H. L. Elvin, Director of the University of London Institute of Education, and there is a concluding summary by W. D. Wall, Director of the N.F.E.R.

Perhaps the most interesting result from the British i.t.a. research is the discovery that children do not seem to be transferring in quite the manner originally envisaged by its inventor, Sir James Pitman. His i.t.a. characters and spelling conventions are supposed to maximize transfer of learning from i.t.a. to t.o. once fluency in the former has been achieved. He based this on the well-known research finding [11] that fluent readers use only minimal cues situated chiefly in the upper part of the line of print. Therefore, as far as possible, the upper part of the i.t.a. configurations of whole words are similar to the upper part of the t.o. configurations of the same words. Study of the errors i.t.a. students make in reading t.o. indicates that we need to consider a smaller unit of processing than the top half of the configurations of whole words. The errors made by children after the transition stage occur often in words which have highly similar configurations, but some misleading individual letter or letters in the t.o. spelling (e.g., *ch* in school, *s* in island, *c* in ceiling, *g* in gnome) seemed to have caused errors in the post-transition t.o. tests. Further evidence of such pro-active interference has been found in McBride's [12] research. He investigated the degree of difficulty with which children were able to transfer from i.t.a. to t.o. reading, using 100 words from the *Janet and John* basal reading series. The six most difficult words contained t.o. letters which had different sound values in i.t.a., i.e., *these, age, huge, whom, fruit, magician.* Therefore an important area in which to seek improvements in i.t.a. is one related to these sources of pro-active interference in individual letters.

Inevitably, these brief extracts cannot do justice to the careful and detailed analysis and discussion of the data which has been carried out by the Reading Research Unit. The fullest treatment is provided in the present author's *Evaluating the Initial Teaching Alphabet.*[13] Specific proposals for changes in i.t.a.'s design have been made in a recent article in *Elementary English.*[14]

In summary, something is wrong with the i.t.a. writing-system itself. Despite i.t.a.'s success, both before and after transition to t.o., there is clearly room for improvement on i.t.a.'s present design. It may even be necessary to evolve a new s.r.w.s. which will eventually supplant i.t.a. What is needed now is a series of experiments to ensure that every element in whatever s.r.w.s. is adopted has been established empirically as the best possible solution in the total complex of problems involved in making the needs of the beginner compatible with maximal transfer efficiency at the later stage.

The view that future progress by further improvements on i.t.a. should be investigated is supported by several other authors, including Artley and

[11] See, for instance, D. G. Patterson and M. A. Tinker, *How To Make Type Readable.* New York: Harper and Row, 1940.

[12] F. McBride, *A Preliminary Study of the Ability of Children Who Have Been Learning To Read in i.t.a. To Transfer to Reading Material in Traditional Print.* London: Reading Research Unit, University of London Institute of Education, 1966. (Mimeographed)

[13] J. A. Downing, *Evaluating the Initial Teaching Alphabet.* London: Cassell, 1967.

[14] J. A. Downing, "Can i.t.a. Be Improved?" *Elementary English,* (in press) 1967.

Holmes.[15] As Artley says, "Indeed, it would be extremely unfortunate if at this stage in the development of the Initial Teaching Alphabet it were to be assumed that both the code system and the method of its use were fixed and established so that no further work on either would be necessary. Were this to take place the chances would be great that we would be operating with something less than the best. This, the profession could hardly condone."

Holmes' comment on this proposition is, "In summary, this reviewer heartily agrees with Downing's call for a series of experiments in the 'psychological laboratory' designed to determine how the forms of i.t.a. characters ought to be modified to maximize their transfer value to t.o.; and further to find what new materials and teaching techniques should be developed to facilitate transfer from i.t.a. to t.o."

WHAT'S WRONG WITH ACCRETIONS

Threatening to submerge the essential issue of the writing-system for beginning readers and writers in English-speaking countries are all the barnacles that have attached themselves to the i.t.a. experiment. i.t.a. cannot be condemned for faults arising from these accretions, but they ought to be corrected in case they lead to misunderstandings about the true nature of i.t.a. If Gillooly had in mind such external growths on i.t.a., then the professional researchers and teachers in the schools who began the i.t.a. experiment in Britain five and a half years ago would have to admit that they are distressed about the events which seem to have led Gans [16] to complain:

As yet there are not enough results from the experimentation going on to warrant the *extravagant claims* that are being made for it.

There seems little doubt that a great number of reasonable educators have been prevented from giving serious consideration to the esstential i.t.a. idea because of panacea claims made by some i.t.a. promoters.

Another thing unnecessarily wrong with i.t.a. is the mystery being created by conflicting statements about property rights in i.t.a. Is i.t.a. private property or is it in the public domain? In 1960, when the i.t.a. experiment began, the University of London Institute of Education [17] announced in a pamphlet appealing for financial and moral support, "NO COPYRIGHT. The particu-

[15] A. S. Artley and J. Holmes each have comments on the i.t.a. research in *The i.t.a. Symposium, op. cit.*

[16] R. Gans, "The Initial Teaching Alphabet," *Grade Teacher*, October, 1964, pp. 35 and 118.

[17] University of London Institute of Education and The National Foundation for Educational Research in England and Wales, *Some Reasons Why We are Initiating an Investigation into the Early Stages of Learning To Read, When the Matter To Be Read Is Printed in a Special Form Alleged To Be Easy To Learn and Leading Easily to a Full Reading Skill.* London: The Institute, 1960.

lar alphabet used above may be obtained (in 12 pt.) from the Monotype Corporation, 43 Fetter Lane, E.C.4. Any designers' rights have been freed for all time for unrestricted use by all." And in the same year Sir James Pitman,[18] who invented i.t.a., declared, "The copyright in the characters has been made free to all." In neither case was any condition or proviso stipulated.

Six years later i.t.a. has become widely used, but a new note—apparently in conflict with the earlier "no copyright" statements—is being sounded, for instance:

But he [Sir James Pitman] retained the right to supervise and, in the last resort, to insist upon conformity. (Patrick Gordon Walker at the Lehigh University i.t.a. Conference, August, 1965)

This service enables publishers to conform to standards of spelling consistency which have been laid down by Sir James as a necessary condition for using the alphabet. (Peter Daffon at the same conference)

When Sir James Pitman developed the Initial Teaching Alphabet, he believed strongly that it should be free from the restraints of copyright and that it should be in the public domain. In doing so,[19] Sir James stipulated that only the characters he designed be the ones referred to as the Initial Teaching Alphabet, and that the spelling rules he formulated be faithfully adhered to in printed materials. (Statement issued by the American i.t.a. Foundation in their first "report")

In contrast, a statement in conformity with the original "no copyright" statement of 1960 was made at the same Lehigh Conference in August, 1965, by Edward Meade of the Ford Foundation: "Sir James has given the copyright for the Initial Teaching Alphabet without condition to the world."

The three statements which conflict with Meade's clear assertion all emanate from the i.t.a. Foundation (British and American). As the i.t.a. Foundation "is an independent, nonprofit, educational institution" dedicated to the "propagation" and dissemination of i.t.a. "without commercial interest," [20] it will no doubt issue a further statement to remove the ambiguity which is being caused by its insertion of provisos and stipulations not in the original declaration of 1960. This ambiguity about i.t.a.'s legal status is something seriously wrong with i.t.a. in America, because it appears to be deterring American publishers from producing i.t.a. materials. In Britain, by the deliberate policy and planning of the Reading Research Unit, over 40 publishers produce i.t.a. materials and there are several competing basal reading series in i.t.a. In America there are few publishers of i.t.a. books,[21] and one particular series dominates the i.t.a. market. This lack of real competition within i.t.a. is another thing wrong with i.t.a. in America.

[18] I. J. Pitman, "Learning To Read: An Experiment," *Journal of Royal Society of Arts*, Vol. 109 (1961), pp. 149–80.

[19] By normal English grammatical usage this apparently refers to "he believed strongly."

[20] *The i.t.a. Foundation Report*, Vol. 1, No. 1 (Spring, 1966), pp. 2–3.

[21] For a complete list of i.t.a. books, see *i.t.a. Books for the Teacher and the Child*, obtainable from the National Book League, 7 Albemarle Street, London, W.1., England.

Perhaps the most seriously wrong thing about i.t.a. at the present time (again this is chiefly an American problem) is that it has allowed itself to get sewn up into a kind of "package deal." In the minds of all too many American educators, i.t.a. has become irrevocably linked with a whole lot of other ideas which have really got nothing to do with this experimental s.r.w.s. In the i.t.a. package deal the American educator is being sold ideas from Rudolf Flesch's *Why Johnny Can't Read* and Arthur S. Trace, Jr.'s *What Ivan Knows That Johnny Doesn't*, along with a sort of salvation-through-innovation complex.

The British teachers and educational researchers who began the i.t.a. experiment in 1961 just would not recognize the i.t.a. image that has been created in America. (Nor would those American i.t.a. teachers who have kept in close touch with the longitudinal experiments in Britain.) An outstanding example of this incredible abuse of i.t.a. is a recent article by Vera Ohanian [22] in *Elementary English*. Misconceptions crowd one after the other: 1) i.t.a. is "a phonic approach"; 2) "a basic sight word list is not an important consideration"; 3) in i.t.a. "learning phonic clues *precedes* the learning of word wholes"; 4) "the mode of teaching and learning is largely through telling and being told respectively, and much less through guided discovery"; 5) "a single word analysis technique is taught during the first year, at which time also transfer is encouraged and achieved, usually about April and May"; 6) "the characters representing the 40 sounds are called symbol-sounds"; 7) "blends (such as glass, black, and clock) are not taught" in i.t.a.; 8) "the teaching of phonic-analysis principles are unnecessary" in i.t.a.; 9) with i.t.a. the child "must attend to the visual characteristics of a word since he cannot decipher it through a global but a more piecemeal look"; 10) "children are taught to write each symbol-sound after it is introduced"; 11) "the order of [teaching] the symbol-sounds [in i.t.a.] was determined from two studies."

Every one of Ohanian's statements listed above would be regarded as complete nonsense by the British teachers who pioneered the development of i.t.a. in their classrooms. In fact, her description of i.t.a. is so far removed from the reality of the majority of their classrooms that it would produce gasps of incredulity from British teachers experienced in i.t.a.

Ohanian's image of i.t.a. is wrong on two counts: first, she describes only one methodology of teaching with i.t.a., and a very unrepresentative one at that; and second, i.t.a. is a writing-system which is not associated with any particular set of teaching methods.

On the first point: i.t.a. is *not* a phonic method. Most British teachers of i.t.a., for certain, use an eclectic approach which does not begin with formal phonics. Most i.t.a. basal reading series *do* have controlled vocabularies with a basic sight word list, e.g., *Janet and John* and the *Downing Readers* in Britain, and the i.t.a. edition of the well-known Scott, Foresman basal readers in Amer-

[22] V. Ohanian, "Control Populations in i.t.a. Experiments," *Elementary English*, Vol. 43 (1966), pp. 373–80.

ica. Guided discovery *is* the general rule in British i.t.a. classes and in many American i.t.a. classes, too. Transfer is *not* encouraged and achieved in April or May of the first year. This is probably Ohanian's most dangerous misunderstanding. In Britain the average time of transition from i.t.a. to t.o. would be at the end of the second or beginning of the third year. More important, transfer to t.o. is individualized, and research indicates that a much longer period in i.t.a. will help slow learners. No informed teacher in Britain would use such a misnomer as "symbol-sounds." Sounds are symbols in the *spoken* language. Of course, blends may be taught in i.t.a., and, obviously, analysis of sounds will be learned. The teaching of i.t.a. in formal phonic drill, with the characters arranged in one special best order, is absolutely foreign to the way in which i.t.a. has been used in British schools. It is inconceivable that we would put the clock back to such dreary, formal, meaningless methods. If they really were an integral part of i.t.a., then it would never have found its way into our classrooms. But, fortunately, Ohanian's image of i.t.a. is, to say the least, quite unrepresentative of real-life i.t.a. classes.

The fundamental error in Ohanian's description of i.t.a. is her association of i.t.a. with any one teaching method. Perhaps, in the future, after appropriate experiment and research, we may modify teaching methods in i.t.a. classes, but until then i.t.a. should be regarded as a writing-system which is available for teaching by any methodology. This fundamental error has been the cause of serious mistakes in most American i.t.a. researches. The i.t.a. package deal has been contrasted with some other package deal such as "language-experience" or "basal reader," The present author has shown elsewhere [23] how this has invalidated most i.t.a. research so far conducted in America. Basal readers can be printed in t.o. or in i.t.a. or some other s.r.w.s. Similarly, the writing in the "language-experience" can be in t.o. or in i.t.a., etc. It is doubtful if an orthodox i.t.a. method will ever emerge. Hopefully, there will continue to be room for a choice of approaches based on the professional judgment of teachers.

These, then, are the more important things wrong with i.t.a.'s accretions: extravagant claims, ambiguity about i.t.a.'s copyright status, the consequent lack of competitive i.t.a. programs, and the false notion that i.t.a. comes in a package along with outmoded formal phonic drills. Other wrongs might be mentioned, e.g., teachers' indoctrination in i.t.a. instead of education about i.t.a. But these complaints relate *only to i.t.a.'s accretions*. Sufficient examples have been given to show how i.t.a. is in danger from these side issues. But clear thinking should overcome the danger in time.

The really interesting recent development in the i.t.a. experiment is the discovery that the process of transition from i.t.a. to t.o. seems to be different from the one predicted when the experiment began. Here is "something

[23] J. A. Downing, "Conflicts and Confusions in i.t.a. Experiments," in J. A. Figurel (ed.), *Proceedings of the 1966 I.R.A. Convention, Dallas, Texas*. Newark, Delaware: International Reading Association, 1966.

wrong with i.t.a." which is exciting because it indicates a fruitful line for further research on the s.r.w.s. idea.

THE PROMISE OF i.t.a.
IS A DELUSION *

Yes!

William B. Gillooly

No!

Albert J. Mazurkiewicz
and Theodore B. Dolmatch

By William B. Gillooly

If the grapheme-phoneme (symbol-sound) correspondences of our writing system were regular (that is, if each sound was represented by one letter), children would only need to learn the sounds for which the letters of the alphabet stand before they could read. However, since English uses twenty-six symbols to encode 40-odd sounds, the result is an irregular writing system which, at present, uses about 2,000 or so ways of representing the sounds of the language. Consequently, readers face such inconsistencies in the sounds represented by symbols as exhibited by the letters "ough" in the following words: cough, furlough, ought, plough, thorough, though, through, and tough. Another frequently encountered example of inconsistency is the sound "eye," which is spelled in about twenty different ways.

One of the prices we seem to pay for such inconsistency is a relatively high rate of failure among beginning readers. Another is the ubiquitous spelling error. By comparison, the children of countries which use more regular writing systems seem to have little difficulty learning to read and spell.[1] It has been reasoned that if the writing of our language could be altered so as to correspond more closely with the spoken form, the learning of reading and writing skills in this country would be facilitated.

Since the possibility of spelling reform is quite remote, proponents have suggested that its benefits may be derived, nevertheless, from beginning read-

* REPRINTED by permission of the publisher from *Phi Delta Kappan*, June, 1966, pp. 545–53.

[1] Roger Brown, *Words And Things*. New York: The Free Press, 1958, p. 66.

ing instruction with a more regular writing system.[2] After developing sufficient competence in this system, they would presumably be in a better position to deal with the traditional orthography (t.o.) and all its inconsistencies. The result should be better readers and spellers in t.o.

The writing system proposed to bring this innovation about is the Initial Teaching Alphabet (i.t.a.), which shares twenty-four symbols with our conventional alphabet and augments these with twenty additional symbols. By means of these forty-four symbols, the sounds of English are represented in approximately eighty-eight ways.

The investigation of this issue has led to several experiments and a considerable amount of controversy. It is the goal of this paper to review these experiments and to ascertain the benefits, if any, which derive from the use of i.t.a.

Another system for increasing grapheme-phoneme correspondences is Edward B. Fry's Diacritical Marking System (DMS).[3] We will have an opportunity to view the results of a comparison of this system with i.t.a. as well as with t.o.

The criteria used in selecting studies for review in this paper (in addition to their availability) are as follows:

1. Only those studies which report the results of investigations conducted in this country will be included. The number of these studies is such that we do not have to depend upon data collected abroad, with the attendant concern about generalizing these findings.

2. Because there is an insufficiency of data beyond the first grade, only data collected to this point is treated.

3. Only reading achievement data in the form of test results (not, for example, the instructional level of the most recently completed reading book) are reported.

4. Only the results of tests administered in the conventional alphabet are included.

5. Insofar as possible, only data on the total sample groups will be considered. That is, data collected on subsamples of the experimental and control conditions will be avoided. This restriction seems necessary in the light of the finding from an early analysis that at least one researcher has reported data on an unrepresentative subsample of the total experimental group.[4]

The Control Condition in i.t.a. Research. In evaluating the effectiveness of any particular factor (such as i.t.a.) in an educational setting, there are a

[2] For an interesting treatment of this whole issue, the reader should consult Maurice Harrison, *The Story of the Initial Teaching Alphabet.* New York: Pitman Publishing Corporation, 1964.

[3] Edward B. Fry, "A Diacritical Marking System To Aid Beginning Reading Instruction," *Elementary English,* 1964, pp. 526–30.

[4] William B. Gillooly, "A Critical Analysis of the i.t.a. Interim Reports," 1966, unpublished.

host of other factors which must be taken into consideration and controlled or else their effects will be confounded with those of the experimental (the to-be-evaluated) variable. These extraneous factors include: the students (their intelligence, cognitive factors associated with sex, etc.), the teachers (their age, experience, level of training, competence, etc.), the teaching methods, the materials of instruction, and novelty (the so-called Hawthorne effects). The manner and degree of control exerted over these factors varies from study to study but the following treatment will provide a flavor of the kind of controls used in the research on i.t.a. Of course, it goes without saying nowadays that there will be control groups; therefore our concern is for the way in which these groups are formed and treated.

Student factors: The most frequent, explicitly stated practice was to assign the pupils to classrooms according to the usual administrative practice and to assign these "intact classes" to the i.t.a. or t.o. condition in random fashion.[5] The pre-experimental equivalence of the groups was evaluated by means of a variety of measures. In three studies, the pretests showed significant differences favoring one or the other group: i.t.a. in one case [6] and t.o. in the other two cases.[7] In two of these situations, the magnitude of the difference was 2.7 points [8] and 2.3 points,[9] both on the Pinter-Cunningham General Ability Test.

Teacher variables: Usually, the teachers (who were most often volunteers, by the way) were assigned randomly to the two conditions [10] or they were matched on some measure of competence and then randomly assigned.[11] However, in Chasnoff's study one teacher taught reading and related language activities to both groups (i.t.a. and t.o.) in the same school and another teacher taught the other activities.

Teaching method: Chasnoff and Mazurkiewicz seem to have done the best job of controlling this factor, with the edge going to Mazurkiewicz. He provided specific training for his t.o. teachers in the methods to be used by the i.t.a. teachers in devolping reading, writing, speaking, and listening skills with

[5] Robert E. Chasnoff, *Comparison of the Initial Teaching Alphabet with the Traditional Alphabet in First-Grade Reading.* Report of Cooperative Research Project No. S-210 of the U.S. Office of Education 1965; Edward B. Fry, *First Grade Reading Instruction Using a Diacritical Marking System, the Initial Teaching Alphabet, and a Basal Reading System.* Report of Cooperative Research Project No. 2745 of the U.S. Office of Education, 1965.

[6] H. J. Tanyzer, H. Alpert, and L. Sandel, *Beginning Reading—The Effectiveness of Different Media.* Report of the Nassau School Development Council, Mineola, New York, 1965.

[7] Albert J. Mazurkiewicz, *First Grade Reading Using Modified Co-Basal Versus the Initial Teaching Alphabet.* Report of Cooperative Research Project No. 2676 of the U.S. Office of Education, 1965; H. Tanyzer and H. Alpert, *Effectiveness of Three Different Basal Reading Systems on First-Grade Reading Achievement.* Report of Cooperative Research Project No. 2720 of the U.S. Office of Education, 1965, a summary.

[8] Tanyzer, Alpert, and Sandel, *op. cit.*

[9] Mazurkiewicz, *op. cit.*

[10] Fry, *op. cit.,* Tanyzer and Alpert, *op. cit.*

[11] Tanyzer, Alpert and Sandel, *op. cit.*

instructions for them to use the same methods. Other studies left the decision to the teacher (therefore, for those studies, this factor is confounded with the teacher variables discussed above).

All studies introduced some measure of control over the amount of time spent on reading instruction; however, Tanyzer, Alpert, and Sandel tested the significance of the difference between their groups on this factor. The difference was not significant (at the P = .05 level). Evidence that reading and related language skills were not pursued to the detriment of other skills is reported by Chasnoff in the form of data from the arithmetic section of the Stanford Achievement Test administered on the 160th day of instruction. Not only was there no difference between the i.t.a. and t.o. groups but both scored approximately at the expected grade level (2.01, to be exact).

Materials: Most of the reported studies did not attempt any control over this factor and, as a result, the effects due to the materials themselves have been confounded with the writing medium (i.t.a. or t.o.). Strictly speaking, therefore, these studies did not compare i.t.a. with t.o. More precisely, they compared different reading systems which employ a different alphabet in addition to different stories, etc. In some of Chasnoff's schools, however, the materials were controlled. That is, the i.t.a. children used transliterated editions of the t.o. readers. And, in addition, Fry was able to introduce a considerable degree of control between the DMS and the t.o. groups. The DMS children used a reprinted form of the Allyn and Bacon Sheldon Readers which, in addition to the added diacritical marks, differed only with respect to the pictures, which were black and white in the DMS edition.

The reading series used by the control groups in other studies include the Lippincott *Basic Reading* series and the Scott, Foresman *New Basic Readers*. The most often used i.t.a. materials were Albert J. Mazurkiewicz and Harold J. Tanyzer's *Early-To-Read* series. All researchers exerted a considerable amount of effort to provide the i.t.a. groups with supplementary reading materials. In some cases, this was accomplished by transliterating t.o. materials into i.t.a.

Hawthorne effects: All studies provided some control for Hawthorne effects, but the most effective control was exercised in the study by Edward Fry. There, two experimental groups were used (i.t.a. and DMS). Since both methods are equally novel, comparisons between them are free of novelty effects. Further, the number of visitors and the duration of teacher training were equalized for all groups (as they were in the other studies as well).

The sample size of these studies ranged from 338 in Chasnoff's study to 926 in Mazurkiewicz's. The mean number of subjects was 630 and the total was 3,147.

Some Thoughts About Criteria for Evaluating i.t.a. In recent correspondence with this writer, Albert J. Mazurkiewicz stated that the comparison of i.t.a. with t.o. using a test of reading comprehension (such as the Paragraph Meaning subtest of the Stanford Achievement Test) is inappropriate in evaluating i.t.a. because comprehension does not reflect simply the alphabetic aspects of the reading program. For this reason, he believes that the word-attack skills developed by experience with i.t.a. are better assessed with other tests—the Detroit Word Recognition Test or the Word Reading subtest of the Stanford, perhaps.

To give the reader some idea of the extent of disagreement on this important issue, we will turn to the words of another researcher: "We feel that probably the Paragraph Meaning subtest (of the Stanford) is the most important, as this represents a true complex reading task." [12]

It is true that word recognition skills are important, but they are so only to the extent that they influence comprehension. Comprehension is, after all, the purpose of reading. Further, in the studies reported here, as has already been pointed out, comparisons have been made between reading systems—programs which have differed in several respects. Only in Chasnoff's study has there been a concerted effort to control the effects due to the materials themselves (the actual stories employed, etc.) and even there, although one can state that control has been approximated, the author himself does not claim it has been attained.

Consequently, we must employ measures which do in fact provide us with a total assessment of the effectiveness of the reading programs. Most of the studies reported in this paper have used the Stanford Achievement Test [13] and some have, in addition, collected data with the California Reading Test and the Detroit Word Recognition Test on their total sample group. If there are relevant differences between the reading systems under consideration, these tests should be sensitive to those differences.

Nor does this writer agree with Mazurkiewicz when he states, "Further, a truer test of a child's spelling ability is not that of standardized tests but rather that found in his written expression in daily activity." [14] Examining the written work of children may be quite deceptive, due to the possibility that children will mask their deficiencies by choosing only those words they believe they can spell correctly. Because the inferior spellers would seem to have more opportunity to learn the set to mask spelling deficiencies, they might be mistaken for the better spellers in a free-writing situation. Moreover, this writer considers that the standardized spelling tests (such as the spelling subtest of the Stanford) are not inappropriate (subject to the limitations of spelling tests in general in evaluating competence in this area).[15]

[12] Fry, *op. cit.*, p. 4.

[13] The relevant subsections of this test are: Word Reading, Paragraph Meaning, Vocabulary, Word Study Skills, and Spelling.

[14] Albert Mazurkiewicz, "Lehigh-Bethlehem ITA Study," Interim Report Ten, *Journal for the Reading Specialist*, March, 1966, p. 119.

[15] William B. Gillooly, *op. cit.* There is reason to believe that error rates for i.t.a. children spelling in t.o. vary according to the class of word (regular or irregular) involved, with fewer errors being made on the regular words (those spelled identically in the two systems). Such a state of affairs prevents our use of test results as a basis for making inferences about the i.t.a. group's general spelling proficiency in English until an analysis of the composition of our language by word class determines whether those tests include the correct proportions of the two word classes.

What the Data Show. We turn now to an examination of the evidence which has accumulated with respect to children's achievement in three skills: reading, writing, and spelling.

Reading: When the i.t.a. and t.o. groups' reading in the traditional alphabet is compared on the Stanford Achievement Test, there is no statistically significant difference between them. The result is the same whether the groups are compared in terms of: 1) the total score on the Stanford,[16] 2) a composite of several reading subtests of the Stanford,[17] or 3) each separate subtest.[18] In addition, the Diactrical Marking System is not significantly different from either i.t.a. or t.o.

Further, there is concurrence with the data collected from other reading tests. No significant i.t.a.-t.o. differences have been found at the end of the first grade on the total raw scores of the California Reading Test, or on the mean grade scores of the Reading Vocabulary and Comprehension subsections of that test.[19] Finally, the Detroit Word Recognition Test shows no differences among i.t.a., t.o., and DMS.[20]

This finding is stable enough to withstand the small but significant pre-experimental differences in the intelligence of the i.t.a. and t.o. groups in three of the studies.[21]

Spelling: The spelling data tell a different story. Analysis of the results obtained on the Spelling subtest of the Stanford Achievement Test shows that the t.o.-trained children are significantly better spellers (in t.o.) than the i.t.a.-trained. Chasnoff's data indicate that the difference may be as great as three and one-half months at the end of first grade.[22]

Fry has found that when i.t.a. spelling is scored as correct there is no significant difference between the i.t.a. and t.o. groups. Therefore, as one would expect, the i.t.a. group's spelling deficiency is the result of the group's having learned inappropriate spellings. The DMS group, by the way, spells equally as well as the t.o. controls in the conventional alphabet.

Writing: Our ignorance of the effects of using i.t.a. are, perhaps, greatest in this area. In Chasnoff's study, 616 writing samples were collected after 120

[16] Chasnoff, *op. cit.*

[17] Tanyzer, Alpert, and Sandel, *op. cit.* For Tanyzer and Alpert, *op. cit.*, the finding holds only for the comparison of the i.t.a. group with the Lippincott controls. Both of these groups (i.t.a. and Lippincott t.o.) were significantly superior to the Scott, Foresman (t.o.) controls.

[18] Fry, *op. cit.*; Mazurkiewicz, *op. cit.*; Tanyzer, Alpert, and Sandel, *op. cit.*; and Tanyzer and Alpert, *op. cit.*, with the exception that Lippincott t.o. is superior to i.t.a. on the Vocabulary subtest. However, I believe this is due to the pre-experimental differences in intelligence which favored the Lippincott group in this study. Vocabulary tests are highly related to general intelligence in children.

[19] Chasnoff, *op. cit.*

[20] Fry, *op. cit.*

[21] See footnotes 6 and 7.

[22] However, Fry has collected data in the middle of the second year which indicate that although the i.t.a. children are still inferior, they are no longer significantly so.

days of instruction. The samples were transformed so that the four judges could not tell in which group they originated. They were then rated for "communication of meaning." A significant difference favored the i.t.a. group.

Fry collected writing data from a random subsample of forty youngsters from each of his three conditions. There it was found that although the i.t.a. children wrote longer stories, they were significantly inferior in writing mechanics (punctuation, capitalization, indentation). He attributed the differences to the different training given the children, not the use of a different alphabet. The i.t.a. teachers had been urged throughout the year to encourage their children to write.

There are two studies whose data do not agree with the above treatment. The i.t.a. program receives strong support from both Shapiro [23] and Dunn and Mueller.[24] However, neither of these studies employs as stringent control over extraneous variables as do the studies cited above. For example, the post-tests in the Dunn and Mueller study were administered over a seven-week period. That this in itself could account for most of the post-test differences is not taken into account.

In the study reported by Shapiro, in addition to the fact that there was no attempt to control Hawthorne effects, there is small reason to believe that the student factors are controlled. Starting with a sample of 3,600 pupils in twenty-three school districts, final analyses were made on 1,018 pupils in ten districts. The latter group was quite atypical, since both i.t.a. and t.o. pupils averaged five months ahead of grade placement on the Stanford Achievement Test at the end of the first grade. That the final comparison groups were not equivalent is indicated by the fact that reported significance levels are based on an analysis of covariance, a technique used for adjusting the scores of non-equivalent groups. However, in this writer's judgment the assumptions on which the use of analysis of covariance depends seem risky here.

In the light of this analysis, it was decided to discount the findings of these two studies.

The results of a questionnaire: It will be informative to determine if the conclusions about i.t.a. will be the same if we radically alter our evaluative techniques. What would be the outcome if, instead of examining test data, we asked teachers for their opinions about i.t.a.? Tanyzer *et al.* administered a

[23] Bernard J. Shapiro, *A Comparison of the Reading Achievement of i.t.a. and t.o. Groups in the First Grade, 1964–65: A Report for Classroom Teachers and School Administrators,* Evaluation and Testing Department of the Educational Research Council of Greater Cleveland, February, 1966.

[24] Lloyd M. Dunn and Max W. Mueller, *PLDK and ITA in Nashville—After One Year:* An Interim Report on the Efficacy of the Initial Teaching Alphabet and the Peabody Language Development Kit with Grade One Disadvantaged Children. Report of the Institute on Mental Retardation and Intellectual Development, George Peabody College for Teachers, Nashville, Tennessee, 1965. (In collaboration with M. D. Neely, Nashville Metropolitan Public Schools.)

questionnaire to their teachers and some of their findings will be summarized here.

Ninety-four per cent of the i.t.a. teachers agreed that their bright, average, and slow pupils made more progress in i.t.a. than previous youngsters had made by using the conventional alphabet. Further, 88 per cent of the teachers stated that they preferred to continue teaching with i.t.a.

However, only 41 per cent of the i.t.a. teachers thought all first-grade children should be i.t.a.-taught. The major reservation concerned those who already could read t.o. when they came to school. These, it was often stated, should be spared i.t.a.

Fifty-three per cent of the teachers reported that they had received complaints from parents about the i.t.a. program. The reasons for complaining were varied, but spelling was mentioned quite often. In commenting, teachers often mentioned the beneficial effects of i.t.a. on children's creative writing.

In general, teachers' responses do not lead to the same conclusions as the data. The use of i.t.a. seems to have generated considerable enthusiasm among the teaching staff. This disparity should alert those educational administrators who depend upon their competent teachers' impressions to forecast end-of-year test results.

Is i.t.a. Better for the Dull Children? So far, we have been examining the performance of children without regard for their individuality. However, one could suppose that using i.t.a. might not affect all children in the same way. In fact, i.t.a. might be beneficial only for slower children. We turn now to evidence which bears on this question.

None of the studies which have investigated the issue have found any evidence that i.t.a. is better than t.o. for the dull or for the average—or for the bright child, for that matter.[25] In other words, i.t.a. affects all children in a consistent way—it is no better than widely available t.o. reading programs for any subgroup.

Will Weaning Children from i.t.a. Be Difficult? To this writer's knowledge, no detailed treatment of the difficulties some children experience in making the transition to t.o. is yet available. That sizeable numbers do have trouble is indicated by the following figures from Mazurkiewicz's study: Thirty-five per cent of the i.t.a. children had not transferred to t.o. by the tenth week of the second grade and 5.5 per cent still clung to i.t.a. on April 15, 1965 (approximately thirty weeks into the second grade).[26] It should become an important part of longitudinal studies to tell us more about these children.

[25] Chasnoff, op. cit.; Fry, op. cit.; Tanyzer, Alpert, and Sandel, op. cit.; and Tanyzer and Alpert, op. cit.

[26] Albert J. Mazurkiewicz, Second Annual Report on the Lehigh-University-Bethlehem Area Joint School System Demonstration and Evaluation Project: Use of the Initial Teaching Alphabet in Reading Instruction, unpublished, undated.

In responding to the Tanyzer, Alpert, and Sandel questionnaire, one teacher indicated that the transition to t.o. may produce undesirable emotional effects in some children.[27] These, too, ought to be investigated further.

Concluding Remarks. The call for more data is indeed, as Roger Brown states, "a stale tune." [28] Psychologists are obliged to advise educators concerning procedures which are justified by the available data. But before doing so we will draw some conclusions from the data.

There is no reason yet to believe that i.t.a. is more effective in teaching children to read the traditional alphabet than other widely used conventional reading programs. There is, however, evidence which strongly supports the conclusion that the i.t.a. children are inferior spellers, although these effects may be surprisingly transient. The possibility that some children experience difficulty in making the transfer to t.o. deserves investigation, as do the effects of i.t.a. on writing. It is difficult to tell yet whether it is i.t.a. or other aspects of the training situation (such as the instructions used in the Fry study, "Don't worry about your spelling, go ahead and write") which have led the i.t.a. group to write longer, more effective (at communicating meaning) stories.[29]

The present situation certainly does not justify the widespread adoption of reading materials which use the Initial Teaching Alphabet. Their continued use on a limited scale ought to be undertaken with all of the caution which should accompany any experimental innovation in such an important academic area.

In addition to his responsibilities to professional educators, the educational psychologist has a responsibility to speak to the researchers. It would seem that there is no longer any need to conduct additional research with the same level of control as exerted in these studies. There is need now for longitudinal studies using more and tighter controls so that the effects due to i.t.a. alone can be evaluated. Perhaps some American researchers can learn about controlling the effects due to the materials from their British counterparts.[30] For the purposes of their research, the British transliterated their most widely used reading series into i.t.a.[31]

Greater control over the materials and other extraneous aspects of reading

---

[27] Tanyzer, Alpert, and Sandel, *op. cit.*, p. 34.

[28] Roger Brown, *op. cit.*, p. 78.

[29] Fry believes that the instructions are the responsible factor. If it is the instructions producing the effect, there seems to be no reason why we can't exploit the phenomenon, if we wish, using t.o. Edmund H. Henderson (University of Delaware), for one, has undertaken the investigation of this possibility.

[30] That the effect of the materials is considerable is indicated by the finding from the Tanyzer and Alpert study that differences between t.o. reading programs are as great as those which exist between i.t.a. and t.o. reading programs.

[31] John Downing, *The i.t.a. Reading Experiment*. London: Evans Brothers, Ltd., 1964, p. 26.

programs, coupled with a policy of collecting data with more and varied post-tests, will eventually lead to precise knowledge of the role played by grapheme-phoneme correspondences in beginning reading instruction.[32]

COMMENTS ON MR. GILLOOLY'S REVIEW

I. By Theodore B. Dolmatch

In terms of his criteria, which Mr. Gillooly very explicitly presents to the reader, his review is unexceptionable. Unfortunately, these criteria—which are both his privilege and his responsibility—make his conclusions less useful than they might otherwise be. This is a vital point, lest the reader accept his conclusions as being really relevant to an evaluation of i.t.a.

Analyses of i.t.a. research that are more comprehensive than Mr. Gillooly's are now in preparation; one of them which I have seen reviews scores of research projects, as compared to Mr. Gillooly's rather small and selective sample. When these and other analyses appear, they will undoubtedly be useful.

In this response I must confine myself to just a few remarks on Mr. Gillooly's criteria:

1. The results of British research just cannot be disregarded, particularly since the British experience with i.t.a. has extended longer than that in the United States. In addition, since there are scores of U.S. research studies on i.t.a. available (as Mr. Gillooly himself points out), why he selected only three is a reasonable question.

2. Two of the projects on which Mr. Gillooly reports were one-year projects with relatively small populations. Mazurkiewicz's and others are both larger and have extended longer. Most of the researchers recognize the inadequacy of their one-year studies and have requested extensions. Although most children in the U.S. have transferred to the conventional alphabet by the end of the first year, perhaps 20 per cent have not. It might be reasonable to assume that testing children as a group at an arbitrary point of time in a writing system with which they have insufficient familiarity might be misleading, particularly if an evaluation of i.t.a.'s worth confines itself to this kind of testing. And what about the teacher whose work is evaluated after one year and one year only in a completely new program?

[32] Another study was received too late to be given detailed treatment in this paper. It is Robert B. Hayes and Joseph S. Nemeth, *An Attempt To Secure Additional Evidence Concerning Factors Affecting Learning To Read*, Report of Cooperative Research Project No. 2697, U.S. Office of Education, 1966. The results of this study add support to the findings of Chasnoff, Fry, Mazurkiewicz, Tanyzer *et al.*, and Tanyzer and Alpert. The i.t.a. group's reading is not significantly different from the Lippincott t.o. or the Scott, Foresman t.o. program supplemented by a phonics and a word power program. However, the i.t.a. children are inferior spellers (in t.o.).

3. Most of us have so many reservations about reading tests generally that Mr. Gillooly might have mentioned a few that are particularly germane here. Thus, all the tests to which he refers are conventional measures with content validity determined in terms of the basal readers conventionally used. But most of the experimental groups used i.t.a. materials which departed significantly from those by which these tests were validated—the same tests that were used in one form or another by the t.o. population. Also, most populations were matched before testing in "intelligence" (comprehension?) and finally tested for "comprehension" (intelligence?). The differences were slight, and only a few of us were surprised. I'll not deal with the fact that i.t.a. is measured here only as a reading vehicle when its implications reach far beyond the decoding process.

4. This point is covered above. It's a pity that no one thought to install a control by testing the t.o. populations with i.t.a. versions of the tests used. Something might be learned from this procedure.

5. Mr. Gillooly cites his own findings to justify his eliminating the available data on subsamples. But he later departs from this principle to cite one lone teacher who had something negative to say about i.t.a. It is in just these subsamples of the three research projects selected by Mr. Gillooly and others—all larger than one teacher—that one can see so many positive aspects of i.t.a.

If Mr. Gillooly's criteria are so structured that they limit the usefulness of his study, one might wonder why they were selected. It cannot be that Mr. Gillooly was unaware of other research. Even we have most studies available for examination. Had Mr. Gillooly identified his purpose on his only visit to our office, we would have been pleased to spend the time and provide the detailed information that we freely offer to professional visitors. Two of the questions that he asked, only of our sales representative—"You can tell me, isn't there anything wrong with i.t.a.?" and "How are i.t.a. books selling?"— might have been answered with more authority by me or another available executive. However, let me answer them now:

1. None of the data show that i.t.a. is less effective than t.o. Most of the data show that i.t.a. is significantly better than t.o. as a medium for beginning reading. Tens of thousands of children in hundreds of schools in forty-seven states and countries around the world demonstrate this better than I can. I wonder whether Mr. Gillooly has visited any i.t.a. classrooms.

2. Our own books are selling very well. There are almost forty publishers in England and at least a dozen others here now producing i.t.a. books. I assume that theirs are selling well too.

Let me place one final question in the researcher's mouth: Why do I take issue here, in this "educator's domain"? The answer is that we, as publishers of educational materials, take our responsibilities at least as seriously as some educators do, and that we must protect ourselves against irrelevancy and bias in order to do so.

II. By Albert J. Mazurkiewicz

Mr. Gillooly's report suffers from bias, selective reporting, and quoting out of context. There is deliberate non-use of data which would negate the position taken.

Harris, Sheldon, and others, in their first-grade studies, all note the weakness of the outcome-variable testing. Harris [1] states, "Available reading tests, including those prescribed for the cooperating studies, tend to be inherently biased for or against particular teaching procedures." He notes that the vocabulary section of the Stanford test, for example, "seems to emphasize the words commonly taught in basal reader series for the primary grades," and cautions against generalizing from such results. Mr. Gillooly apparently cares nothing about this, since he accepts unquestioned such outcome variables as the *only* basis for his analysis and even rejects any other view as unthinkable.

Mr. Gillooly quotes selectively a statement on spelling, which, out of context, does not show that second-grade spelling was first tested on the Stanford Achievement Spelling Test and that the i.t.a. children's results were significantly better than their t.o. counterparts whether the raw (and most unequivalent) or the matched-pair sample results were used. He ignores the data because they don't support his position, and further rejects the view that spelling in creative writing may be more meaningful than that found on biased standardized tests.

Mr. Gillooly states that "there is an insufficiency of data beyond the first-grade level," hence he deals only with data from the first grade. Yet it seems peculiar that he quotes Fry in a personal conversation about his second-grade findings and selectively quotes from my Second Annual Report to justify his position.

Later, Gillooly notes that there is no statistically significant difference between the i.t.a. and t.o. groups and neglects to mention that in every one of the studies a large segment of the i.t.a. population had not had any school experience with the t.o. medium on which they were tested (they had not transferred). He neglects to point out the remarkable fact that despite this the raw populations' results were as good as the results with t.o. children who had been taught only in that medium. We might conclude that there is something drastically wrong with our t.o. programs under these circumstances, but Gillooly avoids the obvious in order to justify his position.

Still later, Mr. Gillooly seems to ignore the fact that children are different and learn at different rates. He quotes my statement that by the tenth week of the second grade (my second-year report, by the way) 35 per cent of the population had not transferred to t.o., and apparently believes that all children should have stopped reading i.t.a. material in the first grade. He forgets that an educator's first concerns are the child's security and ego strength, accept-

---

[1] Albert J. Harris, *Comparison of Reading Approaches in First Grade Reading with Disadvantaged Children,* Cooperative Project No. 2677, p. 98.

ance of the laws of learning, and the effects of intelligence on learning (in this population I.Q.'s range from 55 to 146). The well-grounded educator would not presume to think that all children should accomplish the same amount of work in the same length of time. The view that transition to t.o. is a difficulty is wholly incorrect; Mr. Gillooly appears to discount the rates of learning or the learning difficulties of the mentally slow and the effects of cultural deprivation on language learning. He should note that when the slowest children made the transition to t.o., in May and June, 1965, they were effectively reading second-grade material. For a child with an I.Q. of 55 to 75, such achievement is remarkable. No one, to my knowledge at least, has presumed to say that all children will leave i.t.a. at the same time. Rather, every anagologist has, from the outset, assumed that in i.t.a. (even though it is vastly easier), as in t.o., children will learn at different rates and gain confidence and security in their command of the reading process at different rates. Transition should not be pushed but may be expected when that point of confidence is reached.

Mr. Gillooly's offhand dismissal of the interesting findings of Nemeth and Hayes is curious, since I made these results available to him at the same time he acquired much of the other data. His interpretation of the Nemeth-Hayes study is contrary to their statements.

The most glaring faults in this review, however, appear to be a result of his predetermined view to accept uncritically *only* data from unequivalent populations. Apparently, equivalency may be disregarded in research—a most peculiar view and one which effectively cuts off any consideration of the positive results in favor of the i.t.a. populations when covariance or matched-pair studies are done.

MR. GILLOOLY REPLIES

The Messrs. Dolmatch and Mazurkiewicz hold two contradictory positions at the same time. The first is that I have been too selective in collecting studies, and the second is that none of the present studies are of much use anyway, since they have employed currently available reading tests which are inappropriate for evaluating i.t.a. If the second is true, the first is irrelevant.

The decision concerning whether or not a test is suitable for the task assigned it ought to be made before the results of its use are known. Otherwise, researchers could reject, as inappropriate, test results which do not conform to their expectation—a very unsatisfactory situation indeed. It is relevant to note that the tests used for evaluating i.t.a. were selected by twenty-seven recipients of U.S. Office of Education grants. The group included Jeanne Chall, Edward Fry, William Sheldon, George Spache, Harold Tanyzer, and *Albert Mazurkiewicz*. Whatever misgivings Mr. Mazurkiewicz entertains should have been voiced to the other researchers at that time. To quarrel about the tests after the results start going against i.t.a. is out of order.

In this writer's judgment, the most effective defense of the Pitman Publishing Corporation and Mr. Mazurkiewicz's interests would be for them to cite the studies which support their views on the matter. Each of them had the opportunity to do so this spring when I visited with them in their home offices. Again, I invite them to produce those studies. After they are produced, we can discuss each on its merits. But let it be known now that the studies will have to be quite good to be of a caliber equal to the six studies (not three, as Mr. Dolmatch reports) which support the position expressed in my review. The Hayes and Nemeth study, by the way, was received by this writer on April 7, 1966—five days before my manuscript had to leave to meet the publication deadline. Hence, it could be treated only in a footnote. Mr. Mazurkiewicz seems to be under the impression that I should have included their findings (which, by the way, do agree with the five others in support of the position taken in my review) because he told me about them when we talked in Bethlehem. I must comment here that it is not my policy to report and comment on research results obtained in conversation with a third party. All of the data I reported were treated only after I received a *written* copy of the researcher's formal report. To proceed on hearsay in such an important matter would have been inexcusable.

The charge of bias against me is a curious one, unsupported by the inclusion of a motive. But for the record, let me state now that I stand to gain nothing material from the success or failure of i.t.a. My concern is for the discovery of the facts in this issue and my bias, if any, is toward careful, well-controlled research—regardless of its outcome. I am disturbed by the thought of large numbers of children using a new writing medium the claims for which are not supported by presently available, carefully designed studies. I wonder if my accusors are prepared to make an equally frank evaluation of their motives in this issue.

D. Phonics—Linguistics

BREAKING THE CODE: WHAT METHOD? *

Introducing an Integrated
Linguistic Approach to
Beginning Reading

Rose Sabaroff

Reading is undoubtedly the most researched area in the curriculum. Yet we know that some children still have difficulty in learning to read. Many new beginning reading programs described as linguistic are appearing on the market. Why? What is lacking in the basal reading approach? What is unsatisfactory in a phonic approach? A brief analysis of approaches to beginning reading may provide some answers.

There is much research to show that at the earliest stages in reading, a word has much more meaning for a child than a letter: the word *man* carries meaning; the letters *m, a, n* do not. The word method was first suggested by Comenius more than three hundred years ago. In 1657 he wrote in his *Orbis Pictus:* "The very looking upon the picture suggesting the name of the thing will tell the child how the title of the picture is to be read. And thus the whole book being gone over by the bare titles of the pictures, reading cannot but be learned—and indeed, too, without using any ordinary tedious spelling— that most troublesome torture of wits" (1).

Nevertheless, we know that children cannot go on indefinitely learning whole words by sight, using configuration and context alone. At first, it is easy to differentiate such totally different looking words as *red* and *yellow* or *one* and *three.* But eventually, and very soon for some children, additional cues are needed to help retain and differentiate words. Words like *was* and *saw, went* and *want, horse* and *house,* whose configuration is similar, cause trouble. If a child learns the word *look* because of the "two eyes" in the middle, what does he do with the words *book, hook,* and *took?* If a child "recognizes" *monkey* because of the tail at the end, what does he do with the word *money?* If a teacher simultaneously shows a child a picture of a cat and the word *cat,* what does the child do when he cannot recall the word and no

---

* REPRINTED FROM *The Elementary School Journal* (November, 1966, pp. 95–103) by Rose Sabaroff by permission of The University of Chicago Press. Copyright 1966 by The University of Chicago.

longer has the picture to help him? On many occasions I have seen a teacher point to her eyes or her nose to help a child who is having difficulty reading the words *eyes* or *nose*. Does this technique help children learn how words are put together?

There is a system in which our English language is encoded. This coding system is not the easiest or the most consistent one, but it is helpful with many words despite the fact that there is not a one-to-one correspondence beween the sounds in our language and the letters we use to represent these sounds. We use more than one letter to represent a given sound; we use the same letters to represent different sounds. Yet there is a way of organizing our presentation of words in beginning reading so that children can break the code rather than try to learn each word independently of all others.

THE MODIFIED SIGHT METHOD

Despite an abundance of materials, modern reading programs generally depend on one of two methods. The approach most popular currently uses the sight method at first and then introduces children gradually to the consonants. This approach is here called *the modified sight method*. Sounds of consonants are more regular than sounds of vowels. Also, consonants appear at the beginning of most words and hence are considered most helpful. Take the example, "The boy ran down the *r*———." In the context of that sentence, a child would most likely guess the last word to be *road*; "*p*———" in that position would probably be read as *path*; "*str*———" in that position would probably be read as *street*. Hence, the modified sight method, which is used in most basal readers, stresses the principle that every letter in a word need not be analyzed to read that word. Context plus the use of the first letter or letters of a word are often enough for the child to guess the word.

This method also stresses consonant substitution: *toy* becomes *boy* by substituting *b* for *t*; again, there is no need to sound all elements in the new word. Gradually children are taught to make substitutions in ending consonants as well as in beginning consonants: *map* can be figured out by comparing it with *man* and noting that a *p* has replaced the *n*. Eventually, a child begins to concern himself with vowels also.

THE PHONIC METHOD

Modern phonic approaches, like sight approaches, generally start with whole words. However, unlike the modified sight method in which primarily consonants are stressed, in phonic approaches each letter is considered equally important. The sounds for letters, letter combinations, and their variations are learned separately and then blended together to "sound out" the word. Phonic approaches are usually carefully structured, and sound elements are taught in a systematic way. The Spalding approach, for example, introduces first-graders to seventy elements of which twenty-three have an additional two to six variations, or one hundred and ten elements in all (2). This is a tremendous array of separate elements to be learned; all elements are presented in first grade and repeated in second grade and again in third grade as needed. Other phonic approaches introduce the elements to be learned more gradually, and each phonic approach has its own sequence.

Most schools use one or another of these two basic methods: a modified sight method that gradually takes cognizance of consonants and then vowels, or a phonic method in which individual letter sounds are learned and blended into words. With each of these methods we have children who are having too much difficulty learning to read. Why?

THE SIGHT METHOD—PROBLEMS

When beginning reading is based on a sight vocabulary, the following difficulties arise:

1. Children get the idea that reading is memorizing or guessing.

2. Some children have poor visual memories and, without additional cues, soon decide they cannot learn to read.

3. Eventually, even children who have fairly good visual memories begin to have difficulty as words are introduced more rapidly and begin to overlap in appearance.

4. Since the sight method, while it is working, is fast, children later resist more analytic approaches to words when they arrive at the stage where the pure sight method is no longer adequate.

5. The words generally used in a sight approach to beginning reading are the most highly irregular: *look, come, mother, go.* In a sight approach, it is extremely difficult for the child to make any discoveries about the relation of sound to letter. For example, what discovery can a child make about the sound represented by *o* as the letter appears in the words *look, come, mother, go?*

The teaching of phonic elements in the modified sight method usually begins with initial consonants. Children who recognize the value of the initial consonant as a clue thereafter look at the first letter of a word and guess the rest of the word from the context. Many children who have been taught by this method never get beyond guessing alone, or guessing with the aid of the initial consonant, and will not look carefully at the remainder of the word.

THE PHONIC METHOD—PROBLEMS

But, when emphasis in beginning reading is placed on learning the letters and their sounds and then blending them into words, difficulties still arise for some children:

1. Letters or sounds as such do not have meaning apart from words. It is hard for many children in the beginning stages of reading to think of words as sounds blended in a given sequence.

2. Learning of the names or the sounds of isolated letters often does not transfer to reading new words. The child may know the sounds of the individual letters but may not be able to use the information in attacking words. Many studies show that a moderate amount of phonics taught in a functional way is more effective than isolated phonic drill (3–5).

3. Some children learn the letters and their sounds but cannot blend them into words.

4. Letter-by-letter phonics is laborious and may destroy the desire to learn to read.

5. One letter may represent more than one sound; one sound may be represented in several ways.

6. More and more phonic elements must be introduced to take care of the irregularities of the spelling in our language.

7. Even if some children learn this way, is it the best method for all children? Research seems to show that great emphasis on phonics at the early stages may make for some early advantages, but that over time, the advantage is lost (6).

LINGUISTICS

Linguists have recently made available knowledge about the structure of words and the structure of sentences in English. This newly available knowledge needs to be incorporated into what we educators already know about the reading process. We are not starting from scratch. From the psychology of learning we have some information about motivation for learning. We know something about the advantages and the disadvantages of various materials and methods of instruction. We know something about the comparative value of systematic and less systematic methods of teaching reading. And now the linguists have made available to us a systematic analysis of the structure of English words and English syntax. But we know that all children do not learn equaly well by any single method. And we know that there is more to reading than decoding, which the linguists tend to emphasize.

The writer has been developing and testing an integrated linguistic approach to beginning reading that uses knowledge from psychology, from best current practices, and from linguistics. In the past when educators have swung to something new, they have been too willing to give up what experience has taught them is worthwhile. Instead, we should keep what is good of the known and incorporate from the new only what is valuable for our purposes.

The integrated linguistic approach offers many advantages. It helps children break the code. It helps them discover how our spoken language is set down in writing. It helps children get at the system that is operating. It helps them find out how words are structured. It helps them become aware that the arrangement of letters in a word controls the way these letters function.

One does not ask, "What is the sound of *o*?" When an *o* appears alone at the end of a one-syllable word or at the end of an accented syllable, it usually represents the long *o* as in *no* or *going*. But *o* in combination with *y* as in *boy* has quite a different sound. There are many arrangements or patterns in which *o* can occur in a word. Thus, the sound represented by *o* in a given word depends on the pattern of consonants and vowels in that word.

Since there are not nearly so many patterns in words as there are isolated phonic elements, the linguists have given us a way of looking at the structure of words that should make the decoding task infinitely less difficult for children who are learning to read.

FIVE PATTERNS

Here are five basic patterns that should be most useful in beginning reading. The patterns are based on the relation of vowels and consonants in a word.

The single (or short) vowel pattern.—Pattern 1 contains a single vowel followed by a consonant or consonants. Examples of this pattern using the *a* as a single vowel follow: *at, man, that, mash, strap, catch, pass, pack*. As is obvious in the examples just given, one or more consonants may precede the single vowel; more than one consonant may follow. It does not matter. The important elements are a single vowel followed by a single consonant. This pattern is the most common way of representing the short sound of a vowel. Words representing short *a*, short *i*, short *u*, short *o*, and short *e* are variations of this same pattern. Visually, we see a single vowel within a word. Auditorially, the single vowel with the word represents the short vowel sound. This pattern is often designated the (consonant-) vowel-consonant pattern.

The open vowel pattern:—Pattern 2 consists of a single vowel as the terminal element of a one-syllable word: *go, so, no; my, by, cry; he, she, be; I.* The open vowel may also appear at the end of an accented syllable within a word: *ba-by, di-al, po-em, du-ty*. In each case the single vowel in this pattern represents a long vowel sound.

The vowel with final e *pattern:*—Pattern 3 contains a vowel, followed by a consonant, followed by a final *e*. Examples are *rate, ride, use rope*. The *a–e*, *i–e*, *u–e*, *o–e* combinations regularly represent a long vowel sound. Instead of short *a* in *rat*, we have long *a* in *rate*. Instead of short *i* in *rid*, we have long *i* in *ride*.

The double vowel pattern:—Pattern 4 contains a double vowel element as in the words *seed, each; coat; rain, ray; coin, toy; out, down; raw, auto; good; toot; new*. (Notice that in some of these words—*down, raw, new*—the *w* acts like the *u* in *out, fault, neutral*. Notice also that *y* replaces *i* at the end of a word: *rain→ray; coin→toy*). These double vowel combinations are consistent enough and appear frequently enough to be of considerable help to a beginning reader.

The modified vowel pattern:—Pattern 5 contains a vowel whose sound is modified by a consonant. A vowel and *r* represent a special sound as in *or, for; art, harm; her, bird, burn*. In the words *or* and *for* the *o* is neither long nor short. Instead, we now have a modified vowel sound that is represented by the element *or*. *Ar* as in *barn*, and *er, ir, ur* as in *her, bird, burn* also represent modified vowel sounds. The vowel + *r* is the most important of the modified vowel combinations.

In turn, the *w* preceeding an *or* element as in *word* or *work* modifies the sound of *or*. The *w* also affects the sound of *a* as in *want* or *water*. The vowel *a* with *l* in combination often represents a modified sound as in *all, ball,* or *salt*.

SPECIAL CONSONANT COMBINATIONS

In addition to the five basic vowel patterns described, there are also several common consonant combinations that should be called to children's attention:

1. *c* in combination with *e, i, y* as in *cent, city, cyst*; where *ce, ci, cy* represent the soft sound of *c*.
2. *g* in combination with *e, i, y* as in *gem, gist, gym*; where *ge, gi, gy* represent the soft sound of *g*.
3. *kn* as in *knee, know, knife*.
4. *gn* as in *gnaw, gnat, gnarl*.
5. *wr* as in *write, wring, wrap*.

These consonant combinations have a one-to-one relation with a given sound. We therefore accept them as regular, and words in which they appear can be grouped in the appropriate vowel pattern.

MULTISYLLABLE WORDS

In multisyllable words certain phenomena occur repeatedly because of variations in stress. Children's attention is called to those structural elements that will extend the usefulness of the five basic patterns.

1. Inflectional endings. An *s, es, 's; d, ed; ing* are added to words in the patterns children already know.
2. The unaccented *y* at the end of words of more than one syllable represents a consistent sound in words like *fun-ny, ba-by, cit-y*.
3. The unaccented *e* in a syllable composed of consonant + *le* has a characteristic pronunciation in words like *lit-tle, cir-cle, pur-ple*.
4. The unaccented *a* standing first in a word of more than one syllable as in *a-way, a-round, a-bout* represents a consistent sound.

5. There are many multisyllable words like be-gan, rab-bit, bet-ter, in which the vowel elements do not receive their full sound value in the unstressed syllable. In decoding, however, the child usually stresses each syllable. Once the word is recognized as familiar, the child easily switches to the unstressed pronunciation. Hence, in such words, no special attention is given to the unstressed vowel in the initial decoding.

6. Irregular end syllables. Certain common end syllables are spelled irregularly but have a consistent pronunciation: *tion, sion, ture, tive*. If these are taught as common syllable elements and not analyzed phonically, no reading problem is created.

Those who wish to read in greater detail about linguistic patterns and about the relation of sound and spelling in English should see Bloomfield, Fries, and Hall (7–9).

The integrated linguistic approach developed by the author starts with familiar words that are phonemically regular; that is, each consonant element and each vowel element used has a consistent one-to-one relation with the sound it represents, as in the words *pan, sit, rub*, and *fox*. However, the reading is not limited to three-letter words. Digraphs and blends are introduced in words like *dish, sick, slip, glad*; and common inflectional endings appear soon: *sit→sits, man→man's, jump→jumped, swim→swimming*.

The program is systematic and carefully programmed. The child is introduced to phoneme-grapheme (sound-sight) relationships gradually (only a few at a time). He is expected to achieve mastery or near-mastery of these elements before further elements are introduced. The learning of a new element draws on prior learnings. The material is presented in such a way that the child must discover the structure in words. When he is faced with the words *cat* and *rat*, he is forced to differentiate between them. When he sees *man* and *mat*, he must pay attention to the important difference. While he is learning his first consonants, he is also discovering the position in which a short *a* is found in a word: *cat, man's, and, flat, that, at, glad, naps*. The program begins with words in Pattern 1. It does not matter how many consonants come before or after the vowel, as long as one consonant follows the single vowel. The child learns that the pattern holds true for all short vowels, not only the short *a*.

Thus the child is led to discover the characteristic sounds of consonants and vowels as they appear in certain positions in words. The program is designed to help the child notice from the start the relation between elements of the spoken word and its written counterpart; only the most common, the most regular, the most frequently occurring elements are brought to his attention.

In the first materials presented to the child only the short *a* is used. He thus learns to differentiate consonants while the vowel is held constant. Next he must differentiate short-*i* words from short-*a* words. Immediately, the vowel takes on tremendous importance. All the previous consonants can now be used with the new vowel. This approach is markedly different from approaches that stress consonants almost exclusively in the first year. As noted earlier, in a linguistic program, the patterns are built around the relation of vowels and consonants in a word. Vowels are important and are to be differentiated from consonants. A blend or a digraph is an element because of its relation to the vowel: *gl* in *glad* is the consonant element before the vowel; *th* in *that* is the digraph before the vowel; *nd* in *and* is a blend following the vowel; *ck* in *sick* is a digraph following the vowel.

A single vowel such as *a* in a word has its characteristic sound: *sat, sand, stand, strand.* A double vowel element such as *ai* has quite a different characteristic sound: *maid, chain, braid, strain.* An *a* with an *r* is quite different again: *star, start, farm, barn.* Patterns are built around the vowel elements, as the five basic patterns described show.

The materials presented to children progress systematically from the short vowel pattern through patterns that have more complex vowel combinations. New blends and digraphs continue to appear. Structural analysis is introduced to extend the use of the basic patterns to words of more than one syllable.

ADVANTAGES

The integrated linguistic approach is different from a phonic approach. In a phonic approach, the child often learns a particular combination of letters in isolation such as the *at* in *hat, pat, cat,* and *fat,* but he may not be able to transfer the knowledge from the drill situation to the decoding of a new word in connected reading. In a phonic approach, a child learns so many isolated bits of information that he is often unable to organize this information when it is needed to attack a new word. Even phonic approaches that start with whole words treat each letter in a word as of equal importance. Often, too, the child is concerned only with sounding a particular word. He is not trying to discover an underlying pattern but merely wishes to decode the given word in question.

The problem of blending, which is common in a phonic approach, is avoided in the linguistic approach. In the linguistic approach the child becomes aware of the sound represented by a letter as he analyzes the difference between two similar words. He is not asked to sound letters in isolation and then blend sounds to make a word. The fragmentation that occurs in learning many isolated sight-sound relations is overcome. The major sound elements fit into five basic patterns that help a child organize or generalize his knowledge in such a way that it is more readily available for use.

The integrated linguistic method is also different from the sight method. In the sight method each word is learned for its own sake: each new word is one more word added to the repertoire. In the integrated linguistic approach, each word is an opportunity to discover how the coding system works. For example, when a child discovers how to recognize the short *a* (within his repertoire of consonants), he has made a major step toward the decoding of all short-*a* words. When he learns how a single *i* functions in a word, a whole new group of short-*i* words becomes available to him.

In a linguistic approach, most words presented in beginning reading are phonemically regular and fit a pattern. It is much easier to discover the underlying system and "break the code" when letters in words behave consistently.

A new pattern opens a whole new array of words that draw on all previously learned information. Since the number of new words a child can decode expands rapidly, a large repertoire of words becomes available quickly.

Stories are built on phonemically regular patterns. (Basic service words of our language that are phonemically irregular but vitally important in building good sentences are introduced gradually as sight words.) A child checks his decoding skills in meaningful story content. What he decodes makes sense; thus, the context provides a check on the correctness of his decoding.

An Integrated Approach

This approach to beginning reading is called an *integrated linguistic approach* for several reasons. On the one hand, words are consistently presented for linguistic-analysis; on the other hand, words are constantly checked in connected story content: the concern is always with decoding and meaning. Words to be analyzed are based on linguistic patterns that are phonemically regular. Sound elements are learned by analyzing word patterns rather than by blending isolated sounds into words. The approach combines the use of sight, sound, and meaning. Writing is used as a reinforcement. Breaking the code involves analyzing the basic spelling patterns of our language; hence, spelling becomes an incidental but important learning. Thus, the approach is integrated in that it combines reading, writing, speaking, spelling, and meaning in a total language approach to reading.

REFERENCES

1. Irving H. Anderson and Walter F. Dearborn. *The Psychology of Teaching Reading,* p. 211. New York: Ronald Press Company, 1952.
2. Romalda Bishop Spalding and Walter T. Spalding. *The Writing Road to Reading,* pp. 43–66. New York: Whiteside, Inc., and William Morrow and Company, 1962.
3. John B. McDowell. "A Report on the Phonetic Method of Teaching Children To Read," *Catholic Educational Review,* 51 (October, 1953), 506–19.
4. Arthur Gates and David H. Russell. "Types of Material, Vocabulary Burden, Word Analysis, and Other Factors in Beginning Reading," *Elementary School Journal,* 39 (September, 1938), 27–35; (October, 1938), 119–28.
5. Harry L. Tate, Theresa Herbert, and Josephine K. Zerman. "Non-Phonic Primary Reading," *Elementary School Journal,* 40 (March, 1940), 529–37.

6. Paul E. Sparks and Leo C. Fay. "An Evolution of Two Methods of Teaching Reading," *Elementary School Journal*, 56 (April, 1957), 386–90.
7. Leonard Bloomfield and Clarence Barnhart. *Let's Read*. Detroit: Wayne State University Press, 1961.
8. Charles C. Fries. *Linguistics and Reading*. Chapter 7. New York: Holt, Rinehart and Winston, 1963.
9. Robert A. Hall, Jr. *Sound and Spelling in English*. Philadelphia: Chilton Company, 1961.

READING: LINGUISTICS *

Emmett Albert Betts

Reading instruction is being given another dimension: linguistics. At the same time, linguistics is being broadened into a more comprehensive dimension: psycholinguistics (7, 44).

Linguistics as a science was given momentum by the publication of Edward Sapir's *language* in 1921 (43) and of Leonard Bloomfield's *Language* in 1933 (5). Moreover, Bloomfield's Chapter 28 on "Applications and Outlook" still serves as a pattern for several present-day linguists who would improve reading instruction via linguistics.

That there has been a revolution in the field of grammar cannot be gainsaid. But why is traditional grammar under heavy assault? Linguists offer at least three values of the newer structural English:

1. To update thinking about language and to put the study of language on a scientific basis.
2. To provide a scientific basis for teaching English as a foreign language.
3. To improve communication by providing insight regarding the structure of English and by increasing user proficiency.

LINGUISTICS

Linguistics—the scientific study of language—deals with two basic units, or elements, in the expression *system:*

1. The *phoneme* (or group of related speech sounds), or the smallest unit which differentiates the meaning of words: e.g., the phonemes *b* and *p* differentiate between *bit* and *pit*. Phonemes "are distinguishers only" and with-

---

* REPRINTED FROM the May, 1963, issue of *Education*. Copyright 1963 by The Bobbs-Merrill Company, Inc., Indianapolis, Indiana.

out meaning themselves. (This facet of descriptive linguistics is called *pho-nology*, the study of phonemes and sequences of phonemes.)

2. The *morpheme*, or smallest unit of expression that has meaning; e.g., *boy* is a morpheme, but *boys* embraces two morphemes, *boy* and *s*. (This facet of descriptive linguistics, including word groups, is called *grammar*, the study of morphemes and their combinations.)

Characteristics of Language

Linguists have called attention to these and other significant characteristics of language:

1. *Language is a set of sounds*. Linguists have emphasized that language can and has existed without writing but that writing cannot exist without speech. In other words, they have demonstrated the primacy of speech.

Speech is a system of sounds which differentiates the meaning of words, as *bet-bit, bet-pet*, etc. The sounds of language have distinctive patterns, grouped as functional units called phonemes. These phonemes, joined together, became the basic elements of continuous speech.

Writing is the representation of speech by means of the alphabet, punctuation, numbers, etc. Hence, writing is a code system called encoding; reading is the decoding or translation into speech which signals structural meaning and carries referential meaning (the content of a message).

Writing has speech as its base, and is a derivative of speech; however, there is no one-to-one relationship between writing and speech, as evidenced by spelling inconsistencies and incompleteness of punctuation.

Language, therefore, is speech activity producing a set of sounds.

2. *Language is a set of symbols*. The speaker puts (encodes) meaning into sound; that is, he goes from the lexicogrammatical level to the phonological level. On the other hand, the listener puts (decodes) sound into meaning; that is, he goes from the phonological level to the lexicogrammatical level.

But the situation is even more complex for the listener. The speaker (en coder), for example, knows whether he means *bear* or *bare*, but the listener (decoder) depends on the context to decide on the meaning.

Furthermore, language is used to refer to "things" (e.g., potatoes, airplanes, etc.) in the world, within the range of hearing, sight, or other senses and beyond their range. Language, therefore, is a system of arbitrary symbols composed of sounds structured in complex patterns (8, 14, 21, 28, 34, 43, 45).

3. *Language has system*. The sound of *ch* as in *each* recurs in *church, catch, nature*, and a great many other words. So does the sound of *ap* as in *cap, lap, map, lappet, lapse*, etc. In English, there are a limited number of phonemes and combinations of phonemes which serve as auditory signals to meaning— as a part of the *system* of language.

Consider the allomorphs *s* and *es* (sounds of *s* and *z*) in *laps, tubs, buses*. These are distributed according to the environments in which they occur;

namely, following voiceless consonants, voiced consonants (or vowels), and sibilants (or affricates) respectively. This complementary distribution of allomorphs is a part of the system of language.

Attention, birds, bicycles, etc., are the same part of speech: nouns. *Attend* is a verb. Both *attention* and *attend* involve action, doing something. But *attention* may have noun markers: determiners *the, all, his,* etc. and position before the verb.

Word order, intonation, function (or structure) words, inflection, and derivational contrasts—all of those systematic signals of structure are used in determining parts of speech.

Parts of speech, in turn, enter into larger and more complex structures; for example, the sentence. That is, the sentence consists of word-group patterns —a part of the system of language.

4. *Language is complete.* Language is complete in the sense that it permits its users to talk about all of their experiences. Each of the parts of speech, for example, may be expanded by coining new words to meet new situations (21, p. 8).

5. *Language has built-in redundancy* (41, p. 19). Consider the following sentence:

Many lawyers were at the party. The plural meaning of *lawyers* is signalled by *many,* the *s* ending of lawyers, and the verb *were.* The word *lawyers* is signalled as a noun by its position in the sentence and the noun marker *many.* And so on. These multiple signals of structural meaning are the patterns of language.

Referential and Linguistic Meaning

Can referential and linguistic meanings be isolated? Is it a matter of referential *and* linguistic meanings or referential-linguistic meaning? The linguist recognizes both kinds of meanings, but for purposes of research in descriptive linguistics, emphasizes *linguistic* meaning. Referential meaning, embracing the study of cultural systems, is categorized as *mentalinguistics* or *exolinguistics* (7).

In 1933, Leonard Bloomfield (5) helped to set the stage for differentiating between "practical events," and "the act of speech" (5, p. 23), between *"practical* stimuli" and *"speech* (or *substitute*) stimuli" (5, p. 25), between "speechless reaction" and "reaction mediated by speech" (5, p. 26). In short, he distinguished "between language . . . and *real* or *practical* events stimuli and reactions" (5, p. 27).

Referential Meaning. When the young child points to an apple and asks, "What is it?" he is concerned with the labeling of a thing in the physical world. When he is told, "apple," he is given a word—or in this case a morpheme—that designates this class of fruit. As he gains more experience with different kinds of apples, he becomes consciously or unconsciously aware that *apple* is an abstraction and generalization covering Winesaps, Grimes Golden, Delicious, and other kinds of apples.

The three phonemes of *apple* ('ap-l) designate a thing in the physical world —called a *referent*. The spoken word *apple* has extensional (real life) meaning. This referential meaning is meaning in the usual, but not the linguistic, sense of the word.

The meaning of the word *apple* shifts from one situation to another, depending upon the experience, attitudes, etc., of the speaker and the listener. The word *apple*, for example, may have one meaning for a healthy, hungry individual and a different meaning for an ulcer patient. Then, again, an "apple to eat" is quite different from "the apple of his mother's eye."

The study of referential meanings is called *semantics*. These are the meanings of the content of the message.

Linguistic Meaning. Linguists view language as a "*system* of signalling"; therefore, they are concerned with the meanings of linguistic signals (14).

Hall states the case this way: "In any utterance, meaning is conveyed by morphemes and their combinations into phrases and clauses; by the term *meaning* we refer to the way in which these linguistic features symbolize the facts of the universe in which we live." (19, p. 5)

Sequences of speech sounds—language—form a system, or code, of symbols by means of which the content of a message is "sent" by the speaker to the listener.

In his *The Structure of English*, Fries warns: "The total linguistic meaning of any utterance consists of the lexical [dictionary] meanings of the separate words plus . . . structural meanings. No utterance is intelligible without both lexical meanings and structural meanings." (14, p. 56)

PARTS OF SPEECH

For generations, parts of speech have been ambiguously defined in terms of their referential rather than their structural meanings. As a result, the study of this aspect of grammar deteriorated into the mere labeling of *words* in terms of *the* eight parts of speech: nouns, pronouns, adjectives, adverbs, prepositions, conjunctions, and interjections.

Gleason identifies the crux of the resulting confusion: "But, if our understanding of structure is based on [referential] meaning, and our understanding of meaning on structure, we are in a most vicious circle." (15, p. 94)

In 1933, Leonard Bloomfield recommended the determination of "English parts of speech not by their correspondence with different aspects of the practical world [referential meanings], but merely by their functions in English syntax." (5, p. 271)

The classification of morphemes or words results in "form classes." These form classes usually are referred to as "parts of speech." However, the form classes identified by the linguist only approximate the "parts of speech" of traditional grammar.

Fries (14) refers to the parts of speech as:

Class 1 words; e.g., The *man* is here.

Class 2 words; e.g., Our mail *arrived*.

Class 3 words; e.g., The apple is *good*, or The *happy* boy is here.

Class 4 words; e.g., He called the facts *accurately*.

The four form classes, or parts of speech, may be recognized by:

1. Contrastive, or distinctive, positions in which the word occurs

> Change jobs men.
> Men change jobs.
> Jobs change men.

These three words have only lexical (dictionary) meaning:

> change job men

When the words are arranged in an order, they carry a message and the class form is indicated:

> Men change jobs.
> Jobs change men.

Men and *jobs* are Class I words, or "nouns"; *change* is a Class II word, or "verb." Different sentence meanings result from different word orders, or patterns.

2. Word features

> Tom seemed cheerful.

In the above sentence, the verb is marked by the *ed* ending of *seemed;* the objective, by the *ful* suffix. In this sentence both the word order and the characteristics of *seemed* and *cheerful* signal the use of *seemed* as a verb and of *cheerful* as an adjective.

3. Structure words

> The man was early.

In the above sentence, *the* is a marker of a noun, called a noun determiner. Words like *the, that, this, each, some, my,* etc., pattern with nouns and enhance the meaning. As to position, they occur before nouns, as below:

> *The* airplane was late.
> *The* huge airplane was late.

FUNCTION WORDS

A very few words—e.g., *the, a, an, can, not, most, and, at, do, there, when, now,* etc.—may account for one-third of the running words in free utterances. These words—identified and labeled *function* words by Charles Fries—"differ sharply from the four classes" parts of speech and belong "in 'expanded' free utterances." (14, p. 88)

These function words are "those words which, although some of them may have also full-word meaning content, primarily or largely operate as means of expressing relations of grammatical structure." (14, p. 44)

Function words (1) may have very little if any lexical meaning of their own, (2) are quite indispensable, (3) occur often, and (4) are used in combining words into complex (large) structures.

Fries categorized his 154 function words into fifteen groups. For example, his Group A function words—*the each, all,* etc.—serve as markers, or determiners, of Class 1 words in these positions:

The men were working.
Both men were working.
Pepper's collar broke.
Every man was at work.

INTONATION

Intonation has been called the punctuation of speech. While there is no one-to-one relationship between speech and punctuation, intonation does signal grammatical structure. These signals include:

1. Pitch, tone or relative voice frequency
2. Stress, or relative voice loudness
3. Juncture, or the transition between contiguous speech sounds.

Pitch. Sentence melody is analyzed by most linguists into the rising or falling of the voice from one pitch level to another—into sequences of relative pitch. Hence, pitch contour is a "sequence of pitches with only one peak." (21, p. 28) Pitch contrasts, as a feature of intonation, signal meaning.

Linguists identify four relative levels of pitch:

1. Low (Unstressed and lesser stressed syllables)
2. Mid (Normal voice of speaker)
3. High (Stressed points of utterances)
4. Extra high (Special emphasis seldom used in normal conversational speech)

Stress. When one-syllable words— e.g., *one, it, with*—are said in isolation from a phrase or sentence context, they are given strong, or heavy, stress. Two-syllable words—e.g., *again* and *silver*—are given strong stress on one syllable and weak stress on the other. The three-syllable word *reinstate* is given medium stress on the first syllable, weak stress on the second syllable and strong stress on the last syllable. Three degrees of stress are indicated in most dictionaries.

The part of speech, or form class, of homographs is often signalled primarily by heavy stress on the first or second syllable; e.g., *content, produce, subject, object, contract*, etc. Stress plus contrasting consonant sounds signal the part of speech of *refuse*.

Stress is the loudness or softness—emphasis or force (energy)—given to sounds of speech. Contrastive differences in "loudness"—one of the characteristics of language structure which signal meaning—characterize stretches of speech utterances.

Some linguists identify four contrasting levels of stress:

1. Primary stress (strongest)
2. Secondary stress (next strongest)
3. Tertiary stress (next to softest)
4. Weak stress (softest or zero)

Juncture. Count aloud *one, two, three, four*, etc., and listen to the breaks—separations or slight delays—in the flow of speech sounds. This and other ways of joining sounds are called junctures. They signal the boundaries of utterances and of parts of utterances.

There are several types of juncture (juncture phonemes?), depending upon how they are classified: close juncture, joining phonemes within a syllable; open juncture, joining phonemes with shifts in allophones as in *I scream* and *ice cream*; and terminal junctures, joining groups of words and emphasizing pitch and stress for contrast.

1. Close Juncture. In the spoken word *it*, the phonemes *i t* are distinctively different but they are closely joined in the syllable without a pause. This rapid transition from one phoneme to another in the syllable is called *close juncture*.
2. Open Juncture. Linguists often use pairs of expressions to demonstrate open juncture, as in the phrases:

a name	an aim
that stuff	that's rough
why choose	white shoes
gray train	great rain
I laid	I'll aid
neat owl	knee towel
I scream	ice cream

A very slight pause between *a* and *name* produces *a name*. But a slight pause between *an* and *aim* produces *an aim*. The spoken expression of *a name* contrasts with *an aim*; therefore, the two constructions carry different meanings.

3. Rising Terminal Juncture. In counting aloud, each number except the last one is said with an upturn in level of pitch, or rising inflection. This transition from one word to the next—in counting—is called rising terminal, or double bar, juncture.

   Listen to the difference in levels of pitch and to the "pause" after each of these two sentences:

Fred is here.
Fred is here?

As contrasted in the first sentence, the second has an upturn in the level of pitch on the last word before the pause. This signal is called a rising *terminal* juncture.

In writing, this rising terminal juncture is usually signalled by a question mark. In counting—one, two, three, etc.—a comma signals this type of juncture.

4. Falling Terminal Juncture. In the sentence "Fred is here," the pause after *here* is preceded by a downturn in level of pitch, or falling inflection. This signal is called falling *terminal* juncture.

   Note also the falling terminal juncture on *four*, in counting *one, two, three, four.*

   Rising terminal juncture and falling terminal juncture most frequently mark the ends of sentences.

5. Sustained Juncture. Some utterances, especially incomplete ones, are joined with neither a rising nor a falling juncture, as the appositive in: The pilot, Joe McConnell, arrived on time. This sustained terminal juncture is heard before and after the appositive.

   This sustained juncture is commonly called "single bar."

The contribution of linguistics to reading instruction may be under- or over-emphasized. Hence, an inter-disciplinary approach to the teaching of reading provides perspective.

Factors Emphasized

Linguists emphasize:

1. The primacy of spoken language—of spoken language as a code or system and writing as a graphic, derived system
2. Pupil control over the structure of spoken language as a prerequisite or background for learning to read

3. Phonemics—distinctive speech sounds—rather than phonetics (phonemes and their allophones)
4. Consistency of phoneme-grapheme relationships for large groups of words have the "same" spelling patterns, with significant implications for word learning
5. Function and limitations of graphemes, especially the alphabet and punctuation as representations of phonemes and intonation contours
6. Patterns, or structure of language; e.g., spelling patterns (consistent phoneme-grapheme relationships), intonation patterns, classes of morphemes, et cetera
7. Word order (position, or order of sentence functions), grammatical inflections (number, tense, possession), function words (e.g., *the*, *all*, *may*, *very*, *not*) and intonation (pitch, stress, juncture) as signals of structural meaning
8. The sentence as a sequence of "grammatical functions" rather than as a sequence of words with only lexical meanings
9. Structural (differential) meaning as well as referential meaning
10. Listening, speaking, reading, and writing as integral processes

Factors Overemphasized

Some linguists tend to over-emphasize:

1. Oral reading, especially for beginners
2. Structural (versus referential) meaning in beginning reading
3. The child's inability to translate audio-language skills into the graphic representations as *the* cause or a cause of learning disability
4. The child's control over the basic structure, or system, of spoken languages as *the* reading readiness factor or a reading readiness factor, minimizing perceptual, visual-motor, and other skills known to psychologists and many reading specialists
5. The need for a more rigidly controlled vocabulary in beginning reading, especially in terms of phoneme-grapheme consistencies as in *an*, *pan*, etc.
6. Gradation of basic readers in terms of the "difficulty" or irregularity of their spelling patterns (phoneme-grapheme relationships)
7. The difference between inductive generalizations regarding phoneme-phonogram relationships (e.g., in *at*, *sat*; *make*, *lake*; *boat*, *goat*) and analogical reasoning regarding the "spelling pattern" plan of some linguists
8. Linguistics as *the* foundation of the teaching of reading and writing, minimizing semantics, perception, concept, formation, etc.

In spite of over/under emphases by a few linguists, linguistics offers a wealth of scholarship for those concerned with instruction in listening, speaking, reading, and writing. Through scholarly collaboration there can be a meeting of minds and emotions regarding basic issues.

DIVERGENT OPINIONS

Linguists offer highly divergent opinions regarding:

1. The value of the look-and-see, or sight "method" used in beginning reading (19, 46)
2. Relative emphases to be given structural and referential meanings in beginning reading (2, 7, 8, 14)
3. Allographs (A, a, etc.) to be used in beginning reading (5, 13)
4. The validity of attacks on "how much phonics" and "what brand of phonics" can be justified (5, 13, 19)
5. Classification of parts of speech and function words, especially the emphasis on phonology (2, 14, 20)

Divergencies in concepts, procedures, and therefore, findings abound in the literature on linguistics—indeed, as they do in the teaching of reading! Compare or contrast, for example, Fries (14) and Sleed (2), Fries (14) and Chomsky (8), Fries (14) and Pooley (35), Kenyon (2) and Pooley (35), Smith (46) and Hall (18, 19), Whitehall (2) and Trager and Smith (55), and so on. These honest differences of opinion stimulate rather than impede progress in the scientific study of language and in the application of findings to practical problems.

Being neither teachers of reading nor reading specialists, some linguists appear to be unaware of:

1. Methods for teaching new "skills" at a time when the pupil recognizes his need (3)
2. Methods of teaching a child how to *apply* a skill, usually during his silent reading and when the pupil needs to learn how to apply it
3. The value of silent before oral reading (3)
4. The pupil's independent and teaching, or instructional, "levels" of reading, basic concepts in reading instruction (3)
5. The causes of word-by-word reading, lip movement, etc. (3)

LINGUISTICS AND READING INSTRUCTION

Teachers of reading do need basic understandings of phonemics, grammar, etc. However, teachers of reading need not be linguists; instead, they need to use the findings and conclusions of these dedicated scholars. On the other hand, teachers and authors of professional and pupil text books do need some depth of scholarship in linguistics so they are prepared to collaborate with linguists for the improvement of reading instruction.

For depth and breadth of scholarship in the highly specialized field of linguistics, the educator solicits the cooperation of researchers in that field. In doing so, the educator observes two cautions:

First, linguists tend to have specialized research interests in phonemics (e.g., Charles K. Thomas), in grammar (e.g., Noam Chomsky), and other facets of linguistics.

Second, linguists—not qualifying as either educators or psychologists—may make proposals that are neither pedagogically nor psychologically acceptable. Hence, there is a need for collaboration between educators and linguists.

An inter-disciplinary approach to reading instruction has been "in the making" for a long time. Phonemicists have provided significant concepts for structuring a phonics program. Experimental psychologists have provided equally important concepts of perception on which to base instruction in phonics.

But neither of these disciplines offers *the* answer to the word learning needs of pupils. Furthermore, the conclusions of scholars in different disciplines are being sorted out, evaluated, and tried out in classroom situations by those responsible for instruction; namely, educators.

Likewise, students of morphology and syntax have contributed significantly to the thinking facet of reading instruction. But so have the semanticists. And so have researchers on the psychology of thinking. However, conclusions of these and other scholars are being identified, evaluated, and tried out in classrooms.

No one can justify the status quo of reading instruction or any other curriculum area. Some phonic programs in use today are significant improvements over those of yesteryear. The same is true regarding motivation (including interest) and thinking. Moreover, a great deal of progress has been made in the differentiation of instruction.

But effective reading instruction is based on far more scholarship than that offered by linguistics. Methods and materials would be distorted, indeed, if they were based on the limited, though important, contributions of linguists.

Evidence of this point is ample, for there have been linguists' recommendations and materials—including outright tirades—bordering on the ridiculous. However, other linguists working with psychologists and educators are making significant contributions to the improvement of reading instruction.

What can linguists contribute to reading instruction? There are several answers, including:

1. A phonemic basis of word perception and recognition
2. An understanding of incorrect spellings which reflect correct pronunciations, as *use to* for *used to*—which offers a rational basis for remediation
3. An understanding of incorrect pronunciations which reflect interpretation of spellings, as saying *Wednesday* in three syllables or pronouncing the *t* in *often* but not in *soften*

4. A phonemic basis for the consistent use of pronunciation symbols in dictionary respellings.
5. A structural, or differential, dimension to "meaning"
6. An intonational, especially pitch and juncture, basis for understanding the use of punctuation and the structure of sentences
7. A grammatical basis for teaching comprehension of higher level structures, especially the sentence.

LINGUISTICS: FAD OR CONTRIBUTION?

Linguistics can become a new fad in reading instruction. Or, this relatively new approach to the scientific study of language can contribute to the restructuring of both materials and methods and, therefore, contribute to pupil achievement.

Linguistics can easily become a fad when too many educators fail to come to close grips with findings and with the *different* interpretations of them. For example, there are educators who limit their view of linguistics to phoneme-grapheme relationships—to one facet of word perception and recognition. But linguistics also embraces higher structural levels: morphemes, morpheme classes and function words, syntax, etc.

Faddists lay claim to a knowledge of linguistics when they make superficial mention of phonemes and their allophones, morphs and their allomorphs, classes of morphemes (parts of speech), kernel sentences and transforms, intonation contours, phrase structure grammar, and other terms. But scholars in education master the concepts—often divergent—and use them as a basis for improving reading instruction.

Faddists rush into linguistics as a panacea for all reading ills as they have into the sight-word "method," a phonic method, semantics, group and individualized reading, and so on. But linguistics cannot be equated with reading instruction. Instead, linguistics is a body of knowledge that provides a systematic insight in regard to (1) word perception and recognition and (2) the ability to think in a language.

In fact, phonemics has already provided a scientific basis for a phonics program and for respelling (pronunciations) in at least one set of dictionaries.

REFERENCES

1. Albright, Robert W. "A Linguistic Approach to Reading and Spelling," *North Dakota Teacher* (January, 1957).
2. Allen, Harold B. *Readings in Applied English Linguistics* (New York: Appleton-Century-Crofts, 1958).
3. Betts, Emmett A. *Foundations of Reading Instruction* (New York: American Book Company, 1963).
4. Block, Bernard, and Trager, George L. *Outline of Linguistic Analysis* (Baltimore: Linguistic Society of America, 1942).

5. Bloomfield, Leonard. *Language* (New York: Henry Holt and Company, Inc., 1933).

6. Bloomfield, Leonard. "Linguistics and Reading," *The Elementary English Review*, XIX, No. 4 (April, 1942), pp. 125–130; XIX, No. 5 (May, 1942), pp. 183–186.

7. Carroll, John B. *The Study of Language* (Cambridge, Massachusetts: Harvard University Press, 1961).

8. Chomsky, Noam. *Syntactic Structures* (The Hague, The Netherlands: Mouton & Co., 1956).

9. Church, Joseph. *Language and the Discovery of Reality* (New York: Random House, 1961).

10. Edfeldt, Ake W. *Silent Speech and Silent Reading* (Chicago: The University of Chicago Press, 1960).

11. Francis, W. Nelson. *The Structure of American English* (New York: The Ronald Press Company, 1958).

12. Fries, Charles Carpenter. *American English Grammar* (New York: D. Appleton-Century Company, 1940).

13. Fries, Charles Carpenter. *Linguistics and Reading* (New York: Holt, Rinehart, and Winston, Inc., 1963).

14. Fries, Charles Carpenter. *The Structure of English* (New York: Harcourt, Brace & World, Inc., 1952).

15. Gleason, H. A. *An Introduction to Descriptive Linguistics* (New York: Henry Holt and Company, 1955).

16. Hall, Frances Adkins. *Sounds and Letters* (Ithaca, New York: Linguistica, 1956).

17. Hall, Frances Adkins, and Brenes, Eleanor H. *Spelling Patterns* (Ithaca, New York: Linguistica, 1960).

18. Hall, Robert A., Jr. *Linguistics and Your Language* (Garden City, New York: Anchor Books, Doubleday & Company, Inc., 1960).

19. Hall, Robert A., Jr. *Sound and Spelling in English* (New York: Chilton Company-Book Division, 1961).

20. Harris, Zellig S. *Methods in Structural Linguistics* (Chicago: The University of Chicago Press, 1951).

21. Hill, Archibald A. *Introduction to Linguistic Structures* (New York: Harcourt, Brace and Company, 1958).

22. Hockett, Charles Francis. *A Course in Modern Linguistics* (New York: The Macmillan Company, 1958).

23. Jespersen, Otto. *Language, Its Nature, Development and Origin* (London: George Allen & Unwin Ltd., 1922).

24. Kennedy, Arthur G., and Sands, Donald B. *A Concise Bibliography for Students of English* (Stanford, California: Stanford University Press, 1960).

25. Lloyd, Donald J., and Warfel, Harry R. *American English in Its Cultural Setting* (New York: Alfred A. Knopf, Inc., 1956).

26. Marckwardt, Albert H. *Introduction to the English Language* (New York: Oxford University Press, 1952).

27. Miller, George A. *Language and Communication* (New York: McGraw-Hill Book Company, Inc., 1951).

28. Morris, Charles. *Signs, Language and Behavior* (New York: Prentice-Hall, Inc., 1946).

29. Neurath, Otto; Carnap, Rudolf; and Morris, Charles (Editors). *International Encyclopedia of Unified Science*, Vol. 1, Nos. 1–5 (Chicago, Illinois: The University of Chicago Press, 1955).

30. Osgood, C. E.; Suci, G.; and Tannenbaum, P. *The Measurement of Meaning* (Urbana, Illinois: University of Illinois Press, 1957).

31. Pike, Kenneth L. *The Intonation of American English* (Ann Arbor, Michigan: The University of Michigan Press, 1945).

32. Pike, Kenneth L. *Phonemich* (Ann Arbor: The University of Michigan Press, 1947).

33. Pike, Kenneth L. *Phonetics* (Ann Arbor: The University of Michigan Press, 1943).

34. Pike, Kenneth L. *Tone Languages* (Ann Arbor: The University of Michigan Press, 1948).

35. Pooley, Robert C. *Teaching English Grammar* (New York: Appleton-Century-Crofts, Inc., 1957).

36. Potter, Simeon. *Modern Linguistics* (London: Andre Deutsch, 1957).

37. Quine, W. V. *From a Logical Point of View* (Cambridge, Massachusetts: Harvard University Press, 1953).

38. Read, Allen Walker. "A Discrimination among Synonyms of the Word 'Meaning,' " *Report of the Sixth Annual Round Table Meeting on Linguistics and Language Teaching*. Washington, D.C.: Georgetown University Press, No. 8 (September, 1955), pp. 123–134.

39. Read, Allen Walker. "An Account of the Word 'Semantics,' " *Word*, IV, No. 2 (August, 1948), pp. 78–92.

40. Roberts, Paul. *English Sentences* (New York: Harcourt, Brace & World, Inc., 1962).

41. Roberts, Paul. *Patterns of English* (New York: Harcourt, Brace and Company, 1956).

42. Roberts, Paul. *Understanding English* (New York: Harper & Bros., 1958).

43. Sapir, Edward. *Language* (New York: Harcourt, Brace and Company, 1921).

44. Saporta, Sol (Editor). *Psycholinguistics* (New York: Holt, Rinehart and Winston, 1961).

45. Smith, Henry Lee, Jr. *Linguistic Science and the Teaching of English* (Cambridge, Massachusetts: Harvard University Press, 1956).

46. Smith, Henry Lee, Jr. "Review of Let's Read: a Linguistic Approach by Leonard Bloomfield and Clarence L. Barnhart," *Language*, XXXIX, No. 1 (January-March, 1963).

47. Smith, Henry Lee, Jr. "Superfixes and Syntactic Markers," *Georgetown University Monographic Series on Language and Linguistics*, IX (December, 1957), pp. 7–24.

48. Soffietti, James P. "Why Children Fail to Read: A Linguistic Analysis." *Harvard Educational Review*, XXIV (1955), pp. 63–84.

49. "Structure of Language and its Mathematical Aspects," *Proceedings of Symposia in Applied Mathematics*, XII (Providence, Rhode Island: American Mathematical Society, 1961).

50. Sturtevant, Edgar H. *An Introduction to Linguistic Science* (New Haven: Yale University Press, 1947).

51. Summey, George, Jr. *American Punctuation* (New York: The Ronald Press Company, 1949).

52. Thomas, Charles Kenneth, Ph.D. *Phonetics of American English*, second edition (New York: The Ronald Press Company, 1958).

53. Trager, Edith Crowell. "Superfix and Semanteme: English Verbal Compounds," *General Linguistics*, II, No. 1 (Fall, 1956), pp. 1–14.

54. Trager, George L. *The Field of Linguistics* (*Studies in Linguistics, Occasional Paper, No. 1*) (Norman, Oklahoma: Battenburg Press, 1949).

55. Trager, George L., and Smith, Henry Lee, Jr. *An Outline of English Structure* (*Studies in Linguistics, Occasional Papers, No. 3*) (Norman, Oklahoma: Battenburg Press, 1951).

56. Whitehall, Harold. *Structural Essentials of English* (New York: Harcourt, Brace & World, Inc., 1951).

57. Whorf, Benjamin Lee. *Language, Thought, and Reality* (New York: John Wiley & Sons, Inc., 1956).

58. Wijk, Axel. "Regularized English: An Investigation into the English Spelling Reform Problem with a New, Detailed Plan for a Possible Solution," *Stockholm Studies in English* VII. Acta Universitatis Stockholmiensis (Stockholm, Sweden: Almquist & Wiksell, 1959).

LINGUISTIC FACTORS IN EARLY READING INSTRUCTION *

Gertrude Hildreth

The current emphasis on the mechanics of reading, sounding out the letters, drilling on perception and oral pronounciation of isolated words and syllables, flash techniques for word-attack skills, and speeding up the eye movements through mechanical devices all too frequently overlooks the fact that reading is primarily a linguistic process, one which requires grasping sentence meanings primarily in an oral context. Here is a sixth grader reading aloud. She inquires anxiously, "Does it sound all right?" This is her first response to reading: "How does it sound?" not "What does it mean?" Has she been able to pronounce each word is her concern, not what do the sentences mean. Too seldom pupils realize that reading is not just pronouncing but associating sound with meaning, and that meaning is expressed not only by single words but by the larger syntactical units of phrases and sentences.

---

* REPRINTED with permission of Gertrude Hildreth and the International Reading Association, from *The Reading Teacher*, Vol. 18, December, 1964, pp. 172–78.

In teaching "phonics" we have traditionally taught the speech sounds represented by letters and groups of letters. We need now to extend the study of "phonics" to include the speech melodies of phrases and sentences, which in print are in part signaled by punctuation marks. That is, we need to teach larger segments of sound than we have traditionally taught. We need, further, to teach these larger segments of sound in association with meaning. Comprehending the meanings of phrases or sentences is the central problem for the reader. The ability to comprehend such meanings is developed by the child's experience primarily and mainly with the oral language. The more extensive the child's experience in the language of speech, therefore, the better equipped he is likely to be in getting an author's meaning.

The experience which a child gets in understanding language from speaking and listening is extended by his experience in reading. The young reader constantly learns more about both vocabulary and sentence sense as he continues to read and to comprehend increasingly difficult material. In writing compositions he also extends this experience in understanding language. He not only uses words and sentences to express his own meanings, but as he spells out his words or "says" his sentences to himself he gets practice in associating the oral with the written language.

Evidence concerning the relation of a child's language experience to his reading achievement comes from various sources:

- Studies of normal children learning to read and write,
- Studies of children with cultural deficiencies and intellectual differences in language and background,
- Problems of foreign-speaking children in learning to read,
- Studies of the mentally handicapped and of those with physical handicaps hindering the acquisition of speech.

The writer's study of a school beginner's progress in learning words supports the view that the oral language with which children are familiar provides the basis for their learning to recognize words (9). Words more often used by the individual in speaking are normally easier to recall in print. A boy nearing six—of average learning ability, without previous reading experience, and of normal language development—was shown flash cards, each containing a single word. As each card was flashed he was told the pronunciation of the word. The results showed that the words more meaningful to him—*pony, boy, orange, candy, mother*—were the more quickly learned.

A brief report of another case will illustrate the relationship between general reading failure and lack of adequate language experience. A boy of twelve, attending Grade 6 in a New York City public school, has a Stanford-Binet I.Q. of 89, with higher ratings on tests not requiring the use of language. The boy is superior in mechanical skill, a practical-minded youngster. On Saturdays he works along with his father, who is an electrician. His ambition, however, is to become a baseball player. The boy's school record shows that he was a reading failure in Grade 1. At the beginning of Grade 6 his reading level stood at Grade 2, but after thirty reading sessions through the year his reading score came up to 3.5. The family's concern is that the boy must reach a reading score of 5.0 in order to enter a vocational junior high school. The boy's speech is also retarded. He speaks slowly, using a limited vocabulary. Records show that he spent the first three years of his life in an orphanage, where he may not have had the many language-learning experiences of children in the usual family situation.

In a study by Ladd (16) a relationship was found between success in reading and the richness of the child's language background. Progress in learning to read was found to be largely dependent upon the child's previous experience with the spoken language. Children from cultivated homes, where ideas, not just weather or the menu, were discussed at the dinner table, tended to be advanced in their general use of the language and, on the whole, had less trouble in learning to read, though there were exceptions due to the effects of other complex factors.

Dr. Brazziel's study of culturally deprived children gave conclusive proof of the close association between substandard language usage in young school children and reading deficiency (3). These language-impoverished children bog down in the intermediate grades when the text moves too far ahead of their grasp of language meanings in everyday usage. In one intermediate grade class the children did not know the term "magazine" referring to weekly periodicals. A junior high school teacher spent the term teaching boys of limited linguistic background the meaning of such common textbook terms as: "out on the frontier," "a ferocious hound," "Eastern hemisphere," "canal locks," "major power."

A large proportion of reading disability cases come from homes where language is used only for everyday, or not particularly intellectual, subjects or where a substandard dialect is used. A child may be native born and grow up in a home where English is the only language and yet be linguistically uneducated and a potential reading problem.

Dr. Martin Deutsch, a New York psychiatrist who has been making recordings of the linguistic development of school entrants, is impressed with the fact that many young children are put at a disadvantage by the linguistic demands that schooling in Grade 1 puts upon them. He reports finding a direct relationship between linguistic development and social factors (7).

The child of migrant parents who speak a dialect that is widely used in a section of the country where the child grew up may be almost unintelligible when he goes to school in a different section of the country where a different dialect is used. Children moving into a new dialect area tend to lag a year or more behind others in reading in spite of regular attendance. The retardation can be ascribed primarily to the oral language differences (3).

The non-English speaking beginner struggling with reading lessons has the handicap also of not knowing the required sound language for comprehending the printed word. The non-English speaking child has a double handicap when he comes from a home of limited cultural attainments and aspirations. In the study by Ladd referred to above, poor readers were often found to come from homes where a foreign language was the major means of communication.

Dr. Tireman's data indicated that Spanish-American children on our southern border have reading problems in the intermediate grades (22). A teacher described the problems of a foreign child struggling to pronounce words in print. Although this child could pronounce the consonant digraph *sh* in words such as *shovel, sheet,* and *should,* these words meant nothing to her. The child thought *selfish* was a kind of fish. She had never heard this English word. Without oral fluency the best these non-English speaking children can do is to learn to associate sounds with certain letters arbitrarily. They can learn to read only as they learn to speak the syntactical units of standard English.

Another line of evidence comes from recent studies in teaching modern foreign languages with attention first to oral-aural responses, leaving reading and textbook work to a later stage. Learning to read a foreign language is a truly formidable task even for a bright learner if he lacks a knowledge of the spoken tongue. In contrast, reading is much like talking to the page when the student can already speak the language. One study demonstrated the ease with which students learned to read German as a second language after they learned to speak it. As in the case of children first learning to read, the oral foundation facilitates memory for word forms and grammatical structures. This was impressed on my mind in learning to read Turkish. The seven-year-old Turkish beginners who knew nothing of the reading process made such good progress in learning to read that by the end of the year they were enjoying easy little storybooks. My progress was much slower due entirely to slowness in learning to speak the language. In spite of having the mechanics of reading well in hand, even the ability to *pronounce* all the commonly used words, the foreign beginner is unable to anticipate word and sentence meanings without knowledge of the oral language.

The relationship of linguistic experiences in speaking, reading, and writing has also been suggested by experimental research. Dr. B. R. Buckingham made the observation that some years ago many pupils who seemed deficient in reading were really deficient in a general language ability (4). A number of reading experts have found substantial relationships between reading problems and other linguistic deficiencies of school children (8, 15, 20, 21, 22, 23). The child with reading problems due to language limitations tends also to be slow in learning to spell and to write connected sentences in written compositions.

Other studies relevant to the general problem of language and reading deal with sex differences, speech immaturities, and general mental incompetence.

Girls show greater linguistic maturity than boys up to the age of nine and a half, and evidence from many sources shows that twice as many boys as girls experience difficulty in learning to read. Durrell reported, moreover, that even when boys and girls were equated for maturation in oral language, backwardness in reading was still more prevalent among boys (8).

Dr. M. D. Vernon, a British psychologist, reported that speech immaturities in young children were linked with reading backwardness. Dr. Vernon followed up preschool children who had been referred to a clinic for delayed language development. Twenty speech defective cases were found to be a year retarded in reading. Cases with hearing loss had been excluded from the study (23). Some years ago Dr. Leta S. Hollingworth described the case of an eleven-year-old boy, I.Q. 85, with a serious reading defect. Extensive examinations proved that there was nothing atypical about this boy except a speech defect. He did not talk plainly until he was six years old: he stuttered and could not say "I" (14).

Mastery of language is one of the most reliable indications of general mental competence. The mentally retarded child tends to be a language retardate, slow in mastering speech and in learning the skills of literacy. Dr. Samuel Kirk reports that these children develop in language at about the rate of their general mental growth, and that progress in learning to read and write depends upon the child's rate of maturation in language (15). The mentally retarded can recognize words in print only to the extent that these words occur in their own speech. Dr. Ovide Decroly found in working with young mentally retarded children that he could do nothing with them in reading approached as a mechanical drill, but that the children could make progress in proportion to their mental capacity when words in print were related to things these children knew and could name (6).

Implications for the Improvement of Reading

All these findings have significant implications for the improvement of reading. It is doubtful whether a child can become a fluent reader, comprehending fully what he reads, without a good oral language foundation and continued attention to oral language improvement.

Large time allotments for improvement of oral language usage in the school curriculum are justified, not only because children need this instruction to improve oral expression, but because learning to speak fluently the standard dialect is part of learning to read. To skimp on the time for oral language in in order to have more time for reading defeats the purpose because work in oral language is actually part of learning to read. The recommendation is to shift some of the time from direct drill in reading to building up general and various skills through activities requiring oral expression.

A good rule is: never begin reading instruction without first taking into account the child's status in oral expression. Until the age of seven a child may still lack precise enunciation of several difficult consonant sounds. The assessment of readiness status should include appraisal of the beginner's use of the school language. Build oral language ahead of and along with reading lessons if children are to learn to read well. Giving children a rich language experience in kindergarten builds readiness for later reading lessons. Considerable attention has been given recently to listening as a neglected aspect of oral language comprehension. Listening with acute understanding carries over to reading with understanding.

Since language deficiencies may be the major handicap of slow learners, for every such child a thorough assessment should be made of oral language proficiency and past history of language development. In remedial work with slow learners and problem cases attention to all phases of language development may be as essential as specific reading drills, especially speech control, work on articulation, accurate pronunciation of words in the child's everyday vocabulary. The non-English speaking child confronted with the task of learning to read merits special attention in the language area. Instruction in English reading should be preceded by oral work until the child has caught up to the typical school beginner's level in English usage. As much time should be spent on oral language as on reading lessons until the child is fairly independent in reading.

Another recommendation is to relate the language arts of oral usage, reading, and written expression in school instruction, that is, not only develop oral language as a background for reading lessons, but develop writing as an adjunct of reading. Spelling can be an aid to sounding better combinations (10) and word discrimination. Composing sentences helps children develop "sentence sense." Reading his own and other pupils' compositions extends the amount of material a child reads in words in his own vocabulary or that of his age group. Large time allotments are justified for written expression not only because the ability to write well is a practical skill everyone needs, but also because writing reinforces general language skills which are related to reading.

Reading should be taught from the beginning as a process of inferring meaning from sentences, rather than merely forming words. "Where did the mother go?" "What do you think the boy did next?" "Why do you think the kitten got lost?" "Where do the baby birds live?" Answering each question gives the child experience with larger units of language expression. The teacher's object is to increase the child's store of word meanings in sentence contexts, to enlarge his vocabulary of syntax patterns along with his vocabulary of words.

These principles have important implications for the preparation of reading materials for both school beginners and older children. They have important implications for control of vocabulary, for attention to sentence structure, as well as sentence length and complexity in reading material prepared for children.

Reading material for beginners should make use of current experiences couched in the everyday spoken language the children know and use as a bridge to the less familiar written language and situations of the reading books. Begin with the words and expressions representing experiences that are close to the child, then the young learner can make fuller use of language clues in interpreting print. Make use of oral narrative, conversation, and dramatization for readiness in the early reading experiences.

Children taught reading in a language-centered program should not only have a more extensive and rewarding learning experience than those taught by mechanical word-drills, but they should develop the important reading skills of extracting meaning from a variety of syntactical patterns and associating appropriate speech melodies with the printed word.

REFERENCES

1. Axelrod, Joseph, and Bigelow, Donald N. *Resources for Language and Area Studies.* Washington, D.C.: American Council on Education, 1962.
2. Bloomfield, Leonard. "Linguistics and Reading," *Elementary English Review,* 19 (1942), 125–130, 183–186.
3. Brazziel, William F. Report given at the American Educational Research Association Meetings, Atlantic City, N.J., February, 1962.
4. Buckingham, B. R. "Language and Reading—A Unified Program," *Elementary English Review,* 17 (1940), 111–116.
5. Carroll, John B. *The Study of Language.* Cambridge: Harvard University Press, 1953.
6. Decroly, Ovide, and Degand, J. "Contributions à la Pedagogie de la Lecture et de l'écriture," *Archives de Psychologie,* 6 (1907), 339–353.
7. Deutsch, Dr. Martin. Report to the New York City Reading Academy, Fall, 1962.
8. Durrell, Donald D. *Improving Reading Instruction.* Yonkers, N.Y.: World Book, 1956.
9. Hildreth, Gertrude. "An Individual Study in Word Recognition," *Elementary School Journal,* 35 (1935), 606–619.
10. Hildreth, Gertrude H. "Interrelationships between Written Expression and the Other Language Arts." In *Interrelationships Among the Language Arts,* Research Bulletin of the National Conference on Research in English, 1954.
11. Hildreth, Gertrude. *Teaching Reading.* New York: Holt, Rinehart & Winston, 1958.
12. Hildreth, Gertrude. "Reading and the Language Arts," *Education,* 79 (1959), 565–569.
13. Hildreth, Gertrude. "Early Writing as an Aid to Reading." *Elementary English.* In press.
14. Hollingworth, Leta S. *Special Talents and Defects.* New York: Macmillan, 1923.
15. Kirk, Samuel A. *Teaching Reading to Slow-Learning Children.* Boston: Houghton-Mifflin, 1940.

16. Ladd, Margaret R. *The Relationship of Social, Economic and Personal Charac-teristics in Reading Ability,* Teachers College Contributions to Education No. 592. New York: Bureau of Publications, Teachers College, Columbia University, 1933.
17. Lefevre, Carl. "Language Patterns and their Graphic Counterparts, A Lin-guistic View of Reading." In *Changing Concepts of Reading Instruction,* International Reading Association Conference Proceedings, Vol. 6, 1961.
18. Lefevre, Carl. "Reading Instruction Related to Primary Language Learnings, A Linguistic View," *Journal of Developmental Reading,* 4 (1961), 147–158.
19. McDavid, Raven I., Jr. "The Role of the Linguist in the Teaching of Read-ing." In *Changing Concepts of Reading Instruction,* International Read-ing Association Conference Proceedings, Vol. 6, 1961.
20. Monroe, Marion. *Children Who Cannot Read.* Chicago: University of Chi-cago Press, 1932.
21. Schonell, Fred J. *Backwardness in the Basic Subjects.* London: Oliver and Boyd, 1942.
22. Tireman, Lloyd S. "A Study of Fourth Grade Reading Vocabulary of Native Spanish-Speaking Children," *Elementary School Journal,* 46 (1945), 223–227.
23. Vernon, M. D. *Backwardness in Reading.* Cambridge: Cambridge University Press, 1957.

A LINGUISTIC APPROACH TO READING —AN EDUCATOR'S VIEW *

Patrick J. Groff

Linguists are not entirely sure what to call themselves. Some believe they are students of the humanities; others, that they are social scientists; some, that they are a combination of both. A few like to say they are cultural anthropologists.

We do know rather exactly what linguists study: human speech—its ori-gins, structure, and changes. This includes grammar, semantics, morphology, and phonetics. It is especially their study of this last discipline that aligns linguists so closely with the work of teachers of reading.

By dint of their training, these specialists are eminently qualified to give educators the knowledge they need to set up phonetic word analysis pro-grams. Educators then can interpret this information in the light of what

* REPRINTED by permission of the Department of Elementary School Principals from *The National Elementary Principal,* Vol. 42, No. 4, February, 1963, pp. 12–15.

they know of child growth and development, child psychology, educational methodology, and the curriculum.

On what grounds is such a melding of information from linguists and educators possible? That is, on what do we agree regarding language and phonetics? Although some statements by linguists are enormously abstruse, and therefore admittedly beyond a nonspecialist's complete comprehension, my reading of the conclusions of modern linguists has led me to believe that they and educators agree on substantially all of the crucial aspects of language that affect both our areas of work.

WHERE LINGUISTS AND EDUCATORS AGREE

We agree that language is an aspect of total human behavior, influenced by the maturity of its learner, by time, and by geographical location. We both know how greatly socio-economic background affects language. Semantics exerts its influence. Linguists tell us that the development of multiple meanings of words is a normal development, not something accidental or queer. We agree that meaning does not reside in a word, but in a discriminatory response to it.

We both believe in the primacy of speech in teaching language. We see all the other language learnings having their origin in speech, and being dependent upon it. Linguists tell us, in addition, that sounds are the most stable features of language—not vocabulary or grammar as some educators might think.

We concur that language is changing and dynamic. Teachers would heartily agree with linguists that the definition of Standard English (let alone the teaching of it) is an elusive thing. The modern linguist, called the "structural, descriptive, or scientific" linguist, believes with educators that correctness in language rests on usage. With us they say that the only basis for correctness is the usage of native speakers. We are reassured by their studies that have shown that "standard" language historically has risen out of colloquial English. Both educators and linguists would say that the best way to make conclusions about what language truly is, and how it functions, is to observe it directly and to draw conclusions from this firsthand observation, rather than to adopt previously held ideas of what language is or how it should function.

We both hold, on the other hand, that despite its changes, language is inherently and largely orderly and systematic, and that it can therefore be profitably studied and taught. While this is so, both modern linguists and educators are dissatisfied with many traditionally held notions about American English grammar. Many linguists say the American English grammar has yet to be written. They contend, for example, that the old eight parts of speech system will surely be discarded. Smith, a leading linguist, has said that there are really only four parts of speech: nouns, verbs, pronouns, and "adjunctives" (adverbs and adjectives).[1] Other linguists, though agreeing that there are only four major word classes, list them as nouns, verbs, adjectives, and adverbs.

We agree that normal children entering school have developed speaking and aural recognition vocabularies sufficiently large for beginning instruction in reading. Linguists have repeatedly stated that the child at age six has no need to practice grammar further. Smith believes, for example, that if a child upon entering school "is physiologically normal he is in full control of the structure of his language. . . ." [2] Recent evidence on articulation maturity, on the other hand, shows that the average child cannot speak all the sounds correctly until age eight.[3]

From this, our agreements regarding written symbols become clearer. We both see written symbols as graphic expressions of speech. While we recognize that they have their basis in speech, we know that written symbols are a special kind of communication activity—one that is not passive but can, in turn, affect modes of speech. There is accord between us, too, that the major purpose of writing, as well as of speaking, is to serve the present rather than preserve the past.

With regard to phonetics generally and as it relates specifically to the teaching of reading, teachers and linguists together understand several linguistic facts. For instance, teachers know that all sounds in our speech do not have a single letter to represent them. Many teachers—and linguists, too —are unsure at this point of the exact number of extra letters there are, but they do know there are numerous tricky variations. One linguist has said there are 230 spellings for the approximately 40 different sounds in our language.[4]

Teachers realize that there are a greater number of additional letters that represent the relatively small number of vowel sounds than there are that represent the larger number of consonant sounds. No single group in our society, including linguists, is subject so directly to these unfortunate conditions as are teachers of reading and spelling.

Finally, teachers and most linguists have rejected the old-style phonics that required children to practice sounds in isolation—single letters or phonograms (*ack, at, otch, ble, tion, udge, ry*)—before these letters were seen in words or in meaningful context. Now we agree that phonics should begin with the sounds represented by letters heard and seen in words. I emphasize, *heard and seen in words.* Generally acceptable to both teachers and linguists

---

[1] Smith, Henry Lee. *Linguistic Science and the Teaching of English.* Cambridge: Harvard University Press, 1956.

[2] *Ibid.,* p. 18.

[3] Templin, Mildred C. *Certain Language Skills in Children.* Minneapolis: University of Minnesota Press, 1957.

[4] Barnhart, Clarence L. "Establishing and Maintaining Standard Patterns of Speech." *Quarterly Journal of Speech* 43:73–75; February 1957.

is a procedure of taking words apart, or analyzing them, and then fitting them back together again, or synthesizing them. Hence, neither analytic nor synthetic phonics need be neglected—which is good, since phonics rarely is ever purely analytical or synthetic. Most linguists further agree that reading should begin with a meaningful use of words in a visually attractive setting.

Disagreements Between Linguists and Educators

In spite of the numerous agreements, linguists have protested that educators are using the wrong approach to the teaching of reading. Some charge that their advice on this matter has been largely ignored and that, as a result, educators have greatly jeopardized the effectiveness of their teaching of reading. The large numbers of children who, in spite of their innate abilities, have not learned to read are cited as proof.

Both educators and linguists believe that the child will best learn to read if he understands that letters or groups of letters stand for sounds which are pronounced in the order they are printed. Linguists, so far, insist that the first reading material should consist of regularly spelled words, rather than frequently used words.

They would introduce the different vowel and consonant sounds in terms of their degree of phonetic complexity or irregularity. The easiest, regularly spelled material would be presented first. The reading of letters in words that represent these sounds would be mastered before more complex sounds were introduced. Linguists see the child who fails to grasp the meaning of the material he reads as usually a poor reader in the mechanical sense, and therefore in need of better training in associating letters and sounds. They say that the definition of reading should focus on the nature of the reading process, on the sounding or vocalization of written forms, rather than on the end purpose—comprehension. Otherwise, they feel the full process of reading will not be emphasized.

Soffietti has said: "Reading specialists are likely to say, 'The printed word merely acts as the trigger that releases a meaning we already possess'." [5] Linguists strongly believe that letters and words do not become triggers to meaning until vocalized. They believe that internal speech or vocalization is always present in reading, although served by internal substitute movements in mature readers. Writing, as well, is a response to vocalization, not to thought. Vocalization always stands between thought and symbol. Reading will be easy only as the vocalization of the written forms is easy.

The Linguist's Approach

How, precisely, do linguists say reading should be taught? First, and foremost, they would control the introduction of sounds in words. As has been

[5] Soffietti, James P. "Why Children Fail to Read: A Linguistic Analysis." *Harvard Educational Review* 25:63–85; Spring 1955.

said, the first reading material they would present is made up of regularly spelled words. The irregularly spelled vowel and consonant sounds in words are then slowly and systematically introduced.

Since the sounds of consonants are fewer and more reliable, the child would first learn to read these in short, two or three letter words—e.g., *hat, get, rip, hop, gun.* Constant checks would be made to insure that the child understands the meaning of what he is reading. The words are presented in pictorial, meaningful settings so that the analysis and synthesis of sounds and a visual confirmation of this can be used to complement each other. Only the short sounds of the vowels and the consonants, excluding *q* and sometimes *x*, are found in the first words the child reads. The hard sounds of *c* and *g* appear first. Some linguists would teach as sight words a few "special" words such as *you, to, do, is, was,* and *have* that are used very frequently but do not have phonetic regularity.

Generally, after this, words containing digraphs and double consonants are introduced. Among these, for example, are *ss, ng, ck, th, sh, ch, ee, ea, oa, oo.*

Then "semi-irregularly spelled" words usually follow—for example *line, hole, shine, butter, winter.* Finally, the "irregularly spelled" words appear. These would be, for example, *father, mother, all, rough, cough, through.* All of these latter words are taught as separate items that must be memorized.

EDUCATORS' CRITICISMS

What criticisms should educators make of these proposals? Can we say this approach will make children so conscious of word analysis that word meaning will suffer? Not, I feel, if all activities stress the meaning of what is read. Can not almost all children learn to read meaningful sentences such as these? "Put your book on the desk." "Is Tom in the tree?" One should remember that comprehension implies a certain level of word analysis but not necessarily vice versa.

Under this approach, will children develop into slow readers? Will they become overly meticulous and deliberate, and have small recognition spans? The rise of the currently used incidental or integrated phonics reputedly stemmed from a protest that isolated phonics created slow readers. One should remember, however, that the linguistic approach is an improved kind of phonics. We do know, too, that single word vocabulary tests are a reasonably valid method of estimating the child's ability to read in a wider sense (as well as being a quick estimate of his intelligence); so single word recognition is important. One way to avoid slow reading is to stop word analysis periodically and allow children to practice their speed on materials that are not too demanding, and where the objective of reading is pleasure.

Is the linguistic approach a natural mode of learning? This question assumes that effective reading can be taught largely by imitation and repetition through a "natural" way, such as speaking. It must be asked in return whether, through reading, children ever can be given the same concentration of language they have had in learning to speak. Is it likely that children will ever be exposed to words in print with the same frequency that they hear these words? If so, word analysis might not be needed at all. Word analysis is a short cut to language that need not be taken in learning to speak. Linguists, too, say that children naturally like to puzzle out the sounds of words—to solve reading puzzles.

Does not the linguists' approach to teaching reading assume that all children learn best in the same way—the phonetic way? Some recent evidence has been gathered that certain children seem to learn better by other than phonetic methods.[6] Perhaps the answer here is that the large majority of children could profit by the linguistic approach, while a different method—a structural, a kinesthetic, or a combination approach—could be held in reserve for those who do not respond. A question has also been raised about whether children whose speech is affected by regional dialect will have trouble with the linguistic approach.[7]

One criticism of this approach is not entirely acceptable. This is that the stories written under the controlled sound scheme suffer badly in style, result in a stilted vocabulary, have little continuity of thought, and therefore lack interest for the child. Some linguistic material deserves this criticism.[8] However, there need not be a reduction of interest in stories that use a controlled sound vocabulary. For example, the *Royal Road Readers*, which are so controlled, have a more interesting over-all content, are more realistically life-like, reflect less the values of a single socio-economic class, employ a larger, more exciting vocabulary, have content that appeals to a wider age range, and have a greater measure of literary quality than do the readers now ordinarily used.[9, 10] To read some stories from the first book of this British series and then from a typical American primer is convincing proof of this.

A Proposed Reading Program

How, then, can the linguistic approach best be used while accounting for the major objections made to it? I would organize the reading program using the linguistic approach in this way.

[6] Mills, Robert E. "An Evaluation of Techniques for Teaching Word Recognition." *Elementary School Journal* 56:221–225; January 1956.

[7] Bloomfield, Leonard, and Barnhart, Clarence L. *Let's Read, A Linguistic Approach.* Detroit: Wayne State University Press, 1961. Chapter, "Speech Variation and the Bloomfield System," Faust, George P. pp. 43–44.

[8] Bloomfield, Leonard, and Barnhart, Clarence L. *Let's Read, A Linguistic Approach.* Detroit: Wayne State University Press, 1961.

[9] Daniels, J. C., and Diack, H. *Royal Road Readers.* London: Chatto and Windus, 1959–1960.

[10] Daniels, J. C., and Diack, H. *Progress in Reading.* Nottingham, England: University of Nottingham, 1956.

First, I would take children through the first steps of phonics, using what have been called here "regularly spelled" words. After this, for a time, I would direct the children to read widely in easy-to-read materials of many kinds. Here they would be required to put to use the phonics they have previously learned—to make a transfer of training. Reading here would be largely individualized. Review and re-teaching in groups would be necessary, of course, for those who fail to make an effective transfer of their phonic training. All the irregularly spelled words would be given to the children at this time as they asked for them. Their reading would not be interrupted for the additional phonics that are needed with irregularly spelled words. Instead, the irregularly spelled words would be slowly and systematically given and studied at separate times, with periodic opportunities for wide, extensive reading to practice them, to increase comprehension and speed, and to allow children to develop their reading ability at an individual pace.

The program outlined here would be the combination of an individualized reading program and a strong linguistic phonics program. Neither would necessarily dominate the other. Hopefully, all the advantages of both could be realized.

The linguistic approach deserves the opportunity to be tried out in the United States in some such manner.

PHONIC SKILLS IN
BEGINNING READING *

A. Sterl Artley

It would be relatively easy to discuss the question of phonic skills in beginning reading if there could be some semblance of agreement on the general approach to initial instruction. Obviously what should be taught in beginning phonics is conditioned by one's point of view toward the way reading is introduced.

There is no argument over the question of whether phonics should be taught, for the answer is an unqualified "yes." Sharp differences do arise among those representing various approaches to instruction over "what" and "when." Hence we shall deal with the phonic skills that might be developed under three approaches to initial reading—the phonic approach, the linguistic approach, and the integrated approach through basal materials.

* REPRINTED FROM the May, 1962, issue of *Education*. Copyright, 1962, by The Bobbs-Merrill Company, Inc., Indianapolis, Indiana.

THE PHONIC APPROACH

Within the past decade a number of phonic systems of reading instruction have sprung up (2, 3, 4, 5, 6, 8). Although we have used the term "phonic system," Spache rightly contends that there is no accepted set of beliefs and practices that would constitute *a* phonic method (7). The reason for this contention is that there is so little agreement among those who espouse an all-out phonic approach as to what is to be included and by what method the content is to be taught.

In spite of disagreement as to the content and method, there is essential agreement as to the rationale of their approach. It is based on the contention that since the English language is phonetic, the basic process of initial reading should be one in which the sounds of the written language elements (letters and letter combinations) are learned and blended into words.

In some of the programs much of this learning and blending is done before the actual process of reading connected discourse is undertaken. The teaching process usually involves a great deal of rote drill in recognizing and manipulating letters and letter combinations and their corresponding sounds in words.

Since there is so little agreement among those who have developed teaching materials for an all-out phonic approach to initial reading, it would be impossible to generalize as to the phonic skills that are ordinarily developed in beginning reading. Consequently we shall refer to the skills included in only one of these phonic programs, the Hay-Wingo *Reading With Phonics.* There is no assumption that the content described is that of any other program.

1. Recognizing short sounds of the vowels (*a* for *apple, e* for *elephant, i* for *Indian,* etc.)
2. Recognizing initial sounds of selected consonants (*s, m, f, r, g, n, b, t, p, d*)
3. Blending one initial consonant with vowels (*sa, se, si, so, su,* etc.)
4. Blending the consonant-vowel combinations above with final consonants to form words (*fat, ran, nap,* etc.)
5. Recognizing sounds of additional consonants and selected consonant digraphs (*e, k, l, ch, sh,* etc.)
6. Blending two initial consonants with vowels (*flu, pli,* etc.)
7. Blending consonant-blend-vowel combination with final consonants to form words (*glint, skunk,* etc.)
8. Recognizing digraphs, diphthongs, and silent letters (*heart, meat, coil,* etc.)
9. Blending three initial consonants with vowel-consonant combinations (*scrap, spray, thrush,* etc.)

The amount of actual reading material in the text is very limited and stresses certain elements that have been taught.

Additional reading material is suggested in stories which the teacher dictates to the children for writing and reading purposes, as well as materials "provided for the regular reading program." No statement is made in the manual as to the portion of this content that should be taught as part of the program of beginning reading. Presumably the entire book is to be taught.

The Linguistic Approach

Recently Clarence Barnhart, co-author of the Thorndike-Barnhart dictionaries, brought out *Let's Read* (1), a program of reading instruction based on the ideas of the late Leonard Bloomfield, a well known linguist. The essential feature of this program is to focus the child's attention upon established patterns of letters and sounds in printed forms representative of those of spoken words under the assumption that the ability to transform these sound-letter constants back into spoken words constitutes the reading process.

Although this program differs materially from other all-out phonics programs, it does have in common with them the practice of drilling the child on the sounds of letters and letter combinations. However, the words on which the child is drilled must follow a regular phonic pattern. This makes for a most rigid control of vocabulary, not in number of words introduced, but in types of words.

The author attaches only passing significance to meaning. In the first lesson he says, "Some of the words will be strange to the child. In fact, a familiar word, such as *an*, when presented alone, is likely to convey no meaning. *There is no harm* in telling the child that 'a van is a big covered truck for moving furniture,' or that 'Nan is a girl's name.'" (The italics are mine.)

Let's Read is a tome of 465 pages, making up 245 lessons which are divided into six parts as follows:

Part I—(Lessons 1–36) Recognizing the short sounds of the five vowels, and combining them with initial and final consonants to form three-letter words (*jut, nub, cud, din, dab,* etc.)

Part II—(Lessons 37–71) Dealing with consonant letters having values assigned as "regular" (*S* suffix; *ng, nk, ch, ck,* etc.)

Part III—(Lessons 72–97) Manipulating certain pairs of vowel letters such as *ee, ea* and combinations of a vowel letter with *y* or *w*; two-syllable words and compounds.

Part IV—(Lessons 98–151) Recognizing the commonest irregular wo' such as *said, you,* etc.

Part V—(Lessons 152–199) Dealing with the commonest irreg' ings of vowel sounds (*a* for *ai, are* for *air* and *care, y* as in *put,* etc.)

Part VI—(Lessons 200–245) Dealing with the commonest irregular spellings of consonant sounds (*e* as in *cent, gh* as in *rough, ui* as in *build,*
etc.)

Each lesson presents words to be studied and pronounced. It is relatively
unimportant if some are unfamiliar to the reader, for they "are useful as nonsense syllables to test the child's relation of letters to phonetics in the lesson."
Each lesson also contains phrases or sentences for practice in "connected
reading."

No statement is made as to the amount of material that should be taught
to "beginning readers" in this program, nor how, if at all, the material is to
be integrated with other reading. Apparently the author assumes that this
is the reading program and these lessons are all that are necessary.

The Integrated Phonic Approach

An integrated phonic approach, developed through the use of basal materials, is based on several assumptions.

First, phonics, though it is an important means of attacking unfamiliar
words, is only *one* approach to word recognition. Structure, context, word-
form, and the use of the dictionary are equally important.

Second, the form and meaning of a word are inseparable.

Third, the word-perception program, should be an integral part of the in-
terpretative process which includes comprehension, emotional and critical
reaction, and the application and use of ideas.

Fourth, the most effective learning takes place when the learner is given
the responsibility to discover for himself the meaning of the elements taught.

Fifth, true reading is a complex act that involves far more than word
perception.

Sixth, the early interest and enthusiasm that a child develops for reading
are potent motivators for continual growth.

Consequently, to enable a child to read immediately, and thus forego
meaningless and monotonous drill on letter sounds and words out of context,
the child is introduced to initial reading through a group of initial words,
sometimes called sight words. Concurrent with the development of these
initial words, is the continued attention to auditory and visual discrimination,
oral language, concept development, and other areas considered important
to growing readiness for word perception.

As soon as the child has developed an initial vocabulary sufficient to enable
him to discover from these known words the elementary phonic understandings, as well as other word recognition principles, these understandings and
principles are taught in a systematic and sequential manner.

Again, it would be impossible to generalize a list of the phonic elements
that are introduced and taught in beginning reading by all the basal series in

current use. From one series to another there will be differences in the elements taught as well as in the time at which they are introduced. However, most of the basal reading series in grade I will include elements such as the following:

1. Auditory perception of initial consonant sounds (similarity of initial sounds as in *mother, me, my*)
2. Auditory perception of rhyme (*run* and *fun, book* and *look,* etc.)
3. Visual-auditory perception of initial consonants (association of sounds with their corresponding letter symbols—*f, b, m, e,* etc.)
4. Visual-auditory perception of final consonants
5. Substitution of initial consonants to derive new words (*pig* from *big, bump* from *jump, toy* from *boy,* etc.)
6. Substitution of final consonants to derive new words (*nod* from *not, hot* from *hop,* etc.)
7. Visual-auditory perception of selected consonant digraphs (*ch, sh, th, wh,* etc.)
8. Perception of silent consonants in words (*ll, gg, ss,* etc.)

On the basis of these beginning phonic understandings, and the skills developed in conjunction with them, the child grows systematically in his ability to attack unknown words.

Conclusion

Space does not permit the discussion of the relative merits of the three approaches described above. The reader undoubtedly is familiar with the claims and counterclaims that have been made for each of them. An objective analysis of the existing studies would lead one to the conclusion that the findings are inconclusive.

However, a question that is frequently overlooked in an attempt to discover which of two approaches is "better" is that of "better for what?" If one is concerned with the development of an early ability to pronounce words, then there should be little question of the content and the approach to be used in doing the job. If, on the other hand, one is concerned with word attack as a means to an end, the end being growth toward maturity *in all* aspects of interpretation, then there is need for an entirely different approach and content.

Essentially it becomes a question of what constitutes reading growth rather than an issue of phonic skills. Truly, it might be said, one "pays his money and takes his choice."

REFERENCES

1. Bloomfield, Leonard, and Barnhart, Clarence. *Let's Read, A Linguistic Approach.* Detroit: Wayne State University Press, 1961.

2. Cox, Mary Aline. *Teach Your Child to Read*. N.Y.: Exposition Press, 1953.
3. Flesch, Rudolf. *Why Johnny Can't Read*. N.Y.: Harper, 1955.
4. Hay, Julie, and Wingo, Charles, *Reading With Phonics*, N.Y.: Lippincott, 1948.
5. Schoolfield, Lucile, and Timberlake, Josephine, *Phonovisual Method*. Washington, D.C.: Phonovisual Products Co.
6. Sloop, Cornelia, Garrison, Harrel, and Creekmore, Mildred. *Phonetic Keys to Reading*, Oklahoma City: Economy Co., 1952.
7. Spache, George. "Limitations of the Phonetic Approach to Developmental and Remedial Reading," in *New Frontiers in Reading*, Annual Proceedings of the International Reading Association, N.Y.: Scholastic Magazine, 1960.
8. Spalding, Rolanda and Spalding, Walter. *The Writing Road to Reading*. N.Y.: William Morrow, 1957.

HOW SHALL WE TEACH PHONICS? *

Roma Gans

Today's teacher is being buffeted about in conflicting pressures regarding the teaching of phonics. She may attend a meeting to hear a lecture on an "all-phonic" approach to teaching reading "through which, if precisely followed, every child will learn to read successfully."

She may shortly thereafter pick up a professional magazine and read that the only scholarly approach to teaching phonics is through linguistic materials, all other approaches lacking scholarship. She need not understand linguistics, but if she follows the materials, all children will become able readers.

Within another short span of time, she may hear an enthusiastic account of research which reveals how young children think and purports to throw light on the teaching of phonics. All the while, she may be teaching thirty children of varied backgrounds and a wide spread of abilities to read independently, and she may be observing their continuing growth in unlocking new words, using phonics among other word recognition techniques, and evidently making progress via her own methods of teaching.

No wonder that this sudden burst of excitement about how to teach phonics causes the alert teacher to wonder, to doubt her own methods and to ask, "What is this all about?" In all the stir, experienced teachers in good schools notice the change in children's reading which has occurred in the

* REPRINTED by permission of Roma Gans from *Grade Teacher*, Vol. 80, November, 1962, pp. 29+.

past several decades. No longer do children confine their reading to assigned work to be memorized. Instead, they are functional readers who read texts and at times assigned work, yes, and who also read newspapers, magazines and books! Books of all varieties, books of old tales and of new stories, books on history and books on science. Their reading is as broad and as essential to them as is the reading in the life of a truly literate adult. They are not only learning how to become mature readers, they already *are* readers.

True, not all children, nor all schools, achieve this high reading quality, but so widespread is its practice that any teacher today can observe it in some school in the vicinity. If the teaching of reading is reaching such high performance, then why be aroused over which way phonics is taught? After all, phonics is only one means of recognizing words which, when recognized, help the child to get at the meaning of what he is reading.

Part of the answer to such a quandary is found in the nature of these times. We are in an edgy condition, an almost perfect state of readiness to be alarmed at a moment's notice. And, with our mass media, we can tune in to any headline in less than twenty-four hours. So, let one alarmist say "Today's Jims and Janes can't read because teachers are not allowed to teach them phonics," and we are off on a new wave of professional terror. Then, in a matter of weeks, the panacea promoters move in and peddle their wares as did the old patent-medicine healers of yesterday.

Much of our pressure can be explained in this way. Not all; there are some points worthy of careful consideration.

Let's look first at the "all phonic" system. Although they vary, they have one point in common, namely, a planned sequence of phonic elements which a teacher is to teach, depending upon the grade level. According to the promoters of certain of these systems, a child first learns the names of the letters of the alphabet and their sounds. Then he progresses to simple words like bat, bed, bit, pronounced b-at, b-ed, b-it. A teacher who has had an elementary course in speech and some awareness of phonetics realizes at once that such stress on letter sounds is a distortion of the actual sound of the initial consonant in the first set or the final one in the second. Also, rules are introduced early—in kindergarten in some systems.

Systems of this type meet serious criticism from scholarly critics. According to Robert C. Pooley writing in an "Introduction to Teachers" in *Let's Read* by Bloomfield and Barnhart, such methods violate "the inseparable relationship . . . between the words as printed and the sounds for which the letters are conventional signs, and that to learn to convert letters to meaning requires from the start a concentration upon letter and sound to bring about as rapidly as possible an automatic association between them." [1]

A child taught to say "bu-ed" or "be-da" adding on extra sounds in pronouncing *bed* must unlearn this sight-sound association later on in order to

[1] *Let's Read* by Leonard Bloomfield and Clarence L. Barnhart, Wayne University Press, 5980 Cass, Detroit 2, Michigan. 1961. $7.50.

say *bed* correctly. Teachers using one of the all-phonic systems are full of examples of the errors in pronunciation which develop and which must be eliminated later on.

The linguists who are scholars in the science of language, its history, its phonetics, its meaning, its inflections and its grammar have recently entered the field of teaching children to read. An experiment by Leonard Bloomfield several decades ago proved successful, but did not win widespread acceptance. A number of linguists are eager to influence the teaching of reading through linguistic principles. "To become an accomplished reader," according to one of the linguistic principles, a child must acquire the habit of "uttering the phoneme of the English language when he sees the letter *p*, another phoneme when he sees the letter *i*, another when he sees the letter *n* . . . In this way he utters the conventionally accepted word when he sees a combination of letters like *pin*."

The first words a child is taught are two- or three-letter words. They are regular in phonics and contain no silent letters or double letters like *tt* or *ll*. They have single sound values and are presented in what is commonly termed by teachers, family style. For example, *bat, cat, fat, hat, mat*, and so forth. Simple "stories" using a family of words follow. (I am reminded of my beginning reading days: The cat. The mat. The cat is on the mat.)

Learning to pronounce words automatically precedes paying attention to meaning. Linguists stress the need for all children to deal first with the mechanics of automatic connection between sound and symbol. Like the all-phonics authority, the approach is the same for all children and the logic is inherent in the letters and words presented, with the assumption that a strictly logical approach is the soundest way for a child to learn.

Now growing stronger in emphasis comes the deeper knowledge of young children's thinking which is important to relate to the present-day stress on specific ways to teach phonics. After all, learning to read does call upon a child's way of thinking. A timely caution by Millie Almy, who is conducting research in children's thinking is appropriate here: "The problem the adult faces is perhaps most acute when the children he wishes to teach are still at an intuitive level of thought (early childhood to age seven or eight) still too caught up in the perceptions of the moment to be able to deal logically with the relationships between various aspects of their experience. To what extent are children in kindergarten, first, and, perhaps, even second grade thinking in these ways, and how is their ability to learn affected?" [2]

Learning to generalize phonic rules which are not related to concrete things which a child can feel and manipulate tactually may be possible for mature Fives, Sixes and Sevens. However, for the majority, this may lead to meaningless verbalization as such specialists as Millie Almy and Jerome S. Bruner call to our attention. Children up to the age of seven or eight learn

[2] Millie C. Almy, *Teachers College Record*, Vol. 62, No. 5, Feb. 1961, Teachers College, Columbia University, 525 West 120th Street, New York 27, N.Y., $4.00 per year.

much from the world close to them in an intuitive way, by examining, exploring, handling and assimilating in a personal way. They do not follow a logical step-by-step method in such learning. Also, each child has a strongly individual way of looking at and sizing up situations and making mental notes.

Points about children's thinking raise serious doubts about the present-day pressure to adopt all-phonic or linguistic approaches to beginning reading for all children of a group. Many children are not ready for the intellectual processes involved although, obviously, some are. The blunt fact to be faced is that children cannot be standardized; their individual personalities, ways of working and thinking and background influences will not be submerged.

How, then, does an up-to-date, alert teacher proceed with the teaching of reading, particularly in the field of phonics? Groups of thirty and more youngsters must be faced daily, and each with all his uniqueness of background and potentialities is to be guided into a reader, one who grows in ability and personal satisfaction in his use of reading. The following general suggestions seem practical in the light of present-day teaching situations, knowledge of how young children learn, facts about the reading mechanics and practices that have been proven helpful:

1. If kindergarten and primary grades continue, as good schools have done over the past several decades, to help children meet a wide array of experiences in science, community life, processes essential in everyday living through which they continue to develop understandings and enlarge their vocabularies.
2. Call attention to signs, labels and printed matter inherent in such experiences, encouraging children to examine and talk about what they notice. Be a good listener and cautious in making deductions about what goes on intellectually in the minds of the glib talkers as well as the silent ones.
3. Have materials for children's personal exploration available, also books for browsing and materials for writing.
4. Write before them essential memos and notices, often describing the writing of each letter and the left-to-right sequence of letters.
5. Help children with their letter forms and with their spelling as soon as they are ready to sprout their first steps in independent writing.
6. Read stories and information materials to them, some which they request, some selected to link with a recent experience or special group interest.
7. Have many books available for the group, in terms of their interests and reading abilities.
8. Find time to listen to individual children and to watch them individually at key moments.

More specifically about phonics:

1. Children grow through experiencing sounds. Attention to the variety of sounds they hear, the relative pitch of bells, gongs and piano keys, the variations in their own voices and the specific sounds of words and letters helps youngsters get tuned-in to hearing sounds and making distinctions in them. Playing games in identifying sounds, noticing similar and dissimilar words and parts of words can be a genuine help.
2. Utilize opportunities to call attention to words that are regular in phonics on charts, notices and books: Peter and Patsy, Jane and Judy, ran and can. Children are ready to share in building families of names and words, working in a group or, abler ones, as individuals.
3. Study the phonic suggestions in manuals for the age being taught and check on what some children are ready for. A teacher's knowledge of the structure of words is essential. Dolores Durkin's *Phonics and the Teaching of Reading* [3] is written particularly to give teachers this kind of help.
4. Encourage children to see relationships in writing and spelling between letters and groups of letters and their corresponding sounds. Many children need much practice in making the sight-sound connection.

The foregoing suggestions were not divided into kindergarten, first and second grade, for a valid reason. Children vary; some in kindergarten have a good beginning sight vocabulary and some beginnings in phonics; some in first and second grade are not that far along. Intelligent teaching demands a personal approach in order to hold no child back, nor discourage any. For the same reason, no one way or one system is recommended. Children cannot be so grouped or organized to fit a common time, approach and material.

This places a tremendous responsibility on classroom teachers. Many, over the years, have demonstrated their worthiness of full confidence by the skillful way in which, under their guidance, children acquired mastery in reading, a love of books and an eager use of reading. In spite of the more vocal and more impressive voices championing specific systems of teaching phonics, a wise teacher will keep abreast with new ideas, try promising practices and materials, but take her cue for her next steps from the response of the children. An easier road may ultimately be found. If and when, it will be grounded in genuine understanding of how children think as they learn.

[3] *Phonics and the Teaching of Reading* by Dolores Durkin, Bureau of Publications, Teachers College, Columbia University, 525 West 120th Street, New York 27, N.Y. 1962. $1.25.

E. Programmed Reading

PROGRAMMED INSTRUCTION IN READING *

Edward Fry

Only about a year ago at the Florida meeting of IRA I told the audience that there were very few programmed instruction materials available in reading. The situation has definitely changed. As we shall see, there are now a number of programs commercially available, but considering the size and range of reading in the curriculum these are relatively few.

Before we look into the specific programs, let's take a quick review of the theory or principles behind programmed instruction. On a practical level we might ask, Just what is a "program" anyway? The word "program" means many things to many people, but in the sense of teaching machines and programmed instruction it generally means:

1. Subject matter is broken into small bits (frames).
2. A student response is required (writing a word, pushing a button, turning to a specific page, or just thinking an answer).
3. The student is immediately told the correctness of his response (feedback) and sometimes why he is wrong.
4. Each student may vary the rate to suit himself.
5. The frames are arranged in careful sequence.
6. The learning goals are specific (stated in such a way that they can be tested—even a long subhead would often help).
7. The audience is specific (fifth grade reading ability required, completed first year algebra, etc.).
8. Revisions of the program are made based on tryouts (tryout group specified so teacher can compare it with her own class).
9. Proof of learning is desirable (there should be some evidence that a specified group has learned, how much, on what test).
10. Additional information, though not always part of programming, will help teachers in selecting the program. This would include name of the author, average working time, specific material covered (table of contents), pre- and post-tests (or criteria frames) readability level, basis of curriculum content, and type of branching.

---

* REPRINTED with permission of Edward Fry and the International Reading Association from *The Reading Teacher*, Vol. 17, March, 1964, pp. 453–59.

After looking over the current crop of reading programs, I can say that most of them meet the first four points, but the sheep are separated from the goats, and the good programs from the poor, by the last six points.

Let us first state what a "program" is not. Such programs as the SRA Reading Laboratories or the Scott Foresman Reading Series are not included because they do not meet the first four criteria. A program instruction expert would call reading labs and reading series a "system" or part of a "system." A system might include programmed instruction as one large part or as a small part.

Let's begin by looking at a minimum program. Publishers Company Incorporated has a Teachall multiple-choice teaching machine that has a "Reading Course" which covers forty-eight nouns and nothing more (15). Already you can see the problems of labels. Each word is allotted exactly three frames. Each frame is on a separate piece of cardboard that is exposed in a simple multiple-choice teaching machine. On the top half of the first frame there is a picture of a box with the word "box" below it. On the bottom half of the card are three pictures each with a word beneath. One of the words is "box." The child presses a button on the machine beneath the "box" picture and one word on the lower half. He then hears a buzzer if he is correct. If he pushes the wrong button, however, nothing happens. The second frame again has the same top half, but the bottom half has only three words, one of which is "box." The child hopefully pushes the button beneath the word "box." On the third frame the word "box" is in the top half, and there are three pictures on the bottom half, one of which is a box. The next frame teaches "cat" in three similar frames and so on for forty-eight words.

Though the Teachall pamphlet mentions that the reading series "is the product of over two years of research by a staff of educators, psychologists, and reading specialists of one of America's most modern universities," no names are mentioned. Why? Similar vague statements are made about tryouts, but there are specific directions about use; for example, "Day 1 Unit 1 (twice) . . . Day 9 Review cards from units 1, 2, 3, and 4." Each unit contains fifteen frames of five new words. About eight units are considered first grade and the remaining four are second grade. This "Reading Course" is obviously intended as material supplementary to some other system of reading instruction. One can at best manage a tolerant smile for the publisher's assertion that "These cards will teach children to recognize new words faster and more effectively than any other educational system." I do not wish to embarrass any particular publishing company (there are many who would make such claims), but rather I would like to warn teachers to take a gulp of salt with such grandiose advertising statements.

Now, jumping to a much more complete program for beginning readers, let's take a look at *Programmed Reading* by Cynthia Buchanan and Sullivan Associates, published by McGraw-Hill (13). This is a series of programmed text workbooks. In general, it is patterned after traditional reading series in that it includes *Programmed Prereading, Programmed Primer, Programmed Reading Book 1, Programmed Reading Book 2,* and more are planned. A teacher's manual mentions something of the background of the author, the name of the schools used in tryouts, and a good bit about the philosophy and curriculum orientation of the series—which interestingly enough has a linguistic slant. The student covers the correct answers by holding a card over a gray area to the left on the workbook page. Then he marks his choice of responses on the right hand portion of the frame, after which he uncovers the answers on the left. Sometimes responses are to be written in. Book 1 is first grade and Book 2 is second grade.

In the Sullivan Associates materials we see a carefully worked out program which covers most of the ten principles. A notable omission is the proof of learning. Publishers are faced with the problem of heavy development costs, but we hope that both they and educational researchers (perhaps someone looking for a master's or doctorate) will begin to supply us with some evidence on this important point. Even though this series is well developed it still has many aspects of a supplemental nature; surely most teachers would want to have their first and second graders also learning reading from a basic series of books or at least many individual reading books. This series does a strong job in phonics, a moderate job on comprehension, but from the standpoint of literature or intrinsic interest (interest in reading material, not interest in performing the tasks in the program), it does not appear to rate high. For example, nowhere in the series does the child have to read a paragraph. This is but another way of saying that the reading teacher must still command the ship and select materials on their strengths for her particular children.

Now let us take a look at another type of program and another level. The first program was a multiple-choice program of a very simple nature. The second program had some multiple choices (Yes-No) but also some constructed responses (N-p). The third type which we will now consider is called a scrambled book. Typically, the student reads a bit of information, is asked a question, and is given three possible answers. If he chooses the first answer, he is told to turn to page 9; if he chooses the second answer, he is told to turn to page 18, etc. When he gets to page 9, he is told that his choice was wrong and why. He is then branched back to the original frame and instructed to read it again. The illustration shows a typical reading comprehension item for weak junior high pupils. Note that the right choice on page 18 tells the student why he is right. This type of programming permits more complex branching: "go back 5 frames because you missed the point of this section" or "skip ahead." This program was written by Gracecarol Bostwick

progress of the human race

No. This is not the main fact expressed in the two-sentence paragraph. Look for the fact which caused the progress. What is it that was necessary before the progress of the human race could take a big step forward? You should find it easily now.

Read No. 25 again. Find the main fact of the paragraph

---

modern way of living

Sorry. No. Modern living is important to us, of course. However, in the two-sentence paragraph in No. 25 the main fact is something else. What made present day living possible?

Read No. 25 again. Find the main fact.

Below are two sentences which are related. Together they make a short paragraph.

The invention of the wheel was a great step forward in the progress of the human race. Man could not have developed the modern way of living without it.

Which of the answers below is the main fact expressed in this two-sentence paragraph? Whichever answer you choose, read all that is said there when you turn to that number in the book. You will learn something from each choice that you make.

progress of the human race (No. 32)

modern way of living (No. 36)

invention of the wheel (No. 40)

---

invention of the wheel

Yes! This is the main fact expressed in the short paragraph in No. 25. In the first sentence we see that the invention of the wheel was a major move forward for mankind. In the second sentence we see that we would not be where we are today without it.

Turn now to No. 41.

(*1*) with the author of this article acting as consultant, and it is part of a series called Lessons for Self Instruction published by the California Test Bureau (*2, 10*). The series is loosely tied to the California Achievement Tests, so there are scrambled booklets to match such skills as Reading Interpretations (comprehension), Reference Skills, and Following Directions at the junior high level, with work at other levels planned. The series is definitely supplemental—to be used at the teacher's discretion or to bolster up areas of weakness as shown by scores on achievement tests. A table of contents, Dale-Chall readability level, and classification of items by Bloom's taxonomy are provided, but again proof of learning is lacking.

Also on the junior high level is *Steps to Better Reading* written by Wilbur Schramm, Herbert Potell, and George D. Spache and published by Harcourt, Brace and World (*11*). This is an enlightened mixture of programming and textbook making technique. Basically, it is a programmed text, which means that most of the frames require a written response of a word. However, the authors have also blended in some multiple-choice items, some workbook-type exercises, and some passages of prose. The book has a clear, well-defined index and frequent review sections. There is even a short section on improving reading rate with timed drill passages, though it is doubtful whether these few selections are enough to effect much change of rate. This three-book series for grades 7, 8, and 9 is designed to accompany the same publishers' Laureate Edition of the Adventures in Literature Series. Despite the fact that there is no information about the tryout and revision procedure or proof of learning, these books have much more of the character of good programming than mundane workbooks.

Vocabulary improvement seems to be a favorite of programmers, but most of them seem to lack a sense of gradual progression, and they tend toward a rote learning of isolated words. A pleasant exception to this is the book *Words* by Susan Meyer Markle, published by Science Research Associates (*9*). Dr. Markle, one of the first really professional programmers, covers all the points even to describing error rate on the tryouts on junior high populations. This program has a noble history beginning in 1957, including some development at Harvard, being reported in the Lumsdaine and Glase classic book on teaching machines (*8*), with final development at the Center for Programmed Instruction.

In contrast, we see *Vocabulary Enrichment,* published by General Education, Inc. (*5*), and presented on a roll of paper in a small plastic "teaching machine." This program has no author's name, no report of tryout and revisions, no proof of learning, no sequencing, and little additional information.

In the Thorndike-Barnhart dictionary you can find the following entry:

haunt 1. to go often to . . . 2. place visited often . . . 3. be often with: Memories of his youth haunted the old man.

The fifth frame in General Education's vocabulary program looks like this:

haunt   Be often with: come or go often to. Memories of his youth . . . the
   ‹   old man, so that he lives in the past.

or later
Thorndike-Barnhart

staple   1. The most important or principal article grown or manufactured in a
            place: Cotton is the staple in many Southern States.

General Education, Inc.

staple   Principal article grown or made in a place. Cotton is the . . . in some
            Southern States.

My only comment is that the Thorndike-Barnhart dictionary is copyrighted
1952 and 1959, while the General Educations, Inc., "program" is copyrighted
in 1963.

What makes this doubly disturbing is that Matthew Israel, the president
of General Education, announced in a brochure that he is a recent student
of B. F. Skinner, and that he holds a Ph.D. from Harvard. In a duplicated
letter over his signature we find the following: "General Education prepares
custom programs for schools, publishers, industry and the armed forces.
Among our satisfied clients are the Harvard Business School, Field Enter-
prises, Science Research Associates. . . ."

Unfortunately, we can't go on discussing programs in detail (not that even
now we have gone into much detail), but we hope that you have received
some idea of the type, level, and quality of programs now being sold to
schools. Though one person or organization can never be completely up to
date, here are a few more reading programs that have come to our attention:

How to Improve Your Reading and Vocabulary Growth. Booklets programmed by Learning, Inc. (Willard Abraham) for Coronet Instructional
Films. Junior high level. Good, brief, 59 pages, clever cardboard masking
arrangement (6).

EDL Word Cues. A series of booklets for grades 7 to 13 by Stanford Taylor,
Helen Frackenpohl, and Nancy Joline, with Arthur McDonald consulting.
Published by Educational Developmental Laboratories. Complete dictionary
entry every third frame, each word gets exactly three frames, very dull programming (14).

Building Words by R. Lepehene. Prepared for Honor Products Company
by Bolt, Beranek and Newman. Seventh grade and above. Two hundred
frames on a roll that fits a small battery-operated, push-button teaching
machine (7).

First Steps in Reading. A Programmed Reading Primer For Children Who
Have Not Yet Mastered the First Steps, by TMI—Grolier. Can be used in

a machine. Parent reads to child on Frame 27, "Can you find the letter with the *buh* sound?" The TMI organization knows programming and psychology but might use some help on reading and phonics (*16*).

Vocabulary Building I. Prepared under the direction of Alexander Schure, Ph.D., Ed.D., for Central Scientific Company. Comes permanently installed in a cardboard box roller type teaching machine. Probably aimed at aspiring parents who read newspapers and go to department stores (*12*).

The Basal Progressive Choice Reading Program. An interesting system developed by research psychologist Myron Woolman, being used in study on the mentally retarded. Strong on reading readiness, crudely prepared (*17*).

Dialogue 1. An aural-oral in phonics by Andrews Brogan and Emily Hotchkiss. Published by Chester Electronics Laboratories. An interesting combination of tape recorded information and programmed workbooks for teaching phonics to beginning readers (*3*).

There is no doubt about it, programmed instruction materials are rapidly becoming available in reading. Teachers should welcome these new materials as *part* of their reading instruction procedures, but it is well to use due caution, since the range in quality, curriculum coverage, and suitable grade level is tremendous.

REFERENCES

1. Bostwick, Gracecarol. *Reading Interpretations I* and *Reading Interpretations II.* Lessons for Self-Instruction in Basic Skills Series. Monterey, Calif.: California Test Bureau, 1963.
2. Bostwick, Gracecarol, and Midloch, Miles. *Reference Skills—The Dictionary.* Lessons for Self-Instruction in Basic Skills Series. Monterey, Calif.: California Test Bureau, 1963.
3. Brogan, Andrews, and Hotchkiss, Emily. *Dialogue 1.* An Aural-Oral Course in Phonics. Chester, Conn.: Chester Electronics Laboratories, Inc., 1963.
4. Fry, Edward B. *Teaching Machines and Programmed Instruction, an Introduction.* New York: McGraw-Hill, 1963. P. 242.
5. General Education (Matthew Israel). *Vocabulary Enrichment 1,* Student Tutor Library. Cambridge, Mass.: General Education, Inc., 1963.
6. Learning Incorporated (Willard Abraham). *How to Improve Your Reading.* Chicago: Coronet Instructional Films, 1963.
7. Lepehene, R. *Building Words, Structural Analysis of Words.* Vocabulary Series Honor Roll No. 402. Prepared by Bolt, Beranek and Newman, Inc., Cambridge, Mass. St. Louis: Honor Products Co., 1962.
8. Lumsdaine, Arthur, and Glaser, Robert. *Teaching Machines and Programmed Learning.* Washington, D.C.: Division of Audio Visual Instruction, National Education Association, 1960.
9. Markle, Susan Meyer. *Words, A Programmed Course in Vocabulary Development.* Chicago: Science Research Associates, 1962.
10. Midloch, Miles, *Following Directions.* Lessons for Self-Instruction in Basic Skills Series. Monterey, Calif.: California Test Bureau, 1963.

11. Schramm, Wilbur, Potell, Herbert, and Spache, George D. *Steps to Better Reading* (Books 1, 2, and 3). New York: Harcourt, Brace & World, 1963.
12. Schure, Alexander. *Vocabulary Building I, Prefixes, Suffixes and Stems, Meaning and Usage*. Published by Educational Aids Publishing Corp. for Central Scientific Company, 1962.
13. Sullivan Associates (Cynthia Dee Buchanan). *Programmed Prereading, Programmed Primer*, and *Programmed Reading Books 1 and 2*. New York: McGraw-Hill, 1963.
14. Taylor, Stanford, Frackenpohl, Helen, McDonald, Arthur, and Joline, Nancy. *EDL Word Clues* (Books G through M). Huntington, N.Y.: Educational Developmental Laboratories, 1962.
15. *Teachall Reading Course* (No author). Washington, D.C.: Publishers Company, Inc., 1962 (180 cards for teaching machine).
16. Teaching Machines Inc. *First Steps in Reading*. Distributed by Teaching Materials Corporation, Grolier, Inc., New York, 1962.
17. Woolman, Myron. *The Progressive Choice Reading Program*. Washington, D.C.: Institute for Education Research Inc., 1962.

PROGRAMMED INSTRUCTION IN READING —A RESEARCH REVIEW *

Robert Glaser

At the present time I am editing a second volume of the book on teaching machines and programmed learning which Lumsdaine and I edited in 1960.[1] This second volume is called *Teaching Machines and Programmed Learning. II: Data and Directions*, and consists of a series of chapters on various topics related to programmed instruction. It contains one chapter entitled "Reading and Related Verbal Learning" by Dr. Harry F. Silberman of the Systems Development Corporation in Santa Monica, California. After thinking about the purpose of this meeting, and after reading Dr. Silberman's chapter, it seemed that I could do no better than to report some of its contents and just add a few remarks of my own. I will do this, but if you wish the benefit of

---

* REPRINTED by permission of Robert Glaser from *New Dimensions in Reading*, D. L. Cleland (ed.). Pittsburgh, Pennsylvania: University of Pittsburgh, 1963, pp. 113–24.

[1] Glaser, R. (Ed.) *Teaching Machines and Programmed Learning I*. Washington, D.C.: National Education Association, 1964.

all of Dr. Silberman's review of research in reading, uncontaminated by some of my side remarks, I urge that you read the book.[2]

The organization of Silberman's chapter differs from the usual division of reading research into such topics as methods, materials, comprehension, and remediation. Instead, the following topics are used: sequencing factors, stimulus-response factors, reinforcement factors, mediating effects, and individual differences. This division of topics is related to the present technology of programmed instruction which specifies that the response made by the student be defined, that stimuli be designed to evoke these responses, that reinforcement be provided so that these responses gain strength, that learning steps be arranged in a systematic sequence with provisions for individual differences, and that instructional procedures be designed on the basis of learner performance.

SEQUENCING OF INSTRUCTIONAL MATERIAL

Let us first consider sequencing factors. Research shows that a difficult discrimination is best learned if it is preceded by training on a similar but easier discrimination. When a young child, on the right occasions, says "dog" and "cat" we say that he has learned to discriminate between these two classes of animals. When he says the word "cat" to a strange cat that he has never seen before, or to the picture of a cat, or to the sound of a cat purring, we say that he has generalized within the class of stimuli that have something to do with cats. When an individual has learned to make discriminations so that he can respond selectively to different stimuli, and when he has learned to generalize these same responses to a variety of situations, we can say that he has learned a concept. In the same way that the child learns the class concept cat and dog, the older child learns the class concepts noun and verb, and the still older child learns the concepts light and sound.

An example from the psychologist's laboratory indicates the kind of instructional procedure used in many programmed instructional sequences for *concept acquisition*, i.e., to teach the student to make the same responses to all stimuli falling within a class and to make different responses to different classes. In teaching a child who does not know colors the concepts of "red" and "blue," we might select objects, some red, some blue, and some other colors. First, we might show the child successive sets of three objects, two red ones and one not red. Each time we present these three objects we would ask, "Which one is not red?" We would also repeat this a number of times with two blue objects and one of another color. In this way we establish discriminations between red and not red, and blue and not blue. The child might then be presented with two objects, one red and one blue and asked, "Which one is red?" or "Which one is blue?" We could then increase the number of

[2] Glaser, R. (Ed.) *Teaching Machines and Programmed Learning II: Data and Direction.* Washington, D.C.: National Education Association, 1964.

non-red and non-blue objects so that only one out of a number of objects is red or blue. In order to carry out such training for generalization,[3] we would include objects with a variety of characteristics. In this sequence of color discrimination training we would include large and small objects, dark and light ones, rough and smooth ones, near and far ones, square, triangle and multi-shaped ones, etc. This would prevent the responses "red" and "blue" from being attached to other than the appropriate stimuli, and with the properties of the objects varied the child would learn to generalize among objects in which the common characteristic is not color. In this way the child is presented with a series of progressively graded experiences by which he acquires the concepts of redness and blueness. Of course this is just a simplified example, and this process can be extended to the learning of many color names or concept dimensions having multi-categories.

The task of sequencing reading material in a progression of increasing difficulty is conceived by Silberman as a problem of finding a solution to the ordering of material on more than one dimension. Word frequency is only one of these dimensions. Other dimensions which need to be considered are letter frequency, syntactic structure, meaningfulness, redundancy, pronounce-ability, word and sentence length, familiarity, stimulus similarity, and grapheme-phoneme correspondence. All of these factors are related to learning difficulty.

With respect to *grapheme-phoneme correspondence* as a dimension in reading difficulty, research indicates that it is indeed a significant aspect of an instructional sequence. A study by Gibson, Osser, and Pick [3] (1963) for example, considered two different possibilities of the way in which spelling-to-sound correspondence rules are learned. Either the child begins by memorizing whole words and later learns to formulate some of the correspondence rules, or simple correspondence rules might develop as soon as he learns to speak. In their experiment they reasoned that, if the first alternative was correct, that children first memorize whole words and then memorize correspondences, children would read words but not pseudo-words that had never been encountered even though the pseudo-words follow certain predictable correspondence rules. But if the second alternative is correct, the first graders would read the pronounceable pseudo-words more efficiently than unpronounceable ones. In brief, the experiment showed that pronounceable trigrams were read more accurately than unpronounceable ones by the same children, and it was concluded that a child in the early stages of reading has learned to generalize certain grapheme-phoneme concepts, probably much in the same way as the concept-formation sequence previously described. These simple rules can be used early in an instructional sequence. At any rate, the dimensions of grapheme-phoneme correspondence is a significant factor to be considered in ordering reading materials.

[3] Gibson, Eleanor J., Osser, H. and Pick, A. A Study of the Development of Grapheme-Phoneme Correspondence. New York: Cornell University, 1963.

Another dimension to be considered in ordering or sequencing reading instruction is *word frequency*. The use of word frequency lists is based upon the assumption that children should learn those words that they will encounter most frequently and should progress from the most common words to the less frequent words. In this respect, however, recent laboratory research suggests that a factor more influential in learning than the frequency of printed sequences is the frequency of spoken sounds. The pronounceability of the verbal units being learned is a predictor of learning that has held up throughout a series of experiments. This suggests that the frequency of specific sounds and sound sequences in verbal behavior may be a more useful guide in bringing the child's behavior under the control of letters and words than frequency counts based on printed texts.

Printed word frequency counts also do not reflect the linguistic structure of the sentences used by children in *active connected speech*. A study by Strickland (1962)[4] indicated that there was a random, haphazard relationship between the sentence structure appearing in the language of elementary school children and the language of reading textbooks. There appears to be no scheme for the development of control over sentence structure that parallels the generally accepted scheme for the development of control over vocabulary. The implication here is that when children have mastered certain language patterns in their speaking these patterns should begin to appear in the materials designed for teaching them to read.

Experimental work is also going on in the measurement of the amount of *letter redundancy* in children's written and spoken language. By redundancy we refer to the influence of the verbal context of the English language. More specifically, redundancy refers to the extent to which the choice of a particular word depends upon the words that precede it. For example, a language favors certain speech patterns as compared with others. If we read the sentence, "Man bites dog," we immediately detect the error. If, however, "dxg" were a more admissible word, we would be less likely to detect the error. As another example, if a speaker says, "Children like to . . ." and then stops, his choice for the next word is already considerably limited. Words like *elephant, punished, loud,* and *George* are highly unlikely continuations. The learning of meaningful material may not be due to any such things as meaningfulness per se, but rather to the greater redundancy in children's speech, which may be a useful guide in sequencing reading instruction.

Another variable which has been studied in verbal learning research and which may be important in designing reading programs is *stimulus similarity*. Where words to be learned are quite similar so that difficult discriminations must be made, errors of generalization are more likely, and learning difficulty will increase, so that *rat, ran, pan,* and *pen* will be harder to learn in a

[4] Strickland, Ruth G. "The Language of Elementary School Children: Its Relationship to the Language of Reading Textbooks and the Quality of Reading of Selected Children." *Bulletin of the School of Education,* Indiana University, July 1962, 38, (4), pp. 1–131.

sequence than words like *boy, children, look,* and *father.* The difficulty involved would discourage the beginning reader from attempting to discriminate between the words on the basis of letter differences, and he will depend more on context cues and other stimuli for his response. This is not what we would like him to do. One solution for this problem is to restrict the extent of dissimilarity so that the irrelevant dimensions can be varied, but the dimension being learned consistently occurs. Some recent reading material by Everett [5] (1960) contains sequences in which the words are restricted to seven letters. Increasingly difficult sentences based on combinations of these letters are presented to the child. The early easy discriminations employ sentences in which the combinations of letters emphasize the differences between them so that they are easily discriminated. If the seven letters were a, h, i, m, n, s, and t, an easy sentence might be "This is a man." A more difficult sentence in which there is an increasing similarity of words might be "It is his hat." As the child learns the initial groups of letters and their combinations, new letters may be more easily discriminated from the members of the original group.

A sequencing question which has received considerable attention is whether reading instruction should be *synthetic,* that is, build wholes out of parts, or *analytic,* that is find parts in previously learned wholes. As I understand it, the synthetic approach is advocated by the "phonickers," and the analytic approach is advocated by the "whole worders." Most of you are much more authoritative on this controversy than I, so that perhaps all I should say is that Silberman's review indicates that no great harm and possibly considerable gain can come from introducing words which follow regular grapheme-phoneme correspondences so that the child builds up these basic "concepts" before going on to irregularly spelled words. Carroll [6] (1961) has indicated that the argument is not between phonics and no phonics, but between good programming and poor programming. By programming instructional sequencing in which new elements are gradually introduced and mastery of these elements is actually assessed before further elements are introduced. Every step of the sequence is guided by the specified student behavior to be mastered, the prerequisite behavior necessary to attain this mastery, and technique to get from one to the other. Programmed instruction is concerned with this kind of sequence and develops such a sequence through repeated revisions of the material and the accumulation of empirical evidence that it is effective for the population for which it is intended.

The question of *individual differences* in learning is tied up with the emotional, mythological notion called *"readiness."* Some writers (McCracken,

---

[5] Everett, R. M., Jr. *Comparison Between Conventional Basic Reading Programs and the Language for Learning Program.* New York: Washington Square Press, 1960.

[6] Carroll, J. B. *Research on Reading and Its Teaching.* Cambridge: Harvard University Press, 1961.

1961) [7] claim that the word was invented to excuse poor reading instruction by shifting the blame to the child. Others feel, as Carroll does, that "it is impossible to draw satisfactory conclusions about individual differences in reading readiness until the relation between readiness factors and success in learning to read has been ascertained in the context of demonstrable optimal methods of teaching" (Carroll, 1961).[8] My own feeling is that the exploration and utilization of sequencing factors will provide much information to reduce the confusion in the concept of readiness. Very simply stated, the notion of sequencing says that a reading program should be developed into specifically stated successive levels of attainment. In order to move to another level, mastery of the previous level is required. The notion of readiness, then, becomes a matter of the behavior the student has when he begins to learn to read and how this has to be used to reach the next level of attainment. Any particular reading program may be developed to begin with children who display a particular level of behavior, and the level chosen may be generally typical of three-year-olds or six-year-olds, depending on where the program wishes to start.

I have mentioned, then, an initial key emphasis which programmed instruction suggests for reading instruction: this is the importance of sequencing factors and the analysis of how these factors can influence learning. Silberman [9] indicates that it is highly likely that future researchers will contribute to the development of a reading program with a synthetic sequence, that is going from parts to wholes, established on the dimensions that have just been mentioned.

STIMULUS—RESPONSE REQUIREMENTS

After the general sequence of a program has been determined, a tenet of programmed instruction is that it is necessary to decide *what specific responses it is desired that the student make and what stimuli will evoke these responses*. A simple matrix can be useful in discussing the stimulus-response requirements in programming. Figure 1 shows a situation in which the stimulus presented to the child can be a pictorial stimulus, a grapheme or a phoneme, and the response the child makes can be a grapheme or a phoneme, either selected as in a multiple-choice problem or constructed by the child, that is, written or spoken directly. In this matrix, number 11, for example, is what might be called reading out loud. The stimulus is a grapheme, that is, a visual stimulus, and the response is a phoneme, a vocal response. Item 14 would be reading to oneself, and 15 would be listening. Covert would refer

[7] McCracken, G. "Reading Readiness in Theory and Practice." In C. Walcutt (ed.) *Tomorrow's Illiterates*, Boston: Little, Brown, 1961.

[8] *Ibid.*

[9] Silberman, H. F. "Reading and Related Verbal Learning," In R. Glaser (Ed.) *Teaching Machines and Programmed Instruction II: Data and Directions*. Washington, D.C.: National Education Association, 1964.

to the immediate response, although we would wish to test reading and listening by some subsequent student activity. Since the process of instruction is taking the student from his present behavior to mastery of the behavior we set up as an instructional objective, the programming task for some cells will depend upon prior acquisition of other cells. For example, cell 11 in Figure 1, which we call reading out loud, might be called a textual skill and presumes completion of cells 2 and 6. Cell 2 is a visual discrimination in which the student is presented with a grapheme and chooses like or different graphemes, and cell 6 is an auditory discrimination in which the student is presented with a phoneme and chooses like or different sounds. The analysis of stimulus and response elements by such a device as this matrix may be useful for determining what goes into a program, but should not be permitted to introduce any artificiality into what the student must learn.

				Stimulus Mode		
				pictorial	grapheme	phoneme
Response Mode	Overt	multiple choice	grapheme	1	2	3
			phoneme	4	5	6
		constructed response	grapheme	7	8	9
			phoneme	10	11	12
	Covert			13	14	15

FIGURE 1. *Stimulus-response combinations in verbal behavior* (*from Silberman, 1964*).

Once the behavioral objectives of a program have been defined and the prerequisite or entering behavior is assessed, the *programming strategy* becomes apparent. For example, if the student is to learn to compose phonemes corresponding to display graphemes and he does not have the appropriate pronunciation of phonemes in his entering repertoire, then the program must begin by shaping this correct pronunciation. If the pronunciation responses already exist, then the program will concentrate on bringing these responses under the control of appropriate graphemic stimuli by the process of discrimination training. Beginning reading programs generally assume that the child has phonemes in his speaking repertoire, and the problem is bringing them under the control of appropriate stimuli. The technique often used for this purpose is to get the child to make the appropriate response in the presence of the appropriate grapheme by using some form of cue or prompt, then withdraw the prompt so that the child can emit the desired response to the grapheme without being prompted. Pictures are often used to evoke the appropriate phonemic responses. However, a number of researchers have indicated that pictures are distracting and ambiguous cues which need to be used extremely carefully to accomplish this process efficiently.

The technical problem is *the transfer of control of the verbal response to letters.* Psychologists interested in programmed instruction have experimented with the way in which this process works. One of the techniques employed has generally been called "fading" in which the prompting cue is gradually faded out. Figure 2 is an example from a program designed to teach eight color names. The figure shows the characteristics of various program cycles

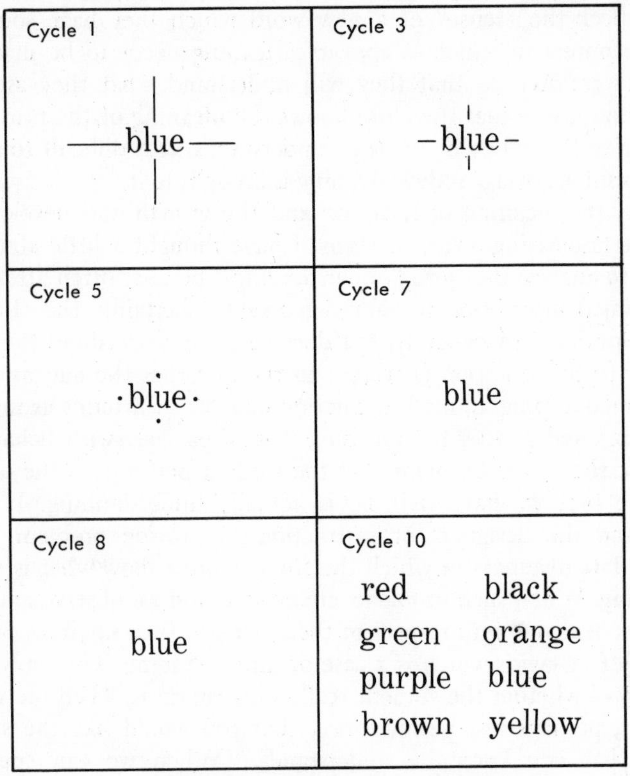

Cycle 1	Cycle 3
——blue——	–blue–
Cycle 5	**Cycle 7**
·blue·	blue
Cycle 8	**Cycle 10**
blue	red black green orange purple blue brown yellow

The halftones in this figure were printed
in blue ink in the actual program.

FIGURE 2. *An example of the "fading" of prompting cues in a program sequence.*

for a particular color; such cycles are interspersed with similar cycles for other colors. The figure indicates how the color prompt for the word "blue" was vanished throughout the program sequence. Squares in the figure illustrate the form in which each of the eight words appeared in cycles 1, 3, 5, 7, 8, and 10. In going through the program, a child read each of the eight words a total of 11 times, the order in which the words appeared was varied from cycle to cycle, and the entire experimental program consisted of a total of 74 frames. At the end of the cycle, the verbal response "blue" was under the control of the written stimulus *blue* and all cues and prompts had vanished.

When the student has acquired units of grapheme-phoneme correspondence and can blend these units into the elements of a word, he can give appropriate vocal response to new words. However, before he can be called a reader, *the child must be able to comprehend the meaning of words in context*. It is for this reason that reading teachers present new words in meaningful contexts drawing attention to them for separate study, and children are taught to check the "sense" of a new word which they have sounded out against the context in which it appears. Meaning needs to be in the repertoires of the children so that they will understand what they are reading. Teachers often insure that the child knows the meaning of the printed words he is reading so that when he reads he understands. It is difficult to get meaning from a printed passage unless meaning is brought to it.

Of course, the meaning of meaning and the growth and development of meaning are fascinating areas for study. I have thought a little about this in attempting to analyze the word *"understanding,"* because often after a lecture on programmed instruction teachers have said, "Certainly the child is performing his problem successfully, but does he really understand the subject?" The answer to this question is related to the fact that the educational technology required in programmed instruction equates such terms as understanding, reasoning, and getting the meaning from a passage, with behavior. This is so because the actual behavior that the student performs is the only tangible evidence that we have that he is actually understanding. It is up to educators and the designers of instruction to provide problem situations which stimulate instances in which the student must show what is defined as understanding. When such problems are devised and we observe and measure the student's behavior with respect to them, we can then say he is performing an instance of behavior which is a case of understanding. The reply, then, to the question of whether the student really understand is, "Tell me what kind of behaviors, perhaps test performance, that you would like the student to display so that you know he understands." When we can specify such terminal behaviors it is the task of a good reading program to determine what combination of experiences result in this behavior.

In general it appears that the instructional objectives defined as understanding seem to be brought about by continuous variations of the experimental context in which the student responds. These variations are set up so that the student gradually receives and discovers new information, learns to make progressively finer discriminations and appropriate generalizations, and also learns to apply his responses to a wide variety of situations. This process helps to enrich the student's breadth of learning, and is an operational way of defining the development of understanding. Programmed instructional sequences can provide a series of well-organized examples leading the student to develop abstractions and complicated concepts. As pointed out by Professor Skinner (1959), "An important goal is to 'enrich' the student's understanding by inducing him to permute and recombine the elements of his repertoire." [10] The goal of instruction is really not concerned with the learner's response to any one situation; the objective is that the student acquires not a uniform and explicit set of responses about a particular concept, but rather a repertoire which is applicable in a variety of situations so that he can use the concept to solve problems, describe it to others, modify it for certain purposes, build a model of it, discover related concepts, and so forth. The terminal behavior can be defined as reasoning with, or understanding, a concept. Appropriately programmed sequences which can be employed with other kinds of learning experiences can provide the stimulus and response variation which contributes to the growth of understanding.

There is another interesting aspect of reading with understanding and this is the fact that as children develop verbal skills their chains of *silent reading* and their chains of covert behavior, e.g., *"thinking"* become longer. In the beginning, much of a child's behavior is overt and vocal, and initial crude behavior consists of long chains of verbalizations. It seems that in the course of behavior development the middle of these long chains is internalized and speeded up so the child can quickly go from the beginning of a long verbal sequence to the end with no apparent overt behavior. Such internalization may be similar to the development of thinking behavior. It may be that study of this process may provide some leads for the technology of reading instruction.

REINFORCEMENT

It has been fairly well established that the kinds of learning that have been described above occur as a result of reinforcement which is an essential component of the learning process. It is perhaps not amiss to attempt to briefly define the term reinforcement, since it is a concept central to programmed instruction. Reinforcement refers to the fact that the consequences of an individual's actions serve to modify and maintain his behavior. New behavior is learned or old behavior changed when the learner's actions produce a consequent event such as a reward. Put another way, when an event that follows the learner's activity results in an increase in that activity, that event is said to be a reinforcer, and the process involved is called reinforcement. For example, when a parent makes sure that a child's desirable performance is followed by a cookie, the parent has provided reinforcement. Or, when the teacher makes sure that a child is permitted to perform an interesting exercise only when he has mastered some basic facts, he is in a sense providing reinforcement. The concept of reinforcement points out that individuals are influenced by the consequences of their behavior so that events such as praise, promotion, good grades, self-satisfaction, and money which follow behavior can serve to reinforce or strengthen on-going activity.

[10] Skinner, B. F. "The Programming of Verbal Knowledge," In E. Galanter (Ed.) *Automatic Teaching: The State of the Art*. New York: Wiley, 1959, pp. 63-68.

In the world in general, reinforcing consequences occur naturally as a function of the environment and society in which we live. In the classroom, *the instructional process deliberately arranges behavioral consequences* so that appropriate learning will occur. Programmed instructional procedures are set up to take advantage of the operation of reinforcement, and one principle in the design of programmed instructional procedures is that provision should be made for specific reinforcement to occur. It is also necessary that reinforcement follow a response a sufficient number of times so that the response becomes strong and well learned. Practice without reinforcement is not very effective, if ever effective at all.

It is also known that the delay of reinforcement may result in little or no learning. In the design of programmed instructional procedures, this fact has been taken seriously so that the student receives rather immediate consequences of his work. In school learning, a major reinforcing event for the student may be "knowledge of results," that is, knowledge of whether or not the response he performs is considered correct. In programmed learning techniques, such confirmation is immediately forthcoming upon the completion of the student's response. The utilization of this fact in learning in educational technology is very dramatic in light of the frequent delay of reinforcement that occurs in many classroom procedures. I must also hasten to add that knowledge of the fact that he is performing correctly may be a less effective reinforcer for the student than arranging learning so that as a result of being correct he is permitted to engage in further and more complex activity. Being able to move on, get into and discover the fine details of the subject matter without being incorrect, frustrated, or punished for being wrong may be the most potent reinforcing consequence in a programmed instructional sequence.

The *search for effective reinforcers* is a persistent activity in research in reading instruction. These include such things as the use of interesting reading material, or permitting the student to self-select his reading material. Selecting interesting reading material means that teachers discuss situations and have the student engage in activities which help establish a purpose in reading for meaning. It is important, however, to remember that the interest value of a story may serve as a reinforcement for some behavior that is being taught, so that it is not interest per se that needs to be considered but the use of interesting material in relation to learning how to be a skilled reader. What needs to be considered is the contingency between the kind of response the student is required to make in reading and the reinforcement of being interesting. One of the advantages of programmed instruction is the fact that it serves to constantly keep one aware of the necessity for providing reinforcement and the particular relationships between stimulus, response, and occurrence of a reinforcing event.

A number of individuals are beginning to develop programmed reading instructional materials considering the ideas that I have been expressing here. The proof of the worth of any of these materials can only be accomplished if we as educators take the time to set down, for all levels of education, the *requirements for student mastery* in terms of demonstrable student behavior. This behavior while it may vary according to the talents and uniqueness of different children and according to requirements of local environments, is nevertheless a demonstrable standard of performance. Such a standard can be best illustrated by the following example. When children learn to swim we set up successive levels of attainment which they must master before they begin to try the next level. So far as I know, in developing such standards, the Red Cross has saved many lives. In doing this, I believe, they have never computed the time and distance that the average child swims and then assigned swimming grades on the basis of percentiles or standard deviations around the average performance. This kind of computation does not seem to make much sense in the context. Perhaps in reading instruction it does not make much sense either, and perhaps we should begin to think about successive levels of mastery rather than some less definitive educational objective in relation to average performance. It is this kind of thinking of the specificity of behavioral objectives and techniques for attaining them which I believe is a major contribution of much of the new work in reading instruction.

THE SRA READING LABORATORY AND FOURTH GRADE PUPILS *

Reginald L. Jones and Earl L. Van Why

The SRA Reading Laboratory is a set of multilevel reading materials designed to provide for a wide range of reading abilities within a single classroom. In using the materials, each pupil begins at the point representative of his present level of functioning and proceeds through the units at his own pace. The exercises are largely of a self-teaching nature with demands on the teacher being minimal. Four editions (elementary, intermediate, secondary, and college prep) have been developed.

This Laboratory, composed of two basic sections, presents materials which emphasize the acquisition of word meaning and word analysis skills, and the "basic reading-thinking skills." Comprehension checks on oral and written material are provided.

Although the materials have been in existence for several years (since

* REPRINTED with permission of the International Reading Association from *Journal of Developmental Reading*, 5 no 1:36–46, Autumn, 1961.

1958), there appears to be little published on their effectiveness. A survey of the literature revealed no studies using the Laboratory. The experimental background of the SRA Reading Laboratory has been stated by the authors as follows:

The SRA Reading Laboratory grew out of six years of preliminary work by the author in Florida, North Carolina, and Westchester County, New York. During this time several thousand students were trained with multilevel materials. In a carefully controlled experiment involving 406 seventh grade students in Charlotte, North Carolina, the group using multilevel materials showed a 112% greater gain than a matched group using one-level materials. Experiments with 4th, 5th and 6th grade students during the past three years show similar gains.[1]

Against this background, the following specific hypotheses have been tested:

1. There are no significant differences in the post-experimental performance on the Vocabulary Subtest of the Iowa Tests of Basic Skills for an unselected group of fourth grade pupils who have been trained with the SRA Reading Laboratory (experimental group) and those pupils who have received no such training (control group).

2. There are no significant differences in post-experimental performance on the Reading Comprehension Subtest of the Iowa Test of Basic Skills of a group of fourth grade pupils who received training with the SRA Reading Laboratory and those pupils who received no such training.

3. There are no significant differences in the pre- to post-experimental changes in vocabulary of pupils in either the experimental or the control group.

4. No significant differences will be found in the pre-to-post change in the reading comprehension scores of either experimental or control subjects.

5. There are no significant differences in the vocabulary changes for pupils in either the experimental or the control group who function at various pre-achievement levels (here labelled low, middle, and high).

6. There are no significant differences in the reading comprehension changes for experimental and control subjects who function at various pre-experimental achievement levels.

7. Fourth grade pupils who achieve in the lower third of their class in vocabulary and who receive training with the SRA Reading Laboratory will perform no higher on a post-training measure of vocabulary than will those fourth grade pupils who receive no training with the SRA Reading Laboratory.

8. Experimental subjects who achieve in the middle third of their class on a measure of vocabulary will perform no better than the control group on a post-training measure of vocabulary.

9. Fourth grade pupils who achieve in the upper third of their class on a

[1] Don H. Parker, et al. SRA Reading Laboratory, Elementary Edition Teachers' Handbook. (Chicago: Science Research Associates, 1958), p. 1.

measure of vocabulary and who receive training with the SRA Laboratory will perform no better than the control group on a post-training measure of vocabulary.

10. Fourth grade pupils who achieve in the lower third of their class in reading comprehension and who receive training with the SRA Reading Laboratory will perform no higher on a post-training measure of reading comprehension than will those fourth grade pupils who receive no training with the SRA Reading Laboratory.

11. Experimental subjects who achieve in the middle third of their class on a measure of reading comprehension will perform no better than the control group on a post-training measure of reading comprehension.

12. Fourth grade pupils who achieve in the upper third of their class on a measure of reading comprehension and who receive training with the SRA Laboratory will perform no better than the control group on a post-training measure of reading comprehension.

Subjects

The subjects of this experiment were four sections of fourth grade classes. Two of these classes were set aside as control subjects, while two groups received training with the SRA Reading Laboratory (experimental). Both experimental and control classes were matched for average level of ability. One hundred and four of the 119 available subjects were used in the analysis reported herein, with pupils who were absent when the pre test or post-test was administered being eliminated from the samples. Eight students were eliminated to effect adequate ability matching.

Procedures

Experimental classes received training with the SRA Reading Laboratory extending over a period of five months beginning in January and ending in June. The procedures outlined in the manual were followed very closely. Experimental and control classes were administered a reading test before the experiment began and again at its close. The data yielded by the reading tests provided the measures for assessing the effectiveness of the SRA Reading Laboratory.

All pupils had been administered the Lorge-Thorndike Tests of Intelligence earlier in the year. The scores on this test were used to equate the experimental and control groups for level of ability.

Reading Test

The Vocabulary and Reading Comprehension Subtests of the Iowa Tests of Basic Skills [2] were used as criterion measures. The two subtests were found

[2] *Iowa Tests of Basic Skills: Manual for Administrators, Supervisors, and Counselors.* Boston: Houghton Mifflin, 1956.

TABLE I

Means, Standard Deviations, and "t" Ratios of Differences Between the Mean I.Q.'s of Experimental and Control Groups

GROUP	N	MEAN I.Q.	S.D.	DM	"t"	P
Control	52	101.70	13.31	2.01	.78	NS*
Experimental	52	103.71	12.57			

* Unless otherwise indicated, P ≤ .05 is adopted as a critical level.

TABLE II

Number of Subjects, Means, Standard Deviations, and "t" Ratios of the Differences Between Pre-Test Standing of Experimental and Control Groups on the Vocabulary and Reading Comprehension Subtests of the Iowa Tests of Basic Skills

GROUP	SUBTEST	N	MEAN	S.D.	DM	"t"	P*
Control	Vocabulary	52	4.33	.77	.14	.82	NS
Experimental	Vocabulary	52	4.36	.91			
Control	Reading Comprehension	52	4.11	.80	.08	.40	NS
Experimental	Reading Comprehension	52	4.19	1.30			

* P > .25 adopted as a critical level.

TABLE III

Number of Subjects, Means, Standard Deviations, "t" Ratios, and Level of Significance of the Post-Test Standing of Control and Experimental Groups on the Vocabulary and Reading Comprehension Subtests of the Iowa Tests of Basic Skills

GROUP	SUBTEST	N	MEAN	S.D.	Dm	"t"	P
Control	Vocabulary	52	5.16	.66			
Experimental	Vocabulary	52	5.27	1.25	.11	.55	NS
Control	Reading Comprehension	52	4.84	1.12			
Experimental	Reading Comprehension	52	5.00	1.59	.16	.62	NS

TABLE IV

"t" Ratios of the Level of Significance of Pre-to-Post Change on the Vocabulary and Reading Comprehension Subtests of the Iowa Tests of Reading Skills

GROUP	SUBTEST	N	PRE-TEST MEAN	POST-TEST MEAN	dm	semd	"t"	P
Control	Vocabulary	52	4.33	5.16	.83	.122	6.80	<.001
Experimental	Vocabulary	52	4.36	5.27	.91	.094	9.68	<.001
Control	Reading Comprehension	52	4.11	4.84	.73	.105	6.95	<.001
Experimental	Reading Comprehension	52	4.19	5.00	.89	.111	8.09	<.001

to possess satisfactory face and concurrent validity. Split half reliabilities of .86 and .96 were reported for the Vocabulary and Reading Comprehension Subtests respectively.

RESULTS

Matching

The results of matching experimental and control groups for I.Q. are presented in Table I. Both groups were found to be closely matched for level as well as range of intellectual functioning.

The pre-experimental standing of experimental and control groups on the Vocabulary and Reading Comprehension Subtests is presented in Table II. These results show that both groups were closely matched on these subtests. Differences in post-experimental measures of vocabulary and reading comprehension, then, must be attributed either to training with the SRA Reading Laboratory or to the absence of such training.

POST-TEST STANDING OF EXPERIMENTAL AND CONTROL GROUPS

Inspection of the post-test measures presented in Table III shows that there are no significant differences between the experimetnal and control groups on the Vocabulary and Reading Comprehension Subtests of the Iowa Tests of Basic Skills. Consequently, hypotheses 1 and 2 are accepted.

Hypotheses 3 and 4 have stated that differences from pre-test to post-test will be greater for the experimental group. Such a difference can occur in spite of the fact that the groups were equated on a pre-test measure of vocabulary and reading comprehension and were not significantly different on a post-experimental measure on these variables. Results bearing on hypotheses 3 and 4 are reported in Table IV. The change from pre-tests to post-tests for both groups was significant at less than .001. However, differences in the values of the individual "t" ratios suggest that the null hypotheses could be rejected at a more stringent level for the experimental subjects.

EFFECTS ON FOURTH GRADE PUPILS FUNCTIONING AT THE LOW, MIDDLE, AND HIGH ACHIEVEMENT LEVELS

Two general questions were raised in this section. First, do pupils of either control or experimental groups benefit from training with the SRA Reading Laboratory or the absence of such training? Second, are there differences in the post-experimental performance *between* control and experimental groups of several achievement levels? (Hypotheses 7–12).

Preparation of Scores for Analysis.—The following procedures were used in preparing this phase of the data:

First, the differences between the standard scores obtained on the first and second test were computed, making certain that the sign of the difference was preserved in each instance. Secondly, all scores of a given individual (i.e., pre-test and post-test score along with the difference between scores) and within a given experimental condition (i.e., experimental or control group by grade level) were ordered sequentially on the basis of the size of the pre-test score. The experimental and control group distributions were then inspected jointly for points which would delineate three groups (here labelled low, middle, and high) which were roughly equal in size and representative of disparate but roughly equidistant points. Thus, these data yielded experimental and control groups which had three subgroups each and were about equal in achievement on pre-experimental measures of vocabulary and reading comprehension. These results permitted evaluation of the magnitude of change within a given experimental condition as well as between experimental conditions. The data were then subjected to the Kruskal Walis Analysis of Variance by Ranks (Question 1) and the Mann-Whitney U Test (Question 2).[3]

Results relating to Question 1 are presented in Table V. Inspection of these data shows that there were significant pre-to-post changes for pupils who functioned at the three achievement levels. However, these differences occurred only with pupils who had been trained with the SRA Reading Laboratory. High achievers were found to make the greatest gain in vocabulary. The low achievers were second in magnitude of gain, while the middle achievers received the least benefit. This pattern did not occur in reading comprehension, however. The low achievers were found to receive the greatest benefit from training with the SRA Reading Laboratory, followed by the middle achievers. High achievers on a pre-experimental measure of reading comprehension benefited least. No significant differences within levels were found for control group participants.

Hypotheses 7–12 raised the question of whether pupils functioning at various achievement levels would benefit from training with the SRA Reading Laboratory more than would pupils not trained with these materials. It was expected that the post-experimental performance of experimental pupils of all achievement levels would be significantly greater than that obtained by pupils who were not trained with the SRA Reading Laboratory. Data bearing on these hypotheses are presented in Table VI. The results do not permit rejection of the null hypotheses. It is concluded that pupils of low, middle, or high achievement will perform no higher on a post-training measure of vocabulary and reading comprehension than will those pupils who received no such training. However, training with the Laboratory did affect, differentially, those who received such training. High achievers made the greatest pre-test to post-test gains in vocabulary, while low achievers made significant gains in reading comprehension.

[3] Sidney Siegel, *Nonparametric Statistics for the Behavioral Sciences* (New York: McGraw-Hill, 1956).

TABLE V

Significance Tests of the Degree of the Pre-Test to Post-Test Change for Low, Middle, and High Achievers Within the Experimental and Control Groups

SUBTEST	GROUP	LEVEL	N	AVERAGE PRE-TEST STANDING	AVERAGE OF RANKED CHANGE SCORES	H	P
Vocabulary	Control	Low	19	3.48	25.68	1.57	NS
		Middle	19	4.31	24.61		
		High	14	5.17	29.46		
Vocabulary	Experimental	Low	18	3.39	26.94	7.70	<.05
		Middle	15	4.34	18.53		
		High	19	5.30	32.52		
Reading Comprehension	Control	Low	19	3.23	27.89	.15	NS
		Middle	16	4.13	27.72		
		High	17	5.06	24.04		
Reading Comprehension	Experimental	Low	19	3.47	28.89	8.82	<.05
		Middle	12	3.96	27.72		
		High	21	5.19	24.04		

TABLE VI

Significance Tests of the Difference Between Experimental and Control Group Subjects Having a Pre-Experimental Status of Low, Middle, and High on the Vocabulary and Reading Comprehension Subtests of the Iowa Tests of Basic Skills

SUBTEST	PRE-EXPERIMENTAL ACHIEVEMENT LEVEL	GROUP	N	AVERAGE OF RANKED CHANGE SCORES	U	P
Vocabulary	Low	Control	19	18.79		
		Experi.	18	18.94	159.5	NS
	Middle	Control	19	17.42		
		Exper.	15	15.50	113.5	NS
	High	Control	14	16.07		
		Experi.	19	17.68	120.0	NS
Reading Comprehension	Low	Control	19	19.13		
		Experi.	19	19.76	173.5	NS
	Middle	Control	16	12.97		
		Experi.	12	15.27	74.0	NS
	High	Control	17	19.79		
		Experi.	21	19.29	$z^* = .15$	NS

* z is used when any value of N_2 exceeds 20.

Summary

One hundred four pupils in the fourth grade were used as subjects in an experiment investigating the effect of training with SRA Reading Laboratory on vocabulary and reading comprehension as measured by the Iowa Tests of Basic Skills. Fifty-two pupils received training with the Reading Laboratory while a matched group of fifty-two pupils received no such training. The following results are noted:

1. No significant differences between experimental and control groups on post-experimental measures of vocabulary or reading comprehension were found.

2. Both control and experimental pupils made significant pre-test to post-test changes.

3. Training with the SRA Reading Laboratory resulted in significant with-in-group differences in the pre-to-post change scores of pupils at different achievement levels. High achievers made the greatest gains in vocabulary followed by low and middle achievers, respectively. Low achievers made the greatest gains in reading comprehension followed by the middle and high achievers, in that order. There were no significant differences in the pre-test to post-test performance of control group pupils of various achievement levels.

4. Experimental pupils of the three achievement levels made no greater post-training vocabulary and reading comprehension gains than did their matched controls.

Chapter 6

ORGANIZING THE SCHOOL
FOR READING

The teacher does not stand alone in efforts to help children gain reading power. The entire school environment affects the situation. In fact, how the school is organized for reading and other purposes strongly influences what the teacher can and cannot do in the classroom.

The school environment is sometimes organized in part or entirely around reading levels of children. Children on a particular level of reading work with a teacher who may not know them outside of reading hour time; sometimes children on a certain level of reading join others in a homogeneous ability class. Likewise arrangements have sometimes attempted to effect shifts in school sessions so that groups of children with similar ability could work on staggered schedules

Whatever the arrangement the problem of centering the organization around children's reading levels needs serious study. If one accepts the premise that reading is a continuous, all-day activity related to realities of living (see Chapter 1), and if one believes that reading power must be viewed in relation to total growth, to broad educational goals, and to the unity of total language communication (see Chapter 2), one must proceed cautiously in organizing groups of children for instructional purposes to avoid violating these conditions.

Grouping children by homogeneous reading ability can deny the specificity of reading growth problems that are not revealed through group testing scores, whether totaled or averaged. Unless each child is diagnosed individually (see Chapter 3) the danger of moving on the basis of a general reading ability is indeed ominous. Grouping makes sense when every member of a group needs exactly what every other member of the group requires for growth in reading power. Anything less than that is likely to lead to inefficient, ineffectual grouping. Furthermore, arrangements of environment that fail to involve the self-selection powers of children to group themselves by choices and discerned specific needs, arrangements that permit little or no control over time and materials for reading by children and teacher, arrangements that make it increasingly difficult for the teacher to know the child in a variety of reading situations—such arrangements are open to serious question.

What value do organizational patterns have for helping children develop reading power? Unless this question is honestly faced, children's reading growth may be seriously skewed.

ORGANIZATIONAL SCHEMES
AND THE IMPROVEMENT OF
READING INSTRUCTION *

Harris A. Taylor

O NE OF THE primary objectives of new organizational schemes utilized
by elementary schools is the improvement of instruction with a stated
or implied emphasis on the improvement of the teaching of reading. Therefore, one interested in the improvement of reading instruction has only to
scan the available literature to find a multitude of organizational schemes,
each promising improvement over the traditional method of teaching. Yet,
with all these schemes, the teaching of reading has not undergone major
revision in the past 25 years. Schools experiment in a limited fashion with a
new organizational scheme and then return to past practices. Many of these
schemes are successful for the experimental teachers, but not for all teachers.
There is no doubt that a dedicated, highly motivated teacher can make most
reasonable schemes work, while teachers not fully committed can meet with
a notable lack of success.

Assuming that a school were composed of highly motivated, intelligent
teachers who wished to improve reading instruction, is there an organizational scheme which will allow maximum development of each pupil in
reading skills?

Before any attempt is made to answer this question, it seems necessary to
list the major organizational schemes utilized at the present time for the
improvement of instruction. Some of the underlying assumptions for each
organizational scheme also need to be listed, since it is possible for differently
labeled organizational schemes to have some of the same basic underlying
assumptions.

DEPARTMENTALIZED ELEMENTARY SCHOOLS

The departmentalized elementary school has been proposed as a way of
improving instruction. Assumptions behind this idea are that departmentalization allows for placing teachers in an instructional setting which utilizes
their major teaching strengths and allows pupils to be grouped, subject by
subject, with other pupils in the same range of achievement.

According to many educators, however, departmentalized elementary

* REPRINTED by permission of the Claremont Reading Conference from the *Claremont
College Reading Conference Yearbook*, Vol. 25, 1961, pp. 45–51.

schools should be avoided since it is felt that elementary school children should not be exposed to a great number of different teachers, but be allowed to identify with one teacher. The term "mother image" is sometimes used to describe the desired relationship between pupil and teacher.

Those educators who oppose departmentalization in the elementary school feel that it could not have the flexibility in allocating teaching time which is normally found in many other organizational schemes since pupils usually come and go by a well regulated schedule. In addition it is assumed that the correlation of subject matter may be difficult to attain.

SELF-CONTAINED CLASSROOM

On the other end of the continuum is found the self-contained classroom organization in which one teacher teaches essentially all subjects. In such an arrangement the development of strong teacher-pupil relationships, the flexible use of time, and the correlation of content is far more easily and naturally obtained. Many feel, however, that most teachers cannot adequately teach *all* the various subjects found in the elementary school curriculum, hence any grouping system which places students in classes on a permanent basis is unrealistic. The variability in achievement of pupils from subject to subject makes the permanent assignment of pupils to a self-contained classroom a difficult task.

THE DUAL PROGRESS PLAN

The *Dual Progress Plan* employed by the Long Beach and Ossining, New York school systems calls for the pupils to be with one teacher for one-half day (the self-contained classroom scheme), and with several other teachers during the other half-day (the departmentalized scheme). It is felt by the originator, Dr. Stoddard of New York University, that this scheme allows a pupil to identify with one "core" teacher who teaches language arts and social studies on a graded basis while being taught other subjects by special teachers on a non-graded basis.

This scheme attempts to capitalize on the specific teaching talents of the staff. It narrows the range in achievement of pupils in several subject matter areas by a non-grading procedure, allows each pupil to "identify" with one teacher and promotes the correlation of content in a limited number of subjects.

The "core" class idea which occupies approximately one-half of the school day may not be enough of a unifying element for elementary school pupils. In the Ossining and Long Beach school districts, the plan starts in grade three and extends through grade eight. Primary grade classes are not involved. The correlation of content is limited and the program does not have the flexibility in the utilization of time that other organizational schemes might enjoy.

The Joplin Plan

This plan, which has been used by so many school districts during the past five years, is another compromise situation. In this scheme the pupils are assigned to one classroom teacher for a full day with the exception of a block of time when the pupils are placed with teachers who have a special teaching talent needed by the pupils, or placed with a group of pupils who have the same or nearly the same achievement pattern. Most of the time both of these factors are taken into consideration. This scheme can cut across grade level lines by having teachers of several grade levels exchange pupils.

The subject most commonly made a part of this scheme is reading, followed by mathematics. Teachers employing this scheme may lose some of the flexibility enjoyed by the typical self-contained classroom teachers since one or two regularly scheduled time-blocks during a school day can make the daily schedule a very rigid affair. Many districts have tried this scheme and have reported successes less than originally anticipated. This could be caused by several factors: 1) the teachers did not have the required skills to teach the group assigned; 2) the pupil's lack of sustained motivation due to the non-graded nature of the classes, and the stigma attached to being a member of a class of slow achievers; 3) the difficulty of moving a pupil from one class to another due to a change in the pupil's achievement pattern, and 4) the possibility that teachers may not be as well motivated teaching pupils other than their own for one block of time daily.

Some school districts have been utilizing the Joplin Plan in the teaching of reading for several years and report that they think it is the best scheme for their pupils.

The Non-Graded Elementary School

At the present time a great interest has been expressed for an organizational plan called the non-graded school. In this plan the theory of continuous pupil progress is primary. This implies that the pupil will be taught in logical steps according to the achievement status of the pupil, and disregards his grade-level assignment and the arbitrary assignment of subject matter to grade levels. In the non-graded school pupils of different ages are formed into achievement groups or other type grouping which demand planned flexibility.

This plan, of course, allows teachers to be very precise about achievement groupings. Pupils with like achievement patterns can be placed into groups which disregard the pupil's chronological age and grade level. Both the slow and the rapid learner can receive the type of instruction demanded by their achievement pattern. The evil effects of acceleration or retention of pupils can be overcome since pupils move through the system on sort of a "broken front" approach which does not formally and officially call to the attention of all just what the current grade placement of any pupil might be at a certain point in the educational career of the pupil in the elementary school.

It is the contention of those who are formulating the theories for this scheme that the pupil will learn more and have a more wholesome attitude in doing so. Whether this is the case remains to be seen. This scheme's strength lies in its ability to set a more favorable climate for learning through greater attention to the findings of child growth and development studies; its major weakness is the difficulty educators find in explaining the program to parents. The necessary techniques for maintaining a sound continuous progress plan may not be generally understood by many teachers. The plan calls for better evaluation procedures and record keeping, deeper insight into the problems of pupil motivation, and better command over a wide range of teaching techniques. If the non-graded organization causes teachers to increase their effectiveness in these areas, it surely will make worthwhile the expenditure of time and energy utilized for change.

TEAM TEACHING

Team Teaching as a way of organizing pupils and teachers is becoming more and more prominent in educational planning. The precise meaning of team teaching is illusive since it can take many forms. Basically a teaching team is composed of a distinct pupil group, and a small faculty group responsible for teaching the student group. From this base a seemingly infinite number of teaching team models can be developed. For example, other professional and para-professional staff members can be included on the team. Sometimes one or more intern teachers, master teachers, teacher aides, auxiliary teachers, community resource personnel and student teachers are found on teams.

The team students can be made up of non-graded pupils, gifted pupils, college preparatory pupils, general education pupils, mentally retarded pupils, or any other special grouping devised by educators.

The non-graded organizational scheme, *The Dual-Progress Plan*, *The Joplin Plan*, the self-contained classroom with modification, and the departmentalized classroom arrangement can all be utilized by some form of team teaching.

To further complicate matters, a teaching team at the elementary school or secondary school level can be composed of several teachers, each teaching his *same* subject matter specialty or with several teachers, each of whom teaches a different subject to the pupil group; or several teachers who each teach the same several subjects to the pupil group in a self-contained classroom arrangement. A great number of variations can be developed from these. For example, sometimes two or three teachers of a subject are formed into a team with two or three teachers of one or more additional subjects. Thus, a team could be composed of two English teachers, two history teachers, and two mathematics teachers, or three English teachers and three history teachers.

An interesting variation calls for two teachers with complementary skills to be formed into a teaching team with permission to be completely flexible as to which teacher will teach which subjects, or parts of a subject, to any of the pupils making up the pupil group. This scheme is being utilized at both the elementary and secondary school levels. No wonder we are finding it difficult to discuss team teaching intelligently. The combination of variables makes possible a great deal of confusion. It seems apparent that much care must be given to avoid misconceptions about team teaching by giving a clear description of the team design being considered. It is also apparent that certain team teaching models are more appropriate for some schools than others. Wise educators first determine what they want to gain from team teaching, then design a teaching team model which promises to give them the outcomes sought.

Generally, team teaching, regardless of the design, is based on at least some of the assumptions listed:

- The particular talents of teachers should be used.
- Members of the faculty cannot function in isolation.
- The best teachers should be given extra pay and recognition for instructional leadership.
- Teachers should have personal knowledge of their students.
- Effective programs for curriculum development require teacher responsibility for an involvement in innovations.
- Relationships among fields of knowledge should be developed.
- Schools should be flexible with respect to scheduling classes and grouping pupils.
- Teachers should be freed from routine, clerical tasks.
- Decision making should be close to the point of action.
- Schools should be flexible enough so that pupils may move ahead according to their abilities.
- Students with difficulties in learning need special assistance when the difficulties appear.
- To operate at peak performance, schools should augment their programs with the talents of citizens.

It is understood that not all of these assumptions have the same importance, but nevertheless, they are not listed in any preferred order.

Summary

It is the fond hope of educators that organizational schemes, both the old and the new, will improve instruction through a realignment of the relationship of pupil to teacher, teacher to pupils, teacher to teacher, and lay citizen to teacher and pupil. Basic weaknesses in the educational program such as a lack of pupil guidance, the apparent lack of teaching skill of some teachers in one or more areas of instruction, the lack of pupil motivation, the failure of schools to retain high calibre teachers for classroom instruction, or the difficulty in maintaining and improving in-service education programs for teachers in the light of an explosion of knowledge, and the demands of modern society for increased knowledge, has caused educators to reëvaluate present organizational schemes and make slight modifications or drastic changes as the situations warrant.

Logically, when a school is confronted with a limited amount of teaching talent in a given classroom, it is necessary to reinforce the talent of the teacher with that of another teacher who has special competence. This can be done through in-service education, or through a system whereby the teacher with skill in the instructional area teaches the pupils of the other teacher. The final alternative is to discharge the teacher and never hire another with a teaching weakness. This does not seem to be a realistic final solution to the problem. A new organizational scheme may make it possible for both a sound in-service training program to be accepted by the teachers with some degree of enthusiasm, and to allow the top talents of teachers to be brought to bear on a greater number of pupils than would be the case under current organizational schemes. Organizational schemes may make possible beneficial changes, since they often release educators from an outmoded plan which has grown restrictive with the years. It may make the staff of a school feel that flexibility is the keynote and that proposals for the improvement of instruction will be examined critically, and not "sloughed off" as impossible due to any one of a hundred reasons used for this purpose.

A staff willing to experiment with a new organizational scheme, provided it is designed with the particular school in mind, should be encouraged by both administrators and parents since it is strong proof that the teaching staff is eager to improve the instructional program and will devote the necessary time and energy to make the plan work. The students can only benefit from such an arrangement.

The improvement of the teaching of reading can come about through a change in school organization; more importantly, the improvement of reading can be accomplished through a *sound* change in classroom organization. An organizational scheme which frees teachers from the restrictions of the traditional, encourages new attempts at solving old problems, allows a redistribution of teaching talent within the school, and allows for inservice growth through mutual help programs, will surely succeed.

READING AND NONGRADING IN
THE ELEMENTARY SCHOOL *

Malcolm P. Douglass

The typical elementary school of the 1960's is organized into a series of graded classrooms, each of which is conceived as "self-contained." That is, one teacher is assigned the responsibility of teaching all skills and subjects to somewhere between twenty-five and forty children of about the same chronological age. In some schools, special teachers may be assigned to teach in such fields as art, music, or physical education. But this is a minor deviation from the classic pattern which holds one teacher responsible for the "basic education" of a group of children of approximately the same chronological age during the school year.

This method of grouping young children for their earliest formal educational experiences emerged as the dominant pattern for organizing the elementary school in the United States during the latter half of the 1800's. It is now beginning its second century, in robust good health, as the most common pattern for grouping children for instructional purposes. This is not to say there are no grumblings of discontent. The self-contained classroom based upon the age-grade hierarchy poses some difficult educational dilemmas which challenge the ingenuity and imagination of the teacher who seeks to adjust instruction to meet the variety of levels of ability and achievement which face him in a graded clasroom. We have therefore witnessed over the years a number of attempts to adjust the organizational pattern within which teachers and children learn.

Because of its central role in the elementary school curriculum, the printed word reading program has provided the focus for much of this activity. Of course, even within the conventional graded classroom, many attempts have been made to solve the problem of individual variation. The most familiar is the three or four group arrangement in the basal reader approach in which different achievement levels use textbooks or readers written at different levels of difficulty. Recently, individualized reading programs in which each child progresses at his own rate, often in a book of his own choice, have grown in popularity. But beyond these adjustments within the conventional pattern has come, particularly since World War II, widespread experimentation with patterns which actually alter the basic framework of the typical elementary school. Some of these patterns represent new departures. Others hark back

---

* REPRINTED by permission of the Claremont Reading Conference from the *Claremont College Reading Conference Yearbook*, Vol. 26, 1962, pp. 85–95.

to experimental programs of the late 1800's and early 1900's. Because they do depart from the familiar graded pattern to a greater or lesser extent, the term "nongrading" has been used to describe them.

It is the purpose of the material which follows to identify five major patterns within which reading programs are being organized and to offer some criteria by which they may be evaluated. It will soon become obvious that the term "nongrading" is a slippery one with many meanings. In some instances, for example, programs which have been assigned this term are, in fact, much more rigidly graded arrangements than the typical graded class. The five which have been selected for discussion here may be identified as departmentalization, staggered sessions, continuous progress, departmentalization within a teaching team structure, and multi-age groupings.

Departmentalization. Departmentalization for reading is among the oldest forms of regrouping, having its origins in the Gary Plan (1907–18) (1) and gaining attention most recently as the Joplin Plan. (2) In such an arrangement, children are regrouped for their work in reading only. The remainder of the day may be spent with one teacher whose responsibility it is to teach all of the remaining "basic subjects," as in a self-contained classroom, or the graded class may move for one or more subjects. Assignment to classes for reading instruction in this arrangement is most often based upon the score attained on a standardized reading test. Teacher judgment and other kinds of information about the child which might affect his assignment are also widely employed criteria.

Departmentalized programs have been roundly criticized at the elementary level. Particularly is this true of those arrangements in which children move several times during a day. The arguments are well-known, the major points of contention being that no one is really familiar with the individual child and with his learning problems and that the child is denied the opportunity to identify closely with any one of his teachers. Departmentalization when it occurs only with respect to the reading program, however, is usually criticized less severely. One such move during a day is not viewed as being disruptive to the values inherent in the self-contained classroom. The assumption is made that such limited regrouping, based as it is on achievement, may be done safely and that it provides learning situations in which children may progress more in accord with their abilities.

Adoption of a Joplin-type program usually brings with it more realistic understanding of the widely varying achievement levels which are to be found as a matter of course among readers, especially in the intermediate grades of the elementary school. As to the general effectiveness of such arrangements, reports are conflicting, but there do seem to be indications that the greatest values accrue to the children in the upper achievement levels. Ceilings become imposed in the standard classroom, apparently, and these tend to disappear. This is perhaps more a criticism of the rigidities within basal reading programs founded on homogeneous groupings than a plus for the departmentalized arrangement. No pattern should be looked upon as a panacea, of course, but the departmentalized arrangement carries with it some assumptions that ought to be clearly understood by those who would adopt it. Primary among these is the notion that children will learn to read better if they are regrouped from basically heterogeneous classes into homogeneous ones. That research fails to provide proof that this in fact happens comes as a surprise to many. Another assumption is that reading should be taught in a more or less similar fashion by all teachers using related materials. In practice, this means a basal reader program for all. It is widely accepted, however, that reading may be taught and learned through varying approaches. The question therefore arises as to how much freedom of choice a teacher should have in selecting an approach to teaching reading. Departmentalization results in an implied if not an explicit agreement that there will be more similarities than differences in the teacher's approach to the teaching of reading and in the materials which he will use in the classroom.

Staggered Sessions. A second pattern, often found as an adjunct to the familiar self-contained classroom, has been termed "staggered session." In such an arrangement, half of the children in a given class come to school, for example, at 8:30 a.m. The second half joins the early risers a half or three quarters of an hour later. The group which comes early to school leaves that many minutes earlier in the afternoon, and the remaining half of the class stays to work with the teacher in a small group setting. Under such an arrangement the teacher may use a basal reader approach, an individualized approach, or some other approach to the teaching of reading. Unlike some other plans, the organizational pattern does not imply a method of teaching reading. Thus, determination of which children will be assigned to the morning or afternoon small groups will depend upon the arrangement which is most comfortable for the teacher under the method which he wishes to use.

The staggered session is utilized for the most part in the primary grades. Intermediate teachers, who normally are required to teach for a longer period of time, do not care to extend their day as readily as do primary teachers. That this scheme has failed to gain wider acceptance in conventionally organized schools has been due to the fact that teachers feel thwarted in their desires by the hard facts of bus schedules, the notion that all teachers must "stagger" or none can, and the feeling that parents would object to the differing times at which they would be asked to dispatch children from their homes in the morning. Where these supposed problems have been faced directly, however, they have become much less important. Apparently, where a faculty wishes to undertake the staggered session, either separately or in concert, and where ability groupings are not viewed as the *sine qua non* of the reading program, the staggered session can be invoked with ease.

Continuous Progress. A third form of adjustment, one which has been growing rapidly in recent years, is the grouping of children for all learning according to printed word reading abilities. This is sometimes called the

"Continuous Progress Plan." (3) In such an arrangement, children are grouped into "reading levels." One, two, or three such "levels" form the basis upon which classes are organized. Usually, three "levels" are equivalent to the conventional grade. Thus, levels one, two, and three are roughly equivalent to grade one; levels four, five, and six equal grade two; and so on. "Levels" may serve as the basis for grouping children throughout the elementary school. More often, however, the "level system" is limited in its application to the primary grades.

Children may be selected for assignment to a particular "level" according to the same general criteria as are employed in a departmentalized plan. More often, however, the assignment is made according to the teacher's perception of which book in the reader series is most appropriate to the child's reading capabilities. Once the child has been assigned to a "level," he presumably makes "continuous progress" through progressively more difficult materials, emerging at the end according to the rapidity with which he masters the material in the textbook.

One or more "levels" may be present at the beginning of the school year in a given class. This is an administrative problem since it obviously requires nine classrooms to form groups which are homogeneous with respect to their level assignment at the beginning of the year. Schools which have fewer than nine classrooms in the primary department will organize classes so that each one will have more than one level in it. As the year progresses, however, it is expected that children will progress at different rates and that they will assume a wider variety of positions within the level or levels present in a given classroom. When an obvious imbalance occurs, therefore, a child may be transferred to another classroom—to a group which is more nearly "on his level." Thus, reassignment is possible at any time of the year. Theoretically more or less time than the conventional three years of the primary program may be spent by any one child moving through the levels. The plan is thereby said to avoid much of the trauma which failure and double promotion are thought to produce in the conventional graded pattern. There is often in this arrangement a conscious effort to eliminate the use of the word "grade" and to substitute "level" for it. In practice this rarely occurs. The level system is more likely to become superimposed upon the graded hierarchy. The complaint is often voiced, therefore, that the Continuous Progress Plan is actually a more rigidly graded system than the one with which we are all so familiar.

Like departmentalization, this plan carries with it the assumption that reading will be taught in a more or less similar fashion by all. Every such arrangement known to this writer, at least, depends in this regard upon a basal reader program to establish the guide for the teaching approach used. Deviations to individualized programs, such as self-selection, are simply not countenanced. This arrangement also includes the idea that groups formed according to a measure of success in reading—in this instance, position in the sequence of readers used in the school—provide the most satisfactory human combinations for learning in all areas of the curriculum. Again, objective evidence which might be used to support or refute this claim is meager and inconclusive. Research is needed which explores the relationship of "Continuous Progress Plans" to achievement in other curriculum areas and which provides information on the impact of such an arrangement upon mental health and motivation for learning. In the meantime, we should recognize that judgments with respect to which pattern may provide optimal learning opportunities in reading are based largely upon unscientific data.

Departmentalization within a Teaching Team Structure. A fourth plan for breaking the graded lockstep in reading is a combination of departmentalization and aspects of the "continuous progress plan." It represents a deliberate effort to account for intra-individual differences. In such an arrangement, it is recognized that within each child there will be varying levels of achievement. The assumption is made that children learn best when they are grouped homogeneously for several, if not all, of the curriculum areas. Therefore, each child is placed in one grouping for reading, another grouping for arithmetic, and possibly other groupings for social studies, language arts, etc. In practice, homogeneous groupings are most often formed for reading and arithmetic and social (age) groups for the remaining portions of the curriculum. A pupil may be moved from one achievement grouping to another at any time, but the amount of such movement is not great in practice. Even with only three major groupings in the organizational pattern, such departmentalization obviously results in fairly tight scheduling and considerable pupil movement from one class to another throughout the day. This fact has raised considerable criticism among those who adhere to the philosophy of the self-contained classroom.

Advocates of this plan for working with children in reading and the other curriculum areas, aware of the allegiance to the underlying principles of the self-contained classroom, have experimented with this pattern in recent years most often within the framework of the Teaching Team concept. The most important experimentation in this regard is currently being conducted in the Lexington and Franklin schools in Massachusetts under the direction of the Harvard University School of Education. (4) In such an arrangement, a group of teachers deliberately plan their work together. For example, five teachers might join together in a team whose responsibility it would be to plan the curriculum experiences for 150 children rather than planning individually for 30 children each. An additional feature in the team plan is selecting children of different age levels (perhaps from what originally amounted to two grades) and keeping them together for two or even three years.

The team is directed by a Team Leader and assisted by a teacher aide. In planning the curriculum experiences for 150 children, the team considers the subjects to be taught, the ability levels of the children in the team, and the manner in which teachers and children may be deployed to achieve the in-structional goals of the team. An important and interesting feature in the process of deploying teaching talent and children is the emphasis upon small group and large group instruction. Classes therefore vary in size according to the subject being taught and its adaptability to a small or large group setting.

Within this framework, the reading program is organized in a fashion simi-lar to the departmentalized plan described earlier. However, the increased flexibility in size and make-up of the instructional groups introduces a new element. Also, the team of teachers, by the very nature of their work with the total group, does have more intimate knowledge of each child's reading capacity and abilities. The consequences of these newer elements has yet to be tested sufficiently long to warrant drawing final conclusions. However, as an experimental design it provides a provocative concept about working with children from which important information should be forthcoming.

Multi-Age Groupings. The fifth arrangement for working with children in reading challenges the assumption that elementary age youngsters can be most successfully taught to read by grouping according to similarities in achievement. In this pattern, children of different ages *and* abilities are de-liberately placed together for most of their learning activities. Planned hetero-genous grouping becomes the dominant pattern of organization rather than homogeneous groups. In one sense, this represents an effort to extract from the Little Red Schoolhouse the advantages which have been sensed in that fading but hardly extinct American institution.

One example of this approach may be seen in Torrance, California. (5) In this plan, a self-contained classroom is composed of children from two, three, or even four different "grades." Each child considers himself to be in a specific "grade," but his class consists of children in several grades. All teach-ing is done within the classroom; it is in fact a multi-graded class. Children arranged in this pattern achieve as well or better than their counterparts in the traditional self-contained classroom. This program, now about ten years in existence, continues to receive solid support from the citizens of the com-munity. It therefore is losing its mark as an "experimental program."

Another example of multi-age groupings forming the basic instructional unit may be seen at the Sycamore School in Claremont, California. This plan is part of an experiment in Team Teaching being conducted under the aegis of the Claremont Graduate School. (6) The Sycamore Elementary School consists of a faculty of thirteen teachers who are supported in their work by six additional people. The teachers and their assistants are divided into three Teaching Teams. Each team is comprised of a Team Leader, three Team Members, an Auxiliary Teacher, and a Teacher Aide. The Auxiliary Teacher provides twenty days of released time for the team each year and is, in addi-tion, always the first person called upon when a substitute is needed for one of the Team Teachers. The Teacher Aide contributes five hours per day of clerical and other duties as assigned by the Team Teachers. The following chart indicates the maner in which the children are organized in to classes. These groupings provide the basic instructional units for the school. Most children will thus spend two years with each Team, remaining with the Team Teacher over that period. At the conclusion of the academic year, half of each class moves to the next Team and half remains. Some movement, or reassignment, within or between Teams occurs during the year as well.

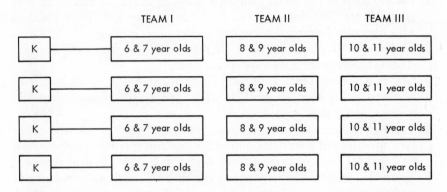

The school day for many, but not all classes, is organized along the lines of the staggered session, described earlier. The decision to go on a staggered session, and the months of the year in which this takes place, is made by the Team, but individuals may demur if they wish. These "staggers" are not conducted during the earliest weeks of the school year nor at other times of stress, such as during the parent conferencing period.

Movement of children to other classes occurs as needs are identified, not according to a schedule worked out in advance. For example, large group instruction takes place from time to time as the need arises. Small groups are also formed in addition to those which result from the staggered session. Such movement may be in groups or as individual needs are perceived by the members of the teams.

The reading program of the school exemplifies the manner in which the Team operates with respect to all areas of the curriculum. It should be noted that this form of organization does not imply a method of teaching reading. It provides a flexible arrangement within which the teacher may teach reading as he thinks best. However, most of the teachers in the school prefer an individualized or self-selection reading program. In addition, the faculty has been impressed by the need to interrelate all language activities (reading, writing, speaking, listening), in developing a sound reading program.

Although the organizational pattern of the Sycamore Plan is based upon multi-age groupings, the flexibility within the plan provides regrouping opportunities which are homogeneous according to specific needs. For example, some reading groupings are formed from time to time which are homogeneous according to some criterion for achievement, other groups are based upon interests, still others upon certain learning needs. The major characteristic of the groups is that they are formed *after* a need has been identified and are maintained only as long as the purposes for which they were initially formed seem to be met. The following are illustrations of regrouping practices in the school:

1. Early readers in the kindergarten are assigned to the six and seven year grouping for "enrichment," *i.e.*, an extended day with older children who have also developed some independence in reading.
2. Children in Team II and Team III read orally to younger children, including kindergartners, on a systematic basis.
3. Children within Team I are sometimes reassigned to work with two teachers during the "stagger" or with even smaller groups than the normal "half a class" provides.
4. Team II children who have become competent readers but who could take advantage of systematic comprehension and speed instruction move to Team III once or twice a week where such instruction is provided.
5. Team III children who have yet to establish thorough independence in reading may move to Team II for remedial work or may be provided other systematic work outside of the regular classroom.
6. Team II and Team III pupils write books for younger children. These books, bound and illustrated, become part of the classroom library for the younger children. In addition, each class writes books for its own use.

Quite obviously, the Sycamore Plan contrasts sharply with most of the other patterns of nongrading described here. As an experimental program, the evidence which is secured from this effort should therefore prove valuable in helping us assess this form of regrouping and, particularly, in providing an interesting contrast to the other patterns which are more widely represented on the educational scene.

CONCLUSION

In conclusion, the observation must be made that no organizational arrangement, no nongraded school, should be viewed as a panacea which will solve even a substantial number of our problems in teaching reading to young children. Providing children with competent and enthusiastic teachers is the basic problem in building a sound reading program. This means more than merely knowing a method of teaching reading and having faith in it. It means, above all, understanding the complex nature of the reading process and how children learn. Teaching methods grow naturally and normally from such knowledge. But the organizational arrangement within which teachers work and children learn does have a potential for good or ill. An understanding of the assumptions underlying the various patterns which we see about us should prevent us from taking too hasty or ill considered steps to change the pattern within which the reading program is conducted.

REFERENCES

1. Cremin, Lawrence A., *The Transformation of the School*, New York: Knopf, 1961, pp. 155–7.
2. Floyd, Cecil, "Meeting Children's Reading Needs in the Middle Grades: A Preliminary Report," *Elementary School Journal*, Vol. LV, No. 2 (October, 1954), pp. 99–103.
3. For example, the Indio (California) Public Schools *Course of Study in Reading* (n.d.), shows twelve developmental levels in reading skills arranged in check-list form.
4. Anderson, Robert H., "School-University Cooperation and the Lexington Project," *Journal of Educational Sociology*, Vol. 34 (April, 1961), pp. 382–386. See also: Robert H. Anderson, "Team Teaching in Action," *Nation's Schools*, Vol. 65 (May, 1960), pp. 62–5 and Robert H. Anderson and others, "Team Teaching in an Elementary School," *School Review*, Vol. 68 (Spring, 1960), pp. 71–84.
5. Hamilton, Warren W. and Walter Rehwoldt, "By Their Differences They Learn," *National Elementary Principal*, Vol. 37 (December, 1957), pp. 27–9.
6. Claremont Graduate School, *Claremont Teaching Team Program* (text by John A. Brownell; Harris A. Taylor, Project Director), Claremont, California: The Claremont Graduate School, 1961.

READING IN THE REORGANIZED ELEMENTARY SCHOOL *

John I. Goodlad

Some Structural Problems and Issues

Schools are organized vertically and horizontally to serve two different administrative functions: (1) the movement of learners upward through the programs; (2) the allotment of kinds and numbers of learners to available teachers and programs in the several divisions of the curriculum. Thus, the educational enterprise is organized vertically into primary, elementary and

* REPRINTED by permission of the Claremont Reading Conference from the *Claremont College Reading Conference Yearbook*, Vol. 25, 1961, pp. 37–44.

junior and senior high schools, and junior colleges, colleges and graduate schools. These units are subdivided, in turn, into grades at the lower levels and years at the higher levels. Similarly, the educational enterprise is organized horizontally into classes, usually of 25 to 40 in elementary and secondary schools, and of more variable numbers in colleges and universities. To accompany these structural units, buildings are constructed egg-crate style, providing 750 to 1200 square feet per room for elementary and secondary schools and only slightly more space variability for collegiate institutions.

Traditionally, adjustments of student placement in the vertical scheme of organization have been effected through retention of the learner for an additional year (nonpromotion) or through acceleration (usually grade-skipping). These alternatives virtually exhaust the possibilities for re-assigning students in the graded scheme. They represent attempts to adjust the learner to the school's organizational framework.

There have been more alternatives for horizontal adjustments in pupil placement. Commonly, in the elementary school, groups which are homogeneous in chronological age are brought together in classes where they are found to be quite heterogeneous in achievement. Inter-class groups are established, too, in order to bring about homogeneity in achievement, ability, interest, or some other factor. Groups that are homogeneous for any one factor usually remain quite heterogeneous in other factors.

These traditional patterns of school structure and pupil placement are now being subjected to widespread critical scrutiny and modification. The scrutiny is of a deductive rather than a research character. And the modifications are of a "best judgment" variety involving much trial-and-error.

Thoughtful re-appraisal of long-standing arrangements in school organization is based on considerations such as the following:

1. Studies into the effects of nonpromotion—a major adjustment mechanism of graded schools—conducted for a half-century show no advantages for retained children in regard to achievement, social acceptance by peers or personal adjustment. In fact, the evidence is in favor of promotion as the more advantageous practice.

2. Studies into trait-variability reveal striking inter-individual and intra-individual differences. In the usual heterogeneous age-grade class, the overall spread in achievement is as many years as the number of the grade level: four years in the fourth grade, five years in the fifth, six in the sixth, and so on. Only three or four children in each class are at grade-level in all subjects at mid-year. The balance score above and below grade-level in various subjects, sometimes many grades above or below. A "fifth-grade" child is merely one who happens to be assigned to "the fifth grade."

3. "Minimum essentials" defined according to grade-level specifications is a stultifying concept. The easy attainment of such standards by the academically-gifted encourages a false sense of accomplishment, perhaps even slothfulness and over-inflated egos. The unattainability of such standards by the

slow-learner encourages a sense of futility, perhaps even of personal failure and worthlessness. Some 25 per cent of our student population receives as much as 80 per cent of class and school failure. Such a condition could hardly be described as an equitable distribution of success and failure.

4. There are periodic upheavals of humanitarianism which direct suspicion to heavily subject-oriented concepts of school function. At present in the United States, however, many educators and parents alike appear, frequently, to be equating more and more, harder and harder, faster and faster with better and better. They tend to look favorably on changes in school practice that permit students to move ahead more rapidly, unimpeded by the progress of slower pupils.

5. From time to time, we develop suspicions about whether or not subject-matter learnings are slighted in self-contained classrooms. Once such suspicions are thoroughly aroused, departmentalization appears again as antidote. The current search for structure in the various fields of knowledge is being accompanied by a downward extension of emphasis on such subjects as geometry, algebra, physics and logic. These developments, in turn, appear related to demands for more subject-matter preparation on the part of teachers.

6. There are persons who believe that the job of the teacher—especially the elementary-school teacher—is impossible. They propose school arrangements and personnel allocations designed, presumably, to simplify the teacher's task.

Foreign visitors comment on what they perceive to be an American propensity to seek structural panaceas for instructional problems. The Pueblo Plan, the Gary Plan, the Platoon System, the Dalton and Winnetka Plans have come and gone. In 1961, we are going around the clock again with ability groups, accelerated groups, homogeneous groups and homogenized groups but we don't yet know how to tell the time.

Proposals for Reorganization and the Reading Program

Two plans, each with several variations, for reorganizing school structure currently are receiving considerable attention. Nongrading—sometimes incompletely referred to as the ungraded primary—is designed to modify the vertical lock-step. Team teaching (or cooperative or associated teaching) is designed to modify the horizontal egg crate. Because of the variety of plans in operation, it is advisable to refrain from describing any one plan for fear of confusing a class of phenomena with a single example. In brief, nongrading may be defined as the removal of grade labels and barriers from two or more conventional grades; team teaching as the cooperative pooling of resources by two or more teachers.[1]

Nongrading and team or cooperative teaching, as proposals for structural

[1] Schools seeking to build a hierarchy of personnel working together wish to restrict the term "team teaching" to these efforts. "Cooperative teaching," therefore, is a more accurate term for the joint teaching plans described in this paper.

reform, have potentiality for affecting the reading program in two, basically different, ways. Nongrading offers opportunity for removing grade-level *pre-scriptions* of learnings and materials as *standard* for all and substituting a wide range of expectancy in traditional "grades." The words "offers the opportunity" are significant. If grade labels are removed but the opportunity for removing expectancy prescriptions is ignored, then we still have a graded school, whatever the name applied to it. Similarly, team teaching offers the opportunity, among others, for greater flexibility and variety in grouping. But, if pupils are merely re-allocated to teachers according to accomplishment in reading and re-arranged for arithmetic and then for spelling or social studies, we simply have departmentalization, whatever the label applied. Nongrading, then, has potentiality for affecting the vertical organization of the reading curriculum; team teaching for affecting the horizontal allocation of teachers to groups of learners.

Reading and Nongrading

The central, vertical problem in designating the reading program is that of determining the bases of pupil progression. Learners must move upward by means of *something*. The need to designate this something in a nongraded plan has led to a description of levels of difficulty through which learners are to progress. Thus, some school systems have designated 8, 12, 20, or even 32 "reading levels" defined according to expected reading accomplishment for each level. The manner of designating these levels varies. Sometimes, kinds of pupil accomplishments are described; sometimes, kinds of materials which ought to be within the reading range of the child are defined. Kinds of materials usually are equated with the reading series of a publishing house.

The above approach to curriculum organization reflects a conception of individual differences and school function that is not acceptable to all educators. The basic provision for individual differences here is differentiated rates of progress through learning prescriptions common to all. The concept of function is that schools are to provide such a set of prescriptions. But, some educators claim that learnings should be differentiated in *kind* as well as *degree*, even within a category such as reading, and that the developmental progression of learners in reading skills does not always proceed according to an arbitrary, pre-determined sequence. Nonetheless, the encouragement of individual rates of progression is a significant move forward from the graded lock-step.

One might argue that good teachers in graded schools provide for such differentiation. In part, they do. But the differentiation in a specific activity such as the selection of materials leaves much still to be desired. Poor readers usually are using at the end of the year what good readers used at the beginning. In other words, a year's spread in difficulty of reading materials is provided. But the spread of reading accomplishment in a graded class usually is from one and one-half to two times the number of the grade level. A range of difficulty in reading material should be provided accordingly.

The "reading levels" approach to the longitudinal arrangement of the reading program in a nongraded school is a step forward—provided the levels do not become an arbitrary set of hurdles. When this occurs, the so-called "nongraded school" becomes only a graded school, with 12 or 32 reading levels replacing 3, 6 or 8 grades. Some school leaders, fearing the levels plan as merely a graded school under a new name, seek more fundamental designation of vertical threads around which a variety of learning opportunities may be organized. Under such a scheme, teachers pay less attention to the progression of books in a reading series and more attention to the skills which the books, presumably, are designed to develop.

This approach transfers emphasis from the progression of materials or activities to the progression of pupil competencies, with certain salutary outcomes. Teacher attention is directed to the child and appropriate next steps for him, rather than to the mere fact of his gross successes and failures. The teacher retains a mental picture of what developmental success in reading looks like, a picture that is useful in diagnosing and remedying reading disabilities. Such an approach tends to avoid both the prescription of arbitrary requirements and meaningless comparisons of more with less able pupils.

Marked differences in school practice exist under the label, "nongraded." The removal of grade labels and grade expectancies creates opportunities for but does not assure continuous and flexible pupil progress through sequential curricular arrangements or, for that matter, does not insure any educational changes whatsoever. The ways in which educators utilize these opportunities, not the mere absence of grade labels, differentiate between graded and nongraded schools.

Reading and Team Teaching

The central, horizontal problems of assigning pupils to teachers have to do with pupil-teacher ratios, curricular bases of pupil distribution, ease and frequency of redistributing learners for instruction, and determining the character of instructional groups. Current team teaching efforts, for the most part, question the validity of the traditional 30 to 1 pupil-teacher ratio; seek to acquire the strengths but avoid the weaknesses of both departmentalization and the self-contained classroom; and strive for flexibility in pupil grouping in line with educational interest. But not all team-teaching efforts possess or even seek to possess these traits.

Intra-individual differences provide one set of motivations for team teaching. Within a given child, the range of achievement from subject area to subject area often is marked, approximating the range in overall, average achievement of the class group. Consequently, grouping children homogeneously on a criterion of general ability or average achievement produces groups within which there are still marked inter-individual differences. Likewise, grouping children homogeneously on a criterion of specific achievement such as reading produces groups which are heterogeneous in all other areas of achievement. To group and re-group children from teacher to teacher and room to room in order to achieve high-level homogeneity in the subject being taught at a given time creates acute organizational problems, may threaten curricular unity and, according to some psychologists, impedes the development of group cohesion and pupil identification with a stable group.

Cooperative teaching plans usually enlarge but sharply define the boundaries of the group within which pupil-teacher interaction and pupil-pupil interaction is to take place. Thus, there is greater flexibility for grouping than exists in the self-contained classroom but not the excessive mobility found when class groups are established departmentally and homogeneously. In team teaching, the self-contained concept can be extended to encompass a "class" of 90 or 150 students. These students constitute a "family" within which almost unlimited grouping and re-grouping may occur. An essential difference between this arrangement and any of the common forms of departmentalization is that *all* teachers assigned to the total group engage in *all* the planning for education, working together in a variety of ways for the actual conduct of the enterprise.

Let us visualize, for example, a simple cooperative teaching arrangement involving three teachers and three third-grade classes. Under usual procedures, reading in each room probably would be conducted in three groups, an A and a B and a C group in each of the three rooms. Thus, there are 3 A groups, 3 B groups and 3 C groups, with the range in reading achievement in each cluster being approximately equivalent. Under the cooperative teaching plan, the three classes embracing perhaps 100 children are viewed as a single class to be subdivided in any number of ways. It would be helpful if moveable partitions separated the three rooms, but simply cutting a doorway in intervening walls contributes materially to space flexibility (or malleability, in the architect's terminology).

These 100 children are arranged and re-arranged to provide, when appropriate, homogeneity of interest, of ability, of achievement, of learning disability, or any of the other traits, according to the purpose of activities underway. For reading they might be divided into five groups, each of which would be more homogeneous than any one of the nine groups set up under the conventional arrangement described in the paragraph above. Thus, there would be three teachers for five rather than nine instructional groups. Or, most of the children might be arranged in the five groups with two teachers while the third teacher, perhaps specialized in clinical reading techniques, worked with a special group of youngsters presenting common reading problems. Many such examples of unique grouping arrangements might be described.

Teachers working in these and comparable team teaching arrangements claim time-saving advantages in effecting the transition from group activity to group activity. They like the opportunity of conferring together over the unique problems of individuals. Likewise, joint diagnoses and prognoses of selected children are carried effectively into parent-teacher conferences. Above all, they appreciate the opportunity of conferring with colleagues throughout the working day over problems which, normally, would be individual, lonely preoccupations in the conventional classroom cell.

Like nongrading, team teaching only creates opportunities; it does not, by itself, change instructional practice. Consequently, a wide range of practices—some promising, some questionable—go on under the label, "team teaching." Combine the division of labor possibilities with separation of the subject-fields and departmentalization may be the result. Overdo the opportunities for large group instruction and mechanistic recitation may be the common mode of teaching. No pattern of school organization is able to withstand human excess. Before condemning a given pattern, we should look carefully into the insights and techniques of those acting in its name.

In Conclusion

The preceding discussion has sought to separate nongrading and team teaching as proposed solutions to two quite different sets of organizational problems. The former is proposed to alleviate certain difficulties of advancing pupils through a vertical structure; the latter to facilitate assignment of learners to teachers and instructional groups. One can proceed without the other. However, many advocates of educational reform link the two, claiming for team teaching and nongrading in combination the creation of far more opportunities for educational reform than either can provide alone.

It is too early to know the full value of such organizational proposals. Practices following from nongrading have not yet been adequately differentiated from practices following from grading. Consequently, we have no model types to compare experimentally. And so comparisons of so-called nongraded schools with graded schools may be nothing more than comparisons of graded schools called "nongraded" with graded schools. Furthermore, because nongrading is being used as the organizational framework by a variety of schools that differ markedly in their concept of function and view of individual differences, practices differ widely in schools labelled nongraded. As in the past, we justify a given structure on the basis of its perceived "fit" with the kind of curriculum and instructional practices we seek.

In applying nongrading or team teaching to the reading program or any other area of teaching and learning, there is always the danger of confusing form with substance. Not nongrading, not team teaching, not any other kind of structured arrangement by itself effects substantive program changes. But such devices do, indeed, block or facilitate a wide range of curricular and instructional procedures, making it easier or more difficult for creative teachers to achieve their ends. It is my personal belief that nongrading and team teaching are natural corollaries of some long-needed changes in the teaching of reading.

GROUPING FOR READING OR FOR READING INSTRUCTION? *

Miriam E. Wilt

Reading, however one wishes to define it, is not an act that can be performed in a group. Reading is communication between an author and an individual.

The title of this article may imply a misconception, for while individuals can be grouped together to learn and practice skills, share ideas and orally interpret printed material, the reading act itself is a visual-mental activity between the writer and his audience of one. The reader internalizes the symbols he sees and finds in the symbols meanings drawn from his own experiential background. Teachers can help children learn to read in groups or individually but reading itself cannot be a group activity. Let us then consider the topic to be "Grouping for Reading Instruction and Interpretation."

Prior to 1930, grouping for reading instruction was almost unheard of, although from the beginning of education learners have been grouped by age levels, interests, needs, abilities, or what have you.

The growth in size of public schools in large population centers brought more and more children together so that divisions had to be made. Sex, academic ability, economic levels, vocational interests, and a multitude of other discriminating techniques were applied until finally one could find school placement based solely on a child's reading level.

Today it is not unusual to find children of a narrow age range or grade level divided into many reading ability groups. When, as so often happens in education, the movement gained momentum, the practice became a prison. The three-ability-reading-groups pattern, self-perpetuating, inflexible and fragmenting, became a ritual worshipped by many supervisors, coordinators and superintendents and followed slavishly by teachers. Several generations of children have been labeled in first grade and have carried that label with

* REPRINTED with permission of the Association for Supervision and Curriculum Development and Miriam E. Wilt from *Educational Leadership*, Vol. 24, February, 1967, pp. 445–51. Copyright © 1967 by the Association for Supervision and Curriculum Development.

them throughout their school years, possibly beyond. Let it be noted, however, that humane and creative teachers have ignored the stereotyping throughout these thirty some years.

STUDIES OF GROUPING

Most of the research studies on grouping have been quite inconclusive, although Halliwell [1] shows some statistical significance and some favorable-though-not-statistically-significant implications for non-graded grouping. However, this researcher notes that the findings were confused by concomitant changes in the school. Evidence concerning grouping seems to be in peripheral implications from a wide variety of researches established to assess teaching methods and materials.

Grouping is not a method of teaching reading. Any method can be used in any group. Grouping, like individualizing instruction, is an organizational technique that is designed to facilitate learning. Basal, phonic, i.t.a., linguistic, experience-content, these are methods. Teaching children individually and/or in groups does not preclude the use of any method. It seems rather obvious that method and organization should not be measured the one against the other. In looking at the research in method, one is impressed by certain conclusions and implications that appear and reappear in a wide cross section of research and from which some conclusions for grouping can be drawn.

In examining the titles of the 264 reading research studies listed in *The Reading Teacher*,[2] researchers have found that less than 2 percent dealt with the thorny question of grouping and yet this is one of the major problems of teachers of reading. Grouping in reading may be as flexible as three children brought together to practice some specific reading skill. On the other hand, grouping in reading can be as highly organized as the Joplin plan, in which children scoring within certain intervals on standardized and/or informal reading tests go daily to a reading teacher who organizes the children into groups as homogeneously as possible.

A review of twenty of the twenty-seven reports of First Grade Reading Studies, funded by the U.S. Office of Education, published in the May 1966 issue of *The Reading Teacher* [3] also revealed an astonishing number of these studies reporting method, but not organization for teaching reading. One is led to believe that with two exceptions the children (26–35) in a class were taught as a whole or in ability groups.

Some of the most positive findings, however, were stated by Doris U.

[1] Joseph W. Halliwell. "A Comparison of Pupil Achievement in Graded and Nongraded Primary Classrooms." *Journal of Experimental Education* 32: 59–64; 1963.

[2] Helen M. Robinson, Samuel Weintraub and Carol A. Hostetter. "Summary of Investigations Relating to Reading, July 1, 1963 to June 30, 1964." *The Reading Teacher* 18: 331–428; 1965.

[3] *The Reading Teacher* 19: 563–675; 1966.

Spencer[4] in summarizing her study, "Individualized First Grade Reading Versus a Basal Reader Program in Rural Communities." Again one might conclude from these brief descriptions that organization may be equally as, if not more important than, method. Classroom organization and the teacher seem especially significant since the attitudes, knowledge of various methods and general interest in improving the teaching of reading appear again and again as implications in many of the studies.

The Hawthorne effect may skew results undesirably in research studies but this peripheral benefit in improved educational programs needs to be fostered in on-going innovative programs in which teachers and children are experimental in trying out new ideas.

It is not grouping that is wrong, but what has been done in the name of grouping that has held teachers and children in a vise. On the positive side, the individualized reading instruction movement, which never really got off the ground although it was a severe threat to the status quo, has catapulted some teachers into thinking about the serious harm that rigid, inflexible grouping has imposed on some children. Yet individualized reading could not expunge the need for grouping, nor did it try. Variety, expediency, common needs, interests provide a kaleidoscope of reasons for establishing and disbanding groups as the needs of children are being met.

In the early grades, when children are introduced to the complexities of our phonemic-graphemic systems, it would seem that children in quite small groups could profit by working together in discovering the regular, semi-regular, and irregular ways in which phonemes pattern. When this is learned, it would seem that the word analysis drills that seem to continue endlessly in some of the reading programs could be discontinued. When these mechanics are under control, the teacher's role changes. Now the teacher becomes a discussion leader, a diagnostician of needs and a planner. All three roles should be shared with children some of the time.

Independence in reading cannot be programmed for groups. The very fact that children achieve independence at varying rates and at varying levels seems to deny the value of rigid A, B and C grouping.

A SOLITARY ACT

Reading is a solitary act and whether the same story is read by one child or many or whether every child reads a different piece, they do it alone. Only at the very beginning do children need to read orally so that they know they are reading and even then they do not really need an audience. Oral reading is speaking and interpreting the author's words to an audience. There are and should be many opportunities for children to read aloud but this is not the reading act, but rather a sharing experience.

[4] Doris U. Spencer. "Individualized First Grade Reading Versus a Basal Reader Program in Rural Communities." *The Reading Teacher* 19: 595–600; 1966.

In the process of education and specifically English education, speaking, listening, reading and writing skills are the foundation of all learnings and are our most useful tools. The mechanics of these skills can be mastered early but the fine polishing requires years of practice in real situations that grow out of the total curriculum. In English impression and expression the "learning to" is only the beginning of a long and exacting program. Knowing about language and how it works; knowing how to write, learning to appreciate writing, being able to evaluate writing and learning to improve one's own writing; knowing how to read the literature of English; and finally being able to use language in its very best sense, these are the purposes of English language education.

How does grouping for reading fit into this statement of goals? There are social, emotional and intellectual reasons for putting learners into groups. Common needs, age, sex, interests and acculturation are a few of them. There are probably some occasions when masses can profit from the same exposure such as seeing plays, storytelling, oral reading, choral speaking, poetry reading and others. Even some of these at times should be shared in small intimate groups where the teacher can get very close to the learners to help them in their evaluation of content, performance, and appropriate treatment.

In "grouping for teaching reading," flexibility is probably the major condition. It is doubtful that there are definitive steps to excellence in reading that can be parceled out month by month and year by year. Many people do not believe that there is such a person as a first grade reader or a fifth grade reader. New and expanded skills should be taught as the need for them occurs regardless of age or grade. The curriculum makers are the arbiters of what content shall be taught. The needs of the children are the dictators of when certain skills are needed.

One child, six or twelve or more, may need to be introduced to new skills, put into situations where he can practice and finally use these skills in the content of literature or other subject matter areas. If this can be done most efficiently in programmed, computer or other individual ways, so be it. If not, probably quite small groups will be most effective: small groups that are set up and disbanded as the needs are met; small groups in which neither age nor ability level are the major determiners but rather "Who can profit from the experience?"

A true "reading group" is one in which the child brings to the discussion table the attitudes, understandings, facts and perplexities he has experienced in reading. Here in a life situation he learns what reading really means. Size of schools or organizational patterns vary but within any framework the grouping of children can and should be planned as needs arise and interests require. Placement in educational levels for extended periods of time should not be determined by reading ability alone but rather by age or maturity levels.

Chapter 7

SUCCESS IN READING

If it is true that all children except for extreme cases achieve speech powers and that reading is closely related to speech, then it seems reasonable to expect all children, except for extreme cases, to meet success in reading.

The problem seems to center not upon the goal of success in reading for all children but upon such factors as the timing of success, the degree of success, and the kinds of success to be expected. If early success is emphasized and the child of six or seven is expected to show independence in reading, then failure to achieve early success causes alarm and anxieties among both children and adults who cannot then take a long-view of success.

If a high degree of success is emphasized and the child of six or seven or even eight or nine is expected to show this marked success in reading, then failure to achieve that degree of success causes alarm and anxieties among both children and adults who cannot then deviate from a standard expectation.

If success is emphasized mainly as a measure of ability to read, then failure to demonstrate ability to read becomes the total range of concern for both adults and children who then cannot envision a broader range of reading powers.

On the other hand, if success is interpreted to mean that every child sooner or later will show independence as a reader, will increase his reading powers on a long-term basis, and will choose to use reading as a satisfying function for self-enhancement, then success in reading should be possible for all children.

To think of a successful reader as one who can read but does not choose to read is as much a denial of the value of reading as to think of a successful reader as one who decodes material but finds no use or satisfaction in his efforts.

Success is an important notion in the American culture; it becomes an even more basic notion in an individual's perception of himself. For the child to perceive himself as a successful reader, as a person with reading powers, and as a citizen who needs to read, may be far more significant in the measure of success than any school or society's satisfaction in teaching reading.

What is success in reading? The way one answers this question is basically the way one chooses to view reading in relation to the elementary school child.

THE TEACHING OF READING*

—*Objective Evidence Versus Opinion*

Arthur I. Gates

THE NOVEMBER 13, 1961, issue of *Newsweek* (page 90) comments as follows: "If there's anything guaranteed to rouse the fears of the modern parent, it's an article or book which sweepingly insists that American children are growing up unable to read. The latest example of this sort of alarmist literature is . . . called *Tomorrow's Illiterates* . . . in which Professor Charles C. Walcutt and six associates estimate that three out of four young Americans are not reading as well as they should or could.

"Without citing any statistical source of this estimate, Walcutt, who teaches English at New York City's Queens College, blames the situation on the 'word recognition' method . . ." which "necessarily limits the reading vocabulary of young children. . . ."

Newsweek states that although Mr. Walcutt's "arguments have some validity for the few schools that still rely solely on word recognition, . . . the overwhelming majority of children today are being taught to read with a variety of methods. . . ."

Another book, *What Ivan Knows That Johnny Doesn't*, by Arthur S. Trace, Jr., appeared at almost the same time and presents views similar to those of Mr. Walcutt. It also offers no objective evidence. It consists of opinions based on a comparison of several characteristics of American and Russian basal readers, such as the number of different words introduced in the two series of books.

EVIDENCE THAT CHILDREN READ BETTER TODAY

Mr. Walcutt states correctly that intensive phonic methods were employed by most schools from 1900 to 1925, when transition to the less formal and less time-consuming procedure was getting under way. This newer program which he attacks had been adopted by most schools by 1930.

These authors present no relevant objective evidence to support their assertion that American children read less well today than comparable youngsters did prior to 1930. The available objective data indicate that the opposite is true. For example, a study reported by D. A. Worcester and Anne Kline, *Reading Achievement in Lincoln, Nebraska, Schools: 1921 and 1947*, a book-

* REPRINTED by permission of the publisher from *Phi Delta Kappan*, Vol. 43, February, 1962, pp. 197–205.

let published by the University of Nebraska Teachers College in 1947, showed that a marked improvement had been made during the quarter century preceding 1947. Pupils in grade five in 1947 made an average reading point or "raw" score of 93.1, as compared with 78.9 for the 1921 fifth-grade pupils. In 1947 there were fewer poor and failing readers: 4.1 per cent achieved a test score of 30 or less in 1947, compared with 23.7 per cent in 1921.

In my recent study, *Reading Attainment in Elementary Schools: 1957 and 1937*,[1] based on a comparison of test scores obtained from approximately 107,000 children in 1937 and 31,000 in 1957 (both groups selected as fair representatives of American schools in general and used in developing norms for the tests), less spectacular but clearly substantial improvement was shown. In tests of vocabulary, speed and accuracy of reading, and level or power of reading comprehension, 1957 children surpassed 1937 youngsters of the same age and scholastic aptitude (intelligence) in grades five and six by at least a half grade. I do not know of any objective evidence which shows that children tested in the last two decades are less able readers than youngsters of equivalent age and intelligence tested prior to 1930.

An important fact that is often not taken into account is that many poor readers who would have dropped out of school prior to 1925 are now kept in school. The study cited in the preceding paragraph presents evidence supporting this statement. Equally important is the fact that children at each of the grade levels, such as those in the middle of the fourth grade (grade position or grade status 4.5), are appreciably younger today than they were a third of a century ago. The recent policy of promoting children who would then have been required to repeat a grade means that the average reading ability of those at any particular grade level today would be much lower were it not compensated for by gains in ability.

Evidence That Intensive Phonics Is Not More Effective

The claim is made in both books, but with more emphasis and detail in Mr. Walcutt's volume, that the one indispensable way of developing ability to recognize words and to read in general is to teach phonics in certain ways. The authors further claim that instruction in reading in American schools today is a "word guessing," or "look-and-say," or "word recognition" method which does not include training in phonics except possibly in the most incidental way. The first of these statements is unproved and the second one is untrue.

The methods of teaching phonics which Mr. Walcutt and his colleagues approve are essentially the same as various systems in wide use between 1900 and 1925. In fact, one system which he warmly recommends was published in

[1] New York: Teachers College Bureau of Publications, 1961.

1913. Mr. Walcutt insists that other methods of teaching children to use the sounds of letters and letter combinations are really not *phonic* methods. The fact that children today read appreciably better than children of equivalent age and scholastic aptitude twenty-five or more years ago implies that the old type of phonic training is not in fact superior to the method of teaching phonics now widely used.

The prevailing method of teaching from 1900 to 1925 required a large amount of time and drill on the mastery of phonics—on teaching children to recognize, name, and sound letters and various letter combinations (phonograms) and to combine the sounds of the parts into a total word sound. The children were taught the names and sounds of the letters and some letter combinations before they learned to recognize words and read meaningful material. Typically, the child was laboriously taught one of the formal systems of phonics. In the last chapter of his book, Mr. Walcutt recommends and gives a brief sketch of a number of the systems.

Although Mr. Walcutt states that other reading programs depend entirely upon "look-and-say" methods, the fact is that all of those in wide use today also teach phonics. In nearly all of these systems, the child is taught from the beginning to read words. Soon he starts to learn the name and sound the letters and letter combinations (blends, phonograms, syllables). This study is kept up until the child can use word sounds along with a number of other techniques of word recognition. Although the amount and kind of phonic instruction recommended by the authors of the programs now in use vary considerably, most of them differ mainly from the phonic programs approved by Mr. Walcutt by introducing phonics more gradually, by teaching other useful methods of figuring out words, and by enabling the child to read from the beginning instead of delaying real reading until an extended period of drill on phonics is completed. The typical programs now in use do teach phonics quite thoroughly, as anyone can discover by examining the teachers' manuals.

During the twenty-five years in which the general type of phonic teaching recommended in these two books was used in most schools, it did not work the magic that Mr. Walcutt and his colleagues now claim for it. It was tried out during more than a quarter century with growing discontent because the load of narrow phonic drill was extremely heavy and it did not work well with many pupils. Contrary to the claims of these authors, the evidence indicates that there were more serious reading failures and general retardation prior to 1925 than there are now. It was for this reason that a number of psychologists and other persons began to study reading disabilities.

Around 1910 Psychologist Augusta F. Bronner began to investigate youngsters retarded or failing in reading. She published an important book on reading difficulties in 1916. Another psychologist, Grace M. Fernald, responding to appeals for help from schools, moved into the field and spent the rest of her life developing methods of teaching nonreaders by kinesthetic or motor tracing procedures, which included relatively little phonic training. These methods were remarkably successful with large numbers of children who had failed to learn by phonic and also by "look-and-say" methods. Between 1915 and 1920 Leta S. Hollingworth, William S. Gray, and many others began to study numerous forms of reading disability. When I first came to Teachers College in 1917, I was told by Edward L. Thorndike (and others) how numerous and serious reading difficulties were. Following Thorndike's suggestion, I soon began to work in this field. My first studies were reported in 1922 in a small book, *The Psychology of Reading and Spelling with Special Reference to Disability*. It describes the many reading difficulties found among the students of superior intelligence in a private school. A report by Walter P. Percival pointed out the seriousness and frequency of reading disability during the years preceding 1925. He found that 99.2 per cent of the failures in grade one, 90 per cent in grade two, 70 per cent of those in grade three, and so on down to 40 per cent in grade five were due to failures in reading.[2]

Experimental Studies of Phonic Methods

Such experiments as were done prior to 1920 consisted mainly of a comparison of a heavy phonic program with a pure look-and-say or unguided learning procedure. The phonic groups seemed usually to do no better than those trained by look-and-say. For example, a study by Lillian B. Currier and Olive C. Duguid, published in the *Elementary School Journal* in 1916, showed that phonic training confused many pupils and had a "discouraging" influence on many other pupils, even many who became quite good readers. The latter learned to read without much enthusiasm for reading.

Karl D. Waldo reported in the *Elementary School Journal* for January, 1915, that youngsters trained by the Ward system of phonic instruction became no better readers than children taught by any one of several other methods. In 1919 and later, Gray reported studies in which he found no consistent difference between schools using the time-consuming phonic method and those using other methods. The studies which I carried out between 1920 and 1930 revealed weaknesses both in the phonic systems popular at that time and in extreme look-and-say methods.

In the final section of my report on my first studies of reading difficulty (*The Psychology of Reading and Spelling with Special Reference to Disability*, 1922), I said:

Learning wholly by the "natural" method or "word" method or otherwise

[2] Walter P. Percival. *A Study of the Causes and Subjects of School Failure*. Unpublished dissertation, Teachers College, 1926.

without training in visual perception or analysis results frequently in inappropriate methods of observing words.

In a later report based on many additional studies (*New Methods in Primary Reading*, 1928) is the following statement:

The "natural method" is really an unabridged trial and error or trial and accidental success procedure, the limitations of which are recognized in the learning of other skills. The frequency of failure, of difficulties of various sorts, and of probable unnecessarily low accomplishment by many whose deficiencies were overcome or compensated for after struggles is sufficient reason for seeking definite methods of instruction which make the development of the basal perceptive skills a definite objective of teaching.

The method which gradually developed and is now most widely used starts off by teaching the children to recognize a few individual words which they begin at once to read in simple narrative selections. Many of these selections are not very exciting, but the child finds it very thrilling to be able to read them. Soon the child will be reading material in the classroom and elsewhere as well as in his basal reader. The modern plan is based squarely on the assumption that the child from the earliest possible moment reads widely both in school and elsewhere.

As soon as a youngster learns a few words, a good teacher begins to attract his attention to the similarities and differences among them. As new words are introduced in the basal readers, the teacher helps the pupil examine them. The teacher shows the child how to study these words, by moving the eyes over them always from left to right and by observing the successive parts of the word. He is then taught to read and sound the letters and many combinations of letters. Skill in recognizing letters and letter combinations and translating them into sounds and blending the sounds into whole-word sounds are carefully developed, but the teaching is not restricted to these devices. Many others, as anyone can easily discover by reading a modern teachers' manual, are taught. The aim is to give the pupil a kit of many tools, not just one, with which to deal with all the types of word recognition problems that he will encounter.

Efforts to compare experimentally this general procedure with those which depend upon more exclusive and extensive phonic approaches are difficult to carry out because it is so hard to control all the variables. I believe, however, that an appraisal of the studies reported within recent years will not support the contention that the more extended and intensive concentration on phonic instruction gives any better results than a typical modern procedure. Mr. Walcutt's book is full of assertions to the contrary. He lists a number of schools in which, he maintains, very superior results have been achieved by the phonic programs. For example, he is especially enthusiastic about one system which is designed to be introduced in the kindergarten and maintained all the way through grade eight (see pages 9–11, and 156–160). John A. McCollum, in a report issued by the Office of the Director of Elementary Education, Berkeley, California, June, 1961, recently compared the test results obtained from a few of these schools with those secured from comparable public schools in Berkeley. In no instance did Mr. Walcutt's preferred phonic methods groups excel those taught by means of other typical American programs.

In the course of standardizing a series of reading tests in 1957, these tests were given to the pupils in a school near New York City which had used one of Mr. Walcutt's favorite phonic programs for more than decade. The average of the grade scores obtained from tests of vocabulary, speed and accuracy of reading, and level of reading comprehension for 243 pupils examined near the end of the school year, and the mental ages of these pupils, computed from the school records of intelligence test scores and converted into mental grades in the usual manner, were as follows:

	MENTAL GRADE	READING GRADE	DIFFER- ENCE
Grade 3.9	5.30	4.86	0.44
Grade 4.9	6.10	5.97	0.13
Grade 5.9	7.00	6.88	0.12

The reading grades shown in the above table do not quite equal the mental grades. This means that the youngsters who received the very extensive phonic training provided by this system were doing no better, if indeed they did quite as well, as the average child of the same mental ability who had been taught in the average American school under average conditions by a teacher of average ability.

The intelligence quotients (IQ's) and consequently the mental ages and grades of the pupils in this school were high. Many of the schools which Mr. Walcutt praises for producing outstanding results are in similar suburban areas near New York City. It is precisely in such schools that one usually finds a relatively large number of children of high IQ, superior teachers, better school facilities, and equipment including books and library services. Since these children are likely also to come from homes of better than average educational, social, and economic status, they should be superior readers. Almost any reading system, even a very inferior one, when taught to intellectually superior children by superior teachers will make a very good showing.

The fact that the extreme phonic method used in these schools did not always produce superior readers can be shown by comparing the mental grades and reading grades of individual pupils. Following are the data for fifteen fifth-grade pupils who had received the extreme form of phonic training during their entire school career:

	READING GRADE	MENTAL GRADE	DIFFERENCE (R.G. —M.G.)		READING GRADE	MENTAL GRADE	DIFFERENCE (R.G. —M.G.)
1.	3.8	6.2	−2.4	9.	5.3	5.7	−0.4
2.	4.4	6.2	−1.8	10.	7.6	7.9	−0.3
3.	5.9	7.5	−1.6	11.	6.4	6.3	+0.1
4.	6.1	7.3	−1.2	12.	6.6	6.5	+0.1
5.	4.0	5.0	−1.0	13.	6.4	6.3	+0.1
6.	5.5	6.4	−0.9	14.	6.6	6.2	+0.4
7.	6.6	7.4	−0.8	15.	10.0	7.5	+2.5
8.	6.6	7.0	−0.4				

The figures for five students who were given no training by this particular phonic method, mainly transfers from other schools, are as follows:

READING GRADE	MENTAL GRADE	DIFFERENCE R.G.—M.G.
7.2	8.7	−1.5
3.2	4.2	−1.0
7.4	7.1	+0.3
6.0	5.4	+0.6
7.4	5.6	+1.8

In another school in the same city, a fifth-grade class contained ten children who had had the same phonic systems during their entire school career, and five, mainly transfers from various other schools, who had had none. The following list gives the amount, in grade scores, by which the mental grade exceeds the reading grade of each of these children. A minus sign (−) means that the reading grade is lower than the mental grade, a plus (+) that it is higher.

Pupils taught four years by phonic method: −2.7, −1.5, −0.6, −0.4, −0.2, −0.2, +0.6, +0.9, +1.1, +1.3

Pupils taught by other methods: −0.9, +0.5, +0.6, +1.3, +1.3

In another fifth-grade class the same figures for individual children are:

Pupils taught four years by phonic method: −1.6, −1.5, −1.2, −1.2, −1.1, −0.8, −0.8, −0.7, −0.3, −0.2, +0.2, +0.4, +0.5, +0.8, +1.0, +2.3

Pupils taught by other methods: +0.2, +0.2, +0.4, +1.2

These differences between the reading grade scores and the mental grade scores are low in reliability in the case of an individual child, *but* the above list gives no support to the claim that the particular phonic method used in this school produced fewer unfavorable scores than the procedures followed in other American schools.

EVIDENCE OF LARGE READING VOCABULARIES AMONG CHILDREN

The assertion made in both books that children in today's schools do not learn how to figure out unfamiliar words or words not taught in the basal readers deserves the most serious consideration. Both authors point out correctly that typical series of basal readers now in use include selections which are less difficult and based on fewer different words than those which were most widely employed during the first quarter of the present century. Mr. Trace's book compares the American program unfavorably with the Russian basal readers in these respects. The two authors state that because of this relatively light basal reader vocabulary, children do not learn to read nearly as many words today as they did a quarter of a century ago in American schools, or as many as the Russian children now learn in their program. Both authors assume that the only words children can read are those found in their basal reader, as illustrated in the following quotation from Mr. Trace's book (page 29):

There can be no question, then, that all students who are taught to read from these basal readers are being seriously shortchanged. Most students begin to study history and geography and science in the fourth grade, and if the texts for these subjects are good texts, they are bound to have a vocabulary of between 6,000 and 8,000 words; and yet fourth-grade students inherit a reading knowledge of only about 1,000 words from their third-grade readers. One wonders how many students really succeed in overcoming the handicap which these basal readers place them under in learning other subjects. . . .

Mr. Trace's major recommendation is to develop new basal readers "that have three to five times the vocabulary and at least twice as much text as the typical reader series now has. . . ." He states that "second-grade readers must have a 2,000-word vocabulary" and "fourth-grade readers should have no less than a 5,000-word vocabulary" and a "sixth-grade reader must have an absolute minimum of a 10,000-word vocabulary." Both authors recommend that this increase in vocabulary in the basal books be accomplished by using the extreme type of phonic drill which they favor.

The purpose of the modern basal reader program is to help the youngsters develop the basic reading skills necessary to enable them to enlarge their vocabulary as well as to enrich their understanding by wide reading in a great variety of other materials. It is assumed that if they develop good methods of working out the recognition, pronunciation, and meaning of unfamiliar words they will be able to read a large amount of literature with understanding and thereby continuously increase their reading vocabulary. The crucial question is whether today's children are limited to the relatively small number of words introduced in their basal reading program. Fortunately, there are objective data bearing on this issue. I shall give only a few examples.

Records are available which show how many words American public school children on the average can pronounce of those included in a word pronunciation test. The test used consists of eighty words, beginning with such words as *so, we, as,* and ending with such words as *superstition, affectionate, philosopher, treacherous, lamentation*. The table of scores based on tests of a large sampling of public school children shows that before he reaches the middle of the sixth grade, the average child recognizes and pronounces correctly all the words in the test without a single error. (See Table XIII, page 35, of the *Manual of Directions for Gates Reading Diagnostic Tests*, Teachers College Bureau of Publications, 1953.)

In another study, published in the November, 1961, issue of *The Reading Teacher*, 75 per cent of the children in grade three in New York City public schools read and understood, in a multiple-choice test, 17 out of 21 words previously studied in their basal readers and nearly as many (16.5 out of 20) which are introduced for the first time in the fourth-grade basal reader. In this and a later study, to be published in the May, 1962, issue of the same journal, second-grade children read and understood 91 per cent as many untaught words from the third-grade readers and 88 per cent from the fourth-grade "new" words as they did of the words previously taught to them in their first- and second-grade basal readers. These children had developed marked ability to tackle untaught words successfully. Using these techniques in a program of wide reading, they learned to read a great many words not encountered in their basal readers.

In another study, by Arthur I. Gates, Guy L. Bond, and David H. Russell, published in the *Journal of Educational Research*, November, 1938, 600 children in grades two to six inclusive in New York City public schools were tested for the sole purpose of comparing the relative difficulty of the successive thousand words comprising the Thorndike list of 20,000 words. By taking every thirty-third or thirty-fourth word, a random sampling of 600 words from this list was secured, making it possible to compute the number of words the children would have read successfully had they been given all twenty thousand. The total number of words pronounced correctly when each was shown alone, or in a sentence, was approximately the same. The number correctly pronounced was, for grade six (second term), 13,800 words; grade four (second term), 10,000; grade three (second term), 7,200; grade two (second term), 3,200. In a test given later to a smaller number of similar pupils, it was found that of the words the children were able to pronounce correctly they could also demonstrate a reasonable understanding of 86 per cent in grade six, 80 per cent in grade four, and 77 per cent in grade three. Grade two was not tested in this study. Applying these percentages to the number of words correctly pronounced (given above), the numbers of words both pronounced and understood are for the sixth grade 11,868, the fourth grade 8,000, and the third grade 5,544.

The Thorndike list of 20,000 words is not a childish list, as some writers have implied. It is heavily loaded with words from the Bible, English classics, and adult reading in all fields. Following are words which appear in the indicated thousand:

6th thousand—*abominable, admonish, apprehension*
8th thousand—*adaptation, adversity, allurement, analysis*
10th thousand—*acquiescence, adjunct, apostolic*
12th thousand—*alluvial, avaunt, Archimedes.*
14th thousand—*archipelago, Aurelius, aboriginal*
16th thousand—*alliteration, appanage, asseveration, avoirdupois*
18th thousand—*acrimonious, Aeschylus, amanuensis, anathematize, apotheosis*
20th thousand—*abnegation, agaric*

The finding that the children were almost as successful on a test in which words were shown alone as when they were contained in a sentence is significant in the light of the assertion that since 1925 children have depended so much on "guessing" on the basis of the context that they are helpless when a word is shown alone. The average sixth-grade pupil demonstrated ability to pronounce approximately 14,000 words from the Thorndike list when they were shown alone without context clues of any sort.

It should not be assumed that the only words a child can read are those contained in the Thorndike list of 20,000 words. The *Thorndike Century Senior Dictionary,* a convenient book for adults, contains "more than 30,000" additional words. Even this is a comparatively small dictionary. Average public school youngsters certainly learn to read many words in this additional 30,000. Among the words in it which are not in the Thorndike 20,000 list are *abacus, abaft, abeam, abrasion, absinthe, acidosis, acne, acoustic, activate, actuary, acuity, adaptable, addiction, ad lib, aeronautics, ageratum, aglitter, agnostic, agog, Akron, Alamo, a la mode, Albany, Alcatraz, alienist, alimony, allergic, altimeter.* These words do not appear to be more difficult than many of the words from the latter part of the Thorndike list.

One needs only to walk through a modern department store or glance through a mail order catalogue to realize how many words a youth runs into, many of them frequently, which are not in the Thorndike lists or in many dictionaries. For example, new words such as *television, electronic, hi-fi, transistor, stereo, feedback, diesel, radar, helicopter, octane, airlift, airline, neutron, proton, aspirin, penicillin, antibiotics, Coca-Cola, Pepsicola, detergent,* and *tabloid* do not appear in the Thorndike list. *Polaroid, Prestone, Brillo, Flako, Kleenex, Kelvinator, Frigidaire,* and many others do not appear. If one spends a few minutes with a Sears catalogue, one will encounter many words not in the Thorndike lists which most sixth-grade youngsters can read today; for example, *bra, orlon, abrasive, acrilan, adapter, additive, aerator, anklet, antifreeze, antihistamine, ascorbic acid,* and scores of trade names.

Edgar Dale and Gerhard Eichholz of Ohio State University began in 1954 to assemble lists of words which were known by 67 per cent or more of the pupils in grades four, six, eight, ten, and twelve. At intervals since that time additional words have been tried out by giving students multiple-choice tests. The latest interim report, published in March, 1960 (*Children's Knowledge of Words,* Bureau of Educational Research and Service), lists the words, the meanings of which were correctly indicated by 67 per cent or more children (except for a few for which the percentage was slightly lower) in several grades. The number for the fourth grade was 4,302 and for the sixth grade was 10,430 words.

The Dale-Eichholz list falls far short of the total number known by fourth- and sixth-grade children. It is limited to words which these investigators have thus far tested. Additions will be made as additional words are tested in future years. There are many thousands of words not as yet tested. The multiple-choice tests such as those used in these studies are often unexpectedly difficult and subtle, even for adults. This list will doubtless be extended greatly in future years. Even in its present incomplete form, it shows that a high percentage of our grade four children know at least 4,302 words (or four times as many as Mr. Trace gives them credit for knowing). Sixth-grade children (tested throughout the school year, and thus representing on the average mid-sixth-grade performance) know well at least 10,430 words. This is more than the total of 8,000 words found in all of Milton's writings and close to the 15,000 in the works of Shakespeare.[3] Indeed, the Dale-Eichholz incomplets lists shows for mid-eighth-grade pupils a total of nearly 15,000 words—14,992, to be exact.

JUSTIFICATION OF MODERN METHODS OF TEACHING READING

During the period 1915 to 1925 a number of persons began to experiment. and theorize about the then-popular phonic method. Efforts were made to find less time-consuming methods. It was felt that unless the extensive phonic drill produced clearly better results, any method which enabled children to do some genuine reading would be preferred. Shortly before 1920 suggestions began to appear. One was that the youngster be equipped to read as soon as possible and that the major activity should be actual reading. This led to efforts to provide more and better reading materials in each classroom, as well as in the school library, and much more time for reading outside of the basal readers. In a general way the teacher of reading was advised to adopt the plan used by most of the best golf instructors, who, after a brief and

[3] See Edwin W. Doran, "A Study of Vocabularies," *The Pedagogical Seminary,* 1907, pp. 401–438.

vigorous lesson in techniques and procedures, would recommend that the learner go out and play golf as much as he could, then return for a later lesson period during which his abilities would be diagnosed again and additional instruction provided.

During the years between 1915 and 1930 many studies were launched in the hope of developing a program of this sort. There was an immediate call for a great increase in suitable reading material for use in the classroom, in the school library, and in the home as a necessary part of the new program. More and better books and magazines, and even children's newspapers, were soon available for all grades from the first up—books on history, science, practical arts, travel, and other fields. New bookcases soon to be filled with attractive new volumes appeared in the typical classroom. A recent survey shows that the average primary grade classroom now contains eighty to one hundred books, intermediate grade classrooms one hundred or more.

In the new program the basal reader is devoted frankly to the task of teaching the abilities and skills needed to read well and to enjoy it. It is understood that this will occupy only a small part of the time devoted to reading in the school program. The basal books are designed to contribute as much help as possible. The teacher must provide the remainder of the guidance needed to enable the pupil to learn how to recognize words and acquire all the other basal skills. Teachers' manuals are prepared to help the teacher round out the program by means of individual and group demonstration and instruction.

The modern basal reader program is designed primarily to teach reading, not literature or science or history or geography or any other subject. It undertakes to develop the skills needed to read books and other material. The teacher is advised to encourage and supervise this wide program of reading as much as necessary. This policy is based in part on a conviction growing out of many observations and studies such as those of James F. Hosic, *Empirical Studies in School Reading*, Teachers College Bureau of Publications, 1921; Theodore W. Irion, *Comprehension Difficulties of Ninth-Grade Students in the Study of Literature*, Teachers College Bureau of Publications, 1925; and May Lazar, *Reading Interests, Activities, and Opportunities of Bright, Average, and Dull Children*, Teachers College Bureau of Publications, 1937.

These studies show that appreciation of literature is more likely to be frustrated than encouraged by using it as a means of laboring through the analyses and practice needed to enable a child to learn to read well. The basal book and the instruction carried on in connection with it should take care of this type of instruction, leaving literature and other materials to be read and studied without the interruptions and distractions which the teaching of reading techniques usually requires.

Authors of basal readers have since 1920 gradually reduced the vocabulary burden, the complexity, and the amount of basal reading material. Teachers found these easier basal books more satisfactory for use in developing the many complex skills involved in reading. It is exceedingly difficult to determine the ideal number of words to introduce in the basal books for the reason that the optimum varies for different pupils and teachers. Current basal readers consequently vary considerably. Some are better for classes of brighter children, others for the less able learners. Each teacher must adjust the kind and amount of teaching to suit very different children. This can be done by cutting down on formal work with a basal reader in some cases and increasing it in others by using other suitable books and practice material. Herein lies the advantage of individual instruction and "remedial" teaching which typically are limited to one child or so few at a time that the teacher is able to teach according to individual needs.

The Nature of Reading Readiness

Mr. Walcutt and others condemn reading readiness. Yet judging reading readiness and acting upon it are merely doing what everyone does in many other areas. Is little Johnny "ready" to carry in the milk bottles or should he have more practice carrying blocks? Is teen-age Johnny "ready" to drive a car on the public highway? Is grown-up John "ready" to take command of a bank or battleship? The idea and practice of "reading readiness" are exactly the same as those employed in other fields. Critics of today's reading methods make capital of mistakes which teachers sometimes commit. Of course they make some mistakes, but so do Casey Stengel and other shrewd persons.

Possibilities of Future Improvement

Mr. Trace and Mr. Walcutt seem to feel that reading is now taught and should continue to be taught as it was in 1900. At that time the teacher often had little or nothing but a single basal reader in each grade with which to teach reading, literature, manners and morals, and American ideals. The basal readers therefore had to be big, complex, and for most pupils discouragingly difficult. As I saw for myself as a ten-year-old in 1900, the results were not happy. This was shown in a report, *Laggards in Our Schools*, Russell Sage Foundation, 1909, by Leonard P. Ayers. He found that children were required to repeat grades and dropped out of school with great frequency. For example, he states that in 1906 the "general tendency of American city school systems is to carry" only "half . . . to the final elementary grade, and only one in ten to the final year of high school." (page 65)

In 1900 books suitable for use in the primary grades were hard to come by. I do not recall having seen a bookcase in the first six classrooms I attended. The "revolution of the Twenties" was due in large measure to recognizing that more and better books and other forms of reading material would be published if they were asked for. The little red school and the big basal reader were passing out of existence. The new world visible in 1920 called for a program based on reading many books, beginning in the first grade. Mr. Trace and Mr. Walcutt seem not to have discovered this change. Mr. Trace bases his major assertions on the assumption that reading skill and vocabulary, literary taste, and an understanding of the American way of life will not be acquired unless they are taught in the basal readers. He has completely missed the point of the educational program prevailing in American schools since 1930.

In spite of several decades of work by many persons, some youngsters still have trouble with reading and the common cold. I hope it will soon be possible to prevent both. I feel, however, that a look toward the future is more promising than a return to the program of the American past or the Russian present. Another new day is dawning now; it promises to be more revolutionary than the one which began in 1920. At times I feel as if I were in a hurricane of new types of electronic devices, teaching machines, television programs, audio-visual devices, scrambled textbooks, minutely detailed printed "programs," and practice materials which were not dreamed of in 1920.

This hurricane contains threats as well as promises. One threat was portrayed a few years ago in a *Punch* cartoon which pictured a half-dozen youngsters and a few parents sitting before a television set. All of the children were looking at the screen, except one little fellow who sat off at the side absorbed in a book. The mother of this child, as she directed another mother's attention to him, exclaimed, "I am really getting terribly worried about Johnny."

The new age has already brought incredible mechanical inventions and great improvements in printed materials. They promise many types of aid for the reading teacher. If they do no more than save time a teacher must now spend in routine activities and laborious oral instruction, they will be of enormous value. The outstanding need today is to provide the time and facilities to enable every teacher to become a more insightful and skilled instructor and to permit her to spend far more time in individual work with her pupils.

It will be advisable also to study the sociological factors which play a vital role in determining the reading activities of old and young alike. Dean E. G. Trotzig, head of the Department of Journalism of the University of South Dakota, stated in the June, 1957, Phi Delta Kappan that "children cannot be expected to do any more reading than their elders." The home which is supplied with a television set, several radios, a phonograph, an automobile or two, and a host of mechanical gadgets and toys but no shelves of books or magazines is not likely to house persons who care much about reading. If Johnny comes home each day to find a conspicuous array of good reading materials and his parents absorbed in reading and in discussing what they have read, he will tend to share this happy home enterprise and make it a permanent part of his pattern of life.

DIMENSIONS OF ASSESSMENT *

Bluma B. Weiner

The current interest in assessing the results of our practices in remedial instruction, particularly in reading, is certainly commendable, but we need to be alert to the notion of assessment as a *process* as well as an end product. In spite of the multitude of materials and machines which have been utilized in remedial reading programs during the past decade or so, much of the effort to help the disabled reader has been rather routine and nonspecific, and much of the effort to determine what progress he has made has been unimaginative and narrow in scope.

The concept of "assessment" is a provocative—even a provoking—one. It implies not only "counting" changes but "accounting" for them. It requires not only that we record data, but that we relate them to a total picture. T. E. Newland (1955, p. 62) has expressed this distinction very well in his discussion of psychological assessment of exceptional children and youth. He states:

> The words *testing* and *assessing* definitely mean different activities. The term *testing* will be used to denote the exposure of a client to any given device, whether group or individual, especially for the purpose of obtaining a quantitative characterization of one or more traits of that client. *Assessing*, on the other hand, includes both this quantitative depiction of the client, and the qualitative and integrated characterization of the client as a dynamic, ongoing, total organism functioning in a social setting.

Newland thus reminds us that assessment of the changes which have occurred in an individual must take into account not only the evidence of performance on testing devices but also the functioning status of the person in a larger setting.

We have selected the term *dimensions* to denote this larger setting. By dictionary definition the word *dimension* means "a measurable extent." We are thus maintaining that, in order to assess progress in the course of remedial reading instruction, we must make several kinds of measurements, and that some of these measurements should occur in the general social environment as contrasted with the special tutoring environment. Whether we prefer an elaborated or a simplified description of reading, the fact remains that the reading process—and the process of learning to read—is quite complex. Evaluation (or assessment) of changes in what we may call "reading behavior"

---

* REPRINTED by permission of The Council for Exceptional Children and Bluma B. Weiner from *Exceptional Children*, Vol. 28, May, 1962, pp. 483–86.

must consider many relevant functions, i.e. perceptual, integrative, and motivational. Only the very naive instructor could be contented with a global "grade level" score. In essence, the assessment process consists of synthesizing evidence which has been obtained on a range of relevant behavior before, during, and following the special instruction. It must include observations of the individual and of his environments, and observations of the individual acting in his several environments, i.e. the tutoring conditions, the classroom conditions, and even the home conditions.

Measurable and Non-measurable Changes

We are accustomed to measuring various aspects of the individual, such as his gross reading performance and achievement (expressed usually in grade scores) in other school subjects. We are also familiar with the procedures for assessing what we presume to be intellectual status as it is expressed in test age (or mental age) or "intelligence quotient." We take for granted that general information about visual and auditory acuity is relevant to the child's success or lack of success. More recently attention has been paid to *perceptual* and *integrative* dysfunctions which appear to interfere with school learning. Observations and comparisons of these types of activity (i.e. behavior) can contribute many clues for investigation and evaluative interpretation by the clinically sensitive reading specialist.

Changes in work habits or "sets" are also important in the total assessment of progress in remedial reading. Impressions of such changes should not be dismissed categorically because they are "subjective." Instead, they should be carefully recorded along with the descriptive behavioral evidence which seems to support them. It is through such procedures that subjective data eventually attain a degree of reliability and objectivity.

Changes in Self Concept

Perhaps the most neglected, yet probably the most significant area for inquiry in the assessment of student progress in the remedial program is that of changes in the student's concept of himself as a person and as a reader. Granted, it is extremely difficult to ascertain how the student views himself, with particular reference to his learning difficulty. The reading instructor without formal training in the use of diagnostic tools for studying personality can nevertheless make valuable observations through informal conversation and "piecing together" of such information as can be gathered from various sources. The significance of this kind of information was dramatically illustrated in the case of Betty Jean, a 13-year-old "non-reader" of at least average IQ who, it was discovered quite unexpectedly, thought that she must be "not right" (i.e. her equivalent for "insane") because she had such difficulty in reading. When it was pointed out to her that the difficulty was due to the fact that somewhere in her school experience someone had failed to help her learn to listen to sounds and to "blend" them (a concept which she readily grasped) the change in outlook was almost miraculous and progress was made at a rapid pace. We do not know how much of this girl's desperate plight was due to her inadequacy in word attack skills and how much was a function of her anxiety about herself.

Not every young person will reveal his burdens so clearly as Betty Jean did, but it has been our experience that the majority of reading clients experience concerns of similar character and equal weight. We, as a profession, are only beginning to appreciate the impact of any type of disability or dysfunctioning upon the individual's estimate of himself as a worthy and competent human being. How the child or teenage student regards himself at the beginning of the remedial program, and the changes which occur during the progress of treatment—whether they can be attributed directly to the instruction or not—are items of critical importance. Granted that the path of progress is seldom smooth or direct, it is nonetheless necessary for the remedial instructor to make every effort to gauge the feelings of students. Evidence of growing independence in suggesting alternatives or in the freer expression of preferences, even of criticism, are useful signs of changes in self-perception.

CONSIDERATION OF CONDITIONS

Gains in reading behavior, whether they be in the traditionally recognized areas of skills or in the area of personality changes, should be assessed not only in terms of the absolute status of the individual's performance but also in terms of the conditions under which he is required to work. Thus, a very small measured gain made against great environmental odds represents an amount of achievement which is better described as a moral victory than reported simply in terms of the small increment of a few months' gain. Data obtained on home and school conditions are frequently recorded but seldom fitted into the situational framework. It is not uncommon to work with children who are beset both at school and at home by antagonistic adult attitudes. Too often the child is expected to master his difficulties without friendliness or support from those adults who we would most reasonably expect should feel a sense of responsibility for his welfare and for his instruction. Such a child is often given "one last chance" to show improvement and then psychologically abandoned.

EVIDENCES OF PROGRESS

The problem of assessment is not simply to determine how much and what kind of change has been effected during the course of remedial instruction, but rather to determine whether the child is making better use of his energies in terms of the conditions under which he has to operate. Observable evi-

dence of such improvement may be expressed in terms of five major considerations: (a) greater accuracy in his responses to printed material; (b) greater
dependability of his responses i.e. retention; (c) greater strength of his
responses, i.e. confidence; (d) greater speed of his responses; and (e) a
reduction in the behavioral symptoms which have been associated with his
reading deficiency. Improvement may be noted in only one characteristic or
in several. It is generally hypothesized, although not yet definitively demonstrated, that alterations in one characteristic are associated with improvements
in the others.

The work of the remedial reading specialist has received increasing recognition from other professions which are concerned with various aspects of
child treatment and rehabilitation. A central consideration in this work, and
one which has not been emphasized as strongly as it deserves, may be thought
of as the "principle of amortization." This principle of amortization, which
is concerned with the gradual extinction of inefficient reading behavior and
the acquisition of efficient patterns, is the foundation of the remedial program. It implies that there must be an allowance made for *recovery* as well
as for new gains; i.e., that time must be allowed for the elimination of er-
roneous or otherwise inadequate reading behavior. Therefore, in assessing the
changes which have been made, we must bear in mind that the seemingly
small gains made during certain phases of instruction may actually conceal a
large measure of "recovery" from the previous condition. This concept is
appreciated in other areas of disability; it is usually overlooked when the
child or adult shows no visible evidence of his special need.

SUMMARY

The purpose of this brief presentation has been to advance a clinical concept of assessment, particularly as it pertains to the evaluation of student
progress in remedial reading. It is hoped that the revival of interest in the
problems of assessment will result in greater concern about the *process* of
assessing rather than in preoccupation with terminal scores as ends in themselves. In this connection it is further hoped that attention will be paid to
the many facets of assessment which we have here labelled *dimensions*.

There are undoubtedly many school workers who long nostalgically for the
good old days when there were few learning problems to cope with simply
because children who presented learning difficulties (or were confronted by
them) were officially discouraged from prolonged school attendance. Presumably things were simpler in those days,—or perhaps they were simpler
only for simple people. Neither then nor now would scientific enlightenment
and professional integrity permit callous disregard for the disabilities, visible
or invisible, which handicap a young learner.

It has been emphasized that assessment should include data gathering *and*
data relating; that evaluation should be based upon comprehensive evidence

of the individual's performance in each of his special environments. Attention has been called to the importance of the pupil's perception of himself and of his reading disability, and to the need for sensitivity to changes in self-perception during the remedial program.

Throughout the discussion emphasis has been placed upon the qualitative aspects of assessment, not because of any desire to minimize the need for quantitative measures (they are necessary), but rather to focus attention on the point that quantitative measures are a necessary but not a sufficient condition for assessment.

Finally, we have suggested a principle which we have called "amortization" to remind the reading specialist and others concerned with the problems of assessing student progress that gains should be measured from the point of actual departure and not from an arbitrary zero point on a grade-level scale. In a very real sense the process of remedial instruction in reading is a rehabilitative process, and the pupils in need of such services start not "from scratch" as the saying goes, but from behind scratch. That is to say that they more often than not have developed maladaptive behavior patterns (both in skills and in attitudes) which must be extinguished. The remedial process (or the rehabilitative process) must be concerned with both the extinguishment of maladaptive patterns and the acquisition of new, more efficient and effective patterns. To disregard this "recovery" feature of remedial instruction and to count gains only in terms of the new acquisitions is to underestimate the investment which the pupil and his instructor have put into the remedial program, and to minimize unrealistically the true measure of the distance which has been travelled.

REFERENCES

Newland, T. "Psychological assessment of exceptional children and youth" in Cruikshank, W. M. (Ed.) *Psychology of exceptional children and youth.* Englewood Cliffs, N.J.: Prentice-Hall, 1955.

THE CHARACTERISTICS
AND EXPERIENCES OF
CHILDREN WHO LEARN TO
READ SUCCESSFULLY *

Jerry G. Keshian

Purpose of the Investigation

This study was conducted in order to discover if there were certain identifiable social, emotional, physical and environmental characteristics and experiences which were common to children who were successful readers.

General Plan of the Investigation

The outline for the study was patterned after the research of Helen Mansfield Robinson, Professor of Education at the University of Chicago. Her study, *Why Pupils Fail in Reading*,[1] was published in 1946 and was a very substantial contribution to the reading field. This study, using a positive approach, might also be called *Why Children Succeed in Reading*.

All of the children in the fifth grades in three schools, each in a different community and each representative of a different socio-economic level, were administered reading and intelligence tests. The schools fell into a low, middle, and high socio-economic level according to the criteria set up by Professor Lloyd Warner in his widely used text, *Social Class Status in America*.[2]

Four hundred and six children were tested, and 362 were found to be reading at or above their mental age. This was determined by taking the scores on the intelligence test and if the reading age was equal to or above the mental age, the child was called a successful reader, so far as this study was concerned. The scores in each school were then divided into three intelligence classifications, low, average, and high. They were then further divided into two groups, boys and girls. Twenty-four children were selected from each school by sampling procedure, for intensive and systematic study,

---

* REPRINTED with the permission of the National Council of Teachers of English and Jerry G. Keshian, from *Elementary English*, Vol. 40, October, 1963, pp. 615–16+.

---

[1] Helen Mansfield Robinson, *Why Pupils Fail in Reading*. Chicago: University of Chicago Press, 1946.

[2] Lloyd Warner, Meeker, Marcher and Eels, *Social Class Status in America*. New York: American Book-Stratford Press, Inc., 1949.

using the case study method. The total number of children in the research was 72.

Each of the 72 children was administered two tests of personality: the *Aspects of Personality*, and the *California Test of Personality*. The *Brace Motor Ability Test* was given in order to collect data on physical ability. Environmental and social information was taken from the pupil questionnaire form, and from the case study interview form. In addition to the information being written up in a narrative case study format, tables were constructed summarizing the data.

What did the data reveal? What were some of the characteristics and experiences of these 72 children, selected at random from among 362 fifth-grade children who were all successful readers?

Characteristics and Experiences of 72 Fifth-Grade Children Who Were Successful Readers

An analysis of the data indicated that:

1. The range in reading ability was very great. There were seven children who were reading just at their mental age, while there were eleven children who were reading two years or more above their mental age.
2. The distribution of the more successful readers among the three communities was fairly even. There was no apparent relationship between reading success and socio-economic level. (This finding supports that of Ladd [3] who found a lack of significant relationship between social characteristics and reading ability.)
3. The children were well-adjusted in terms of personality. Test data indicated that the median score for total adjustment for girls was at the 70th percentile, while it was at the 60th percentile for the boys. However, when a test of Chi-square was used, neither scores were significant at the .05 level. Thus it could not be assumed that these children were better adjusted than the population. Interview data supported the findings of the test data.
4. The parents of these children encouraged them to read. They provided stimulation to read by giving books for gifts, taking their children to the library, and by reading themselves. This latter point is quite significant in the light of what we know about parents' reading habits. In an exploratory investigation of teachers' reading values, Professor Alvina Burrows of New York University found that a child has about one chance in five of seeing his parents reading books daily. [4]

[3] Margaret Ladd, "The Relation of Social, Economic and Personal Characteristics to Reading Ability," *Teachers College Contributions to Education*, No. 582. New York: Bureau of Publications, Columbia University, 1933.

[4] Alvina T. Burrows, *Teachers' Reading Values—An Exploratory Investigation*. New York: New York University, 1957.

5. The parents indicated their strong interest in their children's school work. Examples of this interest was their attendance and participation in PTA work and other school functions.
6. The formal education of the parents was above that of the population. According to the Statistical Abstract of the United States [5] only six per cent of the population 25 years of age and over had four or more years of college. In this study the median for number of years of schooling for fathers was 16. Here again was demonstrated what we have known for a long time—that formal education is a major correlate of reading.
7. All of the children were read to by their parents on a regular sustained basis, throughout their early childhood.
8. General health of the youngsters was excellent. Little time was lost due to illnesses of long duration. No relationship was present between height and reading success and weight and reading success.
9. The children walked and talked at about the same time as the children in the population. Also reading success was not related to the child's relative position among siblings.
10. Most of the children owned their own library cards, and made use of them. This was in spite of the comparative inaccessibility of the public libraries to their homes.
11. The families were strong units—they did things together such as attending athletic events, going to movies, and working at hobbies. The writer suggests that this might be a very important factor in building a strong emotional basis for reading success.
12. Twelve per cent of the children had memberships in book clubs, and 76 per cent had their own subscription to a magazine.
13. These children came from homes where there was a great variety of reading materials. The parents subscribed to more magazines and read more newspapers than did the population.

Conclusions

Several conclusions may be drawn as a result of the analysis of the data. These are:

1. Though the children were well-adjusted both socially and emotionally, they did not fall within any well-defined personality pattern. These children were in a broad range of personality adjustment, with only average adjustment in certain areas of personality and excellent adjustment in some other areas of personality.
2. Reading success appears to be the result of many factors, some of which

[5] United States Bureau of the Census, *Statistical Abstracts of the United States, 1954.* Washington: Government Printing Office, 1954.

apparently lie beyond the control of some individuals with whom the child comes into contact.

3. Factors operating singly, such as a lack of reading materials in the home, do not in themselves prevent a child from becoming a successful reader. Rather, a whole range of characteristics and environmental factors appearing in combination, enable a child to achieve success in reading.

SOME PITFALLS IN EVALUATING PROGRESS IN READING INSTRUCTION *

Arthur S. McDonald

In the past few years, dramatic results have been claimed for one after another "new method" of teaching reading. In the January, 1963, PHI DELTA KAPPAN, the editor warned that most of these results had not been evaluated for possible contamination by the "Hawthorne effect." In point of fact, a number of pitfalls have been overlooked by many researchers in assessing reading instruction.

From the beginning of formalized reading instruction, various kinds of appraisal have been carried on to ascertain progress of an individual and/or a group. Research studies aimed at assessing the effectiveness of different kinds of reading instructional programs have also been conducted.

My own review of published studies in the past ten years shows that the three most commonly used methods for evaluating progress in reading programs are:

1. Determining reading gains by comparison of pre- and post-test scores on alternate test forms of both standardized and informal tests, and finding difference in test performance from that expected (e.g., "Johnny gained six months in reading test performance during a six-week reading program").

2. Comparing test gains with the national average yearly gains made with those made in the local reading program.

3. Comparing test-retest results of the remedial group with test-retest performance of a control group.

Of these three methods, the first one is most commonly used in classroom and reading clinic descriptive reports. The third is most usual in published reports of research studies.

---

* REPRINTED by permission of the publisher from *Phi Delta Kappan*, Vol. 45, April, 1964, pp. 336–38.

SOURCES OF ERROR

In recent years, several writers have pointed out the dangers inherent in these methods. Among pitfalls are these:

1. Failure to correct for regression to the mean. (Most remedial students are selected on the basis of low initial reading test scores. On a second testing, persons so selected are likely to make higher test scores whether or not they have *actually* improved in reading ability.)

2. Treating reading grade scores as empirically obtained indications of month-by-month progress. In reality, reading grade scores are extrapolated from one grade level to another. (Spache has pointed out that experiments using repeated testing indicate that reading growth is not evenly distributed throughout the year but occurs in an initial spurt during the first few weeks or months of the year.[1])

3. Interpretation of test scores on the assumption that the tests used provide reliable and valid measures of the most important aspects of reading.

4. Spurious scores obtained from the use of a single test over wide educational (or performance) levels. (For instance, on one commonly used type of reading test a non-reader can miss all the questions and earn a reading grade score of 1.6. If another level of this test were used with the same child, his score would be approximately third reading grade level.)

5. Use, for checking reading comprehension, of test questions which can be answered by most children from their background knowledge (i.e., without even reading the selection).

6. Errors in interpretation because of use of inappropriate norms, failure to allow for interform differences in equivalence, etc.

7. Failure to select a really comparable control group.

OTHER SOURCES OF ERROR

Even a carefully designed study, however, one carried out with comparable experimental and control groups under conditions providing for control of many important variables (including student and teacher motivation), may still be vitiated by errors. These errors may arise, in part, because too little attention is paid to reading as a *form of behavior* and, in part, because of errors *inherent in the experimental model itself.*

Thus, in the absence of special precautions, the results obtained by use of comparable-groups methods are likely to be confounded by "Hawthorne" and "placebo" effects.

Cook has defined the Hawthorne effect as ". . . a phenomenon charac-

---

[1] George D. Spache, *Toward Better Reading.* Champaign: Gerrard Press, 1963.

terized by an awareness on the part of the subjects of special treatment created by artificial experimental conditions." [2]

As partial explanation of this consequence, Orne has shown that "as far as the subject is able, he will behave in an experimental context in a manner designed to play the role of a "good subject." [3] In other words, the student in either an experimental or control group will try to validate the experiment as he understands it.

A special form of the Hawthorne effect accompanies the use of apparatus, equipment, drugs, special instructional material, ritual, "secret methods," etc. This is called "placebo response."

Following Fischer and Dlin,[4] a "placebo" may be defined as a chemical, mechanical, electronic, or psychological agent or treatment employed, with or without ritual, but always with the suggestion or implication of its powerful and helpful properties. The "placebo response" is that effect of the agent or treatment which cannot be due to the agent or treatment itself but which must be due to some other aspect of the situation.

Thus the placebo effect may be related to the attitude (enthusiasm, belief, optimism, etc.) of the administrator, to the administrator, to the atmosphere (security, insecurity, competitiveness, challenge, etc.), to the treatment situation itself, to the expectancy of *both* the subjects and the experimenter.

Often overlooked in assessment studies, in fact, is the considerable research evidence available that the subject's expectations, the cues provided by the environment and the attitudes and expectations of the instructor or experimenter, may significantly alter the effectiveness of the treatment used and the consequences of the study.

As an example, college students who believed they were getting dexedrine (and who *were* receiving dexedrine) had typical energizer-like reactions, in both mood and psycho-motor performance, while students who received dexedrine (but *believed* they were getting a barbiturate) showed a tendency toward barbiturate-like reactions. It should be noted that the percentage of such typical *student* responses, however, dropped markedly when the *experimenters* knew what drug was being administered.[5]

In another experiment college students were *not* aware that decaffeinated and regular coffee were administered (to the entire group) at different times, but were told that tests were being made to check certain effects of caffeine.

[2] Desmond L. Cook, "The Hawthorne Effect in Educational Research," *Phi Delta Kappan*, 44, 1962, p. 118.

[3] Martin T. Orne, "On the Social Psychology of the Psychological Experiment: With Particular Reference to Demand Characteristics and their Implications," *American Psychologist*, 17, 1962, p. 778.

[4] J. K. Fischer and B. M. Dlin, "The Dynamics of Placebo Therapy: A Clinical Study," *American Journal of Medical Science*, 232, 504–512, 1956.

[5] Jonathan O. Cole, "The Influence of Drugs on the Individual," in Seymour M. Farber and Roger H. L. Wilson (eds), *Control of the Mind*. New York: McGraw-Hill, 1961, 110–120.

The same effects were reported in a similar way for *both* kinds of beverage. When the subjects were told, however, that decaffeinated coffee was being used "just to prove that it was the caffeine that produced the changes" (but *both* regular and decaffeinated coffee were administered as before to all students), *all* effects being measured returned to pre-test conditions.[6] (It is interesting to note that an earlier variation of this experiment, using milk, has often been cited in popular articles as proving that caffeine does not keep one awake.)

Considerable research has shown that the *mere act* of using special treatment or instructional devices, material, drugs, etc., strongly increases their effect. Furthermore, the *intra*individual variation in response to Hawthorne and placebo effects has been shown to be as great as the *inter*individual variation of such responses. The Hawthorne and placebo effects produced depend not only on the particular agent or ritual used and the method of administration but also on the circumstances under which these are used and how the effects are measured. Thus the expectations of the subject, the experimenter, and the nature of the situation in which an agent is administered, a device used, or a course of remediation carried out are important determiners of the effects. Vague means of measuring outcomes, tests with low reliability, and heavy reliance on subjective evaluation strongly favor contamination of results with placebo and Hawthorne responses.

Thus unwanted Hawthorne and placebo contamination is particularly likely in reading programs where the instructors rely heavily on special instrumentation (and themselves believe in the unique beneficial effects of the instruments), or believe strongly in the "powerful" effects of a novel method of instruction, or have found a completely new means of instruction which they believe cannot be measured by existing assessment instruments.

The greater the stress, anxiety, or hope surrounding the circumstances of the treatment or experiment, the greater the desire of the subject to improve, the higher the enthusiastic belief of the experimenter or instructor in the agent and technique used, the greater the tendency for Hawthorne and placebo responses to appear.

Investigations have shown that completely inert substances, useless agents, or exhortations (such as "read faster, comprehend more"), when used with the understanding that they would produce certain effects, did indeed cause such effects to appear in 20 to 60 per cent of the subjects. Lehmann reported that "giving a placebo capsule in a well-controlled, double-blind experimental procedure produced test-retest differences which were larger and of greater significance than the administration of effective doses of psycho-active drugs.[7]

---

[6] L. D. Goodfellow, "Significant Incidental Factors in the Measurement of Auditory Sensitivity," *Journal of General Psychology*, 35, 33–41, 1946.

[7] Heinze E. Lehmann, "The Place and Purpose of Objective Methods in Psychopharmacology," in Leonard Uhr and James G. Miller (eds.), *Drugs and Behavior.* New York: John Wiley and Sons, 1960, pp. 107–127.

EXPERIMENTER MUST BE 'BLIND'

Nash has pointed out the importance of measures taken by the experimenter to increase his "blindness" concerning the subjects in the experiment and the absolute necessity of his paying close attention to his own desires regarding the outcome of the experiment so that he can erect safeguards against the operation of bias or placebo effects arising from experimenter or subject expectancy. He concludes that systematic errors due to suggestion can be reduced if the conditions affecting suggestion and expectancy are kept approximately the same for control and experimental subjects.[8]

Thus in any study of the effects of initial instruction or corrective or remedial treatment, it is absolutely necessary to assess the Hawthorne and placebo reactions. To show that a certain kind of program or type of reading instruction produces more than a nonspecific Hawthorne or placebo response, it must be shown that its effects are stronger, last longer, and are qualitatively different from those produced by placebo agents (as defined in this article) or by the Hawthorne effect, or that the program affects different kinds of subjects than do placebo and Hawthorne reactions.

In this connection, Spache has warned that by dramatic use of novel methods or impressive equipment "it is possible to produce for a brief space of time what appears to be more than normal progress by remedial techniques or methods that are completely contradictory or even irrelevant to the causes of the reading retardation." [9]

My review of relevant research published in the last ten years shows that more than 80 per cent of the studies dealing with evaluation of progress in reading programs of various types at all levels of instruction from elementary to college suffer from serious (but apparently unsuspected or unassessed) contamination due to the Hawthorne and placebo effects.

IMPLICATIONS

Improved evaluation of reading progress requires:

1. Careful delineation of objectives in *operational* terms. (What kinds of reading problems can we help with testable techniques and materials? What kinds of reading problems remain unaffected by our current procedures or show only Hawthorne and placebo reactions?)

2. Appropriate generalization from the experimental or clinical situation to the daily teaching situation *elsewhere*.

3. Controlling for Hawthorne and placebo contamination. (Cook cites

[8] Harvey Nash, "The Design and Conduct of Experiments on the Psychological Effects of Drugs" in Leonard Uhr and James G. Miller (eds), *Drugs and Behavior*. New York: John Wiley and Sons, 1960, pp. 128–156.

[9] Spache, *op. cit.*

suggestions that the placebo treatment be used to control the Hawthorne effect. For example, avoid singling out experimental and control groups. Use some form of special instrumentation, specially scheduled time and instructional material, stamped "Experimental Edition," with all students. This approach must contain safeguards against teacher expectancy.)[10]

4. What conditions and procedures in commonly used remedial programs are especially favorable for the occurrence of Hawthorne and placebo responses? What are the most common responses of the nature encountered?

[10] Cook, *op. cit.*